AUSTRIAN ECONOMICS

CLASSICS
IN
AUSTRIAN ECONOMICS

A Sampling in the History of a Tradition

Edited by
ISRAEL M. KIRZNER

VOLUME II

THE INTERWAR PERIOD

E con £v
6/10/96

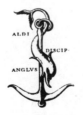

LONDON
WILLIAM PICKERING
1994

Published by Pickering & Chatto (Publishers) Limited
17 Pall Mall, London, SW1Y 5NB

British Library Cataloguing in Publication Data
Classics in Austrian Economics: A Sampling
in the History of a Tradition. – Vol. II: The
Interwar Period
I. Kirzner, Israel M.
330.9436
Set ISBN 1 85196 138 0
This volume ISBN 1 85196 156 9

Printed and bound in Great Britain by
Antony Rowe Limited
Chippenham

CONTENTS

B13

BK Title:

INTRODUCTION

The eight papers in this second volume have been selected to represent the interwar period in the history of Austrian Economics. (Although also several of the papers included in Volume III belong, chronologically, to the interwar period, they have, primarily because of the authorship, been grouped with the other (post-1940) papers representing the 'Age of Mises and Hayek'. On this see further in the Introduction to Volume III.) It was, it will be recalled, our thesis in the Introduction to Volume I that in the interwar period Austrian Economics came to converge more closely than at any other time throughout its history towards mainstream neoclassical economics. We also argued, in that earlier Introduction, against the mainstream view (in histories of modern economic thought) that the Austrian Economics of the 1871–1914 era was nothing more than a separate tributary of ideas which flowed into, merged with, and reinforced the mainstream of modern neoclassical economics. Nonetheless we must emphatically concur in the conventional judgment to the following extent: much of the economics of interwar Vienna, *taken in isolation from post-World War II developments*, does appear thoroughly consistent with that (here rejected) mainstream view of the history of modern economics. The papers in this volume reflect these ambiguities and complexities which characterize interwar Austrian Economics.

In a recent paper on the interwar period in Austrian Economics, Stephan Boehm ably explored some of these (and other) complexities and ambiguities.[1] His perspective was richly informed by his familiarity with the post-1970 revival of interest in the Austrian tradition. For deploying this perspective he was gently taken to task by Mark Blaug[2] for whom, it appears, the interwar period in Austrian Economics is important not in its constituting a background against which subsequent developments in the tradition were to occur, but rather as consisting of a series of resounding Austrian defeats (in debates with mainstream economics) particularly in the areas of capital theory, business cycle theory, and the theory of socialist economic calculation. For Blaug an adequate survey of this period would offer 'a definitive account of how Böhm-Bawerk was vanquished by Frank Knight, how Hayek and Robbins were laid low by Sraffa and Kaldor, and how Mises was buried by Lange.'[3] The papers selected for this volume do not quite coincide with Boehm's emphasis on the Mengerian (rather than the Boehm-Bawerkian) roots of interwar Austrian Economics (and his related interest in potential links between the economics of this period and the later Austrian revival); nor do they at all reflect Blaug's perception of this period in Austrian Economics as substantially consisting of a series of major defeats (presumably responsible for the decisive eclipse of the School by the end of the 1930s). Rather the selection of these papers reflects the (not unrelated) judgments (a) that it was the influence of Böhm-Bawerk and of Wieser (rather than that of Menger) which was most predominant in the Vienna of the 1920s and 1930s, (b) that this influence generated a perspective which naturally converged towards mainstream neoclassical thought (so that 'defeats', both the real and the imagined, at the hands of mainstream economists, can no longer be seen as having been *necessary* for the eclipse of Austrian Economics by the outset of World War II). If, despite all this, we concur in Boehm's broad conclusion, that seeds of the subsequent revival in Austrian Economics are to be sought in some elements of interwar Austrian work, we must at least modify this concurrence by the observation that such a search is likely to demand both patience and persistence.

The Scenery in Vienna: Some Relevant Highlights

The intellectual landscape in Austrian Economics after the conclusion of World War I was rather different from the pre-war scene. Böhm-Bawerk had died in 1914; Menger, who died in 1921, had retired from his university professorship many years earlier; only Wieser, who was to die in 1926, remained still active in teaching after the war's end. A younger generation of economists were coming to the fore, particularly represented in the forceful personalities of Ludwig von Mises (a star veteran of Böhm-Bawerk's seminar) and Hans Mayer ('the favourite pupil of Wieser').[4] For our purposes it will suffice to ignore many other fascinating aspects of the scenery in Viennese economics in the 1920s, and to focus on what Boehm[5] has called the 'interlocking circles' which formed around these two economists. At the University of Vienna Wieser's chair (once occupied by Menger) was given, after his retirement, to Hans Mayer. Around him at the university there came to be formed an important circle of able young economists including Leo Schönfeld-Illy, Paul Rosenstein-Rodan, and Oskar Morgenstern. Mises never did obtain a chair at the university (despite the judgment of many that his scholarly work and international renown rendered this something of an academic scandal).[6] In Mises's own words, a 'university professorship was closed to me inasmuch as the universities were searching for interventionists and socialists.'[7] Yet his title of Associate Professor enabled him to conduct a highly successful seminar at the university (despite what Mises has described as Mayer's occupying 'his time ... with mischievous intrigues against me').[8] Mises's main intellectual influence, however, was exercised outside the university, in his famous *Privatseminar*. This met once in two weeks at Mises's office in the Chamber of Commerce (a tax-supported parliamentary entity formed by businessmen) where he earned his livelihood – and from which he exercised considerable influence at the national level – as the Chamber's economist. In this *Privatseminar* there participated a remarkable group of young scholars, not only economists, but also historians, philosophers and sociologists. One important Austrian scholar in the group was Richard Strigl, who had been trained in the pre-war Böhm-Bawerk seminar. His work was to influence, in particular, that of Lionel Robbins. (For a sample of Strigl's work see in this volume paper 14; for a contemporary Austrian critique of Strigl's major book, see paper 18.) Among the group were also several who were later to become internationally famous scholars in their respective fields, including Friedrich Hayek, Gottfried Haberler, Fritz Machlup, Oskar Morgenstern, Paul Rosenstein-Rodan, Felix Kaufman, Alfred Schütz, and Erich Voegelin. Despite the coolness (to express it mildly) between Mayer and Mises, several (such as Morgenstern and Rosenstein-Rodan) participated both in the Mayer seminar and Mises's *Privatseminar* (hence Boehm's reference to 'interlocking circles'). Almost all of the more important economists in both of these circles are represented in these volumes, with the work of Mises himself, as well as that of Hayek, being collected separately in Volume III. Let us attempt to identify the general perspective on economics which characterized interwar Vienna.

The Character of Interwar Viennese Economics

We have already (in the Introduction to Volume I) drawn attention to Machlup's list of the doctrinal foundations of Austrian Economics as he understood it. There can be little doubt that this list expresses with precision the general perspective which pervaded Austrian Economics in the 1920s, when Machlup began his career, both as student and as scholar. There is also little doubt that this general perspective was broadly shared by economists in both the Mayer and the Mises circles. When Lionel Robbins wrote his 1932 *The Nature and Significance of Economic Science* (which, as we shall see, importantly imported this Austrian perspective into the British scene) his citations were to Austrian scholars both in the

Mises circle (including Mises, Haberler, Hayek, Kaufman, Machlup and Strigl) and in the Mayer circle (including Mayer, Schönfeld-Illy, Rosenstein-Rodan and Morgenstern).

It will be recalled that Machlup's list was made up of 1) methodological individualism, 2) methodological subjectivism, 3) the importance of tastes and preferences, 4) the centrality of the opportunity cost concept, 5) marginalism, 6) the time structure of production. In what follows we shall attempt to show how this list, making up the shared perspective of inter-war Austrian economists, was distinct from that of the dominant British approach of that time, but was nonetheless sufficiently close to that approach as to appear to justify the standard history-of-thought thesis. In this thesis what is valid in Austrian Economics is seen as becoming benignly absorbed (circa 1930) into the neoclassical mainstream. Yet, on the other hand, this list traced its intellectual ancestry to earlier (especially Mengerian) roots. In the fullness of time, this would generate an expansion in Machlup's 'Austrian list' so as to incorporate, especially, explicit attention to the importance of (disequilibrium) *processes* set in motion by entrepreneurial *discovery* in a world of *open-ended ignorance* and *uncertainty*.

This latter development could hardly have been foreseen by an Austrian economist (or any other economist, for that matter) during the 1920s, and was not at all an *obvious* implication of the articulated perspective shared by Austrian economists of the period. This led us to assert earlier that the papers in this volume reflect the influence of Böhm-Bawerk and of Wieser, rather than that of Menger. On the other hand, the fact that the later development (half a century later!) occurred after all permits and compels us, at the same time, to concur with Boehm in recognizing the need to search (in the economics of interwar Vienna) for the seeds of the late twentieth-century Mengerian revival. Boehm suggest that these seeds are likely to be found in the ideas being discussed in the Mayer circle. While we shall certainly recognize, later in this Introduction, the historic significance of Mayer's work in this regard, and will indeed recognize a certain indirect influence exercised by that work upon some late twentieth-century Austrian economists, we find it difficult to attribute the post-1970 Austrian revival, as a whole, to that work. Rather (as will be discussed in the Introduction to Volume III) the post-1970 Austrian revival must, it seems to us, be traced back to seminal insights, discovered and/or articulated by Mises and by Hayek in the 1940s which owed relatively little, it would appear, to Mayer's pioneering work of the early 1930s.[9] Because we have gathered together the relevant work of Mises and of Hayek (including that from the interwar period) in the third Volume of the present work, it follows that the papers in this present Volume can be expected to offer relatively little basis for understanding the subsequent developments in Austrian Economics which were, we have maintained, ultimately to render 'Machlup's list' incomplete. Moreover, it can be argued that, despite important anticipative indications, the work of both Mises and Hayek up until 1940 hardly expressed with any clarity those new insights which they would make explicit in the 1940s. With or without the work of Mises and Hayek, therefore the Machlupian perspective correctly captures what was explicit in the economics of interwar Vienna.

The Austrian and the British Traditions – distinct but convergent

Prior to 1930 the mainstream tradition in English economics did not recognize the centrality of the foundation concepts contained in Machlup's list. It was not so much that the substance of Marshallian economics was antithetical to those concepts. (In fact, as we shall see, Robbins was to argue that the Austrian insights were able to illuminate what British and other neoclassical economists had been doing and saying all the time.) Rather the failure, in British neoclassical economics up until the 1930s, to recognize the centrality of such insights as methodological individualism, subjectivism, and the opportunity cost doctrine, must be attributed to Marshall's vision of his economics as being simply the elaboration and completion of the classical perspective inherited from Smith, Ricardo and Mill. To *this* perspective a doctrine of methodological individualism must indeed appear alien, the notion of opportunity cost must indeed appear awkward and confusing.

For Alfred Marshall or for Edwin Cannan the link between economics and material wealth, while not as straightforward as it had been for Ricardo or Mill, was nonetheless difficult to abandon. In defining economics as studying 'that part of individual and social action which is most closely connected with the attainment and with the use of the material requisites of well-being',[10] or 'the general causes on which the material welfare of human beings depends',[11] Marshall and Cannan are continuing a tradition which was rooted in an explicitly objectivist perspective. What identifies the economic side or department of social life is not, in this perspective, allocative choice, or purposefulness in individual decision-making, but the *material* character of the objects of attention. Although neoclassicism had, unquestionably, vastly enriched the corpus of classical theory by introducing utility considerations (alongside the objective circumstances which identify the costs of production) into the theory of the determination of market values, this was achieved without fundamentally altering the way in which economic science and economic processes were understood. In the picturesque words of Wicksteed's well-known critique of Marshallian economics, the 'new temple, so to speak, has been built up behind the old walls, and the old shell had been so piously preserved and respected that the very builders have often supposed themselves to be merely repairing and strengthening the ancient works'.[12]

So that, while the individual decision was indeed an element in the analytical framework of British neoclassical economics, the *centrality* of that element as capturing the essential, defining character of the entire science – and the subjectivism which must as a consequence surely pervade that analytical framework, were not recognized. It was this which Robbins found frustrating in British economics and which led him to discover, in continental (and, particularly, Austrian) approaches to economics, subjectivist insights which at once simplified and illuminated economic understanding. It was Robbins's genius to distil these insights and articulate them in a manner (and at a moment) which decisively affected the course of mainstream microeconomic thought in Britain and the U.S for decades to come.

Robbins's 1932 book did not require a student of Marshall's *Principles* to *abandon* the substance of his science. Most of Marshall's or Cannan's economics could, for a reader of Robbins, be *appreciated* in a new and satisfying light, once one makes explicit such subjectivist ideas as the defining centrality of allocative, economizing choice, the inescapability of opportunity cost, the utterly individualistic nature of human well-being. To be sure, consistent application of these insights must transform the perspective from which Marshallian or Cannan's economics is understood. (It was to provoke Robbins himself to question the meaningfulness of economic aggregation in general, and of aggregate economic well-being in particular.) To employ Wicksteed's metaphor, these insights permit one to tear down the ancient shell to reveal that neoclassical economics indeed makes up a hitherto unappreciated new temple. It was the discovery of this transformed perspective which excited Robbins and inspired his book.

This importation of Austrian ideas into the British mainstream did not constitute a clash of inconsistent substantive economic doctrines. In fact Robbins saw himself as simply stating clearly what was already implicit in British economics. 'I venture to hope that in one or two instances I have succeeded in giving expository force to certain principles not always clearly stated. But, in the main, my object has been to state, as simply as I could, propositions which are the common property of most modern economics.'[13] Clearly, Robbins saw the elements that would later be grouped in Machlup's list of Austrian fundamentals as thoroughly consistent with British economics. All schools of economics since the marginal utility revolution are, in Robbins's view, ultimately saying the same things. 'At the present day, as a result of the theoretical developments of the last sixty years, there is no longer any ground for serious differences of opinion on these matters, *once the issues are clearly stated*.'[14] What Robbins found in interwar Austrian economics was a set of insights which enabled one to state clearly what economists of *all* post-1871 schools were already saying with greater or lesser clarity.

It is not our purpose here to pursue the story of how, through Robbins's book and related importation of other continental insights into British economics in the early 1930s, Austrian ideas came to play a key (often overlooked) role in the subsequent crystallization of mainstream mid-twentieth-century microeconomics. Our purpose in this Introduction is to draw attention to the presence of these ideas in the contributions of interwar Austrian economists collected in the present volume, and to identify both their distinctness from the British mainstream (as it was understood up until 1932) and the ease with which Lionel Robbins felt himself able to introduce them into that very same British mainstream. The papers in the present volume do illustrate the degree of convergence with mainstream neoclassicism achieved by interwar Austrian Economics.

If our interest in offering the present collection of papers were confined to those in this volume of interwar Austrians, it might perhaps not be important to go much beyond the fact of this 'convergence'. However our purpose in these three volumes is to offer a sampling of Austrian work covering an entire century of intellectual development. We cannot eschew the task of understanding interwar Austrian Economics as it appears in the full sweep of that century-long development. From this longer run perspective any convergence to the British mainstream that occurred during this period must (as we argued in the Introduction to Volume I) appear as something of a short-run sub-plot in a more ambitious intellectual multi-generational saga. That long-run saga offers a story which began in 1871 with Menger's *Principles* and was to lead – through the mid-twentieth-century work of Mises and Hayek – to a late-century revival of the Austrian tradition in a form which sets it almost dramatically apart from mainstream microeconomics (as that microeconomics itself, paradoxically enough, evolved as a result of the Robbinsian, Austrian-inspired, influence!). Although that longer-run story will occupy us more substantively in the Introduction to Volume III, we can hardly avoid an attempt to place interwar Austrian Economics in the context, at least, of this longer-run story. Once again a reference to Robbins's book will offer a clue.

Subjective Value Theory: Menger, Mayer and Mises

Robbins, in his attempt to characterize the central propositions of shared neoclassical theory, found it convenient to refer to the subjective theory of value. 'It does not require much knowledge of modern economic analysis to realise that the foundation of the theory of value is the assumption that the different things that the individual wants to do have a different importance to him, and can be arranged therefore in a certain order. This notion can be expressed in various ways and with varying degrees of precision, from the simple want systems of Menger and the early Austrians to the more refined scales of relative valuation of Wicksteed and Schönfeld and the indifference systems of Pareto and Messrs Hicks and Allen.'[15] From this elementary insight into the character of individual preference, Robbins points out, economic analysis proceeds to derive the idea 'of an equilibrium distribution of goods between different uses, of equilibrium of exchange and of the formation of prices'.[16] Now, this way of seeing these central propositions of microeconomics may certainly have correctly expressed the subjective value theory of the interwar Austrians as Robbins encountered them in his visits to Vienna in the late 1920s. But (as will be seen in Mayer's long paper in this volume, paper 16, and as will be briefly pointed out in our Introduction to Volume III) Austrian Economics itself, even that of the interwar period, was *beginning* to evolve towards an entirely different understanding of value theory. And it was to be this evolution which would result in Austrian Economics turning out, by the second half of the twentieth century, to be unmistakeably different from the theory of subjective value as understood by Robbins (and as subsequently developed in mainstream microeconomics).

Hans Mayer (see paper 16 in this volume) put his finger squarely on the sources of the disagreement, two of which happen to be referred to in the passage we have quoted from Robbins. These are (a) the character of Paretian indifference maps, and (b) the centrality of equilibrium patterns of exchange and of prices. Mayer, in his lengthy critique of Pareto's indifference curve analysis, draws critical attention[17] to Pareto's well-known assertion that, for purposes of understanding economic equilibrium the 'individual can disappear, provided he leaves us this photograph of his tastes'. He also[18] draws attention to a problematic character of equilibrium theory: 'there is an immanent, more or less disguised, fiction at the heart of mathematical equilibrium theories: that is, *they bind together, in simultaneous equations, non-simultaneous magnitudes operative in genetic-causal sequence as if these existed together at the same time*.' One prominent late twentieth-century Austrian economist, Ludwig

M. Lachmann (who was a student at the time Mayer was writing his paper), was deeply influenced by Mayer's critique of 'functional' (rather than genetic causal) theories of price in mainstream microeconomics as it was already presented in its Paretian formulation, and as it was to become even more deeply entrenched as the century was to develop. As we shall see in the Introduction to Volume III, similiar objections to mainstream mid-century microeconomics were to be presented by Mises several years after Mayer's pioneering critique.[19] Although Mises's articulation of his theory of *human action* paralleled the objections of Mayer, and appeared subsequently to Mayer's paper, there is no reason to question the subjective originality of Mises's position (especially in the light of his earlier methodological papers, collected in his 1933 *Grundprobleme der Nationalökonomie*). Regardless of questions of priority, we have here definite signs that, despite the convergence of interwar Austrian Economics (both in the Mayer and Mises circles) towards the neoclassical mainstream, there was already movement towards Austrian rebellion against that mainstream. It was the continuation of that movement that would manifest itself at mid-century in the work of Mises and of Hayek, which would, in turn, nourish the late century revival of the Austrian tradition.

From the perspective of the latter revival, with its emphasis (especially in the work of Lachmann) upon uncertainty and ignorance, the subjectivism of the interwar Austrians, the subjectivism introduced into the mainstream by Robbins, appears severely limited. As will be seen from Rosenstein-Rodan's magisterial survey of the state of utility theory in the 1920s (paper 17 in the present volume) the interwar Austrians saw utility as expressing 'a property attributed to a good, namely its effectiveness in fulfilling the purpose of satisfaction of wants'. It was briefly recognized that 'since only expected anticipated needs are the motive force of economic action, only the expected and not the actually realized utilities are relevant to economic theory'. But this subjectivist recognition was immediately sharply modified by the comforting assurance provided that 'owing to economic experience' actual utility will 'not diverge significantly' from expected utility.[20] Despite the sophistication of the utility analyses surveyed by Rosenstein-Rodan, there is little recognition of human decision-making as grappling with an open-ended future fraught with radical uncertainty. Future wants are treated as given; the capacity of goods to satisfy these wants in the future is treated as given; utility is a property attributed to goods. Given the individual's wants, given the capacity of goods to satisfy these wants, utility analysis can proceed, almost in Paretian fashion, entirely without any decision-making *by* that individual. For the interwar Austrians, as in mainstream neoclassical microeconomics, individual decisions are assumed actually to maximize utility; the perceived ranked options among which choice is assumed to have been made, turn out to have been exactly those that were in fact available. So that the decision outcome is in fact an outcome which is already implicit in the given situation. In other words, subjective value theory, for interwar Austrians, is achieved by drastically abstracting from precisely those aspects of human action which were, for Mises and later Austrians, to supply the driving force for market processes.

As will be seen from Oskar Morgenstern's paper on the role of time in value theory (paper 21 in the present volume), interwar Austrians, especially those influenced by relevant contributions of Hans Mayer, had a lively awareness of the complexities that must be introduced into economic analysis as soon as we take into account the 'dating' of economic events. This will surely come as no surprise in regard to a school of thought steeped in Böhm-Bawerkian doctrines. Yet Morgenstern's paper hardly moves beyond what O'Driscoll and Rizzo have referred to as the 'spatialized' treatment of time.[21] (It is true that Morgenstern's 1928 monograph *Wirtschaftsprognose* went some way beyond such a treatment. However what is presented here in paper 21 seems to have accurately captured the general sense in which time was understood in interwar Viennese economics.) For Morgenstern the economic analysis of economizing decisions made in the face of a multi-period future hardly proceeds beyond what he himself describes as 'some introduction of time-parameters into some systems of equations and the tagging of all economic processes with time indices'.[22] Most perceptively, Morgenstern does, at the very end of his paper, recognize that in order to 'penetrate the problem' more thoroughly, it would be necessary to pay special attention to the entrepreneurial role. But this research programme is merely recognized as a most urgent problem facing economic theory; interwar Austrian economics had not yet attended to this unfinished agenda. And clearly the Austrian perspective which Robbins transmitted to economists in the British mainstream went no further in its subjectivism than these comprehensive treatments by Rosenstein-Rodan and by Morgenstern. All this contrasts with the flavour with which Mises was later to endow his economics of human action (in which a radical subjectivism in regard to time was to transform the analysis of human action in a manner entirely missing from twentieth-century mainstream microeconomics).

The Eclipse of Austrian Economics

No survey of interwar Austrian Economics can ignore perhaps the most arresting relevant feature of that period's history, viz. the precipitous decline in the school's professional fortunes which occurred at the end of the 1930s. At the beginning of the decade the school was held in highest international repute; Robbins and Hayek were introducing Austrian ideas, in microeconomics generally, in capital theory, and in business cycle theory, to the British scene with a degree of success which led to London's being puckishly described as a suburb Vienna. By the end of the decade this repute and success had virtually evaporated. We have already noticed Blaug's impression of the interwar period as being one of resounding Austrian defeats, in capital theory, in business cycle theory, and the theory of socialist economic calculation. We have indicated, on the other hand, that at least part of the eclipse of Austrian Economics in the 1930s can be explained, not so much by reference to doctrinal battles lost to formidable mainstream foes, as by reference to the degree of Austrian *success*. In the view of many Austrians, the extent to which, by the early 1930s, Austrian ideas had been absorbed into the British mainstream was a sufficient reason to believe that there was no longer any good reason to maintain a doctrinally distinct Austrian label. Apparently this feeling was also (and relatedly) partly the expression of the view that all neoclassical schools had faced a common doctrinal enemy, the German Historical School. The unifying effect of such a common foe, and the euphoria generated, at the start of the 1930s by widespread recognition of the final defeat of that common foe, was at least partly responsible, it appears, for the feeling among Austrians that one could now, once for all, lay aside narrow national-doctrinal labels, and join in joint international research programs for the advancement of economic science.

Yet doctrinal defeats were indeed suffered by Austrians during this period. Hayek's (and Mises's) 'Austrian' theory of the business cycle was unquestionably seen as a casualty of the sudden and extraordinary professional success achieved by John Maynard Keynes's 1936 *General Theory*. Böhm-Bawerkian capital theory, seen, in the eyes of many, as the backbone of the Austrian cycle theory, appeared to be another casualty as a result of (or, at any rate, to be very much on the defensive against) the work of Sraffa, Knight, and Kaldor. It is true that at least the Austrians themselves were far from admitting defeat (see especially in the present volume, paper 20 in which Machlup valiantly defends the Austrian position from the Knightian onslaught). Hayek was, at the end of the 1930s, busily at work on his *Pure Theory of Capital* (which would appear in 1941). Yet Austrian capital theory was not to recover the attention and acceptance of the profession for decades to come. Even in the debate concerning socialist economic calculation, in which Austrians had been so influential and successful in stirring up an extraordinarily vigorous debate during the interwar period, it appeared as if, after the 1936 defenses of socialism by Lange and by Lerner, the pendulum of professional favour was moving decisively away from the Misesian position. Again, it would be many decades before the profession would recognize that Lange and Lerner had by no means provided the last word in this debate.

The papers in the present volume do not provide direct insight into these damaging doctrinal wars in which Austrians were (in the court of professional opinion) suffering so badly. This is no accident and should be explained. It is true that business cycle theories were seen as a most important element in interwar Austrian Economics, at least after Hayek made this field his own around 1930; and it is true that Böhm-Bawerkian capital-theoretic ideas were important for those theories. Yet, from the perspective of 1994, the wounds suffered by the Austrians in these wars do not appear as decisive or as historically significant as they must have appeared at the time. Böhm-Bawerkian capital-theoretic ideas have proven themselves, in the long run, to be surprisingly durable. Even outside the narrower scope of the late twentieth-century Austrian revival, those ideas have retained a remarkable degree of appeal.[23] And, while the current Austrian revival has certainly awakened renewed interest in Hayekian business cycle theory,[24] it seems fair to say that from the perspective of this Austrian revival that theory is seen as not at all as so central (and therefore its post-1936 unfashionability as not all as so disastrous) as it may well have appeared during the years of the Great Depression, and at the time of the appearance of Keynes's *General Theory*. A paper (by Mises) which contains a statement of the Austrian Cycle theory is included in Volume III. In that volume there is also included Mises's classic statement concerning what he strongly maintained to be the impossibility of socialist economic calculation. Our assessment of the significance of the widespread (and in our judgment, wholly erroneous) conclusion in the profession that Mises's position had been decisively refuted by Lange and Lerner, will therefore not be provided in this Introduction. We should perhaps here point out, however, that interwar Austrian understanding of Mises's position on this matter was decidedly less than monolithic. The failure on the part of some Austrian-trained economists to appreciate Mises's thesis seems, in fact, paradoxically to be traceable precisely to the interwar Austrian preoccupation with the Imputation Problem. (On this problem, and its significance in interwar Austrian Economics, see in this volume, papers 15 and 19.) This 'problem' was a peculiarly Austrian one, in that Austrian economists had been trained to believe that 'consumers in evaluating ("demanding") consumer goods *ipso facto* evaluate the means of production which enter into the production of those goods'.[25] (Such a belief seems to have been derived from Menger's doctrine of lower- and higher-order goods; the theory of imputation addressed the question of the precise manner in which the prices of resources in fact reflect the values of consumer goods.) Schumpeter at least was tripped up by this Austrian training, to reject Mises's argument as apparently denying a proposition of elementary economics. For this he was properly reproved by Hayek;[26] as we shall see in the Introduction to Volume III, Schumpeter's error arose out of his failure – a failure basically shared by the interwar Austrians in general – to recognize the role of the entrepreneurial market *process* in transmitting consumer valuations of consumer goods to the resources from which these consumer goods are produced.

It is true that the close of the interwar period found the Austrians in eclipse. The story of how the Austrian economic tradition survived and matured in spite of this eclipse is a fascinating one, but belongs to the 'Age of Mises and Hayek', covered in Volume III of the present edition. It will be our task in the Introduction to that volume to show how the contributions made by Mises and by Hayek during the decades following 1940 would ultimately inspire a revival in the Austrian tradition, rendering the eclipse of the late 1930s and the related Austrian 'defeats' of definitely lesser significance than might then have been thought to be the case.

NOTES

1. Stephan Boehm, 'Austrian Economics Between the Wars: Some Historiographical Problems', Bruce J. Caldwell and Stephan Boehm (eds), *Austrian Economics: Tensions and New Directions* (Boston/Dordrecht/London: 1992, Kluwer).
2. Mark Blaug, 'Commentary' [on S. Boehm, op. cit.] in Caldwell and Boehm (eds), op. cit.
3. Blaug, op. cit. p. 31. For further observations by Blaug on this topic, see his 'Comment on O'Brien's "Lionel Robbins and the Austrian Connection"', Bruce J. Caldwell (ed.), *Carl Menger and his Legacy in Economics* (Durham and London: Duke University Press, 1990).
4. L. von Mises, *Notes and Recollections* (South Holland, IL: Libertarian Press, 1978), p. 94.
5. Boehm, op. cit. pp. 6ff.
6. On this point see for example the observations of Felix Kaufman, quoted in Margit Mises, *My Years With Ludwig von Mises*, 2nd edn (Cedar Falls, Iowa: Center for Futures Education, 1984), p. 202. See also that work, pp. 202–10, for additional recollections of the scenery in interwar Viennese economics, by Fritz Machlup, Gottfried Haberler, Paul Rosenstein-Rodan, and others.

7. Mises, op. cit. p. 73.
8. Mises, op. cit. p. 94.
9. On this point see, however, the closing sections of the Introduction to vol. iii, and especially the text there in regard to endnote 16.
10. Alfred Marshall, *Principles of Economics*, 8th edn (London: Macmillan, 1920), p. 1.
11. Edwin Cannan, *Elementary Political Economy*, p. 1. Both this definition, and that of Marshall referenced in the preceding note, are cited by Robbins, in his *The Nature and Significance of Economic Science* [1932], 2nd edn (London: Macmillan, 1935), pp. 1–2n.
12. Philip H. Wicksteed, *The Common Sense of Political Economy* [1910], (London: Routledge and Kegan Paul, 1933), vol. i, p. 2.
13. Robbins, op. cit., p. xv. (This is from the Preface to the 1st edn).
14. Robbins, op. cit., p. xiv (emphasis supplied).
15. Robbins, op. cit., p. 75.
16. Ibid.
17. See in the present volume, p. 111.
18. See in the present volume, p. 92.
19. See Mises, *Nationalökonomie* (1940), which appeared in the English version as *Human Action* (New Haven: Yale University Press, 1949).
20. See in the present volume, p. 173.
21. Gerald P. O'Driscoll and Mario J. Rizzo, *The Economics of Time and Ignorance* (Oxford: Basil Blackwell, 1985), p. 53.
22. See in the present volume, p. 338.
23. See especially J. Hicks, *Capital and Time: A Neo-Austrian Theory* (Oxford: Clarendon Press, 1973); M. Faber, *Introduction to Modern Austrian Capital Theory* (Berlin: Springer, 1979); G. O. Orosel, 'Faber's Modern Austrian Capital Theory: A Critical Survey', *Zeitschrift für Nationalökonomie* (1981), pp. 141–55.
24. See for example, Gerald P. O'Driscoll, *Economics as a Coordination Problem: The Contribution of Friedrich A. Hayek* (Kansas City: Sheed Andrews & McMeel, 1977).
25. Joseph A. Schumpeter, *Capitalism, Socialism and Democracy*, 3rd edn (New York: Harper & Row, 1950), p. 175.
26. See F. A. Hayek, *Individualism and Economic Order* (London: Routledge and Kegan Paul, 1949), pp. 90ff.

The
Interwar Period

Richard von Strigl, 'Wirtschaftstheorie im Dienste Wirtschaftspolitik',
Archiv fur Socialwissenschaft und Sozialpolitik (1928), pp. 353–67.

Richard von Strigl (1891–1942) was perhaps the youngest member
of Böhm-Bawerk's seminar in the years before World War I. He was
a leading figure in Austrian Economics in the interwar period,
providing a link between the generation of Böhm-Bawerk and the
subsequent one that emerged after the war. An important early
book that foreshadowed some of the insights contained in Lionel
Robbins's *Nature and Significance of Economic Science* (1932) was
his *Die Ökonomischen Kategorien und die Organisation der Wirtschaft* (1923). For a contemporary review essay analysing and criti-
cising Strigl's book, see paper no. 18, pp. 215–25. F. A. Hayek, in
his obituary (*Economic Journal*, June–September 1944, pp. 284–
6), described him as an 'eminently successful teacher' and one upon
whom had rested 'one's hope for a preservation of the tradition of
Vienna as a centre of economic teaching and of a future revival of
the "Austrian School"'. This paper has been translated into English
especially for this volume.

14

Economic Theory in the Service of Economic Policy[1]

RICHARD von STRIGL

Translated by

PATRICK CAMILLER

I. Theory and Practice

It is no wonder that the relationship between theory and practice is not the best in many fields of human activity. If practice approaches theory with the demand that it should answer concrete questions, it finds theory busy exploring remote problems for which practice shows not the slightest understanding or which, in the best of cases, it would like to see demoted as problems of minor importance. Of course, theory can rightly point to the fact that it alone can discover its path, that the handling of theoretical questions must develop from the posing of the problem to its resolution, which then leads to the posing of fresh problems. Only where there is a better relationship between theory and practice can one draw a clear distinction. Some theoreticians are closer to practice while others are further from it, and indeed practitioners and theoreticians working in the practical domain unite against 'pure' theoreticians. I daresay that at any point a split can always be found between practice and pure theory. Hardly anywhere, however, is the split as deep as in the field of economics. The practice of economic policy-makers scarcely consults theory: it does not expect from theory an answer to the questions with which it is concerned – indeed, it goes so far as to deny that theory has a right to exist, that a theory could ever be correct and useful. But if one opens a textbook at the second part – which deals with the practical problems of economic policy – and compares it with the theoretical part, then one must admit

3

that there is no connection at all between the two, that each is concerned with something quite different and takes no account at all of the other, unless the theoretical part is expanded into a 'General Economics' which also deals with concrete questions not closely connected with theory and belonging more to the domain of economic policy. (The inclusion of such expositions under general economics is perhaps mainly due to the fact that they cannot find a proper place in the usual category of economic policy.) The picture I have drawn may be rather too darkly coloured, and in particular fields there may be some collaboration between theory and practice. It cannot be denied, however, that there is no close connection between economic theory and economic policy. Of course, that is not a welcome state of affairs. We can grant that economic theory goes its own way – but for a long time people have been urging it to allow some demands of practice, to show that its theorems lead to the answering of questions with a practical import. And should not the practice of economic policy, which is far from always completely satisfying, not also be able to gain something from theory? Even if economic theory should be placed in the service of economic policy, there can be no question of their being fused in a single complex. The split between theory and practice is too deeply rooted in the nature of things. But is it not possible at least to build a bridge between economic theory and economic policy? If I am to consider whether theoretical knowledge can be made useful to practical economic policy, I must first ask how the present relationship between the two was reached, whether *mistakes* were made in one area or the other, and finally what *preconditions* have to be met before a more satisfactory collaboration can be expected.[2]

2. *Economic Policy and Liberal Economics*

If we look back at the time when scientific economics first began, we see quite plainly that the relationship of science to practice was then rather different.[3] However great the distance may otherwise be between the doctrines of the physiocrats and the English classical economists, they are completely in agreement on one point which, for our present purposes, is precisely the decisive issue: that is, they both require the economic policy of laissez-faire liberalism to follow from their theoretical train of thought; and both try to furnish proof that the traditional policy of economic interventionism can do nothing but harm. As the teachings of Adam Smith and his disciples were disseminated, liberalism became the prevailing trend in economic policy. Thus, economic policy was dominated by liberalism which was in turn supported by and closely associated with the spirit of theory. And if liberalism was not carried through sooner in economic policy, if its victory was in fact never complete, if it often seemed to have been overcome before it could have its full effect, this was possible only because economic policy separated itself from the dominant theory. Characteristically, where a reaction set in against liberal economic policy, an attempt was also made to find a special theoretical justification for a policy of intervention – as was partly the case, for example, with the German literature in the first half of the nineteenth century. When it comes to liberalism, however, one thing stands out in the relationship between theory and practice. Theory must discover *connections* and try to bring them together in a *system*: its task is *knowledge*. Policy must set *goals* and indicate the means for their fulfilment. How then could theory and policy form a unity within liberal economics? It is clear that such unity was only *apparent*. If classical economics thought it could offer more than knowledge and also placed demands upon economic policy, it had to assume a goal for economic policy. Adam Smith revealed this goal of liberal economic policy when he entitled his famous work 'An Inquiry into the Nature and Causes of the Wealth of Nations'. The *wealth of nations* – that is the goal of liberal economic policy. I shall explain that this formula of the wealth of nations can also be interpreted in quite diverse ways. But broadly speaking it did provide a direction for economic policy, and it may be useful if I take a concrete application to clarify all the consequences which this objective may have for economic policy.

One of the most splendid conceptions that we find in classical economics is the doctrine of the *international division of labour*.[4] In the system of all national economies, as in each one taken separately, it is not only the sum of capital ownership but also the advances in the division of labour which determine how large is the output available for distribution. In conditions of free trade, the international division of labour leads each country to produce exactly what it can do most cheaply with its *naturally given position in production*; the international division of labour will prevent a country from producing at great expense what it can obtain more cheaply elsewhere, and thus from forgoing potentially advantageous lines of production because it has to employ its means of production in other, less profitable lines. Here is an example given by Adam Smith: with tariff protection it is possible to produce wine even in Scotland by means of glass houses and hotbeds, but wine can be brought from France more cheaply.[5] Protective tariffs do not increase a country's capital and cannot make it wealthier; they obstruct the division of labour and make all countries poorer. I have no wish to examine here whether some modifications are necessary or possible in Smith's argument for free trade once it is assumed that wealth is the goal of economic policy. It is quite beyond

5

doubt, however, that the pursuit of this goal with these means can have significant *side-effects*, and that from various points of view – which may ultimately also determine the goal of politics in general and of economic policy in particular – it may be essential for these to be rejected. I will just mention that a full international division of labour would have to relocate all movable means of production in accordance with the scope for exploiting the most favourable production opportunities. In this connection there would also have to be a relocation of labour between the various countries, which would involve major changes in the division of the world among the nations. We can see clearly that the liberal concept of free trade pushes economic results right into the foreground. And that is precisely what has earned economic liberalism most of its enemies, who have not failed to point out that Adam Smith himself calmly dropped the principle of liberalism when he saw this to be in his country's interests.

Nor is that all. I just said that the formula of popular welfare by no means provides an unambiguous goal for economics.[6] There is no measure for the *quantity of welfare*. In the sphere of material goods that is quite evident: one cannot total up different kinds of goods, and greater provision with one may be offset by weaker provision with another. Not even the value of the national wealth or the national income can here serve as the measure, for the currency value itself – even when monetary relations are perfectly healthy – displays not insignificant interlocal differences. But let us imagine that a formula were found for calculating the wealth of nations as a whole. What would that achieve? Is the greatest wealth desirable *per se* in all circumstances – for example, where mass poverty exists alongside riches accumulated in a few hands? Is it not better if less wealth is distributed rather more evenly, so that the condition of the poorest layers of society is somewhat raised or at least fewer are completely excluded from the distribution of property? It is not the scale of wealth alone, but also the *type of property distribution*, which determines the extent to which needs are satisfied in the national economy. Although individual wealth has an undeniably important function in the supply of goods in the economy – if for no other reason than that even wealth used for consumption will give other employment and earnings to a very narrow layer of the population – and although *wealth as such* is desirable for the national economy and the satisfaction of needs insofar as it is compatible with other goals of economic policy and of politics in general, nevertheless the question of the *distribution of wealth* must be considered at the same time. This was already an acute problem in the age of the classical economists. And their inability to provide a satisfactory answer has greatly contributed to the fact that the classical teachings have been rejected *because of their consequences*. Here the liberal rejection of interventionism

6

is founded on the idea that economic events have the force of *natural law*. Here too one cannot deny the ambitiousness of classical theory. The laws of the free market determine the extent to which each layer of the population participates in the fruits of production. It would be pointless for people to try to fight the power of such laws. As the destiny of the labour force is mainly decided in accordance with the laws of economics, artificial intervention cannot yield any results. Wages cannot be raised above subsistence level: an artificial increase in the wages of one group of workers will be at the expense of other groups; and relief works will waste capital in a way that can only exert renewed pressure on the level of wages. I cannot here take on the task of critically examining, by means of tiresome expositions of economic theory, the foregoing law of wages, the wages-fund theory and so on. What is crucial for us here is a certain tension in classical doctrine which we can best explain by referring to the so-called law of wages.

If the workers' wage rises above the subsistence level corresponding to the standard of living, then the supply of labour-power will increase: among other factors, a favourable set of conditions will operate for the reproduction of the workforce. By contrast, there will be fewer new recruits to the workforce if wages fall below their natural level. It has been shown, in more recent times, that this connection no longer holds,[7] that new recruits are often fewer precisely in the top layers of the workforce and more plentiful in the bottom layers. But what matters here is the train of thought. Should theoretical economics ever argue in such a way? Does it not thereby overreach the bounds of what it can handle with its method? It is quite clear that the former law of wages is here argued in a way which careful use of a consciously constructed method must necessarily reject. And this *overstepping of the bounds of the purely economic* in theoretical argument can also be found in the classical economists and perhaps even more strongly in their successors. I will just mention the justification of private property and all the consequences following from its given distribution, from the idea that property came into being through the labour of competent people, that in the free competitive struggle the competent were victorious and acquired wealth for themselves. I shall not touch upon the content of this thesis.[8] I shall not ask whether competence is the source of wealth, nor whether the acquirer of wealth is always competent, nor even – and that would come next – whether the thesis that the competent prosper does not contain a circular definition of the competent as those who are economically successful, so that the measure of competence is given by a quite narrow goal; it may be, finally, that another yardstick would produce a negative evaluation of the economically competent. I shall only mention briefly the *consequence* for a general assessment of the

7

classical doctrine. A theory which regards as just the given distribution of property, which holds this order to be immutable and rejects any interference as harmful, will suit the interests of those layers of the population who have been raised up by the expansive, wealth-creating capitalist economy. Economic liberalism, then, is more than an economic theory: it is the *world-view of the rising bourgeoisie*; it is – to repeat a striking expression – the theodicy of new bourgeois wealth, whose owners wish not only to be rich but also to see their wealth established as just (Max Weber). And it is clear that liberal economics had to reject everything which sought to represent other interests.

Economic policy simply tried to disregard the natural laws of classical theory: it just declared them null and void, dethroned theoretical economics and – was successful. Or at least it thought it was successful. Again, it is not essential here whether, as many argued, appearances were deceptive, whether much at least of what appeared as the success of economic interventionism and especially social policy would have happened just as well without them as growing wealth and productivity increases expanded the realm of the economically possible. The old economics certainly lived on: it lost prestige and support, condemned as liberal, vanquished and refuted by the facts of experience. And, in one of the drollest episodes in the history of ideas, it had to tolerate being forced to supply the stones for the economic theory of Marxism, for the system which opposed the doctrine of class struggle to the liberal gospel of harmony à la Bastiat, and which used the theory of implacable economic laws to prophesy that immanent tendencies would soon have the effect of bringing capitalism to an end. We might say that the classical theories nowhere have a stronger resonance today than in the theory of Karl Marx, even if that system, precisely in its theoretical economic aspects, has proved incapable of development and become a rigid system of dogmas. It is also quite beyond doubt that the major importance which the Marxist doctrine has often had for practical economic policy stems not so much from the theoretical content of the system – which is in keeping with conventional economic theory – as from those theses which strove to grasp the moving forces in the economy. The propagandistic power of Marxism, on the other hand, is largely based on the fact that it knew how to incorporate the classical theories in an appropriate form. Little attention was given, however, to what had remained of the classical doctrines after the collapse of the school: this legacy was respected by only a few and driven into the background, where it slowly underwent a far-reaching process of transformation.

3. Vulgar Economics

The practice of economic policy all the more readily believed that it could abandon theory because it was faced with something which appeared to offer a complete substitute for theory: namely, *historical economics*. This solution seemed perfectly natural. If one rejected the enquiries of liberal theory into natural laws governing the evolution of the modern economy, and if one also considered that economic relations had changed quite fundamentally in the course of historical development, then the next step was to attempt to gain knowledge from the study of history. There was no lack of examples for the historical method in other domains. Nor can it be denied that, in any field of human social life, anyone who wishes to take a scientifically grounded position must have learnt from history. In particular, a training in the acquisition of ethical values will always need history as its teacher. And economic policy will also need it. But the relationship between historical economics and economic policy has hardly been close. Economic policy may perhaps have learnt from history which measures have been taken at one time or another in similar situations, but discussion of economic policy measures has scarcely learnt from history what effects are to be expected in particular cases. For the general structure of the economy has changed quite fast and far too deeply in the course of history for a complete analogy always to be drawn between the situation today and one from the past. In practice, then, economic policy had to fend for itself. But can economic policy be content with this? Does it not perhaps require the additional help of a theory? I have spoken earlier of the mistakes of the old liberalism. Now I would like to ask what mistakes an economic policy detached from theory is bound to make.

Economic policy, through the measures it takes, seeks to achieve *certain effects* in the economy which are different from those that would have occurred through the 'free play of forces'. And much can in fact be achieved without further ado.[9] If one wants the price of a commodity not to rise above a certain level or not to fall below a certain level, then an order can be issued to set a maximum or minimum price. If one wants to encourage a certain line of production, there are various means such as subsidies, protective tariffs and export premiums. If one wants to do something that will benefit the workforce, social policy has never been at a loss for things to recommend. And when social policy, and many other tasks of the state or public bodies, required means that could not be obtained through purchase, a whole array of taxes presented themselves: one had only to choose which one to go for. There seemed to be nothing as simple as social policy. Once one had decided to achieve a certain goal,

9

there was only the question of the administrative techniques through which the end was to be reached. Tasks presented themselves in abundant quantity, nor was there any shortage of means. But it was also necessary to ponder and discuss the various means, and it is not just in the present day that the discussion of economic policy measures largely determines the final course of action. Such discussion of economic policy measures has always occupied a large area. It was always quite clear that administrative measures and their immediate effect would not settle everything; there was also the question of the consequences that might attach themselves to the immediate effects. One had to try to identify the correlations, so that, if necessary, undesired side-effects could also be countered through administrative measures. This discussion of economic policy measures had to investigate the effects of certain states of affairs and sought to draw up correlations; anyway it was *theory*, and it is clear that it was largely bad and wrong theory. This had to be the case, mainly because such discussion has always been most closely connected with human interests. A link was missing between such thinking about economic matters and pure theory. Where the discussion had first been triggered by a particular search for results, this inevitably led thought to go astray. And then what came under discussion was not the factual basis for actual links to the object of the dispute, but rather the ill will of those who had different interests or to whom others thought they could attribute different interests. In this discussion on economic policy measures, a vulgar economics came into being which was at once crudely formed and self-contradictory and presented a caricature of scientific theory. A major basis for this was provided by fragments from the system of the classical economists, particularly through the mediation of Karl Marx's doctrine, which was well known in some of its essentials. (There is also such a thing as 'vulgar Marxism'.) Different theories which used the concept of exploitation had in the nature of things to be acceptable to those whose class position seemed to correspond to them. Moreover, the views of wide layers of the population stem from the line of vision in which the consumer sees the economy – and not only when his economic position really depends little on the relations of production. Thus, the technical-administrative measures of economic policy often go in a direction where the primary goal is to keep down the prices of consumer goods. It would be quite a job to define a 'system' of vulgar economics.[10] Let us just mention a few examples of its theoretical scaffolding: the view that the ill will of businessmen can drive up prices; the view that increased consumption has the direct effect of stimulating production, that faster circulation of money is a suitable way of reviving the economy. Even when vulgar economics does not directly draw false conclusions, it does not identify the deeper causes; it will often attach too much significance to superficially remarkable phenomena in the chain of causes. Many of the theses of vulgar economics are naturally presented differently according to the general attitude of the individual in question, but there is broad agreement in the *mode of derivation* of practical consequences. Far-reaching speculations are remote from the practical orientation of vulgar economics, and it will endeavour to find in a single formula the causes of a particular social evil; social policy will then be called upon to overcome those causes. The upshot is that social policy will try to cure by tackling symptoms. It lacks more sophisticated, roundabout ways of achieving its goals, and it often works against its own goals because it is ignorant of the real correlations.

4. Pure Theory as a Foundation for Economic Policy

I said above that after the collapse of the classical school economic theory was driven far into the background, so that for a long time it lost nearly all practical significance for economic policy. The revival of theory dates from the seventies of the last century, when the use of marginal analysis brought with it a fundamental change in the *content* of economic theory. I shall not speak here of this material content, but rather about the fact that the new theory *makes possible quite a different basic approach to the questions which concern us here*. And it should be stressed at once that although the change which has taken place was already partly prepared by older writers – just as the principle of marginal analysis had from time to time been brought into use – what is presented here as the standpoint of recent theory cannot yet be fully considered as simply the common property of economic theory. But I have the right to set out what seems to me of paramount importance for our enquiry into the new directions of theory, and to do so in a pure form without taking into account the other views that are also held.[11]

Let us now consider the central question of conformity to laws. Can economic theory really give a full and complete account of what happens in the economy? Quite varied meanings can be given to this question, but let us begin by extending its scope a little.

Any theoretical science must start out from the general forms of some *primum*, regardless of whether this is grasped as a conceptual necessity or taken from experience. Necessary inferences can then be drawn from this *primum*, so that the type of law and the way in which it is to be grasped are here a matter of indifference. If we then want to see how things work out in reality, we fill in the general formulae with *concrete facts*. In so doing, these facts may to a greater or lesser extent be broken down into particulars, up to the ideal situation where experience is completely inserted in every detail into these formulae so that it appears entirely as the fulfilment of general laws. This ideal of the complete capturing of reality in every detail cannot usually be attained, but nor is that at all necessary. However, according to *which facts* are inserted into the most general formulae of a theoretical science, the *mode of operation of the most general laws* of that science will also vary. Different effects will be expected from the insertion of data group A or data group B. Thus in economic theory, for example, we will obtain different results if we employ groups of data from a simple economy or a commercial economy; we will obtain different results if we take an economy with free competition or one dominated by monopolies; we will have to distinguish between a commercial economy driven by completely free competition and one in which strong frictions exist. The law of costs, for instance, will work itself out quite differently in these two forms of economy. In the field of economics, as in every field tackled by a theoretical science, it must be the case that laws operate differently according to the given data. The 'natural laws' of the freely competitive economy cannot, however, be the most general laws of economics, if only because there are also other forms of economy, because more general laws have been identified for which those of the freely competitive economy are only applications under particular preconditions.

What, then, are the special preconditions of the economy that exists at a given time, the concrete facts of an economy? Immutable necessities of nature are certainly not the only givens. In addition, the social organization of an economy is one of the most important factors determining its concrete shape, and hence people themselves with their qualities and abilities. Never will the blind rule of natural forces alone shape the conditions of an economy. The overall organization of society is changeable, as are individual people and their goals, and this makes possible a change in the premises of economic events and the concrete facts of the economy. In this light, economic policy measures mean nothing other than the exertion of influence over the facts of the economy; the task of theory will be to grasp the effects which such factual changes bring about and the laws which prevail within the factual changes.[12] The classical economists also envisaged the possibility of interfering in the economy. That liberalism nevertheless utterly rejected such interference is to be explained by a particularity of that school: namely, its lack of any theory of facts and its acceptance of natural conditions, although the economy is actually based in large measure upon the shifting foundations of social relationships. In particular, liberalism considered the motives lying within people to be at least partly determined by economic laws; and it regarded a certain social organization of the economy – following the conceptions of natural law – to be a natural order of things. The old theory has already been reproached for all this by the historical school, and our expositions can only show how much its critique was justified.[13] However, when historicism thought it could explain the economy from social relations, without attending to specifically economic connections, it fell into the opposite error. Classical thought, in the end, brought theoretical knowledge into a connection with ideas of justice. And even in this factor lies something of decisive significance.

The history of a science ought to be the history of a path to better knowledge, and when a science deals with a field in which human intentions are so strongly implicated – as is the case with economics – its most important step forward will be to makes its investigations completely independent of what people want to see happen in that field – whether because they approve of the present state of things, or because they would like to replace it with another. So long as the striving for knowledge is influenced by a striving to influence the object of knowledge, it remains a long way from pure science. However much one values the knowledge which new economic theory has produced, it has not brought a *decisive advance* in science if it has not succeeded in making science independent in this regard. But in fact science has made such an advance by developing the most general theory within a sphere in which a clash of political opinions can no longer make itself heard. *The fact that the classical economists started out from experiences of the actual economy may be appealing to many, but this very feature holds a great danger for theory –* for here the object of science must from the beginning be grasped in a form in which it could become the object of a clash of opinions. The pure theory of the modern school is assembling a pure system of knowledge amid the unworldly peaks, but it is only by climbing down from them that it will be possible to reach the questions in dispute in social policy. And a lot would thereby be gained. The true gods could not prevent the summoning up of false gods, and true science has not been able to prevent the establishment of false teachings.[14] *But if the purest general theory is well established, if the questions underlying the clash of opinions can be tackled only in such a way that they descend from the propositions of pure theory through the introduction of particular facts, then one can test a tenet by whether it is capable of being fitted into that solid edifice of scientific theory.*

This is what is new in the basic attitude of modern theory. It can safely say that never before has an economic theory upheld with all its consequences the principle that theorems are not first developed by reference to current questions, but that a theoretical system is erected which can arrive at concrete cases by application. Only in this form can our science serve the practice of economic policy. It will prove better up to this task if 'applied theory' is further cultivated – that is, theory which fits particular concrete facts into the most general formulae and establishes their effects with regard to changes in the facts. Theory is undoubtedly following this path: one day it will perhaps be able to take another decisive step, when it successfully arrives at a quantitative analysis which measures the scale of these effects. But for economic theory to be really useful to economic policy, it is also necessary that economic policy and the discussion of measures relating to it should be *detached from vulgar economics* and established on the material basis of theoretical knowledge. Complete agreement is therefore still not to be expected in economic policy: what the goal of economic policy should be will always remain disputed. But at least it will be known what consequences are to be expected from a particular measure, and one will have to ask oneself whether one wishes to bear them. People will no longer deceive themselves and others. Let us take just one example. If a tax is to be introduced, there will be a struggle to prevent any burdening of agriculture, industry, labour or consumers (who are always depicted as an independent economic layer). It is already much if people recognize that a burden on one layer of the population can also have an effect on others; that a burdening of agriculture might, under certain circumstances, strengthen the social pressure on the countryside, which would in turn sharpen supply pressure on the industrial labour market, and so forth. But what is never asked in the discussion is whether a tax will tend to increase the costs of production and therefore to limit production possibilities; or whether the source of the tax is such that it will be impossible to offload it onto production costs. But when will financial policies ever pose such a question?

If economic theory thinks differently from vulgar economics, it will also critically assess the measures which the latter proposes. It will identify the effects of such measures, which will then often have to be rejected. Economic policy founded on theory will thus easily appear 'liberal' *in comparison with vulgar economics*. But *anyone who understands economic theory will see that this has absolutely nothing to do with the old liberalism.* An unscientific economic policy can promise the moon, but the realities are determined by the scale of wants and the wealth of the national economy; and while wealth has quadrupled over the centuries, so too have people's wants. It is impossible to distribute more than is produced: all that counts in these matters is not experiments but to work and to save. Economic policy can conjure up nothing more. But if it is guided by true knowledge, it will go beyond the primitive tactic of direct interference in the economy and learn to shape more advantageously – when that is possible – the conditions for an increase in production. And in this it will certainly have greater success than the uncritical economic policy of interventionism, which blindly sets off towards a goal and thinks it can chalk up a success even if the side-effects of its measures have brought more harm than any good which has been achieved. But if wants are growing and expanding, they are less and less determined by the physical nature of man alone. Spiritual values are ever more important in determining the goal of the economy. And so for the individual, economics increasingly becomes a means in the service of the ethical ideal. But that is also true for the social community. The goal of economic policy, as long as the economy is poor, will be to improve as far as possible the supply of people with material goods. Economic policy will be able to set other goals all the more easily, the more plentifully the national economy is endowed with material goods. For economic policy, the setting of a goal will always stand outside the field discernible to a theory. But when a goal is set, the task is to discover the means of realizing it. Economics too does not only serve the satisfaction of the baser wants; it can stand in the service of higher ends. And economic theory can teach us how to apply our means to the satisfaction of such ends.

NOTES

1. From a lecture delivered at the Association of Political Scientists of the Karl Franzens University in Graz.
2. As the proofs were being corrected I received a copy of E. Schuster's *Wirtschaftstheorie und Wirtschaftspraxis* (Mannheim, 1928), which addresses in a stimulating way the question of how economic theory can provide rules for *correct* management.
3. For the following section, compare the well-known accounts by Oncken, Hasbach, Gide and Rist, among others.
4. Cf. L. Mises, 'Vom Ziel der Handelspolitik', *Archiv für Sozialwissenschaft und Sozialpolitik*, vol. 42 (1916).
5. Adam Smith, *An Inquiry into the Nature and Causes of the Wealth of Nations*, book 4, ch. ii [quoted here from Methuen edition: London, 1961, vol. 1, p. 480].
6. See A. C. Pigou's way of posing the problem in his *The Economics of Welfare*, 2nd edn (London, 1924).
7. See P. Mombert, *Wirtschaft und Bevölkerung (Grundriß der Sozialökonomik)*, section ii, 1914: 'The worker's life is...not production in the sense in which Ricardo, under the influence of Malthusian ideas, believed it to be.'

15

8. See O. Hertwig, *Zur Abwehr des ethischen, des sozialen, des politischen Darwinismus* (Jena, 1918).

9. See the essays by L. Mises: 'Interventionismus', *Archiv für Sozialwissenschaft und Sozialpolitik*, vol. 56 (1926); and 'Sozialliberalismus', *Zeitschrift für die gesamte Staatswissenschaft*, vol. 81 (1926).

10. H. Herkner makes an interesting contribution to the analysis of vulgar economics in 'Die Lohntheorien der deutschen Arbeiter- und Arbeitergeberverbände seit der Stabilisierung der Valuta', in Hans Mayer *et al.*, eds, *Die Wirtschaftstheorie der Gegenwart*, 3 vols (Vienna, 1928).

11. For a more detailed theoretical justification of the views set out below, see my book *Die ökonomischen Kategorien und die Organisation der Wirtschaft* (Jena, 1923).

12. See my essay: 'Änderungen in den Daten der Wirtschaft', *Jahrbücher für Nationalökonomie und Statistik*, vol. 128 (1928).

13. See, most recently, Louise Sommer, 'Zur Methode der exakten und historischen Nationalökonomie', *Schmollers Jahrbuch*, 52nd year (1928).

14. Even today it happens that 'new' theories, mostly made up of old writers' mistakes that have long been overcome, are taken seriously even though the fact that they directly lead to 'practical' consequences should make their bias evident even to an outside observer.

Hans Mayer, 'Zurechnung', *Handwörterbuch der Staatswissenschaften*, 4th edn, vol 8 (Jena: Gustav Fischer, 1928), pp. 1206–28.

Hans Mayer (1879–1955) was a dominant figure in the interwar Austrian School. He was a close disciple of Wieser and, after Wieser's death, assumed his chair at the University of Vienna. It is well known that a coolness, to say the least, governed the relations between Hans Mayer and Ludwig von Mises. (For Mises's views of Mayer see his *Notes and Recollections*, p. 94.) Mises and most of the younger economists who frequented his seminars found it necessary to leave Vienna before the Nazi takeover in the mid-1930s. Mayer remained in Vienna and dominated economics at the University of Vienna until well after World War II. In this expository paper Mayer surveys a topic which, while it is no longer of substantive interest to modern Austrian economics, was at the time a central theme for discussion among Austrian economists. This paper has been translated into English especially for this volume.

15

Imputation

HANS MAYER

Translated by

PATRICK CAMILLER

I. *The problem*. 1. Its emergence and its content. 2. Demarcation of the economic from the moral and technical problem of imputation. 3. The importance of imputation for economic theory. II. *Historical development of the problem*. 1. The older literature. 2. The present state of attempted solutions. (a) The Austrian School: Böhm-Bawerk (Menger) and Wieser. (b) Anglo-American marginal productivity theory (Clark). III. *Critique of the attempted solutions*. 1. The objection of insolubility in principle. 2. Objections to some attempted solutions. IV. *Positive presentation of the solution*. A. Formation of the total productive combination. B. Establishment of the values of means of production without imputation. C. Ascertaining value through imputation. D. The material determinants of the value of productive goods. V. *The role of imputation in distribution of the national production yield: formation of the prices of means of production*.

I. The Problem

1. *Its emergence and its content*

In recent economic theory the term 'imputation' refers to the question of the determinants of value formation and of the resultant pricing of the means of production in a commercial economy.[1] The most general way of posing the problem is as follows: *How do the values (prices) of first-order goods (i.e., consumption goods) give rise to certain values (prices) of the higher-order goods (means of production) which serve to produce them?* In addition we find – particularly in Wieser, whose locution gave the problem its name – special formulations which already point towards certain attempted solutions. Which laws determine the portions of value that are imputed from products to the means of their production? Or: according to which laws is the production yield *distributed* among the factors combining in its formation?

The problem could emerge only in modern economic theory basing itself on the value of wants, but it also *had to* arise there. If it is ultimately wants which, according to their degree of importance, induce economic man to attach value to things as a means to their satisfaction, then the laws of the valuation of consumption goods can be immediately derived from them. Raw materials, auxiliary materials, labour output, soil yield and the numerous intermediate products – whose concrete forms and properties are not inherently suitable for the satisfaction of wants – can be objects of economic interest and thus of valuation only insofar as the procurement of value-containing means to the satisfaction of wants (i.e., of enjoyable products) is dependent upon them. It is from the value of their products that the means of production receive their value. But in the process, an exceptionally significant complication arises for the derivation of the value of the means of production in comparison with that of consumption goods. No means of production can by itself create a consumption good and thus originate economic utility; it can only ever do this in combination with others. The means of production stand in a relation of *technical complementarity* to one another. Hence there are always whole complexes of means of production – productive *combinations* – which as potential consumption goods have the value of those goods transferred to them. But with knowledge of the values of the productive combinations as a whole, the economic system does not find all that it needs. Knowledge of the values of the different means of production is also required to control the economic efficiency of all dispositions with regard to individual means of production, both in production itself and in exchange – whether the exchange is of means of production for consumption goods, of means of production for one another, or of consumption goods for means of production. On the one hand, individual means of production are simply members of productive combinations (mere components of goods); on the other hand, they have a physical existence of their own, are given independently of one another in definite quantities – land, natural resources, quantities of labour etc. – and undergo change. These two facts force the economy to pay special attention to both of them, to weigh their use potentials against each other so that the one which yields the greater utility can be put into effect. For this, knowledge is required not only of the utility of the productive combinations as a whole, but of the economic utility which depends on command over one more or one less of each *separate* means of production. Where the available quantities and their changes stand in a harmonious relationship to one another – as is the case with the various kinds of intermediate product – this is already a consequence of the systematic gearing of the economy to the utility of the various means of production. The individualist commercial economy thus involves, on the one hand, a lack of economic autonomy of the means of production, as mere members of productive combinations, with regard to the achievement of utility; on the other hand, autonomous physical existence of individuals, with the resulting compulsion to form a judgement about the utilities dependent upon each individual. This situation finds its special expression in the distribution of the various complementary means of production among numerous different owners, whereby they are acquired on the part of the producers who set up the productive combinations, by way of exchange for special compensation which again presupposes knowledge of the utilities dependent upon each individual.

Thus the question of the values of individual means of production *necessarily* arises in practical economy – in fact, in every economic organization – and with it the problem of imputation in the theory by which practical economy is to be explained. However inadequate, and sometimes misleading, may be the definitions of various authors, however great the difficulty of reaching a solution, the problem exists and is solved in practice. And it cannot be removed from the world – as some have tried to do – by denying its reality or simply declaring it to be insoluble. It is no objection, rather a misunderstanding of the problem and of the general cognitive tasks of theoretical economics, to suggest that since the prices of means of production are always already given as 'costs' for the entrepreneur, and since his role in the regulation of production is exclusively to attain the highest possible profit at the given prices, the question of imputation does not arise at all in a commercial economy. For what requires explanation is precisely how the prices of the means of production are 'always given'; and, in general, it is a much more important and incomparably more difficult task of economic research to show how prices reach a particular level, than to describe what happens when prices are given. (See sections IV and V below on the point in the overall production process at which the imputation question asserts itself for the individual kinds of means of production.)

In the valuation of the means of production, as in the formation of any value in practical economic life, the issue is their marginal value, *marginal utility*.[2] Practical economy is never faced with the question of the value (or 'generic value') which a factor of production such as 'labour' or 'land' has *in abstracto* as a species of good, or how much total production in the abstract depends upon land or labour as generic means of production. The

21

answer to this question (if one were possible at all) would be of no significance for what actually happens with the means of production. And so, we can say that the question was wrongly posed in the older theory. And its only conclusion was that nothing can be produced without the factor land, any more than without the factor labour, since both are indispensable as means of production for any good and therefore have the generic value 'infinite'. Practical economy always has to do only with *concrete quantities of goods*, fractions of the total amount in existence, and so – as regards disposal of the means of production – with the question of how concrete amounts of the means of production are to be utilized, and which concrete amounts are to be either added or exchanged for other commodities. The general theory of value shows that, on these practical premises, the value of each part-quantity is determined in accordance with marginal utility. Hence, the theory of imputation also has to deal only with ascertaining the marginal utilities of the means of production.[3] In irregular cases which throw up the question, not of an abstract and economically meaningless generic value, but of the value of a certain *total* combination of the required *total* amounts of a means of production – as when a unionized workforce presents an entrepreneur with the danger of losing all the labour necessary to continue production – a univocal solution cannot be given by means of general theory, but is possible only on the assumption that special determinants are operating in the particular concrete situation.[4]

2. *Demarcation of the economic from the moral and technical problem of imputation*

The *economic* problem of imputation is to be sharply distinguished from the quite separate question of *moral* imputation. Although the economists who have developed the theory of imputation always do this with the necessary clarity, confusion or amalgamation of the two problems is still very often found in the literature, and arguments about the scientific impossibility of grounding moral imputation are even advanced against the theory of economic imputation. The question as to which part of the production yield should *rightfully* accrue to those who participated with their labour-power, and which to those who own the relevant material means of production, is much more popular and arose much earlier than the scientific question as to the determinants of the *actual* distribution of profits. The answer inevitably varied according to perceptions of what was 'right': some demanded that the distribution should reflect the individual 'sacrifice', especially in terms of labour effort; others that it should be according to need, or according to some estimated share in the generation of the profit – or finally, a combination of some or all of these demands.

However, an arbitrary character attaches to all these postulates; they play their role in the construction of social utopias, in social philosophy and even in the formulation of social and political demands; but they offer nothing in the way of *knowledge* about actual events in the economy. These are the focus of the question of *economic* imputation, with which economic theory is alone concerned. Even the question of economic imputation often appears in normative guise, when consideration of the laws whereby the value of the means of production is actually determined, goes together with formulations about the values which 'are to be imputed' or 'should be imputed' to the means of production. But the 'should' in this defective mode of expression refers not to some ideal of justice but to the final goal of all economy: the achievement of the greatest total utility (aggregate satisfaction of wants), which is itself possible only if the partial utility which depends upon the disposition of each individual means of production for the total utility is correctly recognized and 'imputed' to it. And since each inaccuracy in this valuation leads to inaccurate dispositions (ones which do not secure the greatest possible total utility), while the economic subjects, generally guided by experience about what is and is not in their interest, very soon correct such inaccuracies in future calculations, it can be broadly assumed that the actually practised valuations of the means of production (the actually imputed values) will coincide with those derived from knowledge of the utility which is dependent upon them (that is, to be economically imputed to them).

More difficult than the separation of economic and moral imputation, but more important for the successful handling of the problem, is a clear definition of the relationship between, on the one hand, physical-causal tracing of the share of the individual factors of production in shaping output, and on the other hand, imputation of definite values to the individual factors of production out of the value of the profit; or, in a widely used formulation, between *physical* (or technical) and *economic* imputation. The overwhelming majority of economic theorists regard as too general – or in most cases simply impossible – the idea of physically tracing back separate parts of the production yield to certain means of production; one would only be able to establish the general physical determination of the product by the totality of its factors of production. Most representatives of imputation theory therefore consider that a solution of the problem does not require us to ascertain the parts of the product which are physically imputable to the individual factors of production, because what matters in this problem is not *physical causation* but the *economic dependence* of the production yield upon its individual conditions. For their part, however, the opponents of imputation theory maintain that the problem cannot be solved within this framework, because economic imputation is unthinkable without prior technical imputation. This brings us to the heart of the difficulties.

If we look more closely at the emergence of whole productive combinations,[5] which results in the formation of the value of individual means of production, it actually does transpire that each judgement of economic imputation (that is, about the utility which depends upon the disposition of a concrete quantity of a means of production) necessarily presupposes a judgement of technical imputation (that is, knowledge of the effect in the physical or *natural* outcome, whether the effect is understood in quantitative or qualitative terms); and that this effect is to be traced back causally – or, to be more precise, conditionally – to the involvement of a particular means of production in the procurement of the result. For this quantitative or qualitative effect is the material substratum without which utility or value in the economic sense is inconceivable. If, then, each economic imputation is based upon a natural imputation, it by no means follows that, conversely, each means of production which has a technical share in forming the production yield must therefore be imputed a share of the *value* of those results. This can be clearly seen in the example of 'free' means of production (available in abundance); for although their concrete quantities are causally implicated in the obtaining of the product, the practically boundless substitutability contained in the concept of abundance means that no part of the results is *economically dependent* upon those quantities. How this natural imputation is possible, and how it occurs in economic practice, will be considered below in sections III and IV.

3. *The importance of imputation for economic theory*
The theory of imputation is first and foremost a theory of value: it constitutes, qua derivation of the value of the means of production, an indispensable complement to the theory of the value of consumption goods. Since any economy must necessarily extend its reach from the dispositions of consumer goods to some means of production and incorporate these into its calculations, the questions associated with imputation theory do not present special problems but are rather an elementary problem of economic theory as a whole. For the theory of commercial economy, it is impossible to derive the laws governing formation of the prices of the means of production, without knowledge of the laws of value of the means of production. Like the general value-correlation of all products and means of production in a closed economy, so here the general correlation of prices in a commercial economy cannot be given representation without the lessons of imputation theory.

But the prices of the means of production have a dual function: for those who purchase means of production (i.e., the producers) they represent the 'costs' of production; for the economic subjects who sell means of production – workers who sell their labour-power, landowners their land, capitalists the uses of capital – they represent *income* as wages, ground rent and interest on capital. The path to knowledge of the *formative laws and determinants of income* in individual lines of business must therefore lead through the theory of the formation of the value and price of the means of production. Since, moreover, the purchasing power and demand of income-recipients on the products market is determined together with the level of income, and since the participation of the individual economic subjects or classes of the population thereby flows into the production yield of the whole economy, the theory of imputation forms the key to knowledge of the *laws of distribution* of the national income. It is therefore absolutely right that it should be seen as the *central problem* of modern economic theory.

II. *Historical development of the problem*

1. *The older literature*

Questions of 'distribution' – both of national income among the *classes* and of output value among the *factors of production* – emerged very early in the literature of economic science. John Locke already asked what share 'of the products of the earth useful to the life of man...[is] purely owing to Nature and what to labour', and concluded that 'in most of them ninety-nine hundredths are wholly to be put on the account of labour', because 'the benefit [of land without labour] amount to little more than nothing'.[6] This way of posing the question, later extended to the third factor of production, capital, would often appear again. The whole *physiocratic* system constitutes a theory of distribution erected upon an admittedly very one-sided theory of production, and even Ricardo held that the main task of economics was to explain the establishment of the laws which determine the share of rent for land, profit for capital and wages for labour. But all these theories, like the socialist labour theory of value at a later date, focused on costs in a way that made them misunderstand the essence and origin of economic value. Taking as primary a supposedly 'objective' value determined by physical-technical facts, and then deriving as secondary the value ('natural price') of goods, they were completely unable to pose the specific problem of economic imputation. (In classical theory, the duality of 'natural' and 'market' price was seen as a fundamental determinant of final supply and demand, so that the lack of a precise analysis of these factors prevented a breakthrough to the imputation problem.) If these systems now and then display lines of thought that recall imputation theory, this is always because physical-technical and moral imputation judgements are involved. Thus, when the physiocrats made of the factor nature (land) the only pure source of wealth, they became caught up in an erroneous technical imputation, as socialist writers have done in analysing labour as the only factor of production.[7]

Even Ricardo's theory of ground rent – that inorganic element of his system in which the principle of tracing product-value to (labour) costs is abandoned and the values (prices) of higher-quality land or its potential are derived from the values (prices) of its produce – is based upon a special case of genuine economic imputation, although the spell of the labour theory of value did not allow it to pose the problem in a general and systematic manner. J.B. Say's approach showed a constant fluctuation: sometimes the value (exchange-value) of the 'productive services' of the factors of production is derived from the want-value of the products, and sometimes the value of the products from the prices of the productive services, whose relationship shapes the distribution of the product-value among the owners of the means of the production.

As to those who upheld and continued the classical doctrine in Germany, they also came close to the imputation problem insofar as their development of the fundamental concept of use-value, totally neglected in classical theory, paved the way for the modern theory of value. This is expressed in many different phrases, although admittedly they lack a clear distinction between moral or technical and economic imputation.

Thus Jacob describes it as natural 'that the product or its value is distributed among those who created it, in proportion to their actual contribution'.[8] Lotz argues that to ascertain the production costs of a commodity, we must investigate 'what in the yield of the various branches of human endeavour must be *posted to the account* of one or the other conditions that were effective in it'; and he considers it 'imperiously required by natural law' that 'just as much' of the yield is distributed to each as 'is his due according to the ratio of his powers that were effective in it'.[9] Storch explains that each of the three classes corresponding to the chief sources of wealth creation – workers, capitalists and landowners – 'can demand their share in proportion to their participation in production, so that the whole is divided among working people, landlords and capitalists'.[10] Kuddler thinks that 'the share of each follows the importance of the participation of his means of production in the creation of the good'.[11] For A. F. Riedel, the *importance of each part of the (productive) association* can easily be recognized, but 'any definite numerical determination' is not possible when it comes to 'precise measurement of the *size* of the participation of each means of production in their communal effect'.[12]

H. Rössler maintains that we must conceptually distinguish the share of the production yield due to the participation of capital from the shares which have arisen from labour or the free forces of nature, and that *a certain part of the product-value should be put down to the account of capital, another part to the account of labour, and so on.*[13]

Of greater significance for the development of the problem and ways of solving it were J. H. von Thünen's investigations into the 'natural distribution of the labour product among workers, capitalists and landowners'.[14] Still essentially placing himself on the ground of classical value and price theory, Thünen also poses the problem not as one of value but as one of the distribution of the production yield in accordance with *technical and price factors.* From the *law of diminishing returns*[15] – according to which each new growth in capital increases the labour product to a lesser degree than is done by the previously invested capital, and thus causes a fall in the price for use of capital accompanying the fall in the surplus yield – and from the law of *substitution* – according to which two different interest rates (prices for use of capital) cannot exist at the same time for the capital deployed first and later – Thünen concludes that the price for use of the total capital *'is determined by the use of the last-invested portion of capital'*, and that the growth in the total product brought about by the labour of the last-employed worker determines the wages of all workers' (with the same skill). Thus Thünen was the first to delineate the concept of 'marginal productivity', which has become so fundamental for the whole modern theory of distribution. And he also practised a method for solving the imputation problem which was later painstakingly perfected by theoreticians in America (especially J. B. Clark, Carver and Seligman) and Italy (Montemartini) and is today almost universally accepted. (That Thünen also thought he could derive a method of 'correct' imputation from knowledge of technical and economic connections, cannot diminish the value of his achievement.)

Thünen's method for a solution applied to cases where different means of production work together, so that the productive combination is not completely inflexible and there is *variability of the production coefficients* within certain limits – the necessary condition for the law of diminishing returns to hold. His method therefore encompassed the overwhelming mass of empirical production data, but it left unanalysed the case where the value of the individual factors of production is formed within an inflexible combination or a one-sided relation of complementarity. It was H.H. Gossen – here again the representative of modern value theory – who first recognized and clearly formulated the problem in its general form,[16] and who gave a solution at least for the limiting case of strict complementarity which, in its essential features, coincides with Böhm-

27

Bawerk's attempt some decades later, without knowing Gossen's work, to solve the 'eliminating' alternate imputation. Since Gossen's work went missing for decades and had no influence on the development of economic theory,[17] the founders of modern value theory who are known under the name of the 'Austrian School' – Carl Menger, Böhm-Bawerk and Wieser – are justly regarded as the originators of the general theory of imputation, within which Thünen's theory of marginal productivity counts as a special case, albeit an extremely important one in its field of empirical application.

2. The present state of attempted solutions

a) *The Austrian School: Böhm-Bawerk (Menger) and Wieser.* The considerable differences, in both formulation and solution of the problem, between Menger or Böhm-Bawerk and Wieser require a separate analysis. It will not be necessary, however, to reproduce Menger's solution, as it is contained in Böhm-Bawerk's theory which is comprehensively built upon the same basic ideas.

Böhm-Bawerk starts from the fact of complementary goods, which produce a certain useful effect only in combination. To ascertain the value of individual members of the complementary group, he makes use of the very idea which modern value theory employs to establish the value of consumption goods. The value of a good, he argues, is equal to the utility which depends, directly or indirectly, upon that good: that is, the utility which is forfeited if the good is lost, or which, in the case of addition to the stock of goods held by an economic subject, accrues to the previous total utility. This is what is known as the differential method or as operating with 'notional loss', and it has been amply justified and tested in general value theory. In answering the question of how the marginal utility of a complementary group of goods is divided among its individual members, Böhm-Bawerk distinguishes the following cases according to their characteristic presuppositions.

1. If none of the members allows a use other than the one common to the complementary group, and if none can be replaced in its effects, then *according to the concrete supply situation* the piece which alternately has the full total value of the whole group is the *final* one needed to complete the group; the other, already available complementary members have no value, because they can afford no utility without the missing piece.

2. If, *outside the common use*, some members of the group are in a position to originate value, albeit less of it, the value of the individual piece varies between the magnitude of the marginal utility it is able to originate in isolation (the minimum) and the sum of the common marginal utility minus the isolated marginal utility of the other members (the maximum).

Here too, the specifics of the case are decided by which of the group members is assessed as the 'final piece' and which as isolated pieces.

3. If some members of the group are not simply useable as auxiliary to other purposes but also *replaceable* by others of their kind, then the replaceable members never have a higher value than their *substitution value* – that is, the value attaching to them from the loss of utility in the branches from which the substitute specimens are procured. This is why, the more numerous these specimens and the more the uses to which they can be put, the more restricted is the space for establishing the value of the individual good which is appraised now as a 'final piece', now as an isolated piece. If, apart from this potential use, a good in the complementary group has many others from which it can be enlisted to replace a loss in the complementary group, the value of such a *replaceable* member is established at a particular level independently of its concrete complementary use – a level at which it then participates in distribution of the group's total value among the individual members. The distribution then proceeds in such a way that, out of the total group value determined by the marginal utility of the common use, a *fixed value* is first assigned to the replaceable members, and the remainder – according to the magnitude of the marginal utility variable – is imputed to the non-replaceable members as their individual value.

Since the presuppositions introduced in para. 3 – random replaceability of most complementary goods and multiple other uses – are most often by far those of the empirical economy, *the formation of the value of complementary goods is,* according to Böhm-Bawerk, *also overwhelmingly governed by the above formula.* In particular, it is applicable to *the imputation of production yields to the means of production.* Workers' output of raw materials, auxiliary materials, tools etc. is usually replaceable at will, and only a minority of means of production – e.g., the real estate, the mine, the factory plant, the specially skilled activity of the entrepreneurs – are not at all or not easily replaceable. In practical economic life, therefore, it is the 'costs' which are first deducted from the total yield: that is, precisely the *expenditure on replaceable means of production with a given substitution value* (wage-labour, raw and auxiliary materials, wear and tear on tools, etc.). The remainder is attributed as 'net proceeds' or 'pure profit' to the non-replaceable member or members (land, mines, factory plant, entrepreneurship etc.).

4. If, finally, several members at once are not replaceable – a rare combination in practice – then with regard to the remainder left over by the replaceable members they appear as being in the same relation to one another as do several non-replaceable members in types 1 and 2.

In addition to his use of the differential or variational method (assumption of loss), it is characteristic that Böhm-Bawerk brings '*substitution*

29

values' into his attempted solution. It should be stressed at once that the conditions raised under 3 – which, according to Böhm-Bawerk, apply to the empirically normal case of imputation – cannot provide a solution to the problem, precisely because of the enlistment of the substitution principle. For knowledge of substitution values itself assumes prior imputation in those combinations from which the replacement pieces are withdrawn, and thus leads to the two situations in 1 and 2, so that the problem is simply referred back. Of all the typical situations mentioned by Böhm-Bawerk, the problem is only really contained in these two cases, 1 and 2. His solution for both, however – and this is also especially characteristic – is not to ascertain the distribution of the yield or value among the individual members, nor to establish the *simultaneous* values of the individual means of production whose sum would again constitute the total value of the complementary group, nor, in other words, to identify the '*productive contribution*' (the kind of solution Böhm-Bawerk considers impossible[18]), but simply to establish the '*share of the yield depending upon the contribution of an individual factor of production*', which may vary for one and the same piece according to whether its possession is already secure or whether its loss or acquisition is being considered. Only *alternately* applicable values of the means of production of a complementary group, which as merely alternate do not allow of summation, could be ascertained – so that the imputation quotas partly overlap. Distribution of the yield is not directly given, however, through imputation quotas obtained in this way, but only in a 'two-stage' derivation. First, these imputation quotas determine the highest price bids on the market for means of production, and only then, as a result of these bids, do the market prices of the various means of production, and hence the distribution of the production yield, take shape in accordance with the known laws of price.

Wieser's attempted solution follows a quite different path.[19] He too starts out from the complementarity of the means of production, but he poses the problem as a question concerning the *distribution of the production yield*, after the '*productive contribution*' has been ascertained. Ever since there has been such a thing as economy, Wieser argues, every producer has had to acquire practical judgement through experience and trial and error, in order to carry on production according to plan. This judgement concerns 'the extent to which each of the many combined means of production participates in generating the output, the proportion in which the common result is to be distributed among the combined means of production, the contribution which is made by each worker, each machine and each new installation'. That is the problem which theory has to solve. The aim here is not to delve exhaustively into the physical causes – as Wieser convincingly shows by referring to the analogy of legal imputation – but to ascertain which of the many factors causally related to output is relevant in *practical-economic terms* for the achievement of the yield, and to what extent it matters.

The differential or 'notional loss' method of Menger and Böhm-Bawerk is not suitable for this purpose, because the values for individual components must be quite different according to which member of the group is left out. Moreover, precisely on the assumption of a loss, the value is ascertained not on the basis of the total combination which can be achieved with the actually available means of production, but on that of a less productive combination, so that there would have to be an undivided remainder of the yield arising in the case of trouble-free production. Wieser's own attempt at a solution rests upon the empirical fact that the individual means of production do not rigidly combine to produce only one kind of good, but can be associated in quantitatively and qualitatively distinct ways to produce many different items. Hence there are a number of different productive combinations, and at least as many equations expressing the value of their products as there are productive components. And with the help of these equations it is possible to calculate the unknown quantities – that is, the (value) quotas – of each component's participation in the yield. From this system of simultaneous equations are derived the *simultaneously* (and not, as in Böhm-Bawerk, just alternately) applicable values of the means of production, so that the sum of these 'productive contributions' of the individual members of a combination exactly coincides with the value of the yield.

For the actual imputation Wieser distinguishes between two typical cases: (i) the 'common' imputation which occurs when the product is composed only out of means of production with multiple use ('cost-defining means of production [*Kostenproduktivmitteln*]'); and (ii) 'specific' imputation, which refers to ascertainment of the value of a 'specific' means of production (that is, useable for only one or a few kinds of product), which produces its effect in collaboration with cost-defining means of production. The fundamental case, and the more difficult one for which Wieser's equation system tries to provide a solution, is that of common imputation. Here the value of a specific means of production is simply a residual after deduction of the value of the 'cost-defining means of production' from the value of the yield; so the yield quota is imputable to agricultural land or to mines or to entrepreneurship through deduction of the yield quotas of the cost-defining means of production labour and capital from the total yield.

(b) *Anglo-American marginal productivity theory (Clark)*. The instrument of marginal productivity, already used by Thünen, Jevons and L. Walras, was perfected by J. B. Clark and Marshall in their development of Austrian marginal utility theory and became the main explanatory principle

31

of the modern Anglo-American theory of distribution. Its employment presupposes not only the general law that the marginal utility of a product declines with its increasing quantity, and not only the possibility of substitution, but also the operation of the technical law of diminishing returns.[20] It therefore applies – like Wieser's equation system – to the certainly regular case of *variable production coefficients*. On these assumptions, and where the quantity of one factor varies while the quantity of the other remains constant, it is possible to ascertain what growth in the quantity and therefore utility of the yield depends upon the last-employed unit of this factor of production. Such growth is to be imputed to the factor in question as its product through 'economic causation' – and not only to the marginal unit but, by the principle of substitution, to any given unit of that factor. The residue of the yield left over after deduction of this share is to be imputed to the other factor as its product. (Clark and recent American theorists identify only two factors of production, labour and capital, with land being subsumed under the category of capital.) It does not matter for which of the two factors one ascertains the marginal productivity directly (by variation) and for which indirectly (by residual imputation); both methods would give equal magnitudes for the same factor.

Although no factor of production can by itself produce even the smallest fraction of a yield, the part of the yield which is lost with the loss of a small part-quantity of a factor is imputed to that factor as its product. The justification for this is as follows. If we assume that the loss of factor of production A (e.g., labour) is 'very small' – not in the sense of infinitesimal calculus, which does not come into the picture for practical economy, but in comparison with the total quantity used of the other factor B (e.g., land) – then the effect of this loss is distributed among so many units of factor B that the practical efficacy of one unit of factor B may be assumed to be almost unchanged. If, with the loss of a small part-quantity of factor A, there is then a fall in the total product, the amount of the fall must be regarded as the fraction caused by that part-quantity of factor A.

The theory of marginal productivity seeks to unify the solution methods contained in Böhm-Bawerk's 'eliminating' and Wieser's 'dividing' imputation. By applying the differential method (variation, notional loss), it manages to ascertain 'the shares dependent upon collaboration'; but the values ascertained in this way should also have simultaneous validity and thus, collected together as 'productive contributions', should precisely exhaust the value of the yield.

III. *Critique of the attempted solutions*

1. *The objection of insolubility in principle*

Of the objections to the theory of imputation, we can straightaway exclude those made by writers who still stand on the ground of objective, cost-based theories of value; for they run counter to the whole modern theory of economic value and not just the theory of imputation, and an assessment has already been made of them in the articles on 'Value' and 'Marginal Utility'.[21] The most general objection, in fact, which is frequently made against the solubility of the imputation problem, was best argued in the much-quoted words of John Stuart Mill: 'When two conditions are equally necessary for producing the effect at all, it is useless to say that so much of it is produced by one and so much by the other; it is like attempting to decide which half of a pair of scissors has most to do in the act of cutting; or which of the factors, five and six, contributes most to the production of thirty. The form which this conceit usually assumes is that of supposing that nature lends more assistance to human endeavours in agriculture than in manufactures.'[22] These logically unassailable arguments refer quite unambiguously to *physical* imputation: to the attempt to ascertain which physical parts of the product are brought about by the different factors. Only this way of posing the question existed in Mill's time; the specifically economic question of imputation had not yet been clearly formulated in the literature. Moreover, Mill's statement refers only to cases of physical imputation in which several factors are *necessary in the same way* to achieve any result at all, so that the loss of any one factor makes the *whole* yield impossible. But in these cases the problem is falsely posed: it would be impossible to identify the physical causation of certain parts of the yield by individual factors, as theorists of the Austrian School have most clearly shown.[23] These are the cases where individual factors equally indispensable to the production yield are mingled indistinguishably together in the product, which represents their 'success in general'. None of the factors causes, by its addition or loss, a simple increase or decrease in the quantity of the product or a change in its quality; but each one is absolutely indispensable. They are cases of completely fixed, univocal combination: for Wieser, 'several unknowns and only one equation' and therefore insoluble; for Böhm-Bawerk, case 1 with its bald assertion (which provides no solution to the imputation problem) that the final missing piece of the group alternately has the total value of the product, while the other members have nil value.

This proves the impossibility of physical or natural imputation for a relatively small fraction of practical cases, but it in no way demonstrates the *essential* and *universal* impossibility of imputation. A closer look at this core of the problem, which has not received even a close to adequate clarification in the literature, has now become inescapable.

Opponents of imputation theory impermissibly generalize from Mill's objection – which, as we have seen, only applies on very narrow assumptions (several conditions equally necessary to achieve 'the effect at all') – and deny that *any* physical imputation is possible. As to those who maintain that the economic imputation problem can be solved, they have all too readily believed that the objection can be met only by establishing the general insolubility of the problem of physical imputation. By distinguishing between the economic and the physical problem of imputation, they have certainly shown that the latter is of no significance for economic theory, which is concerned to ascertain the *value-shares* and not the physical shares of the factors in the product. But the imputation theorists never demonstrate how this share of a factor of production in the value yield can be ascertained without prior establishment of its *natural* share in the output. On the other hand, in the derivations of the value of the means of production, one continually finds concepts and modes of expression which can only be understood in the sense of *physical* imputation. This is especially true of Wieser, when he speaks of 'the effect which is due to each *part-cause* of the yield', or when he states that, because the combinations of the means of production are variable, 'it must be possible to determine, for each [means of production], the *scope of the effect* which it exercises as *part-cause*', and so on. With research in this state, the opponents of imputation theory might seem justified in claiming that since the question of physical shares is admitted to be insoluble, and since economic shares cannot be ascertained without prior physical imputation, the whole economic problem of imputation must be an illusory problem.

A few points may bring some order into the matter.

(a) On what assumptions and in what sense can one speak of the physical share of a means of production in the physical product? Evidently the expression has meaning only if it refers to a property of the product which can be grasped separately in respect of quality or quantity, or to a component part of the product, and only if that property or component has 'utility' (that is, relates to the satisfaction of wants) and is shown by experience to be physically determined through the involvement of a particular means of production. In such cases, which form a major part of those involving practical valuation of production goods, physical imputation is definitely possible and is actually carried out. Synthetically these cases may be described as all those involving means of production which *increase the return*: that is, which are not essential for the creation of the product 'at all', but which are necessary for the product to have a *more special quality* or a *greater quantity* than in cases where only the 'indispensable' factors are employed. This higher quality or greater quantity is thus, strictly speaking, the natural share in the product which is brought about by the participation of yield-increasing means of production, and the increased satisfaction of wants – in comparison with that produced by only the indispensable means of production – should be causally traced back to this natural share. The better quality or greater quantity is visible, for example, in the more plentiful harvest produced with a certain fertilizer, in the enjoyability of a literary work afforded by the book's artistic presentation, the nourishment to be derived from a food as a result of certain additional ingredients, the greater durability of a useful object due to the use of especially long-lasting material, or its enhanced value bound up with the accompanying satisfaction of aesthetic needs which is attributable to the artistic form given it by the use of especially skilled labour, and so on. If it is certain that the yield-increasing means of production can produce nothing by themselves, it is also evident that the *greater result* obtained through their presence is brought about only by them, so that logically the causal imputation can quite properly follow. So much for the *physical* imputation. Whether the utility generated by this physical share is also *economically dependent* upon it (that is, economically imputable utility), is not yet settled and will also depend on the postulates introduced in Section IV below. The overwhelming mass of production goods, but also many of the various kinds of labour, have this yield-increasing function which finds expression in a certain property of the product.

(b) Apart from this broadly applicable qualitative improvement or quantitative increase in the product as a result of yield-enhancing means of production, it is not possible to ascertain the physical shares which are due to the particular types of means of production. For precisely with regard to the indispensable means of production, not even a tiny part of a unit of the product can be produced by only the one or only the other factor. However, another form of natural imputation is then also possible: namely, *ascertainment of the natural yield which, given the quantities of the various means of production, depends in the concrete case upon the gain or loss of a concrete part-quantity of a means of production*; or, to use the customary expression, ascertainment of the 'share dependent upon joint efficacy [*Mitwirkung*]'. The main application of this method is in the very common instances of quantitatively variable productive combinations (typical case: cooperation of land and labour in a certain quantitative proportion). But it is also valid for cases of yield-increasing means of production and even for the rigid combination of indispensable means of production. At first, the method of ascertaining the share dependent upon joint efficacy also provides only parts of the natural yield; contrary to a

35

widespread misunderstanding, it is not in itself by any means the same as imputation of value or determination of economic shares. The difference between this method and the one of identifying physical-causal shares – discussed under (a) above – is nowhere fully brought out in the literature. *Physical* imputation means that of a product's bundle of useful properties, one or another can be traced back *in accordance with natural law* to the participating effect [*Mitwirkung*] of a certain type of means of production, and that this determination of a particular share in the product by a particular type of means of production – and hence the result of the physical imputation, because it operates with natural laws – is valid in general, that is, regardless of which types and amounts of means of production are concretely available to an economic subject. *Natural* imputation, on the other hand, by the method of ascertaining the share dependent upon joint efficacy, starts from the *actual determination* of the share in the yield achieved through the participating effect of a certain part-quantity of any means of production – determination, that is, by the actually available quantities of all other complementary means of production. The share in the yield which depends upon one additional day's labour varies according to whether a large or a small area of land is involved, and this shows by way of experiment (variation) what in the natural yield depends *in concreto*, with the given provision of goods, upon the addition or subtraction of one unit of a means of production. This is the more comprehensive method: it includes (from the point of view of *economics*) the cases of possible physical imputation as special cases.

The share which depends upon the participating effect of any quantity of a means of production can thus be established without exception in terms of certain natural quantities of goods – whether in the results of a particular area of production, or in the aggregate production (aggregate productive combination) of an economy. The objection of insolubility in principle – on the grounds that there is no material basis for value imputation and that 'the imputed value-shares are left hanging in the air' – has thus turned out to be mistaken. (On the possibility and meaning of cumulative imputation see Section IV below.)

2. *Objections to some attempted solutions*

(a) To Böhm-Bawerk's solution. Many reservations have been expressed, especially by Wieser, about the solution proposed by Böhm-Bawerk (and also by Menger). It is said that the introduction of substitution-values in Böhm-Bawerk's case 3 does not provide a solution but only pushes back the problem – for the substitution-values are not assumed as given but must themselves first be derived through imputation from the values of the marginal combinations (marginal product of the particular type of means of production). Derivation of the substitution-values therefore necessarily leads to cases 1 and 2, as Böhm-Bawerk admits in his later consideration of the problem. But cases 1 and 2 gives us only *alternately* applicable values, so that their sum does not coincide with the product-value. According to Böhm-Bawerk, however, this is not necessary for the subjective values of the means of production (but only for *prices*, which result from the coming together of these subjective values); indeed, he considers it illegitimate to make such a summation, essentially because the value of a plurality of goods is not equal to the sum of their individual values. It is not true, however, that economic theory and practice is never faced with the question of the ratio in which the product-value should be *simultaneously* imputed to the individual means of production – on the contrary, calculation and disposition must regularly apply to *all* productive elements and cannot be based only on alternate assessments of value (see Section IV). And to this question Böhm-Bawerk's attempted solution is incapable of giving any answer. At the same time, there is an internal contradiction in Böhm-Bawerk's own procedure: on the one hand, he considers that the values in the course of substitution can only be alternately valid; on the other hand, he actually treats them as cumulative, adding them to or subtracting them from the total value of the product. It may be argued that Böhm-Bawerk's attempted solution is also inadequate because in employing the idea of loss he establishes the values of the means of production for a situation (subsidiary uses with loss of a unit of a means of production) which is different from the one actually postulated (trouble-free production with the best uses). But this objection is not applicable insofar as what is actually at issue – and that is already enough to ascertain marginal utilities – is small changes in the quantities of the means of production and thus, according to the product-value, subsidiary uses lying close to one another. It is also methodologically unfounded, because the occasion and possibility of ascertaining value only appear in cases of movement and change (variation), and never when the economic system is constant and at rest. A major objection that must be raised against Böhm-Bawerk's solution, however, is that it bases itself upon the *already-finished total productive combination* and thus upon already-given marginal combinations for the individual means of production; it therefore seeks to ascertain *ex post* the values of the individual means of production, whereas in reality they are formed together with the total combination which, without any knowledge of the utilities dependent upon the individual means of production, could not at all be completed in a plan-like manner. The *mistaken demonstration of the material determinants* of the values of the means of production is necessarily bound up with this defect.

(b) Although Wieser's attempted solution offers many fruitful lines of thought, it too fails to clear up the problem as a whole. Apart from the cases of possible physical imputation considered in Section III, 1, it is not possible to determine the 'productive contribution'. What the solution of Wieser's equation-system provides is not shares in the natural yield, but *average values* of the means of production for which the material basis is nevertheless lacking. (In these equations the unknown as well as the given quantities are values.) If it is true that the combinations of most means of production are variable in both quality and quantity – an assumption made for the empirically normal cases – and that many of the resulting equations are used to ascertain values, then it is doubtful, as Wieser himself admits, whether there are normally more equations than unknowns. But this implies that the solution is *indeterminate*. Only if one can take the necessary number of equations *from the margin* – that is, from combinations whose product-values lie within or near the boundary layers of the total combination[24] – can these equations be regarded as even approximately simultaneous. And only then can the average values obtained from their solution approximate to the marginal utilities of the means of production. But if equations are jointly derived for products at higher levels of the (original) scale of values, the resulting average values will lie far beyond the marginal utility of the means of production and – as Wieser knows better than anyone – will have absolutely no significance for practical valuation of the means of production. Moreover, too high values will then always be assigned to the *free* means of production present within the productive combinations. This raises a question which Wieser unfortunately leaves unclear: Are the product-values which constitute the known quantities in the equations, the original want-values of those products, *before* the values of the various products are adjusted to the substitution-values of their means of production as taken from the marginal combinations? Or are they the values which have *already been adjusted* in the course of the substitution? In the first case, as we have seen, the resulting average values may be far above the marginal utility and in practice therefore irrelevant; in the second case, there would be a *petitio principii* because the adjustment resulting from introduction of the marginal utility of the means of production (substitution-values) already supposes *prior* knowledge of the marginal utilities of the individual means of production (the establishment of which is the whole purpose of the equation-system). Wieser's solution cannot, then, be regarded as final and complete. As he too starts out from the already-finished total productive combination, he throws no light upon the law of its formation or the material determinants of the values of the means of production.[25]

(c) A whole series of objections have also been levelled against the theory of *marginal productivity*. First, it is rightly considered illegitimate to regard the rising or falling yield brought about through loss or gain of a small amount of one factor, where the other factors are constant, as the 'product' of that factor or as *caused* by that factor. For a change in the amount of one factor will also influence the degree of the others' effectiveness. Nor is this objection overcome by an appeal to infinitesimal magnitudes in the mathematical sense of the term – for, apart from the fact that infinitesimal magnitudes are never used in practical economic calculation (which does, after all, need to be explained), there is also the inconsistency that the magnitude is too small to have any noticeable effect on the effectiveness of the other factors, but large enough to bring about a noticeable fall in the product. The objection might be dismissed as purely terminological if the expression 'product of a factor' is understood not in the sense of physical imputation (productive contribution), but in that of the share of the product which is 'dependent upon joint efficacy'. But this is contradicted by a fact which constitutes the second main objection to the theory of marginal productivity: namely, that in the view of its representatives, the value quotas established through variation for the different factors must add up precisely to the total yield. *Aftalion*, in particular, has shown that the total yield must then be greater than the one obtained in reality. We cannot go here into other shortcomings of the theory of marginal productivity: those which have to do with an imprecise grasp of the conditions under which it is permissible to valuate supplies of goods by means of marginal utility, and which already pass over into the domain of personal distribution. In its typical forms today, marginal productivity theory also delivers fundamentally incorrect and rather crude approximations to a solution.

IV. *Positive presentation of the solution*

A. Formation of the total productive combination

The inadequacy of these main attempts to solve the value-formation problem for the means of production rests, apart from their internal inconsistency, upon the same grounds. First, they all deal only with the *formal* determinants of the value of the means of production; their method is *simply* that of ascertaining the value magnitudes. But they thereby neglect a problem which is at least equally important: that of revealing the *material* determinants (i.e. the conditions) upon which it depends whether a means of production has greater or lesser value.

Second, they always start from the already-given total productive combination, and its outlying individual marginal combinations, without seeking to establish the *law of its formation*. These two defects are closely related to each other. For the law of formation of the total combination cannot be developed without reference to the use-magnitudes of the individual means of production, nor can these magnitudes be derived without knowledge of the said law of formation. The starting-point cannot therefore be that certain marginal products are given together with their values and technical combinations, and that the economic subject then faces the question of the values of the individual means of production. For it is not the case that production first takes place with the available supplies of means of production and only then *ex post* is the question raised of their utility. On the contrary, the starting-point in practical economic life is that each subject has some means of production at his disposal, if only his own labour-power – otherwise the economy would lack any foundation – and faces the question of how best to make do with it to meet his requirements. This calls for a production plan: it has to be established, with the given goods and wants, which uses of all available means of production will achieve the greatest aggregate utility; and it is necessary to establish the total productive combination in which each part of the supply of means of production, after use-appraisal of various technically possible combinations with other means of production, is brought to the most productive use. Only at the end of the production plan, then, will the marginal employment of the individual means of production and their marginal utility come to light.

In the article 'Produktion',[26] an attempt has already been made to explain how the total productive combination arises and what are the laws of its formation, and the reader is explicitly referred to this as an integral part of the present article. It is shown there that certain factors univocally determine what and how much is produced: the system of wants with its utility scales; the absolute quantities of the various available means of production and their relationship to the quantities required in the different productive combinations; knowledge of the combinations which are technically feasible. The total productive combination is then constructed in such a way that, from the total supply of means of production, the first combinations to be formed are those which satisfy top-layer wants through means of production whose employment keeps to a minimum the loss in the satisfaction of other wants. Then, in similar fashion, the remaining supply takes care of the next most urgent layer of wants, and so on until the margin of production is reached in every kind of product through the using up in full of one or several means of production necessary for that combination. The 'Produktion' article also shows what special significance for the whole economy is contained in those marginal utilities of the means of production which result from the marginal employment (even though they only come to light at the end of their whole process of deployment).

For they are basis, regulator and controller for all dispositions of goods which will become necessary as a result of future changes in the goods situation.

Only in rare, exceptional cases (e.g., complete reconstruction as a result of resettlement) is an empirical economy faced with the task of establishing *uno actu* the *whole* productive combination from beginning to end, in a single production plan which simultaneously determines all uses of all the available means of production. Rather, it is nearly always a matter of partial decisions relating to the total combination which has arisen over time together with the gradual development of the particular economy, the aim being to modify that combination in accordance with changed conditions in the economy – in human wants, technical knowledge and, above all, the means of production (increase or decrease) in particular areas – to reorganize the use of certain means of production, and to make further use only of those increments which complement and consolidate the previous combination. For this purpose, sufficient experience is gained from multiple testing of the utility yield of various combinations. But theory cannot rest content with explaining partial dispositions on the basis of previous experience; it must delve into the whole problem, just to show the form in which such experience arises and what is its content. A distinction must be drawn here between appraisals of value which assist dispositions *during* the process of drawing up the production plan, and for only one stretch of it, and the values ensuing *at the end* of the total disposition as marginal utilities of the means of production. In the first case, it will be enough summarily to compare the total utility increments which can be achieved at the same stage of disposition by use of the same kinds and amounts of means of production in changing partial combinations. And it serves the same purpose to ascertain the average output of the individual means of production within the particular section of the total combination (that is, according to Wieser's equation-system, whose employment in this limited sense is not affected by the earlier considerations, because here it is a matter of partial combinations of products of lesser use-differentiation *within the same section* of the total combination). The question as to the utility yield dependent upon command over one more or one less of a means of production only ever arises as the production plan is taking shape, when harmonious provision for the satisfaction of the various wants is obstructed by the fact that because of the special *scarcity* of one or another type of means of production, it becomes impossible to continue production of the good in whose combination it is indispensable, and the *marginal employment* for that means of production is reached. At this stage, the value of such a specially scarce means of production is not yet definitive but can only be established as a minimum value; it is univocally determined only when all the dispositions have been made and the values are given for the means of production involved in its marginal product. The further one advances in this disposition, the more means of production of increased scarcity are withdrawn with their marginal employment from further disposition, until finally all that are left are combinations of the relatively most common means of production.

Once the total combination with all the available supplies of the means of production has been concluded, the marginal employment is thereby given for each type of means of production – whether this is as part of the combination of a particular kind of product, or of the combinations of several types of product with equal or nearly equal value. The marginal utilities of the means of production must then be derived from these marginal employments.

B. Establishment of the values of means of production
without imputation

This gives us a series of typical cases, some of which enable the values of means of production to be established without their own special process of imputation. It will be easiest to begin by listing them. (1) First, there are those means of production which, in addition to their use in production, also directly yield utility as *consumption goods* (e.g., wood or coal for the heating of living accommodation and as auxiliary materials in production, or electric current for the purposes of both lighting and production). On the assumption that they are always rationally deployed, they can have no other marginal utility in their productive use than they have in their simultaneous use for consumption. As such cases of the dual character of a good are extremely frequent, a large area of the value-formation of the means of production thus causes no further problem with regard to imputation. (2) If the marginal employment of a means of production involves collaboration with *free* means of production, then the product is economically (not technically) the result only of the means of production standing in the relationship of scarcity – for the outcome depends only on each part-quantity of *that* means of production and not on any concrete quantity of any others. From the point of view of economics, it is as if it alone generated the product, and it therefore contains the whole value of the product. Thus, if labour works with materials that are available in abundance, the result in economic terms is only a product of labour. (3) A variant of this case presents itself when a scarce means of production works together with one or several means of production which exist in *relative* abundance. This occurs when the productive combination is completely inflexible, the various means of production are effective only if associated with one another in a quite definite ratio, but they are not available in exactly complementary amounts. Although the uncovered quantities are not free means of production in the sense used earlier – for they could yield utility if more of the scarce factor were available – they have no economic significance and thus no marginal utility as long as this situation persists.[27] Economically, the product depends only upon the scarce means of production, which is thus estimated at the full value of the product. (4) If the marginal employment of a means of production simply serves to *raise output* in the combination of indispensable scarce means of production (see above III, 1a), then its value is given with that of the increased output in the marginal combination.

In all these cases (1–4) the value of a production good results from employment which is to be taken as *isolated* in either the economic or both the economic and technical senses.

(5) The field of genuine imputation is further restricted by the value-formation of *capital goods*. Both technically, as combinations of quantities of primary means of production (labour, soil fertility, gifts of nature), and in terms of their value-formation, these are purely *transient quantities*. In the normal run of things and with static ratios, their value can essentially be none other than that of the primary means of production contained within them. Their function is to raise output, so that products can be produced with more useful properties or in greater quantity than would be the case in direct production with the same amounts of primary means of production. Thus at any one time, in a balanced economy, an appropriate share of the available primary means of production passes into the form of various capital goods, until through their increase, or the increased output produced with their help, the values of the primary means of production in their elementary form and in the form of capital goods are equalized.[28] The value of capital goods is therefore unproblematically *equated* with that of the primary means of production contained within them. Only when such equality is not achieved – when the course of production is disturbed and the capital goods in use cannot be reproduced at the right time from the fund of primary means of production, or when the economy is dynamically advancing and the quantities of primary means of production allocated to the production of capital goods are too small for the increased requirements – only then does the value-formation of capital goods follow the path of true imputation as does that of the primary means of production.

C. Ascertaining value through imputation

If we leave aside the cases we have just discussed, there still remains the derivation of the value-formation of primary means of production, as well as that of capital goods in the case of an unbalanced economy. Essentially, the following typical situations may arise. Either (1) the marginal employment represents a completely inflexible combination. Or (2) the marginal employment is variable, whether because the production coefficients for the marginal product are technically changeable, or because products of several different kinds, from *qualitatively* different combinations of the same (multiple-use) means of production, are present in the marginal layer. In the case of a completely inflexible combination – which is the most unusual in economic practice, because at least one participating factor, labour, can nearly always be varied – if the various members of the combination are available in precisely complementary amounts, the imputation of individual values is inherently impossible; but nor can the imputation question then arise in practice, because there are no economic reasons why the individual values should be ascertained. If, however, the quantities available are not precisely complementary, the case of relatively free components (3 above) applies.

The crucial case of imputation, and by far the most common, occurs where one or more marginal combinations are technically variable. But the moment of variability, which allows a comparison to be made between the utility yields attainable in quantitatively and qualitatively changing distribution of the elements, then affords the possibility of a solution to the problem.

To find our way through the difficulties, we need to establish the meaning of imputation in economic practice, to discover guidelines for the most appropriate disposition by establishing the significant magnitudes of the various means of production. We should distinguish, *on the one hand*, the importance of the means of production *merely in relation to one another*, expressed in the ratios of the last-employed quantities in the form of a series of equations. These equations, which naturally hold only for each basic goods situation (with given types and quantities of means of production), state that in terms of the utility yield $1A = 2B = 1C = 3D$, etc., or, in other words, present the proportion in which the last-employed units of the various means of production contribute to the utility yield. This does not yet say anything about the absolute magnitude of the utility yield obtained through the joint effect of the last units of the means of production. And *on the other hand*, there is the task of establishing these *absolute use-magnitudes themselves*, which are traceable to the joint effect of the last units of the means of production. If these absolute use-magnitudes can be directly established – as in cases 1–4 in B above – then the marginal ratios do not need to be ascertained first: they are produced after the actual imputation and constitute merely a practical means of expressing the value relationship between the means of production. However, if the absolute use-magnitudes attained through the joint effect of the last quantities of the various means of production cannot be directly established – which is the case precisely with multiple-use means of production – whereas the *ratio* between the absolute magnitudes dependent upon the joint effect of the last quantities can be so established, and at the same time the total utility resulting from their combination is known, then it is possible to ascertain from these two determinants the share in the total utility which is due to the effect of the individual magnitudes.[29]

In establishing the above ratios, it is essential to grasp the proportional significance of the various types of means of production for their *aggregate* return – that is, the utility of all the marginal combinations – and not to take this merely as a share in the isolated utility of a *single* product in whose production the relevant means has a part. If the latter approach, which sees an isolated link between an economic means and some partial economic result, already represents in the derivation of consumer-good values a construct which, though legitimate for many purposes, always fundamentally 'stylizes' the facts of the matter because of the systemic interrelation between wants – if this is so then it is of no use at all in ascertaining the relative magnitudes of importance of the means of production with more than one use, since these make their contribution to the aggregate utility precisely by connecting the many different kinds of product in which they participate.

The above ratios can be ascertained according to the variation method, by observation of the utility loss (or utility gain) connected with the decrease (or increase) of a small part-quantity of the various means of production. Of course, only the *effective* loss (or gain) here comes into consideration. If, after the use of all means of production has been determined by the disposition of the economy, a unit of a particular means of production is lost, this will result in the loss of a particular product. Rationally, however, this latter loss is partly compensated by redeployment in different uses of the newly released members of the burst combination, and by the ensuing growth in other products. Only the use difference between the direct loss and the indirect gain constitutes the *effective* loss in utility. Let us now take as established in turn *the effective utility loss which results from the loss of one unit of the various types of means of production present in the marginal combinations* – and nothing

45

stands in the way of its being established, whether by actual experimental means or simply in thought on the basis of experience with production and technology. *We thus obtain a series of use-magnitudes* which do not *yet* represent, however – contrary to what Böhm-Bawerk and the marginal productivity theorists believe – the marginal utility or value or importance of the particular means of production. For these magnitudes are not – and by their mode of procurement cannot be – *simultaneously* valid. As they have been obtained under mutually contradictory conditions, they have only alternate validity and therefore cannot, if summated, give the total utility actually procured by employment of these means of production. It is of no avail to try to get round this point by arguing, as Böhm-Bawerk does, that these magnitudes are only given alternate importance and are never involved in summation. For, precisely in regard to its disposition of the means of production, the economy needs the values which they have in a given situation to apply *simultaneously*. Only in those conceivable but non-empirical cases involving just one isolated disposition which applies to a single means of production – as in the exchange of one single means of production – would the economy make do with such alternate use-magnitudes. In all practical cases, however, rational uniform disposition is impossible under alternately changing conditions – for a decision about the use of quantities of one means of production, precisely because of the characteristic complementarity of the means of production, cannot go ahead without a simultaneous decision about the use of the *other* means of production.

In order to arrive at the share which the various means of production have in the utility yield resulting from the *actual* goods situation, it is necessary to recognize these magnitudes obtained by variation for what they really are: *mere ratios* showing the proportions in which the yield is diminished through the loss of 1A, 1B, 1C etc. *And it is both logical and economically compelling to conclude that the last quantities of individual means of production contribute by their presence and effect to the final yield, in the same proportion in which their loss decreases (or their growth increases) the production yield.*[30] If, then, the actual utility yielded in all the marginal combinations of the means of production is *distributed* among the various means of production in proportion to the diminution caused by loss of the final units, the utility yields obtained in this way constitute the utility of the final units or their *marginal utility*.

D. The material determinants of the value of production goods

So much for the method of *establishing* the values of the means of production, or the solution of the *formal* imputation problem. We have also discussed above the *substantive* imputation problem concerning the *determinants* of the concrete value of the means of production, so that now there is no need for more than a further synthesis. As in any formation of value, so it is with the means of production: the most general determinant is the relationship between *demand and supply*. But whereas, in the case of consumption goods, the size and intensity of the demand is directly given by the gradation structure and the capacity of the individual want for which the consumption good is the means of satisfaction, this is not so with the means of production. In the typical case where they can have multiple uses, the demand for them is constituted from all the scales (and capacities) of the different wants which are satisfied by products created with the help of a type of means of production. That is one major complication in the value-formation of the means of production. But the size of the demand for a means of production also depends upon the quantity in which it is required within the individual productive combinations – that is, upon the technical coefficients of production. And the size of the *effective* demand for a means of production further depends – here lies the second intricacy in the value-formation of the means of production – upon the available *supplies of the complementary means of production*. This is most evident in productive combinations with completely inflexible coefficients, where it may happen that even if the product-value is very high there is no further demand for a means of production necessary to the combination – in which case concrete quantities of it become valueless, because it is impossible to increase the tight supply of other, complementary means of production (see above, B2 and B3).

Supply magnitudes (which, in any full analysis, is how the available amounts of *primary* means of production should be regarded) also have an importance for the formation of value, and this has already been considered in the articles on 'Goods', 'Production', 'Factors of Production', 'Marginal Utility' and 'Value'. For each variable combination of the means of production, and thus also for the total productive combination, there is just one *optimum* proportion in which the various means of production are available. The further the availability of a factor falls below the optimum proportion (in respect of a given factor which is absolutely or relatively fixed), the higher is the value of one unit of that factor; and the more it climbs, the lower is the value. The degree of *intensity* or *extensiveness* of production is determined by the ratio of the available quantities of the variables (labour and capital) to the inflexibly given factors (land and gifts of nature).

47

V. *The role of imputation in distribution of the national production yield:
formation of the prices of means of production*

The law of the value-formation of the means of production must first be
developed as the elementary law of economy for the simplest economic
form – that is, one which is closed or complete in the sense of producing
for its own requirements. The question of the significance of the derived
laws for a commercial economy operating along individualist and entrepreneurial lines, is identical with the question of the laws by which the
prices of the means of production are formed. And with the answer to this
latter question, in terms of the dual function of prices, we also have the
derivation, on the one hand, of the laws of *production costs* and, on the
other, of the *distribution of the production yield* among those who contributed to it with their labour-power or by giving up material means of
production in their ownership. This is what is usually called the question
of the economic 'remuneration' of the different factors of production, or
the question of *'functional distribution'*.

For individual units within the commercial economy which are partly or
wholly engaged in production for their own requirements – such as the
family farms of peasants – the derived laws of the value-formation of the
means of production directly apply. The typical case in an individualist
commercial economy, however, is *entrepreneurial production* for sale on
the market, by means of labour-power and material means of production
that have been acquired for a remuneration. And in this case, the price-
formation of the means of production, unlike the unified *value*-formation
process of a closed economy, is a complex process bound up with the
combined action of different groups of economic subjects, each with
certain partial functions: *consumers* as bearers of demand for products,
producers (entrepreneurs) and *owners of the means of production*. Things
operate in accordance with the following schema. On one side are the
consumers of various kinds of product stratified according to the intensity
of demand, which is in turn graded by their subjective valuations and finds
expression in the price they are willing to pay; on the other side are all the
material and personal means of production present in the economy, distributed among the great mass of their owners who seek to direct them into
the most profitable uses, with the sole aim of obtaining the highest possible remuneration for their relinquishment. And between the two stand the
productive entrepreneurs who, guided by the type, size and intensity of
demand and the anticipated product prices, and driven only by the quest
for the greatest possible net profit, establish the character and extent of
their productive operations and shape the productive combinations with

the factors acquired for some recompense from the owners of the means of production.

Of these three groups, only the consumers present primary subjective valuations. But these subjective valuations set in motion the whole process of production and price-formation. The entrepreneurs alone, however, directly carry out the *distribution* of the product prices resulting from the consumer valuations – as wages to labour, as payment to capitalists for the acquisition of capital goods and the use of capital, as ground rent for the use of the land that is given over. Nevertheless, what is decisive is that this is not at all done in an arbitrary manner, but, in the case of competition, *is strictly determined by precisely the same laws which govern the imputation of the product-value* to the joint factors of production in the simple economy.

Each entrepreneur, competing with all others, tries to make his production as profitable as his abilities, knowledge and means allow, and to expand it in accordance with the expected demand and product-price until further increases would no longer bring him any extra net profit.[31] If the prices of the means of production are not yet given – which is what we must assume to gain insight into the law of their formation – and if, consequently, the margin between product-price and prices of the means of production (which defines the profit level) is also not yet known, production can for a time expand without limits, until the *scarcity* of the means of production within the economy finally calls a halt. That will first occur with means of production (especially rare raw materials, especially skilled labour, etc.) which are relatively more scarce. After these have initially flowed into the most profitable uses (that is, ones paying the most as a result of the high price of the product involved), further available quantities turn towards the next profitable uses in the series – given that, under competitive conditions, their owners cannot keep them back without themselves suffering harm and are forced to offer them for sale. In this way, they increase the product quantities, lower the product price and – for that very reason – obtain an ever lower price until finally the supply is exhausted, the last part-quantities being directed into the least profitable of the uses still covered by the existing supply, where they find their *marginal use* in the economy. Thus, at some point in the aggregate economic process of production, every specific means of production finds its marginal level of use which is higher or lower according to its relative scarcity. But the other multiple-use ('cost-defining') means of production available in relatively large amounts, which apart from complementing the specific means of production also serve in numerous changing conjunctions with one another, also find their marginal use at some point in the overall process of production, higher or lower according to the quantity in which they are present within the economy. If the process is by and large successful – and it takes place all the more swiftly and precisely, the fewer are the constraints on competition from the producers and the owners of the means of production – the scarce supplies of all the means of production are joined together in countless productive combinations. Then, because of competition among those offering means of production for sale and because of the competitive quest for profit among producers in all enterprises which utilize them, the marginal use must be approximately equal for each type of means of production. (Of course, this is not the same as the supposed 'law of the equalization of the rate of profit' laid down by classical theory.)

Now, how do the prices of the various means of production result from this process? Each of the means involved in producing a product (or the owner standing behind it) tries to draw the greatest possible share of the product-price, in the form of a high-as-possible price for handing it over. But together they cannot obtain more than the product-price. By which laws is this distributed among the various means of production? *Here we find repeated, on a different stage, exactly the same process which occurred in imputation in a closed economy.* Each producer can precisely work out – and does so insofar as he is a rational economic actor – what the loss of the last-used quantity of his enterprise's various means of production entails for him in terms of lost physical or monetary returns (and also what additional return would be yielded by a further quantity of the various means of production). But if this is known, then so too is the *proportion* in which the result of the combined action of the last quantities of these factors of production (i.e., the *realized price* for the marginal product) is determined by the effect of the last units of the various factors. It is also thereby established what share of the proceeds of the product-price can be paid as remuneration for the productive involvement of the various factors: how much for the last-used worker of q_1 or q_2 quality, how much for the last-used quantity of raw material r_1 or r_2, and so on.

With these highest price bids resulting from the monetary return on the marginal use of the various means of production in their business, the entrepreneurs act on the market as bearers of the demand for the various means of production. According to how well their respective businesses are placed (organization, market position, etc.), their highest bids will not fully coincide but rather differ to a greater or lesser extent. On the other side stand the owners who have been forced to sell their means of production. In keeping with the well-known general laws of price,[32] when the different levels of demand encounter the supply on the market for means of production, the price bid of entrepreneurs with the lowest level of demand is once again decisive: it must get a look-in if the whole supply of the means of production is to be incorporated. Thus, it is the prices which *marginal undertakings* can still pay (whether a marginal enterprise or a marginal layer of an enterprise) that effectively establish the market prices of means of production for all undertakings.

This is the law governing the formation of the prices of the means of production, and hence too the formation of incomes stemming from participation in the production process. Of course, it also operates in relation to prices of means of production (cost-rates) taken over from the past, as the *law of price changes* of the means of production.

It is now clear that the prices of the means of production are connected to one another by consumer demand for the products through which the producers' demand for the means of production is indirectly determined; that furthermore product-prices are joined together by already-formed prices of the means of production (costs); and that the incomes of demand-bearing consumers themselves result from their share in production. It is through these correlations that the overall price system is given for all products, means of production and incomes, and the process of the commercial economy as a whole presents itself as an organic cycle.[33]

NOTES

1. The author notes that the German term *'ökonomische Zurechnung'* corresponds to 'imputation' in the English and French literature.
2. See the article 'Wert' in this volume of the *Handwörterbuch*, pp. 988ff., and the article 'Grenznutzen' in vol. iv, pp. 1190ff.
3. See the article 'Preis', vol. vi, pp. 994ff., and sect. v below.
4. See the article 'Preis [Monopolpreis]', vol. vi, pp. 1026ff.
5. See the article 'Produktion', vol. vi, pp. 1108ff.
6. John Locke, *Two Treatises of Civil Government* (London: J. M. Dent, 1964), bk ii, ch. 5, pp. 136–7.
7. See the article 'Produktionsfaktoren', vol. vi, pp. 1122ff.
8. *Grundsätze der Nationalökonomie* (1805), p. 165.
9. *Revision der Grundbegriffe* (1815), vol. 3, pp. 125, 322.
10. *Handbuch der Nationalwirtschaftslehre* (1819), vol. 1, p. 130.
11. *Die Grundlehren der Volkswirtschaft* (1846), pp. 88–100.
12. *Nationalökonomie* (1839), vol. 2.
13. *Grundsätze der Volkswirtschaftslehre* (1864), p. 448.
14. *Der isolierte Staat*, vol. 2, pt 1 (Rostock, 1850).
15. See the article 'Produktion', vol. vi, p. 1118.
16. H. H. Gossen, *Entwicklung der Gesetze des menschlichen Verkehrs*

und der daraus fliessenden Regeln für menschliches Handeln (Brunswick, 1854), pp. 25–7.

17. See the foreword by F. A. Hayek to the new edition (Berlin, 1927).
18. See 'Exkurs VII' in the fourth German edition of the *Positive Theory of Capital*: *Positive Theorie des Kapitals* (Jena, 1921).
19. We shall base ourselves here upon Wieser's final version of his solution, as it appears in the *Theory of Social Economy*.
20. See the article 'Abnehmender Ertrag', in vol. i of this *Handwörterbuch*, pp. 11ff.
21. 'Wert' and 'Grenznutzen', in vol. iv, esp. pp. 1007ff. and 1210.
22. *Principles of Political Economy*, vol. 1, ch. 1, p. 34.
23. Cf. Wieser, *Natural Value* (London: Macmillan, 1893), pp. 72–4, and *Social Economics* (London: George Allen & Unwin, 1928), p. 85. See also Böhm-Bawerk, *Positive Theorie des Kapitals*, p. 285, and 'Exkurs VII', p. 179.
24. We may suppose from the separation between 'common' and 'specific' imputation that this is what Wieser had in mind.
25. It has often been objected to Wieser's calculation of utility in general, and his theory of imputation in particular, that the subjective value of a sum of similar goods can never be equal to the sum of the individual values. On the inappropriateness of this point, see my series of articles 'Untersuchung zum Grundgesetz der wirtschaftlichen Wertrechnung', *Zeitschrift für Volkswirtschaft* (1921, 1922, 1928).
26. Sect. ii, vol. vi, pp. 1110ff. of the present *Handwörterbuch*.
27. We cannot consider here the way in which valuation of relatively free means of production is affected by the degree of probability that complementary amounts of the scarce factor will be added at some time *in the future*.
28. We cannot here go into the resulting complication that production with the help of capital goods requires more *time* than does direct production with primary means of production, any more than we can go into the fact of the synchronization of production. See the *Handwörterbuch* articles 'Kapital' (vol. v, pp. 576ff.), 'Zins' (vol. vii, pp. 1130ff.) and 'Produktion' (vol. vi, pp. 1115f.).
29. On the quantifiability of utility, see my series of articles mentioned in note 25.
30. It has been objected to marginal productivity theory that with the loss of a unit of a means of production, not only is the physical effect of that means of production lost, but also the efficiency of its complementarily acting means of production is impaired, so that the loss in yield cannot be regarded as having been 'produced' solely by the missing means of production. However, this objection evidently does

not affect the above derivation. For by basing itself on the *ratio* of product utility losses caused by the loss of units of the various means of production, it already contains within itself the proportion in which the loss of a unit of one means of production and the efficiency of the others influence each other.

31. On the law of diminishing returns, see the articles 'Produktion' (*Handwörterbuch*, vol. vi, pp. 1110ff.) and 'Abnehmender Ertrag' (vol. i, pp. 11ff.).

32. See the *Handwörterbuch* article 'Preis', vol. vi, pp. 994ff., and esp. 1026ff.

33. The text of the German original here includes a lengthy bibliography of sources in various European languages.

Hans Mayer, 'Der Erkenntniswert der Funktionellen Priestheorien',
Mayer (ed.), *Die Wirtschaftheorie der Gegenwart* (Vienna, 1932), vol. 2,
pp. 147–239b.

This paper is probably Hans Mayer's best-known work. It was
published in a multi-volume series of survey papers edited by
Mayer covering the state of economics around 1930, originally
intended as a tribute to Wieser, but appearing only after his death.
It plays an important role in the history of the Austrian tradition,
and has been translated into English especially for this volume.

16

The Cognitive Value of Functional Theories of Price

Critical and Positive Investigations Concerning the Price Problem

HANS MAYER

Translated by

PATRICK CAMILLER

'Happily, there is nothing in the laws of value[1] which remains for the present or any future writer to clear up: the theory of the subject is complete.' 'The intrinsic nature of the pricing process cannot be expressed in any other way [than by...] a system of simultaneous equations like our system.' Nearly a century's development of economic theory lies between the first of these remarks, in which the since famous John Stuart Mill asserts the importance of his theory of exchange-value in establishing the laws of price,[2] and the second, its complete equal in apodeictic certainty, in which Cassel tries to cast his theory of price in a suitable light.[3] In the intervening century masters of theory such as Gossen, W.S. Jevons, Léon Walras, Carl Menger, Böhm-Bawerk, Wieser, Pareto, Marshall and Wicksell – just to mention the most significant names – have devoted their life's work to solving the central problem of commercial economy, the problem of price formation. When we come to the present day, some specialists regard the solutions offered in one or other of the above two systems as unshakeable final truths and see all further work in the casuistic handling of special problems within them; while for others, however sincerely they may admire their achievements, their disappointing and inadequate character is felt ever more strongly, inspiring an ever plainer striving to pass through to solutions which will satisfy a broader cognitive purpose.

Here we need to examine more closely where these inadequacies lie and what should be put in their place. To avoid any misunderstanding, let us say at once that they have nothing to do with those hackneyed phrases which, for want of substantive argument, seek again and again to obstruct the progress of research: for example, the objection that an attempted solution is 'subjective' or 'objective', as if today it were still permissible to claim that a theory can allow man's practical relation to the external world, and more especially, in the economy, man's value relation to goods and the formation of prices, to be determined exclusively by either subjective or objective factors; or, to take another example, the characterization of a purely knowledge-oriented analysis of correlations as 'materialist' or 'idealist' – labels which many still find exceptionally 'profound'; or even that distinction between 'individualist' and 'universalist' theories which may be appropriate for a judgemental (normative) attitude to things but which becomes a meaningless, artificial, illusory opposition if applied to theoretical work whose only aim is to elucidate processes of empirical reality.

Nor do the inadequacies in question here lie in the systems' formal lack of 'unity' [*Geschlossenheit*], in the sense of inner consistency between propositions. On the contrary, as we shall see, many of them are distinguished precisely by their beautifully simple 'coherence', which for knowledge appears as a kind of short-circuit, a dubious approximation to circularity and tautology. It is more likely that many systems display a lack of 'unity' in the other sense of *wholeness*. But even if the price-theory systems so far constructed were *formally* quite faultless, what no longer appears satisfactory is above all their *excessively narrow application* to the processes of economic reality. In a science whose ultimate object is the empirically given economy, the most formally complete system loses its usefulness to the extent that the ideal-typical assumptions underlying its construction deviate from the actually typical preconditions of reality. It is not only that the results produced by the system's apparatus are also discrepant with those of economic reality; far more serious is the fact that that apparatus, because of the way in which it is constructed, cannot even admit and process certain problems thrown up by the actual course of the economy. Research into movements within economic reality ever more urgently requires deeper insight into the *process of price formation* than it is possible to gain through purely 'static' modes of observation or through simple description of finished price relations within an already achieved state of equilibrium. This unsatisfactory aspect of existing theories of price is immediately apparent in the fact that, precisely in the last decade, there has been a rapidly more noticeable shift towards *statistical-realistic* treatment of the correlations between *moving* prices, towards research into developmental phenomena of economic processes and, more specifically, the whole

56

complex of questions concerning the extremely 'dynamic' problem of conjunctures and crises, for the understanding of which the hitherto essentially static systems of price theories have proved to be inadequate.

A classification of modern price theories by their distinctive cognitive tasks and appropriate cognitive instruments will make it easier to clarify their merits and defects as well as the limits of their explanatory power. Two main types may be distinguished:

I. *Genetic-causal theories* which, by explaining the formation of prices, aim to provide an understanding of price correlations through knowledge of the laws of their genesis.

II. *Functional theories* which, by precisely determining the conditions of equilibrium, aim to describe the relation of correspondence between already existing prices in the equilibrium situation.

Both are 'pure' theories: they claim that their (genetic or structural) laws are necessary and thus universally valid, and since the content of every law is a linking of particular phenomena with particular conditions, they have a hypothetical character.

If, as is often the case, one wishes to range 'empirical-realistic' as well as 'pure' theory under the concept of theory, then it would be necessary to identify a further type, statistical price 'theories'. But that would completely blur the concept of theory as a system of necessarily interconnected knowledge. For only an empirical character, not necessity, attaches to the regularities ascertained by statistics: they do furnish empirical material for evaluation by theory, but they cannot themselves be theory in the strict sense of the term. Nothing essential is changed in this respect by the wonderful refinement of statistical methods – for example, the calculation of correlations in the study of movements in the economy, and especially the establishment of 'stochastic' connections replacing the distinctive features of necessity with those of a priori probability.

It is impossible, for all Sombart's ingenious arguments, to shut one's eyes to the fact that the historical scrutiny of prices, the description of how they once emerged and how they developed in concrete cases, is something fundamentally different from theory.[4]

It need scarcely be mentioned that of the numerous actual variants of price theory, hardly a single one realizes either of the basic types in its complete purity. All that are ever involved – and this follows from the nature of an ideal type – are more or less close approximations. This should not suggest that such hybrid types stem from a conscious striving for 'synthesis' or deliberate eclecticism, but rather that one can see in them the struggle to make progress on now one and now the other track – hence, inevitably, that unsatisfactory impression of the system's lack of organic unity. Later we shall have to take a closer critical look at the most

57

important of these variants; here we shall start by examining, in principle, the specificity of the two basic types and how they compare in terms of their resulting efficiency.

The older of the two is undoubtedly the functional type, whose deployment is based on the assumption that certain easily and directly perceivable quantities – prices, wages, interest and revenue, or price, supply and demand – 'settle into equilibrium', tend towards a relation which, if not disturbed from outside, seeks to establish itself again and again. It is an open question whether this idea of an equilibrium situation, which, overtly or otherwise, has always lain at the basis of price theories, first arose from direct observation of the relative constancy of certain connections, or by analogy from processes in (mechanical or organic) nature, or from the postulate of a normal situation. Of the first great system-builders, the Physiocrats presented a distinctly kinetic system of equilibrium, while the Classical equivalent (with its concept of normal price!) produced one which was static at least in its basic character. Nothing essential changed as a result of the attempt to establish a causal underpinning in the Classical theory of labour costs and the theory of supply and demand, which again, as factors genetically independent of each other, are supposed to tend towards equilibrium. The old equilibrium theory reached its peak in John Stuart Mill's system, with the 'discovery' that demand, price and supply do not stand in a one-sided causal relationship to each other but reciprocally determine each other like the components of a mechanism.

The explicitly *causal-genetic* theory of price made its first entry with Gossen's and Jevons's discovery of the significance of the subjective factor for knowledge of economic processes.[5] Its necessity was most strongly emphasized by L. Walras (in the laying of the foundations of his system), and yet in his final overview of price relations the *'inventeur d'équilibre économique'* actually abandoned it again in favour of the functional principle. C. Menger then established it epistemologically with unsurpassable clarity (in the famous Preface to his *Grundsätzen* and in his *Untersuchungen über die Methode der Sozialwissenschaften und der politischen Ökonomie*[6]), and he, together with Böhm-Bawerk, Wieser and the great part of 'Austrian School' theorists doing further work on his foundations, consistently stuck to it in their construction of price theory. Parallel to this was the development of the *new functional* theory which, since Cournot found a way to introduce mathematical forms of thought and expression into theoretical economics, now had at its disposal, in the mathematical concept of function, the requisite instrument for precise handling of equilibrium phenomena, and which, in the work of L. Walras and Pareto, produced those comprehensive and wonderfully coherent systems which, in the judgement of many present-day theorists, make the causal-genetic mode of research and presentation appear definitively superseded. The epistemological problem of causal relations, the unprecedented success achieved by the limitation of research in the exact natural sciences to functional dependences, and not least the occasional mistakes and unhappy formulations – attributable, of course, only to the researcher and not to the method as such – which occurred in applied research, especially the oversubtle talk of 'the cause' of value and price (of which Böhm-Bawerk in particular is not innocent) when in reality a complex of causes act together – all this helped to strengthen the belief that causal-genetic theories of price had had their day. This rejection found its sharpest expressions in the theory of Pareto and the long list of writers who have devoted themselves to further development of the Lausanne School, in Cassel's theory of price, in Schumpeter's theoretical system from the year 1908,[7] and also in Marshall though not in a fully consistent manner.

Nevertheless, it is quite evident that, however much one respects the counter-arguments and critically examines the results achieved on both sides, a return to causal-genetic analysis of the price problem is currently being prepared. It appears as if the functional approach has already extracted from the price problem what is there to be extracted, and unless one completely abandons theory in the strong sense and is content merely to establish statistical regularities, it is necessary to go back to the causal-genetic mode of thinking.

Equilibrium theory sets as its cognitive task to describe precisely the quantitative relations which obtain between the prices, supply and demand of all goods on a unified market once a state of rest is achieved: that is, once no further shifting of goods takes place through acts of exchange. Although this situation is never completely realized in the empirical economy, and although even approximations linger for but a moment, equilibrium theory still believes in it because, with its achievement, all the elements of the economy supposedly tend to establish the cognitive object of price theory. Equilibrium theory therefore seeks to provide the *structural or formal law* of the equilibrium situation by presenting the clear, reciprocal relations between price levels and supply, demand and output quantities, costs and so forth. All elements which reciprocally maintain equilibrium in the state of rest are taken to be simultaneously 'given' (i.e., existent), if not also simultaneously 'known' (in the mathematical sense). No element is given before any other: there is no one-way causal connection between them, but they all mutually determine one another; they relate to one another in *all-round, reversible dependence*, in 'general interdependence', as variable elements of a closed system, so that if one element changes in quantity all the others automatically place themselves in a relation of correspondence. Thus it becomes possible to treat things

59

more geometrico – for in geometry too it is a question of setting out the formal law of a spatial object by presenting the mutual relations among spatial elements (points, lines, surfaces). And such treatment actually does occur, in simpler cases by directly fixing the respective positions of curves, in more complex cases through analytic equations which give a simultaneous system excluding time and causality.

Such equations are said to yield the formal law of the equilibrium situation by mathematically fixing its *conditions* for the freely competitive market (and *mutatis mutandis* for the monopolistic market). They are thus themselves constituted, on the one hand, by the *definition of the equilibrium situation* – cessation of change (or, in mathematical terms, the differential quotients are equal to zero) – and on the other hand, by the *laws of change* to which the reciprocally related elements of the system are subject (by the formal character of the curves), which, for their part, are obtained neither from *experience* nor along the path of *deduction*. As is well known, these conditions must be non-contradictory and independent of one another, and given in such number that it is possible to establish from them precisely the same number of equations as are present in quantities unknown to them. Representatives of the equilibrium theory of price claim that its greatest merit is to have shown that, for the main cases of free competition and monopoly which it considers, precisely as many conditional equations are present as there are unknowns, and that consequently the prevailing level of individual prices and their relationship to one another are not something accidental but are *strongly and unequivocally determined* at any given time.

We must now consider that what equilibrium theories can offer for our *knowledge of the economy* is, without exception, already given by 'calculating thought' in the drawing up of equations; then the process of economic cognition breaks off, and further deduction is left to the automatism of the mathematical apparatus, to begin again only with the interpretation of the results provided by that apparatus. The results will be correct – that is, they will give an accurate picture of economic correlations – if the empirical propositions or deductions which underlie the drawing up of the equations were themselves correct. Everything therefore depends on the content of the propositions which lead to the drawing up of the equations. But even if the relations expressed in the equations, insofar as they do not have a purely definitional character, neither directly contradict experience nor stand in contradiction with each other, the solutions derived from the systems of equations can have very different meanings for the knowledge of economic reality. This meaning will vary according to whether the observation forming the basis of the empirical-propositional content of the equations also applies to the elementary factors of price formation – whose

60

elementary or primary character lies in their being present even without reference to prices (e.g., the mental factors making up demand), whereas prices cannot exist without their being present – or whether the observation is limited simply to relations between quantities themselves resulting from the operation of such elementary factors (e.g., effective demand and effective supply and their relationship to prices), and is therefore restricted to mere surface phenomena both in cognitive purpose and in the tools of explanation. In the latter case, it is evident that little insight could be gained into the process of price formation and movement. To be precise, for these cognitive purposes the systems of simultaneous equations would have to lose their validity even on purely formal grounds, because the relations expressed in the various equations can no longer be established *independently* of one another but partly follow from one another as a result of genetic combination by the elementary factors.

The value of mathematical theories of price cannot be decided with general arguments from a preconceived 'standpoint' which lack any evidential force – arguments such as, 'price theory must be in mathematical form, because the task is to describe quantitative relations', or 'it cannot be mathematical because the mechanical analogy is inappropriate to the organic character of the economy'. It is necessary to follow the surer but far more arduous path of subjecting the main actual types of mathematical price theory to a close critical analysis, whose results will for the first time allow a judgement to be made concerning the limits of the capability of mathematics to deal productively with the problem of price.

The path of development is clear enough. Beginning with Cournot and John Stuart Mill,[8] the line rises from Jevons steeply up to the peak of Léon Walras; it is continued along many ramifications by Vilfredo Pareto and his large number of disciples who today, mainly in the Romance but also in the Slav countries, are active in the same direction. In the Germanic and Anglo-Saxon countries – where, especially in Germany, there was much less inclination and comprehension for functional analysis of economic processes[9] – the work of Edgeworth, Irving Fisher, Marshall, Wicksell and Schumpeter, though not along exactly the same lines, approximates to them to a greater or lesser extent, and today in Germany Cassel's oversimplified presentation, with its maximum elimination of problems, has acquired a dominant position.

It will be useful for critical purposes if we divide into two groups the main representatives of the theories under consideration: older equilibrium theory (older in a purely temporal rather than evaluative sense), which is represented by Jevons and Walras, has as its characteristic feature an attempt to provide a causal substructure for functional analysis; and the more recent, strictly non-causal equilibrium theories of Pareto and Cassel.

61

Cournot, preceding all of them, occupies a special place; connecting threads lead from him more directly to the new than to the older equilibrium theory.

Cournot's Theory of Price

The turn from the inexact 'classical' approach to the exact, mathematical-functional ('neoclassical') analysis was completed by A. Cournot. It is not that he was fundamentally opposed, like Pareto or Cassel, to the investigation of causal connections. He just considered them so complex that he stated: 'How distant we are from being able to solve, in full knowledge of the causal connections, a series of questions which are boldly decided every day.'[10] He speaks of full knowledge of the causes of value changes, arguing that the main thing is to know the laws which bring those changes about.[11] And he is well aware that probability judgements, such as those provided by statistics, are not adequate; 'quite simply, knowledge of the special laws in a particular field, instead of a probability judgement, can establish a binding judgement of certainty.'[12] Nevertheless, the genetic problem of price formation (on the heuristic assumption of barter) is alien to him. For he wrongly identifies it with the *historical* problem, and so 'the contribution of the *original*, triggering forces seems [to him] completely extinct'.[13] He presupposes a ready-made market and a constant value of money – hence a series of basic problems of price formation are excluded at the outset – and he advances 'just one axiom or, if you prefer, just one hypothesis: namely, that everyone seeks to draw the greatest possible value from their property or from their labour'.[14] And then he poses the problem in precisely the opposite manner to that of the Classicists, for whom the market price was the *unknown quantity* they tried to deduce from the combination of the given quantities: supply and demand. Cournot's procedure here has become of such importance for later functional theories that it is worth looking at it more closely.

'"The price of objects", runs the near-unanimous view, "stands in inverse proportion to the quantity supplied and in direct proportion to the quantity demanded"....'[15] 'What is the true content of this principle? Is the idea that the price falls by half if double the amount of commodities are *sold*? Then one should be more straightforward and simply say that the price is inversely proportional to the quantity *supplied*. But that now understandable principle would be false.'[16] For there is no reason why, at the halved price, exactly double the quantity should be sold. 'Moreover, what is understood by the quantity *demanded*? Certainly not the quantity which is actually sold at the buyers' demand; for then the above principle would lead to the absurd general conclusion that the dearer a commodity is, the more one sells of it. But if demand is understood to mean simply the vague wish to own something, abstracted from the price limits which everyone sets to their demand, *then there is no commodity at all for which the demand cannot be regarded as infinite*.[17] And if one must take account of the price at which every demander is prepared to buy and every supplier to sell, what does the principle mean then? It is...not a false assertion, it is an assertion without meaning.' 'Let us try to keep to less barren principles. The demand for a commodity is usually greater, the cheaper it is. The sale or the demand – *for us these two concepts coincide*, and we do not see under what conditions we would have to take account of demand that did not have any corresponding sale – generally grows if the price falls.'[18] And now comes the radical shift: 'Let us assume, then, that the sales or the annual demand D for every commodity is a partial function F (p) of the price p of that commodity. If the shape of that function were known, one would have the law of demand or sale.' But since the shape of that function 'depends' on so many 'moral' factors 'which can be neither counted nor measured' (such as 'obviously the object's degree of usefulness, the kind of service it can perform, the pleasure it produces, the customs and morals of each nation, the average prosperity and the grading according to which wealth is distributed'), 'it should not be expected of this law that it can be expressed by an algebraic formula'. Rather, on the basis of *observations*, one must draw up a table of the accompanying values of D and p and then by interpolation construct an empirical formula or curve to represent the function in question. If, on this basis, one still cannot carry the solution of the problem to the level of numerical application – because of the lack of sufficiently large and exact statistical material 'and also because of the progressive *changes which the law of demand undergoes* in a country that has not yet attained equilibrium'[19] – 'it would nevertheless be justified to introduce the *unknown*[20] law of demand into analytic calculations with the help of an indefinite symbol', for 'as is well known, one of the most important tasks of analysis is precisely to comprehend certain relations between magnitudes which cannot themselves be fully grasped numerically or even in algebraic formulae'. In fact, certain general properties of otherwise unknown functions – for example, to increase or to decrease *ad infinitum*, or to be recurring, or to be real only within certain limits – may lead, with the help of analytic expression, to equally general relations which could hardly have been discovered without such help. Justification of the hypothesis that function F (p) of the law of demand is a *continuous* function – note that, in this deduction, Cournot always understands by demand or sales the *global* and not individual demand or sales, and moreover not sales at a particular point in time, but the 'quantity sold

63

annually in the area of a country or market'[21] – comes from the fact that 'the larger the market is, and the more varied the needs, capacities and even whims of consumers, all the more steadily will function F (p) change with p'. Occasional unsteadiness of function F (p) may be interpreted as 'friction' (the model for the 'frictional phenomena' of modern theory!), which is balanced out through trade. Again and again Cournot expresses the hope that, with the help of quantities to be supplied by statistics, theory will one day be far enough advanced to effect numerical solutions.[22]

Cournot's theory of monopoly price, justly famous though not uncontested for the development of complex cases,[23] presents a brilliant application of his newly formulated relation D $=$ F (p). It also involves a derivation of the relations between product price and price of the means of production,[24] in which one can find an unprecedented and most interesting approximation on Cournot's part to the problematic of modern 'imputation theory'[25] – although it only ever remains an approximation, because Cournot's derivation in the end reverts to the old classical supply-costs theory. It does not require closer exposition in this context, especially as we shall have to look at particular aspects of it in the following critique.

Cournot did not develop a general theory of price (a theory of the formation of competitive prices in their mutual connection). He himself noted this: 'So far we have investigated how the law of demand determines the price for *each individual commodity* in connection with its conditions of production.' 'We examined *the prices of other commodities and the income of other producers as unchangeable given magnitudes*.'[26] Cournot also deserves praise for the first-ever conception of *general interdependence*, which Walras later undertook to carry through in a systematic fashion. It must be noted, however, that Cournot – repeatedly contradicting, of course, his own procedure in the solution of partial problems – upheld a notion of all-round dependence which, unlike the methodical views of those who have created the most recent systems of interdependence, did not exclude the relation of causality: 'In general, system disturbance caused by one element must *gradually show itself in action and counteraction throughout the system*.'[27]

With Cournot's derivation and application of the demand function we have come right to the heart of equilibrium theories as a whole, and so I shall not be going outside my theme of the present state of price theories if I now turn to a critical examination of his work.

The *cognitive value* of an explanatory principle – or, if you prefer, of a principle which serves to describe correlations as Cournot's law of demand seeks to do – depends upon the breadth of the field of problems in which it proves its worth, upon the greater or lesser number of individual problems for the solution of which it proves useful, or, in other words, upon the extent to which the relations constituting its content in the shape of a law have universal validity, so that they permit not only the solution of special or partial problems but also the aggregation of all those partial solutions or areas of knowledge into a *unified system of knowledge*. The more an explanatory principle needs to keep returning to empirical material in moving from one partial problem to another, there to derive further ratios or partial laws or to incorporate further 'independent variables' into the system, the less productive it will be in grasping the overall correlations of the problem area.

Cournot's 'law of demand' is an empirically established ratio between price changes and changes in the quantity of goods sold. From this single ratio obtained by experience ('material assertion'), and from the hypothesis that the seller 'seeks to collect the greatest possible exchange-value from his possession', Cournot derives all his results by purely *deductive* means, through *analytic* judgements expressed in mathematical form. But since, as Kant clearly showed, analytic judgements ('conceptual truths') cannot provide any new knowledge of reality, and since synthetic judgements – as modern epistemology conclusively demonstrates[28] – are possible only on the basis of experience, everything that Cournot's system can offer cognitively in relation to the price problem must stem from that *one* source, his 'law of demand'. Is that source of knowledge sufficiently plenteous? Can the multiple ratios binding the prices of goods to a fixed determination really be grasped as a unity by means of that empirical proposition (the problem of price theory)? It is immediately apparent that Cournot's empirical base for his 'law of demand' is too small to cope with this comprehensive task of the general theory of prices. In reality, one can observe not only Cournot's base ratio between price and sales but also numerous others: for example, sales of a commodity change in a definite way with shifts in income stratification, with movements in the prices of other commodities, with changes in the nature and scale of wants among the population, and so on; or sales and price vary together with changes in a third magnitude – the scale of production, the price of the means of production, changes in technology, etc.[29] But it is not only in terms of content but also temporally that Cournot's field of observation is too narrow to serve as the foundation for knowledge of price correlations in the real world. His observation extends only to simultaneous processes on the market: the relation he establishes between sales and price is timeless, just like the relations of analytic geometry. But we now know from experience that the *association of changes in the magnitudes that concern us here takes place in time, often over quite considerable periods*; and that *members of the series in which it takes place lie spread out in time in an immutable order (causal relation!)*. Thus, if one takes no notice of the 'remote effects' of change in one of these factors (price, sales, demand, supply, scale of production, requirements, income stratification, production technology, etc.), it is impossible, even with the most precise deductions (analytic judgements), to grasp the price correlations in the real world. But that is exactly the procedure of the whole 'static' theory of price and its father Cournot. And that is why the *process of price formation* remains impenetrable to it.

On what grounds, then, does Cournot arbitrarily single out the ratio between price and sales among the whole list in which prices are linked to other 'magnitudes'? On grounds of usefulness, no doubt. For that ratio does deal with directly 'tangible', numerically available magnitudes, and hence is accessible to exact, mathematical capture. But such usefulness in terms of exactitude and simplicity does not coincide with usefulness in terms of cognitive range – as Cournot himself has to admit in the end. It proves its worth only for the solution of individual, isolated problems of a very special kind: in the derivation of monopoly price where the assumptions are highly simplified, and in the calculation of the competitive price for one individual commodity, where the prices of all other commodities and especially of the means of production are always taken as *given* – that is, in the description of narrowly defined partial equilibrium, but not in the derivation of general market price equilibrium.

This inadequacy of Cournot's demand function as a tool for explaining price formation already attaches to the manner in which it is obtained. There is no complaint about the postulate that the curve must always be continuous: the opposite would have been very disagreeable for further mathematical derivations, and older mathematicians therefore said quite bluntly that any 'rational' curve must be continuous – evidently the same axiom as that which is expressed in the long-abandoned *Natura non facit saltum*. At any event, in the case of Cournot – who works with the aggregate supply curve of a whole area of the economy and refers to the great disparities in income, property, needs, taste, etc. among the population – the grounds for the curve's continuousness are given far more accurately than they are in the oversubtle and self-contradictory attempts of some recent equilibrium theorists to justify the assumption of continuousness for their individual demand curves.[30] The crucial point is that, as Cournot himself had to confess, the only general statement he was able to make about the *formal character* of the curves was that, if the changing prices are drawn on the abscissa axis and the simultaneously changing sale quantities on the ordinate, then the curves run from left to right of the abscissa. But this means that the *concrete* form of the curve has to be determined for every commodity – and everything depends on the concrete form, because with every change the price–sales ratios are completely altered. Thus, for Cournot there can be no exact formula, given the multiplicity and diversity of the interacting conditions; it must be ascertained by statistics in every single case, for each commodity and each market and each point in time. (That is precisely how things stand today, nearly a century later. A range of the most up-to-date equilibrium theorists and a whole host of institutes are busy preparing statistics for the price movements of all particular commodities, in order to arrive from the results at the formal character of the curves, now known by the name of the elasticity of demand.)[31]

What, then, has been achieved with this new starting-point? The Classical economists identified a functional dependence between absolute demand and price, on the one hand, and between supply and price on the other, even if they did not use the exact mathematical terms for this. Cournot established in exact form a functional dependence between price and *effective* demand. Both relations correspond to experience and do not contradict each other. But the Classicists were not satisfied with that: they searched for the *link connecting* the prices of *all different commodities*, for the law which regulates how the *exchange-values of all commodities are related to one another*. They could go on asking and searching because their use of absolute demand and supply kept open the outward-looking quest for their determinants; they were also able to build other, more comprehensive relations into the system; and they thought they had found one such in the ratio between the exchange-value of commodities and the outlay on labour costs. But Cournot then immediately shut out this question of a more comprehensive relation, precisely by letting prices be *given* as independent variables and by placing *effective* demand (that is, turnover) in relation to them. For Cournot there are only isolated curves (price–sales ratios) for any given commodity; and the question of the determinants of effective demand is removed on the grounds that it is a function of price which *in theory cannot be determined more precisely*. For to determine it theoretically is to demonstrate the *general* relation from which the respective concrete form of the demand function results, and 'knowledge of the laws which bring about changes in value' is here assumed, while such 'knowledge of the causes of value changes' is said to be determined in turn by 'knowledge of the special laws of the field' to which those causes belong. But instead of investigating these unknown 'special laws of the field' – which, in fact, become *laws of price formation* as soon as they are seen to be decisive for the form of the demand function – Cournot rests content with references to statistics. In each concrete case, he thus sets up unanalysed, empirical raw material, in place of laws which can only be gained through the analysis of comprehensive empirical material. Instead

67

of the formulation of definite, universally valid relations, we are referred to the 'brute facts'.[32] That means no less than completely abandoning a *theoretical* solution to the problem.

Here we can see the full inadequacy of the starting-point. The 'law of demand' is supposed to give the fundamental ratio from which the link between prices and demand can be derived for each commodity. But this law *changes* (as Cournot himself has to state explicitly) from place to place, from time to time, from commodity to commodity, and these changes of the 'law' are only ascertained by statistics; nothing at all can be said about the law which brings about changes in the 'law of demand' – that is, changes in the formal character of the demand curves. But a 'law' which itself changes in accordance with external circumstances cannot contain a *fundamental ratio*, because it does not state any universally valid connection, independent of concrete time and place; in fact *it is not a law in the strict sense of the term*, but only sets the researcher the task of *discovering* the law which governs changes in that pseudo-law through changing external circumstances. Or, to remain with mathematical terms, it only throws up the problem of discovering the *independent* variable or variables in relation to which the variables assumed as independent in Cournot's 'law of demand' – that is, prices and implicitly also their (for Cournot) dependent variables which are the demand quantities – are themselves the variable magnitudes. Only then would one have established the law which yields the changing price-and-demand ratios of all commodities and thus the global correlations of prices and demand for all commodities (as Jevons, Walras and the Austrians have tried to do with their law, branded by some as 'psychological', of the constitution of demand by need utility; or Edgeworth, Irving Fisher and Pareto with their structural laws of indifference-curve analysis). Only then would one have discovered a magnitude which, rather than being determined by a ready-made system, would itself be 'system-determining'.[33] (System is used here in a double sense: on the one hand, as the system of real prices and quantitative demand actually prevailing on the market; on the other hand, as the theoretical schema which is adequate to that system and serves to explain it.)

But if Cournot's law of demand thus fails completely as a tool for the derivation of competitive prices in their mutual connections, it has proved entirely successful – as Cournot himself showed in masterly fashion – for the narrowly defined problem of monopoly price derivation in the simplest cases of complete monopoly and cost-free control by the monopolist over the monopoly good. However, precisely the same result can be obtained without the higher-level analysis,[34] and in any case *this* special problem has to do not so much with social as with individual economics: that is, it is a problem of the *calculation of profitability*. For the task here is to discover the prices at which the monopolistic entrepreneur obtains the highest total proceeds – the proceeds being the product of the unit price and sales at that price (p F (p) must be at its maximum) – *so that the sales total varying with the price is assumed to be already empirically known, and thus the derivative for the social-economic problem is given*. It is even more evident that when Cournot's 'law' goes beyond questions of private economic calculation,[35] it is no longer effective in the next case it deals with: the still elementary one of full monopoly with *production costs*. Here, apart from the sales quantities varying with the price changes (demand function), the monopolist's costs 'which must be paid'[36] also determine the maximum net proceeds. But these costs are assumed to be *given* from outside – by the prices for productive means which have already been somehow formed on the competitive market in which the monopoly is inserted. The mathematical derivation which Cournot gives here for the 'law' of cost changes with varying prices of the monopoly product – that is, for the construction of the costs curve – cannot actually be regarded in the slightest as a *derivation of the prices and price changes of the means of production (cost goods)*. Cournot establishes the relation of costs to his supposedly fundamental law, D = F (p), by making costs – which explicitly include *total financial outlay* for a given product quantity (D) – dependent on product sales, in some form left indeterminate for the time being. Costs therefore become another function (ϕ) of D – in which case, as Cournot says, both costs and the sales quantity are functions of the *only independent variable*, p. In itself that would be a correct notion – which modern 'subjective' theories have reached by a different path and with a much greater specification of the content of the relation – provided, first, that one gives up the general perspective in which the price of an individual product is always assumed to be already given as the independent variable, and second – which is more significant in this context – that Cournot is really both able, on his assumptions, and willing to derive a law that the price of the means of production changes together with the price of the product. Instead, however, Cournot is content for the shape of the cost function (curve) to be determined by his perfectly grasped and formulated *technical* law of the declining, rising and constant growth in returns.[37] But if one bases the construction of the cost curve on the fact that, in the operation of the (technical) law of diminishing returns, an additional quantity of a product can only be produced with, for example, twice the number of paid working hours and therefore twice the 'costs' of the previous, equally large quantity of the product, and if one establishes in this way the ratio between output changes and thus indirectly between the product price and the 'cost' expenditure in the sense of the financial

69

outlay for various quantities of means of production, then the *price* of the means of production (in the example, the factor of production labour) has evidently still not been derived in the slightest; rather, it is assumed to be *already given elsewhere* by competitive price formation, so that the solution to the problem is seriously undermined. Only in one case does Cournot appear to offer a derivation of the prices of the means of production: namely, when it is a question of specific means of production which a monopolist can use only to produce one particular article. That is also the case when Cournot demonstrates the derivation of the prices of the means of production from the product prices,[38] thereby approximating to the imputation problem as we have already seen above.

Since, despite its unusual garb, this point is crucial for the productiveness of Cournot's procedure, we must look at it rather more closely. Cournot asks which are 'the laws in accordance with which the various producers participating in the production of a commodity distribute the returns which all these producers can obtain together on the basis of the law of demand for the final product'. Let us take two raw materials, copper (*a*) and zinc (*b*) and make the following assumptions: they can only be used to produce one product, brass (*a b*); the quantities of copper and zinc contained in the brass unit of weight (production coefficients) are $m_1 : m_2$; each of the two raw materials is produced by a monopolist; abstraction is made from the production costs of each raw material and from the costs of working them up into the end-product. The question is how, on these assumptions, the price of the product (p) is spread between the prices (p_1 and p_2) of the two productive resources. This really does raise the problem of the *formation* of production costs – that is, of the productive resources – in a commercial economy. Cournot concludes that, with his presuppositions, the result must be $m_1 p_1 = m_2 p_2 = \frac{1}{2} p$; hence 'the returns are distributed equally between the two monopolists'. 'And in reality,' he adds, 'there is no reason why the distribution should take place unequally to the benefit of one and the disadvantage of the other.' However, if one thinks of the factors operating in the real world of the economy, it is obvious that there can be no question of Cournot's case of univocal determination of the prices of the two means of production. In reality, the solution remains completely undetermined. The producers of the commodities (*a b*) can pay for ($m_1 + m_2$) no more than the whole of their realizable product price p; but they must pay it if unlimited competition takes place between them. However, the way in which p is spread between m_1 and m_2 is completely immaterial to the producer; if he has to pay more for m_1, he can spend proportionately less for m_2. On the other hand, there are the monopolists A and B, each of whom strives to obtain the maximum proceeds from the sale of his raw material by trying to secure for himself the largest possible share of product price p as the price for his raw material. How far he succeeds, which of the two obtains the larger share of p for his raw material, which has to be satisfied with the remainder: this all remains, economically speaking, completely *open*. The problem precisely coincides with case (1) figuring in Böhm-Bawerk's theory of imputation, where there is a single combination of two factors with rigid production coefficients, the solution to which remains open. If Cournot thinks that 'there is no reason why the distribution should take place unequally to the benefit of one and the disadvantage of the other', we can answer him with just as much right that there is no reason why the distribution must take place equally for them both.[39]

Equally open remains the other problem that Cournot sets himself: namely, how to derive the prices of the two raw materials, assuming that they are suitable for many different uses. Cournot puts it aside with the remark that then 'the equations appear too developed for general conclusions to be drawn from them'.

All the rest of Cournot's derivations, presuppose that the prices of the means of production and changes in those prices have already been given somewhere independently of the basic function $D = F (p)$. (This is true especially of his investigations into the effect of changes in production costs on price movements,[40] – where price is made dependent upon production costs and so there would not be an inconsistency only if the determination of production costs as a function of some production prices had previously been shown to be beyond doubt – which, as we have seen, is not actually the case.) Since, moreover, the fundamental law-based correlation between product price and price of the means of production is not amenable to Cournot's procedure, it is clear that his law: $D = F (p)$ has only very limited explanatory value.

Thus, the radical shift which Cournot saw between the classical school and his own theory only partly constituted an advance. By starting out from a ratio between empirically given, calculable magnitudes (demand functions), he did establish the possibility of mathematically exact treatment of certain narrowly defined special problems. But as a result of the new starting-point, the development of a truly *general correlation in social economy* had perforce to be given up. Since the relations or explanatory tools which the classical economists required for their more comprehensive cognitive task were different from those which Cournot needed for his more narrowly defined task, his sharp polemic against the use of the concepts of supply and demand in classical theory is unjustified and misleading.

By supply and demand, Cournot means *effective* supply and *effective* demand, with prices that are assumed to be already given. Since, on these

71

presuppositions, 'supply' and 'demand' coincide with each other and also with sales, the three concepts become identical and an explanation of price in terms of their reciprocal effect must lead to tautologies. (With all the sharpness one could wish for, this view of supply and demand appears in the expositions of the most modern equilibrium theorist, Pareto: 'In political economy it is customary to distinguish between the quantity of goods which an individual, having arrived at a point of equilibrium, has given up, and what he has received; the first is called his *supply*, the second his *demand*.'[41] And still more sharply, A. de Pietri-Tonelli: 'En effet, l'offre sera constituée *par la quantité donnée et non par la quantité offerte, et la demande sera constituée par la quantité reçue et non par celle qui est demandée*.'[42] But when the Classicists said that supply and demand determine the market price, they had in mind *absolute* supply and demand, which no doubt do have an explanatory function provided that they are thoroughly analysed (although it should be noted that the classical economists did not complete the necessary analysis of supply and demand). The elder Walras drew attention to these points with great acuity.[43]

Despite some fine observations on the varying elasticity of demand according to the kind of commodity,[44] Cournot blocked the path to an understanding of the general determinants of prices (and thus to an account of their general correlation). We can see this in his assessment that whereas 'the abstract concept of wealth or *exchange-value* is a determinate concept which is therefore suited to exact development', this is not the case with the concepts of '*utility, scarcity, suitability for the satisfaction of needs and for human enjoyment....*, for these are concepts which by their nature are changeable and indeterminate and which therefore cannot be used as the basis for any scientific theory. For everyone estimates utility in their own way, because there is no fixed measure for the utility of goods'; and 'truth or falsity is not amenable to proof in judgements concerning the utility of goods: these are questions of valuation which are not amenable to any calculation or logical demonstration'.[45]

Cournot, in such reflections, might have remembered his own words: 'for, as is well known, one of the most important tasks of analysis is precisely to grasp certain *relations* between magnitudes which cannot be fully grasped in purely numerical terms or even in algebraic formulae'; or, in reference to quite another problem: 'what is involved here is *not a quantitative relation but one governed by laws; the magnitudes can certainly be signalled but not measured*'. If he had done so, not only would he have arrived at a quite different assessment of the explanatory function of the laws of subjective utility for the theory of price formation; he would have passed directly to the construction of Pareto's index functions of ophelimity.

And so, the circle of Cournot's followers in exact theory have extended his original mathematical form of expression to the study of how the *subjective factor* operates in price formation, and have thus moved beyond merely partial equilibrium to the derivation of the *aggregate equilibrium* of price formation.

Older Theories of Equilibrium
Jevons's Theory of Price

W. S. Jevons, who did not know Cournot's theory when he was writing the first edition of his work,[46] at first posed the problem in *genetic-causal* terms by setting out to investigate the laws which govern the process of price formation. He started at once with an enquiry into the determinants of price operating on the demand side. Whereas demand had previously been treated *in globo* as aggregate demand, he broke it down into its component, *individual demands*. And in seeking to formulate the law of individual demand formation as laws of *utility* or subjective value[40] – an approach which, as is well known, was adopted almost simultaneously and independently by Carl Menger and Léon Walras, and first of all by Heinrich Gossen[48] – Jevons already outlined the essential features of those theories which people today often try to label as 'psychological'. Like Walras, he offered a distinctive and, it should be said, extremely fruitful synthesis between causal-genetic *derivation* of consequences and *representational* application of the mathematical-mechanical concept of equilibrium. This synthesis of causal-theoretical and functional approaches became quite evident in Jevons's introduction of the concept of equilibrium in the foreword to the first edition: 'The Theory of Economy thus treated presents a close analogy to the science of Static Mechanics, and the Laws of Exchange are found to resemble the Laws of Equilibrium of a lever as determined by the principle of virtual velocities. The nature of Wealth and Value is explained by the consideration of indefinitely small amounts of pleasure and pain, just as the Theory of Statics is made to rest upon the equality of indefinitely small amounts of energy.'[49] Jevons's causal-genetic view of the problem was made explicit not only in his view that Cournot – whom he otherwise held in high regard – 'did not frame any ultimate theory of the ground and nature of utility and value',[50] or in his studies on the 'origin of value',[51] or in the drawing up of *non-reversible relations*: 'Cost of production determines supply; supply determines final degree of utility; final degree of utility determines value',[52] or 'that the value of labour...must be determined by the value of the produce, not the value of the produce by that of the labour.'[53] His causal-genetic approach informs the whole structure of his enquiries.

As Jevons's conclusions have largely become the stock-in-trade of recent theory which may be assumed to be common knowledge, and as we are concerned here exclusively with evaluating his cognitive *path* and demonstrating still unresolved problems or ones only apparently resolved, we may limit ourselves to the most essential points.

The starting-point is the individual systems of wants and the positive or negative quantities of pleasure produced by consumption or the effort of labour. These constitute the degrees of economic utility which Jevons, though at first very sceptical about their *measurability*[54] and convinced only of their *comparability*, treated as fully measurable quantities in his later investigations.[55] He developed the law of the *diminishing utility* of finite subsets given a rising quantity of goods (Gossen's Law), whereby the resulting curves are assumed to be *continuous*; he formulated in exemplary manner the concept of *final degree of utility* that is basic to his whole system,[56] as 'the degree of utility of the last addition...of a very small, or infinitely small, quantity to the existing stock', or as differential coefficients

$$\left(\frac{\Delta u}{\Delta x}\right)$$

of utility aggregates (u) obtained through employment of a total quantity of a good (x) as a function of that quantity.[57] With the establishment of the law of diminishing marginal utility with a growing quantity of goods, Jevons actually discovered a *fundamental ratio* governing all economies, and it is evident that this law must be constitutive precisely for the formation of demand. But this single fundamental ratio cannot be enough in itself for the derivation of prices. It certainly gives the demand-curve law for every commodity in isolation from price formation, but it does not provide the law for the correlation of all demand and all prices of the various commodities. For this, other determinants are also required. Jevons thought he had found them in what later writers called the 'law of the equalization of marginal utility' or the 'law of the equal level of marginal utility'. And it is extremely interesting – as well as providing greater insight into the relationship of functional (equilibrium) theories to causal-genetic theories – that from now on the ways diverge. Everything developed by Jevons up to the law of the equalization of marginal utility completely coincided with what the Austrians developed with their pure focus on causal theory. The concept of marginal utility too, already prepared in its essentials by Carl Menger though not explicitly formulated, was independently derived in its entirety by Wieser. But the Austrians did not put forward the law of a uniform level of marginal utility;[58] they expressly rejected it.[59] On the other hand, the law of the level of marginal utility, as the basic ratio essential to further derivations, can be found without exception in all mathematicians operating with the subjective factor – whether in the elementary form developed by Jevons, or, as in Walras and Pareto, in the form of the equality of the weighted (that is, divided by price) utilities of the last-acquired units of goods, the *weighted ophelimities*, as Pareto calls them. Superficially, the difference in the application or non-application of this 'law' by functional or causal theories appears to be a detail of little significance, especially as, in the following derivations of price, there are many parallels between the two theoretical orientations. In reality, however, the basis is thereby laid for that system of equilibrium which comes to light from the later, purely formal derivations. What John Stuart Mill said about the theory of value literally applies here: 'The smallest error in that subject infects with corresponding error all our other conclusions; and anything vague or misty in our conception of it, creates uncertainty and confusion in everything else.'[60]

It is worth dwelling a little more on this 'law'. Jevons develops it in his enquiry into 'the distribution of commodity in different uses'.[61] A stock of some commodity is divided into x_1 and y_1 according to the 'two distinct uses' of which it is capable.[62] Then, given the striving after the greatest possible total utility, 'when the person remains satisfied with the distribution he has made, it follows that no alteration would yield him more pleasure; which amounts to saying (!) *that an increment of commodity would yield as much utility in one use as in another*. Let Δu_1, Δu_2, be the increments of utility which might arise respectively from consuming an increment of commodity in the two different ways. When the distribution is completed, we ought to have $\Delta u_1 = \Delta u_2$; or at the limit we have the

$$\frac{du_1}{dx} = \frac{du_2}{dy}$$

equation, which is true when x, y are respectively equal to x_1, y_1. We must, in other words, have the *final degrees of utility* in the two uses equal. The same reasoning...will evidently apply to any two uses, and hence to all uses simultaneously, *so that we obtain a series of equations less numerous by a unit than the number of ways of using the commodity*.'[63] That is the derivation. Jevons at once adds the perfectly correct remark: 'We should often find these equations to fail. Even when x is equal to 99/100 of the stock, its degree of utility might still exceed the utility attaching to the remaining 1/100 part in either of the other uses. This would mean that it was preferable to give the whole commodity to the first use. *Such a case might perhaps be said to be not the exception but the rule*.'[64] And then Jevons goes completely astray with *a confusion of economically permitted and technically possible uses*: 'For, whenever a commodity is *capable* of only one use, the circumstance is theoretically represented by saying that the final degree of utility in this employment always exceeds that in any other employment.'[65] Jevons concludes this investigation by arguing that in times of scarcity 'things of great utility in other respects are ruthlessly applied to strange purposes'; that, for example, people ate a large quantity of horses during the siege of Paris because they needed them more urgently for this purpose than for others, although 'a certain stock of horses had, indeed, to be retained as a necessary aid to locomotion, so that the equation of the degrees of utility never wholly failed'.[66] And with this Jevons appears to have completely overcome his own serious doubts about the equalization of marginal utility, for in his later derivations in the theory of exchange he never hesitates to make the broadest use of this 'law'.

Such was the development of the elementary system of equilibrium. In fact, this 'law' is fundamental to all equilibrium theories: *if it is valid*, it constitutes the demand ratio for various goods which emanates from each economic subject; it is then a matter of indifference whether the problem of price is posed in such a way that the demands are assumed as independent variables in relation to the prices of goods, or whether the prices of various goods are assumed as given quantities and the demands for them are derived as the independent variables. In the first way of posing the problem, it would follow from the law – insofar as it was valid – that each economic subject always demands such a quantity of each good that the marginal utility of his final demand is the same in each category of goods; in other words, that the funds available for his individual aggregate demand (his income) is divided among the demands for various goods in such a way that the same marginal utility is attained in each branch of consumption. The addition of individual demands for each good gives aggregate social demand for the various goods on the market and their quantitative relationship to one another – hence too the price ratios; so that the *general equilibrium system* of market prices is determined by this meeting up of *individual equilibrium systems*. If, on the other hand, one starts from the assumption that prices are always *given*, the law of the equal level of marginal utility has the effect that individual demand for all categories of goods – and hence also their total, the aggregate social demand for the various goods – may be determined from the division of each economic subject's aggregate demand fund (his income) among various goods in such a way that the final unit of money spent at *given* prices in every category of goods brings about the same degree of marginal utility in all categories. In this case, then, price equilibrium on the market is already predestined by the individual demand equilibria resting upon the law of the equalization of marginal utilities.

It is therefore quite intelligible that, in the groups of *conditional equations* established by later mathematical economists for the derivation of equilibrium prices, there have to be those which state that the law of the level of marginal utility must be fulfilled for every economic subject with regard to all the varied goods coming on to the market. Indeed, it may be said that this group of equations is the only one whose content is a *synthetic judgement*, a claim about real processes or relations. As to the other two groups of conditional equations in play – (i) that after market equilibrium has been attained the sum of the goods delivered and received in exchange by all economic subjects (pluses and minuses) is equal to zero, and (ii) that receipts and expenditure must coincide for every economic subject involved in exchange (budgetary equilibrium for each individual) – they logically (if not also mathematically) express nothing other than identity judgements: namely, that the presuppositions made at the beginning of the investigation – *compensatory* transfers, *given* types and quantities of goods – are not changed on the market in the course of the investigation.

It is now clear that if this fundamental law of the equalization of the level of marginal utility did not hold, the whole theoretical system of equilibrium prices would lose its main support, completely undetermined by Group 1 of conditional equations.

The 'Law of the Level of Marginal Utility'

The question of the *reality* of the basic ratio expressed in this law must therefore be of decisive importance for the usefulness of the price systems erected upon it. Its derivation is the necessary basis for the following two assumptions: first, that all the want or utility curves of each economic subject have a strictly continuous character for the various goods or psychological circumstances which are supposed to be symbolized in those curves; and second, that the curves coexist alongside one other, so that the maximization problem which is posed for each individual through his striving for the greatest possible total of utility or satisfaction can be solved only when he allocates any increase in his economic means – of course, insofar as technical factors do not prevent this – to securing equal growth in satisfaction or utility in *all* the different categories of needs. For, evidently, to use such means for the ampler satisfaction of *one* category of wants at the expense of deprivation in another would signify a lesser

77

growth in aggregate utility than would an equal raising of the level of satisfaction in *all* categories. Attempts have been made to represent this psychological circumstance with all manner of illustrative material. I am referring to the system of coexisting scales of wants or utilities in the Austrian economists (who do not, however, postulate strict continuity), to the system of simultaneously valid, continuous want-curves and utility-curves among the mathematicians, to the system of indifference lines following one another at infinitesimal intervals in Edgeworth, Irving Fisher and Pareto, and to that most graphic symbolization, widely used since Irving Fisher, in which a common liquidity reservoir of communicating tubes represents the wants for various goods, and the state of liquidity, given changing quantity or changing pressure in the reservoir, always appears in equally continuous increase or decrease at precisely the same level. One may also, however, try to represent the imagined state of things at least in part by employing purely external, 'tangible' relations. And since the just mentioned correlations are essentially *mental* – even if their inclusion may appear necessary to unprejudiced researchers – the aim would be first to take into account the very misleading and simplistic accusation of 'overstepping the boundaries' into the domain of 'psychology' or 'metaphysics', an accusation once made by Pareto which has often been repeated with some pleasure, especially as it saves going more deeply into a rather difficult problem and provides the legitimation for remaining tautologically on the surface. We shall return to these points later below.

In order to keep to what is 'visible', then, the idea is to take the *consumption ensembles* made up of the various kinds of goods and the individual economic subjects and to observe the changes within them. Any small rise in income would, according to the hypothesis, be divided among the resulting small increases in *all* species of goods comprising the individual's consumption ensemble, while any small drop in income would show itself in a small decrease in consumption in *all* species of goods. And if, in this kind of 'observation', one is not content with the mere 'fact' of a rise or fall in the quantity of all categories of goods but wishes to establish the extent or the relative end-points of the rise or fall in the particular branches of consumption – which is necessary to preserve the law of the equal level of marginal utility, and again is possible only by bringing in the degree of marginal utility in the various uses – and if, furthermore, one wishes to steer clear of that frowned-upon 'psychological' determination of marginal utility ratios which proceeds by comparing directly experienced and observed intensities of want, then nothing remains but the device of 'questioning' the economic subjects about the utility ratios which hold between the last commodity increases in the various branches of consumption

– or, more precisely, to pretend to question them, since it appears doubtful whether such a trick is practicable – so that the answer can again be the postulated law of the equal level of marginal utility. And this really is how a whole series of writers proceed.[67]

Now, do these postulated or feigned ratios of the law of marginal utility level – which, as we have seen, are called upon to be the main bearers of mathematical systems of equilibrium – actually coincide with relations in the real world? And if the answer is no, is not the divergence between the two merely an allowable imprecision or 'stylized simplification' which changes nothing of substance and therefore does not impair the cognitive value of the results obtained in this way – i.e., their usefulness for our understanding of the formation of price relations in the real world? Thus, after developing the basic law (of the marginal utility level) in simplified form, could one not achieve its applicability to price formation simply through an auxiliary law that removes the imprecisions? That both are not true, cannot be true, stems from the following considerations.

Let us begin by looking at the second of the two derivations outlined above, the one which claims to base itself upon 'tangible' external facts (consumption ensembles). It is immediately apparent that observation of the real world gives a very different picture. If the income of an economic subject rises, say, by a tenth of its previous amount, we can see that this increase is not at all used to bring about equal growth of commodities in *all* branches of consumption; rather, certain kinds of goods in the consumption ensemble will remain constant, others will increase in various proportions and others will decrease, while other kinds of goods will completely disappear and be replaced by 'more sophisticated' ones. If experience shows that this is the case with small rises in income, the effect of a twofold or even greater increase is not that all previously used species of goods undergo the same quantitative growth, but that the whole consumption ensemble, with the exception of a few commodities which remain at their previous level of use, is made up of new kinds of goods. The notion of a uniform, continuous change in the quantities of all goods becomes quite grotesque when one thinks concretely of the consequences. For example, the richer someone became, the more bread he would have to consume every day, the more sugar would be contained in his daily consumption ensemble, the more salt he would have to use at home, the greater would be the quantities of similar objects of use, articles of clothing, and so on. Are these the 'tangible' facts? Conversely, experience shows that any fall in income is not at all followed by a decrease in all branches of consumption; that in such a case the quantity of some goods remains constant, that of others is reduced in varying degrees, more sophisticated items are replaced with cruder ones, and some kinds of

79

goods are given up altogether. *The derivation of the law of marginal utility level from external experience must therefore be regarded as completely unsuccessful.*[68]

Things stand no better with the second 'psychological' derivation, also to be found in Jevons, which is based on the proposition that a stock of variously useable goods (income) produces the maximum total satisfaction when, in all branches of consumption, the final small increments bring about equal 'amounts of pleasure' or marginal utilities, or – according to another mode of expression – satisfy equal intensities of want. This derivation is more difficult to refute because it refers to the realm of mental facts, but the task is more significant in clearing the way to a price theory that explains the real world. This second way of deriving the law of marginal utility level should, according to its advocates, also provide the *explanation* for that supposedly experience-based, but in reality fictitious, construct of the total consumption ensemble, and it again provides it by means of an illusory structural system of wants as the determinant of that fictitious combination of goods, so that, admittedly, the false picture of the system of wants (false when measured against reality) is consistent with the false picture of the consumption ensemble. In fact, as we can clearly see from Jevons's account that we analysed above, this derivation has a *petitio principii* standing behind it: namely, the argument that the final increments in all branches of want or categories of goods *must* have the same degree of marginal utility, *because otherwise they would have been disposed of differently*![69]

As we have already seen, this derivation necessarily starts from the assumption, whether explicit or silent, that the same degrees (intensities) of satisfaction are always of pressing importance at the same time in relation to all kinds of wants, for only then is it possible for the respective final increments of goods to bring about the same increments of utility or satisfaction in the different branches of want. This is supposed to be symbolized by the continuous course of the scales or curves of want.[70] The derivation further presupposes that each occurrence of satisfaction, symbolized by such a scale or curve, has for itself an isolated mental reality in a kind of want, but that all together they simultaneously (at one point in time or over one consumption period) coexist in this way illustrated by a multiplicity of independent curves present alongside one another, so that any degree of intensity of satisfaction appears at the same time in all the scales (curves).

It is enough to be fully aware of these assumptions to realize that the constructed schema of the system of wants is completely different from the facts of mental reality. There is no need of subtle psychological theories or psycho-physical experiments. Everyday experience, accessible to everyone through self-observation, is quite sufficient to establish two things: first, the course of satisfaction in particular kinds of want is not independent of the state of satisfaction in other kinds – a fact which contemporary authors have called the mental complementarity of wants satisfaction or utility;[71] and second – something unnoticed precisely by those authors who have recognized the mental complementarity of wants – the interconnection between different wants is not at all one of general, mutual *dependence*, but largely involves a genetic and thus *unilateral* (causal) determination of the immediacy of particular wants by the process of the satisfaction of other wants (whether total or up to a certain degree of intensity). Thus, we learn from experience that wants of a particular kind (quality) are first triggered, or raised from latency to actuality, when wants of a different kind are already satisfied in part or in full. But if it is the case that all wants differing in kind or quality are not reciprocally present to one another, then the postulate of the law of equal marginal utility – namely, that equal increments of utility or pleasure are realized in all branches of wants through the final use of goods – becomes impossible in the real world of the psyche.[72]

In order to make this result of our critical analysis more secure, but also positively to demonstrate the basic mental fact from which the connection of individual demands to various goods derives, we should return now to the ultimate foundations of economic theory, the structural laws of the system of wants.

First of all: is there not an internal contradiction in the way in which we refuted the law of marginal utility level by showing that numerous kinds of wants only come into existence when wants of a different kind have already been *completely* satisfied – a consideration which goes beyond the fact, basic to the Austrians' system of scales, that various wants with their maximum intensity are installed at a level (on the general scale of intensity) where other wants are already partly satisfied? Is it not a contradiction that a want of a particular kind only becomes existent at a level where another want has already reached rock-bottom? Would that not mean that the first want, with its initial intensity, begins at or below the bottom point of the general scale of intensity? There is indeed a contradiction: not between the facts we have just mentioned, however, but between them and the usual curves and scales of the system of wants, which are not adequate to empirical reality. This inadequacy of the conventional depictions of reality consists in the following main features.

1. The usual accounts, which work with simultaneously applicable curves or scales of want, make it appear irrational to satisfy one or another want *completely* (unless it can be satisfied just with free goods), if *all* other wants are not completely satisfied at the same time. But since *total*

satisfaction of *all* human wants is never possible, then rationally *none* of them should be wholly satisfied but only all of them partially: for example, there should not be a complete but only ever a partial satisfaction of thirst or hunger, because all the countless luxury wants can never be fully satisfied. This is connected to the second point.

2. The usual construction of the various curves or scales is based upon differentiation in various *external kinds of goods*, whose prices are to be derived by means of those curves. And it is then taken for granted that if there is no longer any desire for a species of goods – so that the intensity of desire for it has fallen to zero – the degree of intensity of the 'pleasure' or 'enjoyment' caused by the final unit of that category of goods will be close to bottom on the general scale of intensity. What this overlooks is that the final degree of pleasure or enjoyment in the *different qualities of feeling* or branches of want is differentially high, and that the tension between the last noticeable degree of intensity of pleasure or enjoyment in relation to a particular kind of want and the last degree in other kinds of want – since not all qualities of feeling go through all degrees of intensity – is in many cases so great that there is room within that range for many new scales of other qualities of feeling.[73] What is overlooked, in other words, is that at a certain point of intensity some qualities of feeling turn into others of which other external goods are the correlate; or that at certain points of intensity there is a ramification of basic wants (to which certain external goods correspond) into a series of other, qualitatively different, 'more sophisticated' wants to which other goods correspond. The desire for commodity *A* completely dies out after a certain amount has been consumed; in its place appears the desire for commodities *B, C, D* etc. which was not there before. Thus, the intensity of the want for commodity *A* – according to the conventional view – becomes zero at a point when the wants for commodities *B, C, D* with their initial intensity first make themselves felt.

3. The usual way of conceiving things, with its scales or curves built in isolation but assumed to be simultaneously valid, disregards or cannot express the fact that the quantity of pleasure (the increment of well-being) brought about by any consumption of goods is dependent – according to 'Gossen's first law' – not only upon a previously consumed quantity of that kind of commodity, but also upon the quantity and sequence in the consumption of all other goods.

If one tries formally to define that maximum of 'satisfaction', 'pleasure' or 'well-being' which, insofar as it can be produced at all by external goods, is the goal of consumption and ultimately of the whole disposition of economic goods, it becomes apparent that since each individual satisfaction or pleasure or enjoyment is transitory, it is possible to do this only in the form of a (periodically repeating) *sequence*, a succession of desired (mental) conditions, and not, for example, in the form of constant preservation of a once-achieved state of satisfaction or pleasure – which would be a psychological and physiological impossibility. This sequential character of 'welfare' always raises the question whether the subject's field of vision is narrowly restricted to the shortest period given by the rhythm of life, the daily curve of welfare, or whether it extends to a larger portion of life comprising several such sequences or the welfare curve of the whole of life. For the sequence as a whole (the aggregate pleasure curve), each good in the consumption ensemble signifies a certain partial pleasure whose quality and intensity is jointly determined by all the pleasures which the previously consumed goods brought about. The welfare maximum which economic subjects can procure from the available amounts and varieties of goods is thus a matter of experience for each individual (without his needing to know the underlying physiological and psychological laws); it will depend upon the *sequence* in which the various types and quantities of goods are employed. And the optimum aggregate sequence of consumption (the optimum curve of aggregate pleasure) is characterized by the fact that, in the sequence of consumption, each individual commodity has its place where it secures the greatest possible pleasure in connection with the use of all other goods. This is why the usual system of curves and scales existing alongside one another for each individual kind of commodity is so inadequate, for reality always involves a *total sequence* and not isolated partial sequences for each species of goods. It is thus quite clear that the law of marginal utility level is an impossibility. It assumes a *synchronization* of needs satisfaction in the different branches at a level simultaneously applying to all (a mistake evidently induced by the fact that one can simultaneously *have* the external goods), whereas the essence of things is a *sequence*. It is as if one were to express the experience of aesthetic value on hearing a melody – an experience determined by successive experiences of individual notes – in terms of the aesthetic value of the simultaneous harmonization of all notes making up the melody. Thus, when some recent theoreticians say that the marginal utility of a good is a partial derivative of the aggregate utility function of the whole available stock of various goods, there can be no doubt that they are right. But one can do just as little with that general statement as one can with, for example, the equally indisputable observation that every concrete event is dependent on the total state of the world at that moment, so long as one does not know the precise form – that is, the law – of the dependence. The validity of 'Gossen's first law' remains unaffected; but since that law refers only to the isolated sequence of satisfaction in the consumption of each kind of commodity, it is by itself not sufficient to derive the structural law of the aggregate sequence of satisfaction and hence the law of disposal over various kinds of goods and the marginal utility ratio between them.

We shall not attempt here to deal exhaustively with the problem,[74] but we do need to refer to certain points which are of fundamental importance in grasping the connection between individual demand curves for various goods and hence for the derivation of price formation laws. Since we are talking of a sequence of mental states – of 'pleasure', 'enjoyment' or 'subjective welfare' – the satisfaction or pleasure effected by the various goods exhibits a dependence which is to a large degree unilateral, and not at all a comprehensively reciprocal (reversible) dependence. In this context, consideration should be given above all to the distinction which Pareto drew, but did not use further, between *besoins* and *goûts*.[75] First, the painful circumstances giving rise to needs must be overcome – which may itself be associated with feelings of pleasure – in order to produce the psychic potential for the experiencing of positive states of pleasure. The sequence is not reversible, and this entails that the striving for goods which serve to produce positive states of pleasure can only become immediate, and the demand for such goods can only assert itself, when command is assured over the goods which serve to overcome the mournful states.[76] But this makes untenable the assumption of a *general, reciprocal and thus reversible dependence of individual demands* for the various goods, insofar as this assumption supports itself upon the mental fact of complementary utility.

If the law of marginal utility level falls – and it can no longer be sustained after what has just been said – all its derivatives naturally also fall, and in particular the formula of the equality of *weighted* marginal utilities which is fundamental for the mathematical economists, and the formula of the proportionality of the marginal utilities of different goods for each subject at the prevailing prices.

Jevons's Theory of Exchange

In the theory of exchange which he constructs upon his theory of utility, Jevons gives up the idea of 'a complete solution of the problem in all its natural complexity', which is 'a problem of motion – a problem of dynamics', and confines himself to the 'purely statical problem' of establishing the conditions under which exchange ceases and equilibrium is reached.[77] From a static point of view, it is true that *'the last increments (dx, dy) in an act of exchange must be exchanged in the same ratio as the whole quantities exchanged'*, so that:

$$\frac{dy}{dx} = \frac{y}{x}$$

This follows from the 'law of indifference, one of the central propositions of the theory', according to which different prices cannot prevail on the open market for the same commodity at any point in time, and so all partial quantities must exchange at the same prices. 'The keystone of the whole theory of exchange and of the principal problems of economics, lies in this proposition – *The ratio of exchange of any two commodities will be the reciprocal of the ratio of the final degrees of utility of the quantities of commodity available for consumption after the exchange is completed.*'[78] It remains to be seen whether, in the case of two economic subjects, one of whom possesses a quantity of commodity A and the other a quantity of commodity B, where the ratio is, say, $10a$ to $1b$, the exchange will be advantageously continued until the gain in utility would turn into a loss in utility for both parties as a result of any further exchange acts. Equilibrium will thus emerge at the point where the utility of $10a$ is equal to the utility of $1b$ for each party, or where infinitely small quantities of A and B exchanged in the same ratio (10:1) would no longer bring any additional utility for either of the two. This idea, mathematically formulated, gives the formula for the derivation of Jevons's famous *exchange equations*. If x denotes a small increment of A and y a small increment of its exchange counterpart B, and if x represents the whole exchanged quantity of A and y the whole exchanged quantity of B, then it is necessarily the case that:

$$\frac{\Delta y}{\Delta x} = \frac{y}{x}; \ \Delta y = \frac{y \Delta x}{x}.$$

But since, in the state of equilibrium, the utility magnitudes of these increments must be the same for each party, 'the degrees of utility [i.e., the marginal utility of the last-exchanged of infinitely small partial quantities] of commodities exchanged will be in the inverse proportion of the magnitudes of the increments exchanged'.

If, of the two kinds of commodity A and B, subject I originally possesses quantity a (of A) and subject II originally possesses b (of B), and if quantity x (of A) is exchanged for y (of B), then after the exchange I will hold quantities $(a-x)$ of A and y of B, and II will hold quantities x of A and $(b-y)$ of B. If, furthermore, $\phi_1 (a-x)$ denotes the degree of marginal utility of A for I, $\phi_2 (x)$ the degree of marginal utility of A for II, $\psi_1 (y)$ the degree of marginal utility of B for I and $\psi_2 (b-y)$ the degree of marginal utility of B for II, then the exchange must continue until for I

85

$\phi_1 (a-x) dx = \psi_1 y dy$ and for II $\psi_2 (b-y) dy = \phi_2 x dx$. After the appropriate reformulations and substitutions, this eventually gives:

$$\frac{\phi_1(a-x)}{\psi_1 y} = \frac{y}{x} = \frac{\phi_2 \ x}{\psi_2(b-y)}$$

with the two equations sufficing to determine the result of the exchange.

Jevons applied exactly the same principles, developed for barter of two goods by two subjects, to the case of three or more subjects and goods. This, the *principal case of price theory*, is treated with surprising brevity and simplicity.[79] If subject I holds quantity a of good A and gives x_1 of it to II and x_2 to III; if II holds quantity b of good B and gives y_1 of it to I and y_2 to III; if III holds quantity c of good C and gives z_1 of it to I and z_2 to II, then the six unknown quantities are exchanged as follows:

I gives x_1 for y_1 and x_2 for z_1;
II gives y_1 for x_1 and y_2 for z_2;
III gives z_1 for x_2 and z_2 for y_2.

'*These may be treated as independent exchanges.*'[80] Now, if ϕ_1, ψ_1 and χ_1 denote the marginal utility functions of goods A, B and C for I; ϕ_2, ψ_2 and χ_2 the same functions for II; and ϕ_3, ψ_3 and χ_3 those for III, then by analogy with the earlier case, after completion of the exchange between I and II, the ratio of exchange of y_1 for x_1 is given by:

$$\frac{\phi_1(a-x_1-x_2)}{\psi_1 y_1} = \frac{y_1}{x_1} = \frac{\phi_2 x_1}{\psi_2(b-y_1-y_2)}$$

and similarly, in the exchange between I and III, the following equations are given by the ratio of the marginal utility of the goods A and C:

$$\frac{\phi_1(a-x_1-x_2)}{\chi_1 z_1} = \frac{z_1}{x_2} = \frac{\phi_3 x_2}{\chi_2(c-z_1-z_2)}$$

And similarly for the exchange between II and III, 'which will be independently regulated on similar principles':[81]

$$\frac{\psi_1(b-y_1-y_2)}{\chi_2 z_2} = \frac{z_2}{y_2} = \frac{\psi_3 y_2}{\chi_2(c-z_1-z_2)}$$

Then: 'For every quantity of commodity which is given in exchange something must be received, and if portions of the same kind of commodity be received from several distinct parties, then we may conceive the quantity which is given for that commodity to be broken up into as many distinct portions. The exchanges in the most complicated case may thus always be decomposed into simple exchanges.'[82]

Where there is *competition* the determination of the exchange ratio is handled still more tersely. Jevons does no more than briefly discuss the case where a subject, by giving up part of his stock of goods, acquires the good he wants from two owners of different quantities of the same, and settles precisely the problem of the equation formula as in the first case given above (barter of two goods between two subjects).[83]

In summary, Jevons comes to the following basic conclusions from his theory of exchange. *The ratio in which a person divides up his money or income for the acquisition through exchange of quantities of other commodities 'will partly depend upon the ratio of exchange, partly on the final degree of utility of these commodities'.* And the general rule of exchange is that 'a person procures such quantities of commodities that the final degrees of utility of any pair of commodities are inversely as the ratios of exchange of the commodities'; or in other words, that 'a person *distributes his income in such a way as to equalize the utility of the final increments of all commodities consumed.* As water runs into hollows until it fills them up to the same level, so wealth runs into all the branches of expenditure.'[84] 'It obviously follows that in expending a person's income to the greatest advantage, the algebraic sum of the quantities of commodity received or parted with, each multiplied by its final degree of utility, will be zero.' This is the ratio which later mathematical economists applied under the name of *balanced budget*:[85] namely, that for each economic subject the sum of receipts and expenditure must come to zero.

Jevons considers that the future progress of economics as an exact science will largely depend upon whether the law of changing utility can be grasped in precise numerical terms – which would require 'accurate statistics of the quantities of commodities purchased by the whole population at various prices',[86] where the utility of money would have to be treated for the moment as a constant. But Jevons does not conceal the great difficulties which arise here, especially from the wide scope for substituting goods and from the fact that in reality the 'utility of money' does not remain constant through price changes in articles of mass consumption.[87]

It must be stressed that Jevons – with a rare degree of intellectual honesty which ruthlessly lays bare to the reader the discernible gaps and problems in his own system and already makes his work worthy of great esteem – refers to a whole series of typical cases in which his exchange equations fail to work, especially those numerous ones where goods cannot be divided into infinitely small quantities. Jevons also explicitly states –

and not at all with that lightness of mind which many later mathematical economists have shown when they reinterpret reality without considering the explanatory value of the results, in a way that is most convenient for the applicability of differential calculus – that *'laws which assume a continuity of variation are inapplicable where continuous variation is impossible'.*[88] In this context, where our only concern is with the basic elements of Jevons's theory of exchange, we shall have to refrain from analysing his remarks about the marginal utility ratio of goods used for consumption and for production,[89] which have since become part of the iron rations of the Anglo-American theoretical literature, as well as his theory of costs (work effort) and more especially the connection between price and production costs.

A Critique of the Derivation of Jevons's Exchange Equations

The results of Jevons's investigations set out the basic theorems to which mathematical economics (equilibrium theory) has stuck right up to the present day. They recur in Walras, Marshall, Pareto, Wicksell, Schumpeter, Barone and others. What is new, and indicative of some progress, are the refinements of formulation, the modifications or corrections at one point or another, but the basic propositions have remained the same. Hence, a critical assessment should also distinguish between verification of whether the basic propositions can be sustained, and demonstration of the shortcomings which, in reality or intention, have already been rectified by more recent mathematical theories.

With regard to the basic propositions, the critique has already been largely anticipated in the above proof of the *invalidity of the law of marginal utility level*. For, as is apparent, that law explicitly or implicitly underpins the derivation of the exchange equations in each of the cases that Jevons discusses. It is the content of the law which he sees as *'the keystone of the whole theory of exchange and of the principal problems of economics'*, the law that 'the ratio of exchange of any two commodities will be the reciprocal of the ratio of the final degrees of utility of the quantities of commodity available for consumption after the exchange is completed' – which is in turn, as Jevons himself shows, identical with the equal utility of the last partial quantities acquired and surrendered in exchange. And since this basic assumption behind Jevons's exchange equations most sharply conflicts with reality, those equations lose their cognitive value for exchange processes in the real world.

A second questionable, and self-contradictory, assumption on Jevons's part is that the exchange ratio is *constant* during the aggregate exchange process which he imagines to be composed of successive minor exchanges coming one after the other (always, for example, with one unit of B for ten units of A). Jevons sees that this assumption contradicts his own fundamental statements on the scales of utilities, from which it necessarily follows that with each of these successive displacements the 'determinants of utility' and hence the exchange relations must change for both parties.[90] But he calms himself with the thought that this is a difficult *dynamic* problem, that first the simpler and hitherto unresolved *static* problem must be tackled,[91] and that according to the (static) 'law of indifference' all quantities of two goods which come on to the market – whether small or large part-quantities or total quantities – must, at the same point in time, be exchanged in the same ratio. But therein lies a methodological error, and a false conclusion. Jevons's methodological error is that the problem of *price formation* – as one usually calls it – is always and necessarily a *'dynamic'* problem. His false conclusion starts from the fact that on the big market of a national economy, the *already existing* exchange ratio, which has arisen from the interaction between many thousands of suppliers and demanders, is not changed at all, or not noticeably, as a result of the exchange acts of individuals (the usual definition of unlimited competition). And this, Jevons wrongly argues, allows one to assume that even in the fundamental case for the theory of exchange – the case of exchange between two subjects whose holdings of the goods in question constitute the *total* supply and the *total* demand – the exchange ratio remains unaltered through successive displacements of the goods; in other words, that the marginal exchange ratio, which determines the equilibrium price, must be identical to the previous partial exchange ratios upon which the marginal exchange ratio is genetically constructed.[92]

A further question to be asked from the point of view of the elucidation of reality is whether it is permissible to assume that exchange acts always take place successively and in small quantities of goods – an assumption whose methodological purpose (for the applicability of the differential calculus) is perfectly evident. However, we shall not be able to examine this in more detail here.

Nevertheless, these reservations lead back to a quite fundamental question, because they concern the cognitive value of the static-functional approach as such for the theory of price. Jevons bases his whole theory of exchange on the laws of need and utility, which he recognizes as central and develops in classical form. One might then have expected him to derive, in a closed chain of argument, the determination of the exchange ratios (prices) from the given utility scales and quantities of goods on the side of the exchanging economic subjects, and thus to allow certain exchange ratios to emerge genetically from the premises. Instead, what

89

follows – just as it does later in Walras – is *a sudden turn from the causal-genetic (dynamic) approach to the functional (static)*. Not only the utility scales and quantities of goods of the exchanging subjects, but also the *exchange ratios themselves (that which has to be derived)* are assumed as *already existing and in that sense 'given'* (if only 'for the moment', to quote the formal restriction).[93] And instead of an enquiry into the laws according to which certain exchange ratios must *emerge*, we have only a consideration of the mutual correspondences in which exchange ratios (prices) and the marginal utilities of various goods, and the quantities of goods given up and acquired by each subject, stand for each subject when equilibrium has *already been reached*. It is the *problem* and not only the approach which is thus changed. And although later, in his theory of production and of disutility and costs, Jevons resumes the path of causal-genetic derivation, in his theory of exchange he forsakes it in favour of the functional approach.

Jevons, then, does not enquire into the law governing the *formative process of the exchange ratio* which maintains itself if conditions do not change, or which, more accurately, reproduces itself again and again through the renewal of the same conditions (since, with constant conditions of 'equilibrium' or rest, nothing at all would be exchanged). The question which is posed instead is that of describing the *simultaneous* conditions that must be fulfilled for there to be no further exchange. This static description, which eliminates all movement and causality, does not pass off altogether without contradiction, as one can already see from the expression *'if no further exchange act occurs'* or *'if a state of rest is achieved'*. These amount to saying that the task is to grasp the reciprocal relation of small (infinitesimal) final phases of movements or processes which immediately precede (the differential quotients are equal to zero) the state of rest (the maximum of the mathematical functions). Jevons identifies two such conditions in the conditional equations that he develops to describe the equilibrium exchange ratio. One – already shown to be unreal – is the condition of equal marginal utility for each exchanger; the second is that the exchange ratio must be identical to that of all the quantities exchanged:

$$\frac{\Delta y}{\Delta x} = \frac{Y}{X}$$

As we have seen, Jevons obtains this equation from the 'law of indifference': once the exchange ratio between two commodities exists, so that its formative process is finished, then evidently, if the data remain unchanged, all parts of the total quantity x, y, can continue to be exchanged in the same proportions. But then the problem of the law of origination of a certain exchange ratio is *already behind us*. Since this equation *presupposes the existence of the exchange ratio*, it cannot itself be used for the derivation of the exchange ratio. Here we are truly faced with ὕστερον πρότερον, a circular argument. This can also be proved quite concretely. Jevons, like all theorists working with marginal analysis, assumes that the barter between two persons takes place in partial exchanges gradually following one after the other – and in a ratio which, though originally supposed to be unknown, is nevertheless *constant* for all the successive phases of the exchange. The quality of constancy is, as we have seen, impossible, because it is in contradiction with the utility curves. But let us pass over this assumption of constancy: whether the ratio is constant or not, the exchange totals of the two commodities (x, y) only appear at the end of a barter process working itself out successively in more or less numerous partial exchanges $(\Delta x, \Delta y)$. *Only at the end of the process*, then, do the exchange totals (x, y) ensue through summation of the partial quantities of goods transferred in the individual phases of the barter. They are not known beforehand to the parties to the exchange – if they were, the parties would immediately barter the full totals and there would be no point in the succession of small partial exchanges; nor do they become definitive before the conclusion of the last partial exchange – just as, at the beginning of a game of chess, the result is neither subjectively known to the players nor objectively settled. For the final totals depend upon the exchange ratios which have come into force in the individual, successive partial exchanges, just as each move in a game of chess is dependent upon previous ones and the final result upon all the moves that have gone before. The preceding partial exchange ratios have therefore been formed without any connection with x, y, or any knowledge of their magnitudes, and to speak of a true solution of the problem one would have to show *their* determinants.

The situation can easily be visualized by means of the usual scales or curves, but a simple algebraic observation is also sufficient. Let us assume that, between the holder of a stock of A and the holder of a stock of B, 1 b is initially exchanged for 10 a; then, after the completion of that exchange act, the marginal utilities of a and b will have changed for both parties, and consequently the exchange ratio must be different – say, 1b to 8a – for the following small transfer of goods, 1b to 5a for the next, and 1b to 1a for the next and last through which 'equilibrium' is established (that is, a further exchange act would bring no increase in utility for either party). Then the exchange totals (y, x) are 24b and 4a, but the final exchange ratio

$$\left(\frac{\Delta y}{\Delta x}\right)$$

is 1:1, so it is not at all the case, as Jevons postulated, that

$$\frac{\Delta y}{\Delta x} = \frac{y}{x}.$$

For in the course of the process, the ratio

$$\frac{\Delta y}{\Delta x}$$

has itself changed. But even if, leaving aside for the moment the striking contradiction with the individuals' utility curves, one assumes that the exchange ratio is constant for all the successive phases of the barter and that the final exchange totals x, y, could be derived from this ratio,

$$\left(\frac{\Delta y}{\Delta x}\right)$$

even then the exchange totals would only be given *ex post* and the core of the problem – *how the ratio* ($\Delta y/\Delta x$) *itself has been determined* – would still be unanswered.

In essence, there is an immanent, more or less disguised, fiction at the heart of mathematical equilibrium theories: that is, *they bind together, in simultaneous equations, non-simultaneous magnitudes operative in genetic-causal sequence as if these existed together at the same time*. A state of affairs is *synchronized* in the 'static' approach, whereas in reality we are dealing with a *process*. But one simply cannot consider a *generative process* 'statically' as a *state of rest*, without eliminating precisely that which makes it what it is.[94]

Once stasis has been reached in the economy and there is 'equilibrium' between the prices of various goods, their costs, their supply and demand, etc., the problem of how that equilibrium has been achieved already lies behind us. For the *static economy* itself, in which all ratios appear ready-formed and constant (because the data are immutable), is unproblematic like any state of rest. And it is self-contradictory to attempt – as Jevons did – to derive the laws of motion or formation leading to equilibrium from relations within the state of equilibrium or rest (marginal utilities equalized at the same level; ratios of the already achieved equilibrium of the exchanged totals of goods). We shall have to return to this fundamental problem of method.

In reality – and here present-day theory is united on what Böhm-Bawerk was one of the first to show conclusively[95] – a univocal derivation of the exchange ratio is impossible in Jevons's elementary case of the barter of two goods between two economic subjects; the problem remains *indeterminate*. For, according to the possession of goods and the utility scales of the two parties to the exchange, their subjective utility ratios can be so far from each other that a large number of different exchange ratios are economically possible for both within the given leeway; and only the arrival of competitors – the more there are, the narrower the limits – will settle the exchange ratio.[96]

But perhaps what induced Jevons to change, with only apparent success, to the path of *static* problem-solving was precisely the fact that, for all his overpitched expectations about the productivity of his new theory of utility, the unsatisfactory conclusion imposed itself that in his elementary case no univocal exchange ratio could be derived *genetically* from the utility scales and the possession of goods.

If it is true that, for the reasons shown, Jevons's derivation offers no solution for the case of elementary barter, it is self-evident that the derivation built on the basis of it cannot lead to a solution for the *main case* of price formation, the case of the exchange of three or more commodities among three or more economic subjects. As one can easily see from the equations given above, they recur here as falsely demonstrated ratios: the law of marginal utility level, which must be fulfilled for each party to the exchange; and the relationship of identity between the total quantities of various goods transferred at the *end* of the whole exchange process between any two persons, and the partial exchange relations existing at the *beginning* of the successive exchange acts. The central problem therefore remains unsolved: how are the exchange ratios for the first exchange acts determined – those ratios from which the transfer totals $(x_1, x_2, y_1, y_2, z_1, z_2)$ themselves result?

It is on this problem of exchange of three or more goods among three or more subjects that most theories of price have foundered – although this has not, of course, been noticed by their originators. The proffered solution states that, with given possession of goods and given utility functions of the exchange subjects, prices must eventually settle at a level where each person has given up so much of his commodity and acquired so much of the other's commodity in return that the law of marginal utility level is fulfilled for them – an outcome which could apply, moreover, to many different prices. But quite apart from the unreality of the law of marginal utility level, this is in fact no solution: it is a *hypothesis* that, by analogy with the laws of mechanics by which the collision between several bodies of different velocity and weight must eventually lead to a predictable state of equilibrium, so in the case of dealings between different economic subjects, a definite equilibrium corresponding to the law of marginal utility level and therefore definite exchange ratios must establish themselves after a complicated and, in its details, *unexplained* process has run its course. Our case should not be confused with the competitive market situation where, because of the multiplicity of persons outbidding and undercutting one another in the supply and demand of one of three or more commodities, a certain unit price must eventually emerge for each commodity. For the account to which we have referred only throws light on one particular phase, the *end* of the formation process. Everything that precedes and determines the final phase – *how the competitors on the demand side reach their highest price offer for particular quantities of the various goods* – or, in other words, everything which determines how, *without the prior existence of any prices*, individuals divide their income (in goods or in money) into the demand for different kinds of goods, remains completely obscure even in this partial account of the process. And to illuminate it is precisely the point of returning to the apparently simple case of the exchange of three goods among three persons, because one expects that in this simplified case the law of the *formation* of exchange ratios must show up most clearly – an expectation, however, which on closer inspection is completely illusory. For what is demonstrated here is not the law of formation but the *hypothesis* of a finished state. The data (utility functions and possessions of separate individuals) are thrown into the 'crucible of the mathematical calculus', together with the law of (un-real) equal marginal utility, plus the tautological conditional equations that receipts and expenditure must balance for each individual after the exchange, and that all the quantities and species of goods available to individuals involved in the exchange must be identical before and after it has taken place – and then it is left up to the mysterious process going on in the crucible to ensure that a state of equilibrium with definite exchange ratios is finally produced. But there is no demonstration of the *law* of that process shrouded in darkness, which is supposed to lead to the formation of quite definite exchange ratios. How is it conceivable that, among three persons who each have a need for the goods of the other two, *simultane-ously* univocal exchange ratios take shape which assert themselves for all three? How is that conceivable if one considers that what Subject One gives of his commodity A to Subject Two in return for part of commodity B is dependent not only upon his own utility scales for A and B and on those of Subject Two for the same commodities, but also upon what of A he must give to Subject Three for part of his commodity C, and upon what Subject Three must give of his commodity C to Subject Two in return for part of commodity B, and so on. And all this must be solved simultaneously: each individual must be in a position to know in advance, from a series of new unknown quantities (not yet given either objectively

94

or subjectively) and from them another series of new unknown quantities, how to draw the following conclusions: this is the most of A I will offer for a piece of C, this at the outside is how much of B that I will offer for a piece of A, for a piece of C, and so on. It is not only that, as Jevons rightly said in another context,[97] 'the subject is one in which complicated action and re-action takes place' that cannot be grasped through simultaneous equations; the whole conception of the problem is such that it can never be solved.[98] It is thus a complete diversion to content oneself with the idea of 'reciprocal determination'. *That is not where the problem ends but where it begins.* To show how, in what way, through which links this 'reciprocal determination' must lead to definite exchange ratios – *that precisely is the problem*. The reader will recall here Marshall's well-known ball example: in the same way that several balls in a bowl reciprocally determine their equilibrium through pressure and counter-pressure, so do the economic factors mutually determine one another. The misleading character of the mechanical analogy is here expressed most clearly. The same *constant*, gravity, operates on all the balls: they all bring their own, *invariant* weight into the bowl, thereby exerting pressure and counter-pressure regardless of the order in which they have been placed there. But the marginal utilities for particular goods, and hence the elements stemming from each individual for the formation of the exchange ratio, are *variable* according to whether Subject One first exchanged with Two or Three, Subject Two with One or Three, Subject Three with One or Two, according to the sequence in which the three came into association with one another in the second, third and other partial exchanges of their goods, and finally according to which of the numerous possible exchange ratios was the one in which each of the three first entered into exchange with the other two. But these exchange ratios are not only undetermined but indeterminable. We are not an inch nearer a solution if we take the exchange ratio between Subject One and Subject Two as a function of the exchange ratio between Two and Three and between One and Three, and the exchange ratio between One and Three as a function of the exchange ratio between One and Two and between Two and Three, and the exchange ratio between Two and Three as a function of the exchange ratio between One and Two and between One and Three. For one must be able to say something about the *form* of these functions and of their *reciprocal association* – or one has said no more than one does with the general but quite unavailing statement that, because all events in the world are interdependent, each one determines all the others and is in turn determined by them.

The mechanical analogy and the simultaneous equations based upon it are thus inapplicable to the problem of price formation. 'But practical life solves the problem.' To be sure. But precisely because it cannot be solved theoretically within the framework of functional theories of price, we can already infer that it must be posed in practice under different assumptions from those of mathematical theory, and that everything hinges on how they are fixed if we are to give an account of price formation in the real world.

The functional approach, even in the hands of such an outstandingly acute and painstaking mind as Jevons, has thus no success to show for itself in solving the problem of price formation. If the assumption that economic activity has a mental determination, whose disclosure in the laws of utility and their effects on price formation is the basis of Jevons's immortal fame, is synonymous with the path of *genetic* derivation, and thus with explanation in the narrow sense (as opposed to mere description) and *'understanding'* of the course of the economy, then the turn to *static-functional* analysis at the point of mounting explanatory difficulties signifies a transformation of the problem of the law of price formation into the problem of the *simultaneous relations of price correspondence* to the marginal utilities and goods quantities of the economic subjects.[99] Even if the propositions in use (law of marginal utility level) were materially correct, it would be a mistake to suppose that with this *description of the correspondence relation* of exchange ratios, degrees of marginal utility and individual possessions, or of small changes in them immediately before the state of rest is reached, *the formative process of equilibrium and of its prices has already been implicitly explained*. That could be the case – always assuming that the content of the applied relations is materially correct – only if it were legitimate to suppose two things: first, that during this final phase, just before or, so to speak, on the margins of the establishment of equilibrium, the (infinitesimal) changes in the factors we have just mentioned are either identical, or stand in a constant and already known relationship, to the changing proportions of those magnitudes which arise in the previous phases of the formative process of the exchange ratio (the price); and second, of course, that the factors themselves, which stand in a relationship to one another within each different phase of the process, remain *qualitatively the same* (and so, in particular, the same kinds of needs or intercepts of their curves go through all phases). To put it graphically: *it would be necessary to assume that all successive intercepts which are established through the temporal process forming the equilibrium exchange ratio display the same structure – that is, the same factors and same quantitative relations of those factors to one another; or else that that structure changes according to the same law (in the same ratio) as it does within the final phase of the formative process immediately preceding the state of rest*. But such an assumption – which underlies the claim of equilibrium systems that the simultaneous equations of the state of rest can afford an insight into the process of price formation – not only lacks any empirical foundation whatever, but sharply conflicts with those facts about the construction of the system of wants which were advanced previously against the law of marginal utility level, so sharply indeed that, far from being a useful working hypothesis, it constitutes a fiction which blocks the way to a derivation of the real-world formation of prices.

Actually, the situation is precisely the reverse. Once the broader (dynamic) problem of the process of price formation has been solved, it will necessarily be the case – since the price ratio in the state of equilibrium only represents *one*, final phase of the whole process – that the correspondence relation of prices (exchange ratios), marginal utilities and exchange totals is also implicitly given. This makes it clear why the difficulties of passing from a static to a dynamic approach, and of using the results of static theory for the investigation of economic movements – difficulties only fully recognized in the most recent theoretical research – are so great as to be scarcely capable of being overcome. It is not the case, as is almost universally assumed, that static theory is the preliminary stage on the basis of which dynamic theory can be achieved, in a realm where the *total process* cannot be derived just from knowledge of its final phase. The only path with any real prospect of overcoming the difficulty probably lies in the method of 'comparative statics',[100] that is, static understanding of the structure of each of the numerous successive phases (intercepts) of the process, and subsequent comparison of changes in the structure throughout the phases of the *whole* process, with the aim that the law of motion or change might thereby be obtained. But such a procedure is statics only in name, for the observation and uncovering of changes during a *total process* actually constitutes the essence of the dynamic approach, which is thus shown once again to be identical with causal-genetic investigation.

Léon Walras's Theory of Price

Having discussed a series of basic problems in the context of Jevons's static theory, we may keep within the strictest bounds our critical analysis of applied systems of functional theories.

In the work of Léon Walras,[101] we have the first attempt, still unsurpassed in its admirable unity, to establish a *mathematical system for the whole of economic theory* upon the new foundations of subjective value which he discovered independently of Jevons, Gossen and Menger.[102] What interests us here, where we are examining the foundations of price theory, is only his 'first problem' which he tackles in the section 'Mathematical

Theory of Exchange': namely, the exchange of goods ready for consumption (without reference therefore to the laws of production). 'The quanta of commodities are given; we shall be looking for the system of equations whose roots are the prices of those commodities.'[103] 'We must therefore, if possible, find a theory which explains the *causes* determining those prices – or else remain silent.'[104] 'By reduction or analysis, we trace prices back to their elements', and then 'we shall express the prices and their *causes* numerically and apply the deductive method – that is, *we shall infer the prices themselves from their causes*'.[105] The problem posed by Walras is to find '*the law of the formation of equilibrium prices*'.[106] 'The causes of price formation are also the causes of price changes. These causes are the utilities of commodities and the stocks of those commodities.'[107] The project of *causal-genetic* explanation – for which Pareto, with his purely functional approach, would later severely reproach Walras – could not be expressed more clearly.

It is most interesting to consider whether Walras achieved this goal, and with what results. His own account of his implementation programme comes across loud and clear; the aim is to show '*1. how market or equilibrium prices derive from the demand curves, and 2. how the demand curves themselves derive from the utility and quantity of the commodities*. From this it will be apparent what is the relation between utility and quantity of the goods, on the one side, and their market prices on the other.'[108]

First the conceptual apparatus. It is the same as in Jevons; only the terms are different. '*Intensive utility*' refers both to the urgency or degree of intensity of a want and to the subjective utility produced by a unit or fraction of a unit of a commodity – in other words, Jevons's 'degree of utility'. A 'measure of urgency' is thus assumed, just as 'in physics and mechanics one brings into the calculation certain magnitudes (e.g., masses) which are also in no way directly measurable'.[109] A good's '*extensive utility*' for a subject denotes the amount of the good necessary to satisfy the want up to vanishing point. In the way familiar today, these elements are then used to construct the 'utility or want curve', which may or may not be continuous.[110] It should simply be noted that, unlike in Jevons, the quantity of goods is presented on the vertical axis and the urgency of wants on the horizontal axis (just as prices later appear on the abscissa and quantities on the ordinate). By '*effective utility*' is meant the total use of a quantity of goods. Walras's basic concept of '*rareté*' (*scarcity*) is identical with the concept of *marginal utility*.[111] *Rareté* may be defined 'as the differential quotient of consumption correlated with stocks'.[112] The price of one good expressed in another is the inverted exchange ratio: if A exchanges for B in the ratio of 2:1, the price of A in terms of B is ½ and of B in terms of A 2. *Effective supply* and *effective demand* – that is,

98

supply and demand at definite prices – must be the same in equilibrium with each other.

In his first statement on the problem and the nature of demand curves – which, of course, he does not in the slightest regard as a theoretical solution – Walras shows how they can be *empirically* established by noting the changes in demand totals at various prices, either through direct market observation or on the basis of market statistics or questionnaires. Its algebraic equation, as in Cournot, is:

$$d_a = f_{a_{,1}}(p_a)$$

(effective demand for a commodity as a function of its price). Walras then moves on to the first point in his programme of *theoretical* derivation: '*How market or equilibrium prices derive from the demand curves*'. Making, as always, the assumption of barter, let us take as given the totals of goods A and B and the individual demand curves of a larger number of persons who wish to acquire quantities of A and B. Since the total demand curve (D_a) is derived from the addition of all individual demand curves for A (each of which is in turn a function of prices), the total demand curve of A in terms of B is also a function of the price of A in terms of B, and similarly the total demand curve of B in terms of A (D_b) is a function of the price of B in terms of A. The total effective supply, which in equilibrium must equal the total effective demand, is obtained from the simple consideration: 'To want to acquire D_a units of A at price p_a (of A in terms of B) means to offer O_b (total supply of B) = $D_a.p_a$ units of B at the same price p_a (of A in terms of B) or at the price

$$p_b = \frac{1}{p_a}$$

of B in A; in other words, the supply of one commodity for another equals the demand for this latter commodity multiplied by its price in terms of the first commodity.'[113] The equilibrium price must therefore be formed at the point of intersection of the total demand curve and the total supply curve, because it only exists for this equality of effective demand and effective supply. 'Thus, if the demand curves are given, the prices follow mathematically.' Up to this point in the exposition, one may assume that it only claims to be *definitional* in character, in that it explains the logical correspondence among the concepts of equilibrium price, effective demand and effective supply. Everything therefore hinges upon the theoretical derivation of the demand curves.

Walras now comes to the second point in his programme: '*how the demand curves themselves derive from the utility and quantity of the commodities*.[114] He begins, just as Jevons does, by constructing the utility or want curves of commodities A and B for Subject One and Subject Two. The total utility which One holds from his stock of A and Two from his stock of B is given, in each case, by a certain surface of the graphic representation. Each could increase his total consumption if he exchanged part of the stock of his commodity for part of the stock of the other's commodity at the market price. Since p_a is given, d_a (the demand of Subject Two for A) is determined by the condition that the quantity of his own commodity (B) which he gives up for the other commodity (A) at the current (!) price will be such that, after the exchange has been completed, the total utility from the remaining B quantity and the acquired A quantity will be the maximum.[115] This condition of maximum utility *'is fulfilled when the urgency ratio of the last satisfied wants or the* rareté *ratio after the exchange is equal to the price'*.[116] The proof of this – again just as in Jevons – assumes that the exchange between the two individuals takes place in a series of separate exchanges (regardless of whether they are in infinitesimal or infinite magnitudes) at the *current* price, so that each successive individual exchange is less advantageous for each of the parties, until in the final act the 'individual consumption area' given up with a quantity of the commodity is equal to the 'individual consumption area' acquired with a quantity of the other commodity. For this last individual exchange, 'the baselines of these areas represent the *raretés* and stand in a reciprocal relation to their peaks, which represent the quantities exchanged'. And Walras then concludes the demonstration: 'Thus, to each price p_a of A in terms of B there corresponds a demand d_a which affords the maximum utility, and in this way *the demand curve is consequently determined as a function of the price'*.[117]

The reader will have followed this argument with astonishment. What was the clearly formulated problem? *'How the demand curves derive from the utility and quantity of the commodities'* – which is the heading to this chapter. At the beginning of the derivation, Walras set out the presuppositions with mathematical precision: 'Two commodities A and B and their respective utilities for each of the parties to the exchange are given, as is the stock of each commodity held by each owner; the task is to ascertain the demand curves.' And half-way through the demonstration, Walras suddenly and as if self-evidently *assumes the price as given*! He thus abandons his own programme of *causal-genetic derivation* of price from the demand curves, and these themselves from the 'final elements', the utilities and stocks of the goods. It had been promised that the prices would be traced back to their *elements* through the method of 'reduction and analysis'; but in his account of the causal interaction of these final elements (utilities and stocks) in the formation of price, Walras assumes the participatory action of an *already formed price*! This, in a somewhat different form, is the same as Jevons's shift from *causal-genetic derivation* of price or demonstration of its formative laws to *functional description of the correspondence* of marginal utility, quantities of goods exchanged and acquired, and already existing prices, in the situation of equilibrium.

It seems completely out of the question that Walras should have consciously performed this transformation of the problem. For the next chapter,[118] which carries the heading 'Analytic Definition of the Exchange of Two Commodities. Scarcity as the Cause of Value in Exchange', begins with the (often to be repeated) assurance: 'Utility curves and stocks of commodities are thus ultimately the *necessary and sufficient conditions* for the establishment of market or equilibrium prices. In the first instance, the individual and aggregate demand curves are derived mathematically from these presuppositions. And from the individual and aggregate demand curves are then derived mathematically the market or equilibrium prices. *The demand curves are derived mathematically from the utility curves and the stocks of goods*, on the basis of the fact that each owner will seek to achieve the maximum satisfaction of his wants.'[119] How is it possible that such a clear mind as Walras's could, without even realizing it, have abandoned his own clearly defined path to the solution of the problem of price formation; or that he moved in circles by assuming what was to be explained (the *outcome* of price formation) as the *determinant* of price formation, with data given at the start of the process; or that, in essence, he explained a certain price by that very price itself? If one considers that the straying from the programmatic path of causal-genetic derivation to circular explanation takes place in the same way, and at the same point, that we found in the case of Jevons, then in view of both authors' clear and sharp reasoning, the conclusion strongly suggests itself that their common use of the mathematical-mechanical analogy[120] – already implied by the concept of 'equilibrium' – must be what led them unconsciously in mid-stream *to change the problem and reverse the demonstration*. Mechanics or geometry has to do with magnitudes or forces or elements which are assumed to exist simultaneously, some of them 'known' or 'given', others 'unknown' and requiring to be discovered by means of those that are known. Now, all these elements or partial determinants stand in a relation of simultaneous and reciprocal correspondence with one another: the sides and angles of a triangle, radius and circumference of a circle, the relationship between two arms of a lever, the relationship between energy expended and energy obtained, an example to which Jevons devoted a whole chapter in justifying the mathematical-mechanical analogy in economic theory, etc. And since, moreover, they are logically but not genetically dependent upon one another – what would it mean to

101

imagine genetic dependence between radius and circumference! – it is immaterial which of these elements are 'given' and which 'unknown'. Their law-based and simultaneous correspondence always allows one to deduce the unknown from the known, their magnitude being enough for the necessary equations to be completed. For the same reason, it is quite permissible to use the methodological device: 'Let us for a moment assume as given the (unknown) magnitudes a, α, etc.' Things are quite different, however, when it comes to *processes of development* such as the formation of prices, where certain 'magnitudes' or elements which become existent at a later stage (prices, exchange ratios) are causally produced by other magnitudes existing at an earlier stage (wants, quantities of goods).[121] With the assumption of reciprocal correspondence, this would mean that the later would have to determine the earlier, as well as vice versa; the psychological motives for a concrete action (an action already performed, not just thought about) would have to be determined by the deed as their effective cause, just as much as the deed by the psychological motives! But in fact it is *one* problem to plot the simultaneous relations of correspondence between elements, and *another* problem genetically to derive the final result of a process. Mathematics has no problems of that kind. But psychology, physiology, biology and also economics certainly do. It may be that, despite previous appeals mainly to Kant and Max Weber, one wants to recognize as belonging to, or 'distinctive of', a particular science only those problems which were treated as such throughout its historical development[122] – according to the truly bureaucratic principle *Quod non est in actis, non est in mundo*. Even then, however, it is impossible to shut one's eyes to the fact that, since there has been such a thing as economic science, the cognitive interest of economists has always been directed, at least in part, to the formative processes of the relationships between economic facts, and not simply to the description of simultaneous correspondences between those whose formation is already complete.

It is hardly necessary to stress that the previously mentioned 'law of marginal utility level' has an essential influence in the development of Walras's attempted solution. For both parties to the exchange, equilibrium is established at the point where 'the individual consumption areas...as a result of the last-delivered and last-acquired quantity of goods must be equal' – to which Walras expressly adds: 'regardless of whether they are infinitely small or not'. And he infers from this that 'market or equilibrium prices are equal to the quotients of *raretés*'.[123] But, even if the law of marginal utility level had some reality, the individual equilibrium corresponding to it – that is, maximum satisfaction of individuals after the exchange – would have to be established at a quite different level for one and the same subject, according to the already formed exchange ratio; and for that very reason the price to be derived in exchange between two persons would be indeterminate. Walras, again just like Jevons, seeks to avoid this conclusion by taking a definite price as *already given* in the derivation of price formation.

Like Jevons, Walras takes the solution to the simple case of exchange between two persons as the methodological basis for solutions of greater complexity. But he jumps over the linking case of exchange of three commodities *among three persons*, which is so important in explaining the process of price formation, and moves straight on to consider the price formation of several commodities in conditions of *free competition*.[124]

The assumption is of n commodities, A, B, C, D....., on a freely competitive market; each party to the exchange only holds one kind of commodity and wishes to keep 'a certain amount' of it for himself and 'to off load a certain amount of it in exchange for others kinds of goods'. Then the demand – e.g., of the holder of A for each of the other commodities, B, C, D..... – will 'depend not only on the price of that commodity but on the price of all others. No doubt we are compelled to recognize that the determination of demand for B in terms of A cannot proceed without knowledge of the prices of C, D....., in terms of A; but one is also forced to admit that, if the prices of B, C, D..... in terms of A are all known, this itself makes it possible to determine the demand for B in terms of A. Thus *every individual demand* for B, C, D.....in terms of A is *a function of several variables*: namely, the prices of B, C, D..... in terms of A.' So we have the following equation:

$$d_{b,a} = f_{b,a} \, (p_{b,a} \, p_{c,a} \, p_{d,a} \cdots \cdots),$$

where $d_{b,a}$ denotes the demand for B in terms of A, and $p_{b,a}$, $p_{c,a}$ etc, the prices of B, C etc. in terms of A. Thus, the quantity of B effectively demanded by the holder of A is determined *if prices are given for all other commodities in terms of A*. But because of the number of variables in the exchange of several commodities, individual demands can no longer be expressed by means of curves: 'we must necessarily pass from geometrical to algebraic modes of expression'.

After this general presentation of the problem, Walras proceeds to the strictly theoretical derivation: '*We have to show: 1. how market or equilibrium prices derive from the demand equations, and 2. how the demand equations themselves derive from the utility and quantity of the commodities.*' The second problem is tackled first. 'Given n commodities A, B, C, D,...... and the *utility* of each of these commodities for each of the parties to the exchange, and given the *stocks* which each holds of each of the commodities, the demand equations are to be found. If the stocks of commodities A, B, C, D,..... held by the individual parties are called q_a,

q_b, q_c, q_d..... and the *raretés* (marginal utilities) of the various commodities for each individual are expressed as a function of the quantity of each of those commodities, then for each holder of A the equations are:

$$r_a = \phi_a(q_a), \quad r_b = \phi_b(q_b).....,$$

so that '*these data are sufficient to establish the demand equation for B in terms of A for any holder of A*'.[125] This man gives a certain amount of A for a certain amount $d_{b,a}$ of B at a certain price $p_{b,a}$ of B in terms of A; a certain amount of A for a certain amount $d_{c,a}$ of C at a certain price $p_{c,a}$ of C in terms of A, and so on. Let x be the total quantity of A which he thus gives for B, C etc., and thus q_a-x the quantity which he keeps for himself. Then the following equation results:

$$x = d_{b,a}.p_{b,a} + d_{c,a}.p_{c,a} + ...$$

and from that another one:

$$q_a - x = q_a - d_{b,a}.p_{b,a} - d_{c,a}.p_{c,a} - .....$$

Thus for several commodities as well as for two, we can state that demand is determined by the condition of maximum satisfaction.....and that this condition implies 'that the ratio of *rareté* or urgency of the last-satisfied wants after the exchange is *equal to the price*'. Were this not so, then further exchanges would take place. If the marginal utility (*rareté*) of A after the exchange is $r_a = \phi_a (q_a-x)$; of B, $r_b = \phi_b (d_{b,a})$; and of C, $r_c = \phi_c (d_{c,a})$, then we have the equations:

$$\phi_b(d_{b,a}) = p_{b,a}.\phi_a(q_a-x) = p_{b,a}.\phi_a(q_a - d_{b,a}.p_{b,a} - d_{c,a}.p_{c,a} - d_{d,a}.p_{d,a} - ....)$$

and similarly for $\phi_c (d_{c,a})$ etc., that is, $(n-1)$ equations.[126] And Walras concludes the derivation: '*In this way the individual demand equation of any one commodity is determined as a function of the prices of all*.'[127]

It was necessary to reproduce Walras's derivation in full: first, because it would have been pointless, or even impossible, critically to examine the exact treatment of a complex problem, without presenting the whole derivation; and second, because it should be made possible for the reader to measure the 'progress' of later mathematical systems of price theory against Walras's system. In the few pages of this chapter of the *Mathematische Theorie* is concentrated Walras's masterly achievement,[128] which justifies his fame as *l'inventeur de l'equilibre économique*. There is hardly another achievement in the whole history of economic theory which even approaches it in scale and unity of conception or in the logical rigour of its seemingly effortless combination of economic factors. What Cournot abandoned as an unrealizable task, what for Jevons still lay in the far distance, here appears accomplished. And yet, our wonder at this artistic and logical mastery should not prevent us from soberly examining the value of this closed system for our understanding of economic reality. For, as is well known, the most perfect unity of a system does not in itself prove anything about its explanatory value in relation to the real world.

First, let us look at the factual assumptions. Here the 'law of marginal utility level', which is supposed to comprehend the condition of maximum satisfaction, plays its fatal role in the establishment of the system of equations. Regrettably it must be said that since reality does not do conceptual systems the favour of adapting itself to them, but rather the conceptual systems are obliged to adapt to the real world, the explanatory value of the system of equations is thereby very reduced. One cannot content oneself with the fact that the reality or unreality of the 'law of marginal utility level' only affects concrete quantitative relations among the economic factors, and does not invalidate the nature of their correlations in the system of equations, so long as the essence and purpose of the system in question is to plot the *quantitative connections* among the various factors (price levels, marginal utility, quantities of goods, etc.). In equilibrium systems, the law of marginal utility level passes as a *structural law*.

Now, even if we leave aside its use of the unsustainable law of marginal utility level, this elaborate system of equations gives us no answer to the fundamental question of price theory which Walras himself set out to answer: *whether and how a univocal determination of the prices of various goods results from the wants and holdings of individuals as the final elements*, without anything else – and certainly not prices – being given as well. Nor is there any solution to a question which needs to be asked even before that: how is individual property (or income) divided between demand for the acquisition of certain goods – demand which only then forms the prices of those goods – again, of course, without the prior existence of such prices? For in formulating his equations, Walras *presupposed* a solution of precisely this question. It is already assumed that the holder of A 'gives...a certain amount' of it at a 'certain price' to acquire 'a certain amount of B', and similarly 'a certain amount' of A at a 'certain price' to acquire a 'certain amount' of C, D, etc., while keeping back 'a certain amount' for himself. Walras then rightly takes these 'certain' quantities to be unknowns *for the theorist*; their prevailing values will first emerge out of the equations that have to be established. Yet *the parties to the exchange*, whose dispositions are supposed to be described in the equations, take them to be already *known*; for it is on that assumption that the holder of A etc. actually gives a certain amount of his commodity for a certain amount of B, C, D, etc. But how is the holder of A to know the part-quantities that he must exchange for certain part-quantities of B, C,

D, etc. in order to achieve maximum satisfaction? The 'law of the equalization of marginal utility' is not enough, because the equality can ensue at very different levels according to the prevailing prices. For current prices to be derived on Walras's assumptions, there must already be prices formed in the past, which themselves can only be derived in the same way by recourse to prices from the past, in a kind of historical *regressus in infinitum*! If one tries to avoid this by appealing to *static* assumptions, including the complete identity of previous and current prices, one derives the intended prices from the very same prices (instead of from their *formative elements* in a still priceless condition) and the circularity of the argument – for the *problem of price formation* that Walras wishes to solve – becomes quite evident. Let us put this another way. It is easy to see that individuals' *potential* demand (stemming from their wants) for the various commodities is reduced to *effective* demand once prices exist for those goods. And the degree of this reduction – in other words, the correspondence ratio (which Walras's system of equations seeks to represent) between effective individual (and implicit aggregate) demand for certain goods, prevailing prices and marginal utilities – is both *logically and genetically a secondary problem*. For, as Walras's assumption of already existing prices clearly shows, the problem only arises when prices already exist and the *primary problem of price formation* is behind us. Price theory will never find peace until *this* problem is laid to rest: it raises its head whenever any slightly deep investigation is made into particular theoretical problems; it is in the background of the whole muddled dispute over 'statics' and 'dynamics'; it lies behind the whole question of our cognitive grasp of movements in the economy, which modern theory finds so disturbing. And the system of simultaneous correspondences, such as Walras presented it with his elaborate set of equations, can offer no solution to this primary problem of discovering the law of a process.

Nor can the further demonstrations which Walras develops on this foundation. They start by quite mechanically establishing aggregate demand equations 'by simple addition of individual demand equations' $n(n-1)$. And then, from the proposition that at equilibrium price the aggregate demand equals aggregate supply, and from the further proposition that the supply of one commodity in relation to another always equals the demand for the latter multiplied by its price in terms of the former, a series of *exchange equations*, again $n(n-1)$, are obtained. We thus have a total of $2n(n-1)$ equations – which precisely corresponds to the number of unknown, $n(n-1)$ mutual prices of the n commodities, plus the $n(n-1)$ total quantity of those n mutually exchanged commodities. Finally, Walras turns to a consideration of *general equilibrium*.[129] So far, only 'a certain incomplete equilibrium of any two commodities on the market has been derived'; 'complete or general market equilibrium exists only when the reciprocal prices of any two commodities equal the price ratio of each of the two in terms of any third commodity'. By way of proof, it is assumed that the market falls into as many partial markets 'as there are exchanges made of the two kinds of commodities': thus,

$$\frac{n(n-1)}{2}$$

partial markets. On each of these partial markets the exchange prices, 'established mathematically through the above system of equations', are recorded and made visible: thus, 'exchange of A for B and B for A at the reciprocal prices $p_{a,b}$, $p_{b,a}$; exchange of A for C and C for A at the reciprocal prices $p_{a,c}$, $p_{c,a}$', etc. According to these *given* prices, 'each party to the exchange formulates his demand for each of the commodities in terms of those which he holds'. Then, for example, in accordance with the condition of 'maximum utility' (law of marginal utility level), the following two equations will apply to 'the holder of A who has kept q_{a-x} of A for himself and acquired $d_{b,a}$ of B and $d_{c,a}$ of C':

$$\phi_b(d_{b,a}) = p_{b,a}\phi_a(q_{a-x})$$
$$\phi_c(d_{c,a}) = p_{c,a}\phi_a(q_{a-x})$$

and therefore:

$$\phi_c(d_{c,a}) = \frac{p_{c,a}}{p_{b,a}} \phi_b(d_{b,a})$$

If now, e.g.,

$$p_{c,b} > \frac{p_{c,a}}{p_{b,a}},$$

then:

$$\phi_c(d_{c,a}) < p_{c,b}\phi_b(d_{b,a})$$

'This means that it is advantageous for our man, after his first two exchanges on markets (A, B) and (A, C), to betake himself to market (B, C), and there to sell C and buy B at price $p_{c,a}$ of C in terms of B.' 'This procedure will disturb the market equilibrium (B, C), for there the supply of C will be greater than the demand; and it will be possible to restore this disturbed equilibrium only through a lowering of $p_{c,b}$.' Each holder of B and each holder of C will proceed in a similar way. Only through these later 'complementary exchanges' will the market equilibrium be 'perfect and general'.

107

In this account of the formation of general equilibrium, it is striking that Walras quite rightly tries to grasp the *process character* of the emergence of equilibrium as a sequence of different *phases*, of which the later are built upon the earlier, as a formation of the final general equilibrium out of previous partial, mutually contradictory equilibria (if one gets 1B for 4A and 1C for 1A on the market, the exchange ratio 2C for 1B cannot be in force at the same time – it must be 4C for 1B). Here unfortunately – again as in Jevons – the investigation concerns only the last phase of the whole process which leads to the establishment of general equilibrium,[130] only the generation of market price uniformity on the basis of *already existing prices* (in the light of which the parties to the exchange could already formulate their maximum utility for further operations on the market). What is left unanalysed is the preceding phase in which the already existing prices have developed out of the primary formative elements, and it is upon those that everything later is built. For the emergence of those given prices out of the preceding phase, we are referred instead to the 'mathematical development through the above system of equations', and thus to the earlier derivation of partial equilibrium prices which we have already subjected to critical examination. Furthermore the (correct) assumption of several phases of price formation developing into and out of one another, which is contained in the postulated necessity of later complementary exchanges, is incompatible with a system of simultaneous equations to which Walras is committed. For a system whose structure only permits simultaneous correspondence ratios is unsuitable for the inclusion of genetic processes. Hence Walras – with the expression: 'assuming that no complementary exchanges take place and that the equilibrium of any two commodities on the market is general' – finds himself impelled to introduce a fresh set of conditional equations, the content of which is 'that the reciprocal price of any two commodities equals the price ratio of the one and the other in terms of any third'. And now it is left up to the automatism of the mathematical apparatus of these extensive equations to ensure by itself that certain prices finally arise in equilibrium. Walras thinks that with his system of equations he has given the 'law of equilibrium price formation';[131] he thinks he has proven 'that for several as well as for two commodities, the necessary and sufficient conditions of market or equilibrium price formation are the utility of the commodities for the exchangers and stocks of these commodities in the hands of the holders'.[132] Finally, Walras asserts once more that he has shown 'the *utility and stocks of commodities*' to be 'the *causes of price formation*'. But, with all due admiration for Walras's mastery in *exactly* grasping the structural laws of an already achieved state of equilibrium, our critical examination must come to the conclusion that he leaves the problem of *price formation* unresolved.

Pareto's Theory of Price

The system of Vilfredo Pareto, as it is developed in the *Manuale di economia politica*,[133] represents the pure type of functional price theory. Although Pareto's system is unimaginable without the pioneering work of Walras, he has no intention of restricting himself to consolidation and further elaboration on Walras's foundations; while keeping the load-bearing constructions in the timberwork – Walras's equations expressing certain basic ratios – he does not think that they are sufficiently well laid and will try to replace certain weak points of support with more secure ones. There are two major alterations of this kind, in which Pareto sees posed his reform of Walras's system. First, the *causal* understanding of the way in which elements combine in the economic system is rigorously and without exception replaced with a schema of *reciprocal conditional dependence*; and second, he abandons what seems to him the completely unreal and therefore illegitimate assumption that the urgency and importance of wants can be measured, and replaces it with a system of hierarchies, achieved purely by experimental means and equipped with definite indices – a system of *indifference lines* or *indifference graphs* which, without requiring any quantitative measure, allow correlations to be derived and presented within a system of equations.

Naturally, we can look here only at those parts of Pareto's complex and monumental structure which concern our problem of price formation, and we shall mention the connection with other parts only insofar as it is required for an understanding of the place which the price problem occupies in Pareto's economic system as a whole.

In Pareto's view economic theory has the task of 'investigating the uniformities of phenomena...; these are called *laws*'.[134] 'A law or a uniformity is true only under certain conditions... Some of these conditions are implicit, others explicit... The circumstances surrounding a phenomenon are an integral part of the phenomenon and cannot be separated from it... We only know ideal phenomena, which more or less approximate the concrete phenomena.' Hence 'the method of successive approximations' must also come in, which corresponds to the 'method of decreasing abstraction' among Austrian theorists.[135] Theoretical economics has to account for 'the many logical, repeated actions which men perform to procure the things which satisfy their tastes'. 'In other words, we are concerned only with certain relations between objective facts and subjective facts, principally the tastes of men.'[136] 'The problem is very complex, because the objective facts are very numerous and partly depend upon each other. This mutual dependence makes ordinary logic soon become

109

impotent when we go beyond the first elements of our study. We must then resort to a special logic appropriate to this type of study, that is, to mathematical logic.'[137] After these preliminary methodological remarks, Pareto moves straight on to the 'principal subject' of static theory, 'economic equilibrium', which 'results from the opposition between men's tastes and the obstacles to satisfying them'.[138] The investigation therefore has to extend over tastes, obstacles and the way in which these two elements combine in the establishment of equilibrium. Economic *equilibrium*, which is taken as the basic situation in all mathematical theories, is here defined as '*the state which would maintain itself indefinitely if there were no changes in the conditions under which it is observed*'. Or, an 'equivalent definition': '*equilibrium...is determined in such a way that, if it is but slightly modified, it immediately tends to reestablish itself, to return to its original position.*'[139] 'To determine equilibrium we will set up the condition that at the moment when it occurs, movements permitted by the obstacles are prevented by the tastes...'[140]

In the subsequent investigation of 'tastes', Pareto first presents the concept of 'ophelimity' (utility), already introduced in the *Cours*, as the pleasure afforded by a definite increase in the quantity of a good. He then further distinguishes between 'elementary ophelimity' which corresponds to the concept of marginal utility,[141] and 'weighted elementary ophelimity', that is, the quotient from the division of the elementary ophelimity by the price. However, Pareto immediately puts them to one side as unusable concepts – this is to be one of the main planks of reform – on the grounds that because the ophelimity of a good A depends not only on the quantity consumed of *that* good but also on the quantities consumed of the other goods B, C,...., the lack of a unit of measure means that a good's ophelimity is unmeasurable.[142] If one were actually to employ the concepts of ophelimity, utility and value in use, Pareto argues, one would do better to speak more simply of a *system of indices of ophelimity*. These concepts do facilitate the exposition of the theory of economic equilibrium, but they are not necessary for it. 'Thanks to the use of mathematics', one can construct 'this whole theory...on no more than a fact of experience, that is, on the determination of the quantities of goods which constitute combinations between which the individual is *indifferent*. The theory of economic science thus acquires the rigor of rational mechanics.' Pareto now demonstrates this by deriving the *indifference lines* of tastes which are so fundamental for his new system.[143] If we take, for example, a person who possesses one kilogram of bread and one kilogram of wine, this combination might be equal in respect of his tastes to:

Bread	1.6	1.4	1.2	1.0	0.8	0.6
Wine	0.7	0.8	0.9	1.0	1.4	1.8

And one could find a still greater number of such combinations. 'We call this series, which could be extended indefinitely, an *indifference series*', because the individual's 'choice is indifferent' among all these combinations. If we draw the quantities of the two goods on the two axes of a system of coordinates, corresponding to the indifferent combinations contained in the above series, we obtain a continuous curve, the 'indifference line', which is composed of points of the same ophelimity. Let us then give each combination of goods an arbitrary index, which has only to satisfy two conditions: (i) that two combinations between which the choice is indifferent must have the same index; and (ii) that of two combinations, the one which is preferred to the other must have a larger index. With this we have also the *indices of ophelimity*.[144] If this process is continued still further, the whole plane of the system of coordinates will be covered with an unlimited number of indifference curves (for all commodities and in an unlimited number of combinations), each of which has its own index. We will thus have a complete reproduction of the individual's tastes with regard to these two commodities. 'That is enough to determine economic equilibrium. *The individual can disappear, provided he leaves us this photograph of his tastes.*' The same can be done for all commodities. These indifference curves may be understood as contour lines, whose heights are represented by the indices of ophelimity. Pareto speaks here of 'the hill of the indices of pleasure'. The unlimited possible ascents of indifference curves, shorter at such great heights (great ophelimity), are what Pareto calls *paths* (*sentiers*). He considers these indifference lines of tastes and paths to be the main techniques of representation available to economic theory. The indifference lines of *obstacles* are constructed in a similar way – the obstacles, that is, which oppose the individual's striving for satisfaction: not just necessary production outlays or costs, but also the fact that a good is scarce and that a price has to be paid to acquire it, and all 'the obstacles which arise from social organization'.[145] An especially important obstacle is present when individuals cannot freely choose the exchange ratio of their goods; for of all the numerous possible paths, the one which the individual must follow is determined in the given exchange ratio.[146]

The next task is to find the common point of equilibrium of both the tastes and the obstacles, which constitutes a point of *general equilibrium*.[147] In the discussion of 'equilibrium with respect to tastes', it is now shown in a complicated way – non-mathematical theories are here simpler and equally rigorous – that with *given* production coefficients for the conversion of good B into good A, or with a *given* exchange ratio (price) of A and B (which in Pareto's language is called a given *path*), the quantity of B which the individual will convert into A or exchange for A is determined at that point in the successive transformations or partial ex-

111

changes where the combination of A and B affording the greatest total utility is reached: that is, in Pareto's language, equilibrium with respect to tastes is reached at the point where the stipulated path touches an indifference curve of tastes. If other paths are fixed (if other production coefficients or exchange ratios are given), there will be different points of equilibrium. And if we link up all these points of equilibrium arising in various given paths, we get the *'line of exchanges'*. By adding together the quantities of goods which are 'transformed' for each individual in the given exchange ratios – that is, which are given up and acquired through the exchange – we obtain the 'line of exchanges for the collectivity' (the effective aggregate supply and effective aggregate demand in each exchange ratio). 'Equilibrium with respect to obstacles for the producer' is developed in the same way, with the *'hill of profit'* taking the place of the *'hill of pleasure'*.

In a highly convoluted argument, which cannot be reproduced within the limits of this essay, Pareto now shows that with *given* indifference lines of tastes and obstacles and with *given* paths or lines for the parties to the exchange, definite points of equilibrium must arise.[148] He makes the following assertions: 'If two individuals exchange goods between themselves, the points of equilibrium are at the intersections of the lines of exchange of the two individuals' (to which it should immediately be added that this discovery – that where two-sided exchange ratios correspond to each other, a state of rest will ensue – is not unknown to non-mathematicians; but that it explains nothing if the lines of exchange are taken as given from the outset). Or, more generally: 'If there is a point where a path travelled by the contracting individuals is tangent to the indifference curves of these individuals, it is a point of equilibrium.' And the most general formulation: 'Equilibrium takes place at the points of intersection of the line of equilibrium of tastes and the line of equilibrium of obstacles. These lines are the loci of the points of tangency of the paths to the indifference lines.'[149]

On these foundations Pareto proceeds to the derivation of *prices*.[150] In economic theory, 'prices appear as auxiliary unknowns, very useful for solving economic problems, but which must in the end be eliminated so that only the tastes and the obstacles remain.'[151]

Next, Pareto defines the *supply* and *demand* of an individual as the goods which are *given up* or *acquired* by that individual when he has arrived at the equilibrium point of the exchange, the quantities of course varying with price (and with the shape of the paths on which the equilibrium price has been attained).[152] Accordingly, supply and demand are given *ex post*, after the exchange has ended (exchange equilibrium is reached) and the price has been formed. We therefore have no explanation here of the *formation* of prices. In the exchange of two goods between two individuals at a *given* price, the exchange curve is at the same time the curve of supply and demand. An individual's demand curve for B is also his supply curve for A (as Jevons and Walras already pointed out). In the system of indifference lines, then, if one draws the quantities of A on the abscissa and the quantities of B on the ordinate, the price of A in terms of B is expressed by the slope of the individual's path towards the ordinate axis. The equilibrium price lies where the first individual's demand curve intersects with the second's supply curve; or, more generally, where the demand for a commodity is equal to its supply. This is supposed to show that the *'law of supply and demand' can be derived from the system of indifference lines* through which that law first acquires its exact meaning. In the case of exchange of *two* commodities, then, the demand for a commodity depends only on its price, as does the supply. In the case of exchange of *several* commodities, the supply and demand for a particular commodity are dependent upon the price of *all* other commodities (as Walras already knew).

After these lengthy and complex preparations, a section entitled 'Equilibrium in the General Case'[153] argues that in a freely competitive market, so long as each individual keeps up successive exchanges (at a given *constant* price) between his own commodities and the objects of his demand up to the point of equilibrium, the *ophelimity* (or *index of ophelimity*) *will be precisely the same for the last small quantities of goods which are given up and which are acquired*: the *law of marginal utility level*, long awaited by the reader, is now solemnly enthroned.[154] 'For this reasoning to be rigorous', Pareto interjects, 'the quantities must be infinitesimal', but infinitesimal or not, *'d'une façon ou l'autre* we have a notion of the phenomenon.'[155] 'For very small quantities it can be assumed that the ophelimity is proportional to the quantities. In that case the ophelimity of 5 grams of wine will be in the neighbourhood of half the ophelimity of 10 grams of wine – it would be precisely one-half if we were considering infinitesimal quantities.' (Note that Pareto here falls into the error of suggesting the measurability of ophelimity which he has so often denounced, and for the avoidance of which his whole system of indifference lines has been constructed.) If, for example, bread and wine are exchanged in the constant ratio of 2:1, then 'for equilibrium the ophelimity of a very small quantity of bread must be equal to half the ophelimity of the same very small quantity of wine'. In other words: 'The weighted elementary ophelimity of the bread and of the wine must be equal.' This is true for all individuals and all commodities on a freely competitive market, 'provided that we assume that the satisfaction yielded by the consumption of each good is independent of the consumption of the others'[156] – an

113

assumption which Pareto regards as entirely permissible so long as we are dealing with only small changes in quantity.[157] For at the point of equilibrium the weighted ophelimities of all commodities are the same.

We can already see what is going to follow. Just as in Walras, three *groups of conditional equations* are introduced: category (A), which denotes conditions referring to tastes and obstacles, is established from the *law of marginal utility level*. Category (B) are the budgetary equations which state that for each individual the receipts and outgoings must balance in the exchange agreed for any of the commodities (we have already seen the tautological character of this 'condition' in discussing Walras's theory). The number of these category-B conditional equations is the same as the number of individuals.

Thus, to take Pareto's examples, if there are 100 individuals and 700 goods, category (A) will give us, for each individual, 699 equations (one less than 700 because one commodity must serve as measure of price), and therefore 69,900 equations for 100 individuals. Category (B) will give us 100 other equations, so that we have altogether 70,000 equations. 'In general, this total is equal to the number of individuals multiplied by the number of goods.' The number of unknowns is composed, first, of the 699 prices of the commodities (one less than 700 because one commodity has the function of money); then of the quantities of each commodity acquired (or given up) by each individual, that is, 70,000 quantities; which gives a total of 70,699 unknowns for 70,000 equations. To preserve the missing 699 equations, Pareto constructs the category-C condition (referring to the obstacles), which states that the total quantities of the commodities remain constant before and after the exchange, since what some individuals give up is acquired by other individuals (one equation less than 700 because, if we know the quantities for the other commodities, the category-B equations directly give us the total quantity of a commodity that is bought or sold). In other words, the sum of the commodities bought and sold by all individuals is equal to zero. 'The number of the conditions is now equal to that of the unknowns, and the problem is completely determined.'[158]

The system of algebraic equations corresponding to categories A, B, C, together with their solutions, is given in Pareto's 'Appendix'. There is all the less reason to examine them closely as the presentation and critical analysis of mathematical price theories is not intended to check mechanical *calculations*, but rather to assess the ideas which determine the equations and the cognitive value of the results.

A natural objection, and one anticipated by Pareto, is that the elaboration of such an equation-system absurdly presupposes an impossible knowledge of the ophelimities of all commodities for all individuals, and of an exceedingly large number of other circumstances of production, etc.;

and that, even if one knew all these data for 100 individuals and 700 commodities, 70,699 equations would already be necessary, and in a population of millions with thousands of commodities, the total would grow to fantastic proportions and exceed the human power to solve them. To this, Pareto replies that it is not a question of offering practical, numerical solutions; but such equations 'are the only means as yet known for arriving at a notion of the way in which these quantities and prices vary, or, more exactly, for understanding in a general way how equilibrium takes place'.[159]

With the 'ordinary logic' used exclusively by 'literary economics' – a logic which works with 'nonsensical talk' and always takes just *one* magnitude as known and leaves the rest unknown – it is impossible to reach a solution of the equilibrium problem. There follows a fierce critique of non-mathematical theories which is often unfair, in the sense of failing to do justice to their different (causal-genetic) approach; it accuses them of operating with 'metaphysical entities' that exist only in the imagination, whereas in the real world there is nothing but 'mutual dependence'.[160] And then Pareto concludes: 'It is the mutual dependence of phenomena which makes the use of mathematics indispensable for studying these phenomena; ordinary logic can serve well enough for studying the relations of cause and effect, but soon becomes impotent when it is a matter of relations of mutual dependence. The latter, in rational mechanics and in pure economics, necessitate the use of mathematics. The principal utility which is derived from the theories of pure economics is that it gives us a synthetic notion of economic equilibrium, and for the moment we have no other way to reach that goal.'[161]

Critical Analysis of the Foundations of Pareto's Price Theory

Is Pareto's optimistic assessment of the cognitive value of his system really justified? Its careful critical verification is all the more a scientific duty in that it is shared in full, or almost in full, by the overwhelming majority of mathematical economists. Many see in Pareto's system the highest point which abstract economic theory in general, or at least static theory, can ever reach.

Let us begin by considering the basic construction of *indifference lines* upon which everything else rests, and with whose help the typical relations or 'laws' of economic reality are derived.[162] If these indifference lines are to be useful, they must be obtained from assumptions which are in turn taken from the real world. On closer examination, however, the exact opposite is the case. We must first examine the way in which the indifference curves

115

are obtained; and this is not, as it might perhaps appear, a merely technical question in a system whose superiority over others in this field rests – we are continually assured – precisely upon the fact that all its findings have been secured by *experimental* means. It is this empirical base which is supposed to allow the use of exact mathematical procedures, with the same rigour that distinguishes the derivations of theoretical mechanics which are also grounded upon experimentally secured presuppositions.

How is the indifference of certain combinations, out of the infinite number of possible ones, to be established? Simply through external observation of visible process? That is naturally out of the question, because one cannot read off the various combinations whether or not they are mutually indifferent for an economic subject. It is therefore necessary to include in the experiment the statements of the economic subject who forms these combinations, and that can obviously be done only through 'questionnaires'. The first step, then, is to ask the subject – as Pareto does – which quantitatively changing combinations of two goods (e.g., bread and wine) are 'indifferent' to him and thus equally important; the answers, according to Pareto, will constitute a very large series: indeed, this could be extended *ad infinitum*.[163] But that would be only one small part of the experiment. It would then have to be continued for three commodities, with a still greater number of combinations (the first series was already infinite), and then once again until the infinite number of indifferent combinations is established for all the hundreds or thousands of goods on the market (this is necessary to obtain the necessary amount of equations for the price derivation). Thus, the infinite series of the indifferent combinations of bread and wine; the infinite series of combinations of bread and meat; the infinite series of combinations of wine and meat; the infinite series of combinations of bread, wine and meat, and so on. Then one obtains indifference lines for the indifferent combinations of any two goods, three-dimensional indifference shapes for three goods; and indifference shapes that cannot be imagined for n goods, because they can be expressed only in algebraic equations yet have to be thought of in n-dimensional space: 'varieties in hyperspace'[164] or, as Furlan puts it, n-dimensional manifolds.[165]

Let us now pass over the fact that for the literally infinite number of surveys required for the completion of this experiment, the time and powers of an entire generation of humans would not be sufficient – which is not uninteresting for an experiment which is supposed to be analogous to those in physics.[166] What we cannot treat lightly, however, is the objective (i.e., located in the experimental object) *impossibility* of its being completed, which in our case is psychological in nature. For the respondents are expected to come up with an infinite number of experiences concerning the indifference of an infinite number of combinations of goods, of which only a few are actually familiar to them; and they are further expected to reproduce in their answers, with mathematical precision, this infinite number of (unavailable) experiences. Both are evidently pure make-believe: it is *pretended* that the individual gives the answers which the theorist needs. It is not a genuine experiment but the *illusion* of one, whose purpose is to provide the theorist with the *results* that he has postulated *a priori*. For this kind of experiment there is no analogy in the natural sciences, where the goal of experimentation is to obtain a previously quite unknown result, or to confirm or refute a hypothetical outcome. *Make-believe* changes the meaning and purpose of an experiment into its opposite; with such an 'experiment' one can naturally 'derive' whatever one wishes, any 'law' contradicting reality to any degree. And will such a make-believe experiment really prevent what it is supposed to exclude: namely, starting from ratios between psychological facts (urgency of wants) given by 'inner experience'? To assume that would be a grave self-deception. For what is supposed to be the ultimate basis of the individual's answers concerning the indifference of certain combinations? Either it is the economic subject's own inner experience of what those combinations mean in terms of subjective wellbeing; or else the research theorist – i.e., the experimenter – puts into the respondent's mouth *his* personal inner experience concerning what the different combinations mean in terms of relative wellbeing, so that it can be repeated in 'questionnaires' as a poet has his own thoughts expressed by his figures. This is not experimentation but stagecraft and make-up. The attempt to pass round inner experience of psychological facts must be regarded as a complete failure.

Far more serious than self-deception about the empirical basis of indifference shapes, however, is the unreality or indeed impossibility of the *content* conveyed in the indifference ratios. Here the main emphasis should no longer be placed upon the assumption that the various goods forming the individual combinations can be varied in *infinitesimal quantities* – a fiction which flies in the face of reality and which, as it is essential to the *continuity* of the indifference lines and paths, is not at all as harmless as mathematical economists are at pains to represent. The much-favoured appeal to the infinitesimal variability of magnitudes in theoretical physics completely breaks down here, as anyone recognizes at once in a seriously conducted comparison. Nor is it by any means the case that the numerical results of derivations resting upon this illusory basis precisely correspond to reality (that is, to actually formed prices). Mathematical economists freely allow as much but hold it to be of no importance, arguing that the apparatus of equation-systems is not intended to provide us with numerical solutions, but only to give the nature and form of the general correlations of elements through which equilibrium is established. Of course, this admits one decisive contrast with the derived equations of theoretical physics which are ever being cited in justification, because if they are to be useful these must precisely be applicable to concrete cases with numerically identifiable results. But quite apart from this, not only would prices derived from this fiction and those derived from the assumption corresponding to reality (*non-random* divisibility of goods) yield numerically different price ratios; but *the nature and form of the ratios* by which the prices of the various goods correlate with one another would also be different. If in reality very many goods can produce a satisfaction effect for individuals only in definite, finite dimensions, then the *kind of distribution of income among the demand* for these different goods (and among other, randomly divisible goods), and consequently the *form of demand correlation* emanating from each individual and the *kind of price correlation* among the various goods, will be different from the situation where all goods are infinitely divisible. Mathematical economists slide all too easily over this highly inconvenient fact, and precisely here Pareto's procedure is so typical when he tries to rebut an objection that can no longer be completely ignored.[167] It is true, he writes, that 'in reality...the variations in the quantities occur in a discontinuous fashion'. But that is a 'technical difficulty', because all problems concerning infinitesimally variable magnitudes are – for mathematical theory – much easier to solve than those in which there are only finitely variable elements. 'Hence, every time it is possible, we must replace the latter by the former; this is done in all the physico-natural sciences. We know that an error is thereby committed; but it can be neglected either when it is small absolutely, or when it is smaller than other inevitable errors.' This is precisely the case in political economy, 'for there we consider only average phenomena and those involving large numbers'. We concern ourselves with the individual, 'not in order actually to investigate what one individual consumes or produces, but only to consider one of the elements of a collectivity and then add up the consumption and the production of a large number of individuals.' Then follows the much-rehearsed example of a pocket-watch. 'When we say that an individual consumes one and one-tenth watches, it would be ridiculous to take these words literally... Rather these words simply signify that, for example, one hundred individuals consume 110 watches... When we say that equilibrium takes place when an individual consumes one and one-tenth watches, we simply mean that equilibrium takes place when 100 individuals consume – some one, others two or more watches and some even none at all – in such a way that all together they consume about 110, and the average is 1.1 for each.'

Did Pareto, in his efforts to rescue infinitesimal calculus for economic theory, really overlook the fact that operations with *statistical averages* nullify the approach of pure theory, which is to explain *economic phenomena by the effects and counter-effects of individuals* (wants, possessions, subjective valuations) *upon the formation of the social* (prices), and vice versa? Why indeed should one not start directly from the average marginal utility of a totality, from average indifference lines, average demand, average income etc., in order to derive from them the average price? The way to the 'normal price' of classical theory would then no longer be so far off! Could Pareto really have failed to notice that the resulting price of a total quantity of a good demanded by a sum of individuals must vary fundamentally according to the *distribution* of this total demand among the sum of individual demands, whether concentrated in one or a few or divided among all, and in the latter case according to whether it is divided equally or unequally among all? In the above example, where there is an 'average' demand for 1.1 watches, the one-tenth for each 100 individuals is ineffective for the formation of actual demand and prices. The tenth-of-a-watch demands would have an effect on price formation only if they increased for each individual to ten tenths, or one whole watch; otherwise, the demand fund (income components) allotted by individuals to the 0.1 watches would turn towards demand for *different* goods, and the prices would be quite different from those obtaining if – instead of each individual demanding 0.1 watches – some demanded 2 or 3 and others none at all. The *ex post average figures*, though significant for the statistician's purposes, are of absolutely no use for the derivations of economic *theory*. This device, which is intended to justify the assumption of infinitesimal *economic* divisibility of goods and hence the continuous character of the curves, is therefore not capable of being applied. Nor is it the only one. Another also requiring great astuteness is recommended by Schumpeter, for example. The idea here is to overcome discontinuities in the individual wants or demand curves on the basis that in such cases, where the real point is that a want or demand for a fraction of a commodity is impossible, people assume instead that the demand still refers to a unit of a good, only a unit of lesser quality. Thus, in the above example the one-tenth demand for a gold watch would be roughly equated (or could be so interpreted) to the demand for a whole steel watch, the two-tenths demand would be equivalent to the demand for a nickel watch, the three-tenths demand to the demand for a silver watch, and so on. In this way one would certainly have a *formally* continuous curve, but it would be of no use at all since it is patched together from the demands for *different* goods commanding *different* prices on the market.[168] There is little prospect, of course, of inducing mathematical economists to recognize that it is illegitimate to employ the infinitesimal calculus in general economic theory, for they

119

would have to give up the essential instrument for mathematical analysis of economic phenomena.

But let us turn now to the main weakness of indifference lines. Their construction rests upon the unrestrained generalization of a fact which in reality has only very limited application. Thus, the *boundless substitutability* of the various goods for the satisfaction of wants is presupposed as 'the first characteristic of indifference lines'. Without that premise not a single indifference line can be constructed. Here again, as always in the checking of basic assumptions against the facts, the visualization of concrete facts in the real world provides the most reliable control. Pareto assumes that the quantities of goods making up a combination of particular marginal utilities (a particular index of ophelimity) can be varied 'indefinitely', in such a way that a fall in the quantity of one good is replaced through a rise in the quantity of another, without any change in the total value of the combination, and with this applying to all commodities and all the numerous, qualitatively different combinations. If, for example, a combination of certain quantities of goods A, B, C, D, E, were to take shape, a change of any size in the quantity of A (m_a) would not alter the marginal utilities in the combination, provided only that m_b or m_c or m_d or m_e (singly or cumulatively) were correspondingly increased, and vice versa, in an unlimited number of variations.

But while it is possible for the goods to be substitutable *within very narrow limits*, this leads to the most absurd conclusions if it is elevated to a generally valid rule. Strictly speaking, a completely reciprocal substitutability of goods – if substitutability is taken to mean the possibility of mutual replacement for the achievement of a *particular* (i.e., qualitatively univocal) result – arises only in the category of those *productive goods* which, as auxiliary materials or powers ('working goods', in Wieser's teleological expression), do not themselves enter into and help to shape the product. The concept, then, already ceases to apply in the case of 'material goods', whose substance enters into the product and whose special qualities help to determine the special qualities of the product, insofar as the various qualities of the product are differentially valued by consumers – which is ultimately what matters. But here too, of course, the economic possibility of substitution has its limits in the naturally given fact of complementarity.[169] Only in the rarest of cases, however, are *consumption goods* endowed with economic substitutability. For the fact that economically they are not identical but *different* goods entails that they do not serve precisely the same, but rather qualitatively different, needs or the bringing about of qualitatively different gratifications – which, perhaps with very rare exceptions, leads to their differential evaluation (differential ophelimity). In terms of the subjective total utility effect (ophelimity), it is obviously of no little importance whether a menu 'replaces' one kind of fruit or one brand of cigarettes with another – or *a fortiori*, whether a smaller amount of bread is 'replaced' by a larger amount of wine in the daily consumption basket. But on Pareto's assumptions, this last example of his should be pushed so far ('indefinitely') that even a combination with a close-to-zero minimum of bread and a great deal of wine is equivalent for the individual to a combination with much bread and a minimum of wine. This is striking proof of the unreality of the 'empirical facts' expressed in Pareto's indifference lines – and that is one of the most favourable examples for him. The more goods a combination involves, and the more varied they are, the more grotesque become the implications of the whole fiction: less and less bread or meat, with more and more salt to go on it; every decrease in the consumed quantity of tea is offset by a transfer of the sugar to equivalent (indifferent) daily combinations; the fewer the furnishings, the more space there is for them; the less the heating material, the more the special occasions; a loss of clothing is made good by some extra cigarettes, and so on. More clearly than any abstract argument, these absurdities show the utterly unempirical character of the assumptions underlying the construction of indifference lines.

The ophelimity correlations, 'lines of exchange', demand curves and price ratios which are derived from such a 'photograph of wants' – actually a caricature of reality – are evidently incapable of describing, even approximately, relations in the real world.

We thus come to a paradoxical conclusion. Knowledge of the dependence of each good's ophelimity (utility) upon the consumption total not only of that good but also of others – in other words, knowledge of the thoroughgoing *complementarity* of goods with respect to the satisfaction of wants or 'gratifications' – induced Pareto to give up any attempt to establish quantitatively the ophelimities of *individual* goods and to operate instead with the ophelimities (or indices of ophelimity) for whole *complexes of goods* in the form of indifference shapes. And in the construction of these indifference shapes, what he left right out of the picture was precisely the fact of complementarity.

This state of affairs is all the more remarkable considering that Pareto is one of the writers who have most clearly recognized the absolute necessity of discovering the *structural laws* of the system of needs or tastes, if pure economic theory is to be established on exact foundations. The investigation of tastes occupies a great deal of space in his system,[170] and together with the work of Gossen, Wieser, I. Fisher, Edgeworth, M. Fanno and Čuhel it must be ranked among the most valuable and essential contributions to the subject.

In the belief that he can 'without major error' disregard the consumption

121

sequence of various goods, with its serious difficulties for theory,[171] Pareto argues that in general the ophelimity produced by the consumption of one good can be dependent in two ways upon other goods available to the individual. The *first type of dependence* (D₁) arises from the fact that 'the pleasure from one consumption is connected with the pleasure from other consumption' – what later writers have termed 'psychological complementarity'. The *second type of dependence* (D₂) relates to substitution and 'manifests itself in the fact that one thing may be *substituted* for another to produce sensations, if not identical, at least approximately equal'.[172] Within the first type (D₁) Pareto further distinguishes between two variants. First, there is the quite general dependence of the ophelimity of one consumption upon the individual's total situation with regard to the goods – a dependence which one may disregard if it involves not substantial but only trifling variations in the quantity of the goods, and if one only studies the phenomena in the proximity of a given equilibrium position. The second variant of dependence (D₁), to which Pareto refers under the heading 'complementary goods',[173] consists in the fact that 'certain things must be used jointly in order to yield us pleasure'. But here too, within this very narrow definition, Pareto comes to the conclusion that the ophelimity of a complementary good may be regarded as independent of quantity variations in other complementary goods,[174] for the following reason: 'The error may be negligible when there are only small variations in the quantities of the goods because in that case we can assume approximately that the consumption of the good under consideration takes place under certain average conditions with respect to the accessory goods.'[175] And with this Pareto bids farewell to that dependence of far-reaching complementarity which he correctly identified a short time ago. From now on, it will be treated only as a special case, and Pareto will concern himself almost exclusively with the second variant (dependence through substitution) for which he showed his preference at the outset because he needs it for the construction of his indifference lines. In accordance with his examples of the mutual substitutability of bread and potatoes in stilling hunger or beer and wine in quenching thirst, or of wool and cotton for clothing, or oil and paraffin for lighting, Pareto maintains that 'a certain equivalence can be established between the goods which correspond to a certain need'.[176] 'If,' he continues, 'the relation of equivalence refers strictly to the tastes of the individual', it is the same as that which underlies the indifference curves. But sometimes it refers not to tastes but to *needs*. In satisfying a need, one can substitute for each other goods of the same type but of very different quality, and according to changes in income one actually will replace, say, corn meal with bread, or imitation pearls with real ones. In the theoretical analysis of this fact, Pareto again thinks it most useful to operate with 'approximations' and, for a large number of human tastes and needs, 'to assume equivalent certain quantities of goods which are substitutable for each other...with regard to nourishment, for example,...between quantities of bread, potatoes, kidney beans, meat, etc. In this case, we would only need to take account of the total ophelimity of these equivalent quantities.' In this approximation too, we should not stray too far from a certain 'limited region'. And this special kind of substitution – through replacement goods – is thereby given the theoretical credentials for inclusion in the equivalent combinations of the indifference lines. The unlimited possibility of substituting different goods in such combinations thus becomes the autocratic principle, and *the fact of complementarity is completely shut out*. Indeed, in his efforts to establish substitution as the universal basis for the general applicability of indifference lines, Pareto goes so far as to constitute indifference lines even for the strongest case of complementarity, when two goods produce an effect of satisfaction only through their interaction in strictly defined proportions.[177] This is an impossible, self-contradictory enterprise, inconsistent with its own premises, because the rigidly defined proportion excludes compensation for a decrease in one good through an increase in another. All that remains in reality of the whole imaginary 'indifference line' is therefore one single *point*, which is precisely this proportion.

We are constantly assured by Pareto that the indifference lines are the core of his system from which the whole of pure economics can be derived. But although he sees in them the advance over his predecessors, we certainly cannot regard this as a correct view of the matter. We have already referred to the unbridgeable gulf between the content of the formal assumptions underlying the construction of the indifference lines and the premises of empirical reality. But there is a still more serious fallacy in his argument.

The more generally we conceive the overall goal or purpose to which the individual disposition of goods is directed, and the more it is reduced from a qualitative determination or composition to a purely quantitative one – in other words, the more purely formal and therefore abstract is the concept of 'maximum ophelimity' – all the more can various goods or combinations of goods be related to that overall goal as means to its fulfilment. If the starting-point is an inherently undifferentiated 'need aggregate' or 'pleasure aggregate', then all possible goods can be placed in relation to it and substituted one for the other. But that would obviously bring us no further knowledge of the factors determining the ophelimity of the various kinds of goods and the ophelimity correlations which are needed for the derivations of theoretical economics. Besides, our own inner experience, as well as the testimony of other economic subjects raised into knowledge, demonstrates that in reality people are guided not by a universal goal of 'maximum gratification' or 'greatest sum of pleasure', so abstract as to be unimaginable, but by a multiplicity of qualitatively different 'needs' or 'gratifications', for the achievement of which only goods of a certain type and quality are suitable. And it is in their acquisition and utilization that we find the range of everything that can be characterized as pertaining to economics.[178] To have based theoretical economics upon this knowledge is the fundamental novelty and advance which the 'moderns', since Gossen, Jevons and Carl Menger, have achieved in relation to the procedure of classical economics, which started from an 'economic principle' at once correct and barren in its lack of content: the greatest possible results with the least means.

Let us be clear about this. The starting-point for the derivation of every process in classical economics is that the final goal guiding economic subjects is to achieve the greatest possible sum of money or exchange-value, a quantitative entity whose homogeneity makes it very easy to grasp. Within this businessman's framework, the various kinds of goods can replace one another without restriction, provided that they represent nothing other than exchange-value. The starting-point of recent theory, on the other hand, which in principle is also adopted by Pareto, is that the final goal of human economic aspirations is to achieve, with the available resources, the greatest possible satisfaction of a psychologically or physiologically determined multiplicity of qualitatively different needs, symbolized not by a homogeneous magnitude (exchange-value, money) but by a system of qualities with different degrees of importance, which cannot as such be replaced by one another.[179]

For the construction of his indifference lines, Pareto makes an assumption which comes very close to the first of the two typical ones presented earlier on. The goal of what individuals do with their goods, he argues, is to satisfy intrinsically undifferentiated 'species of need' or 'generic needs' (this is the meaning of *besoins*, as opposed to *goûts* and *plaisirs*): the 'need for nourishment', for 'clothing', for 'thirst-quenching liquids', for 'lighting', and so on. A whole variety of actual goods are suitable for this generally defined purpose (potatoes, bread, meat, beans, etc.), and in this they may be substituted for one another. Next, Pareto quite improperly transfers that mutual substitutability of goods – which would follow from the *formal* assumption that the goal of economy is to satisfy whole species of need as such – to the fundamentally different circumstances of the real world: that is, to *the hierarchical multiplicity of numerous, qualitatively distinct, particular needs, where the satisfaction of one cannot be replaced with the satisfaction of another*. For these qualitatively different

124

satisfaction-effects are subject to individual interpretations of welfare, and the evaluation of the appropriate kinds of goods will vary not only with the specific quality of the need, but also with the order of the consumption sequence (psychological complementarity) through which they are assigned a place according to the degree of command over quantities of other kinds of goods. This whole question of sequence is ignored by Pareto, however, and everything is turned into its opposite by his postulate of the most far-reaching substitution. As his sensitive investigations show, no one is more aware than Pareto himself that among civilized humans the final goal of economy is the satisfaction not of a *species* of need as such, but of highly differentiated tastes and pleasures. Species of need come into it only in those exceptional situations where mere survival is at stake and people are reduced to the most primal necessities of life. At the front in wartime, for example, a shortage of food may mean that not only potatoes, rye, barley or maize but even ground tree-bark can 'substitute' for one another; or a shortage of smoking material, that cigarette tobacco is 'replaced' by hay. But those are not the subjective connections with goods which operate in the formation of market prices. In reality all the combinations which Pareto regards as equivalent by substitution have different ophelimities or indices of ophelimity, since even if they serve the same need they are adapted to very different tastes. The indifference lines have thus turned out to be imaginary shapes. If this is so – and I believe it cannot be challenged in scrupulous analysis – then Pareto's elaborate system appears as follows. Imaginary basic ratios (the indifference lines) are linked up through an unreal total relation (the law of marginal utility level) to a hypothetical and actually non-existent situation of equilibrium. It is therefore only natural that the prices and price correlations derived from this construct are not those of the real world.

Cassel's Theory of Price

Cassel's theory of price has the advantage of admirable simplicity over all the others we have considered. This is also the main reason why broad circles of German economists began to take an interest in the mathematical-functional approach to the price problem only after the appearance of Cassel's *Theory of Social Economy*.[180] After all, the postulated relational schema of general, univocal interdependence among all the elements of the economy offered a welcome legitimation for the abandonment of difficult investigations into intricate causal connections. At that time, the ideas of Jevons, Walras and Pareto were mostly known in Germany only from hearsay. As for 'Austrian' theory, long-lasting disgruntlement at the unnecessary bitterness of the 'methodological dispute' (G. Schmoller/C. Menger) meant either that it was rejected out of hand because it offered systematic theory instead of historical material; or else, insofar as people were aware of it, that it was held from the start to be 'too complicated' on one side and 'too simplistic' on the other, but in either case useless in explaining *social*-economic price phenomena because it also included *subjective* facts in the basic structure.[181] However, the time came when it was no longer possible to suppress the knowledge that theoretical analysis of the economic totality is indispensable and cannot be replaced by the most thorough accumulation of historical material. And then the ground was very favourable for the reception of a system which, with great simplicity and an exact mathematical form of presentation, had the inestimable 'merit' of offering a *theory of price without a theory of value*, thus sparing any close attention to the mental relations of subjective valuation that were regarded as intrinsically suspect.[182] The enlistment of such valuations to explain economic processes and especially price formation, with their usual turns of phrase so understandable in terms of their origin, was supposed to represent a lapse into the realm of 'metaphysics' or at least an impermissible 'crossing of boundaries into the domain of psychology'.

To be sure, the situation has improved fundamentally in the last twenty years, so that Schumpeter, for instance, largely repeating points in his *Wesen und Inhalt*, can now say of Cassel's polemic against marginal utility theory: 'He takes on objections to it which fall well below his usual level – relating, for example, to the supposedly "psychological drives" of theorists within this orientation.'[183] Before, any caviller could hurl at a researcher guilty of this procedure the dreaded words 'μετάβαϐις εἰς ἄλλο γένος!', thereby damaging him in the eyes of his colleagues: as if the fertility and explanatory value of a theory could be destroyed with logic; as if the whole advance of science in every field had not proceeded precisely in defiance of logic! Today we much more rarely encounter such curt dismissals of the inclusion of mental facts (also wrongly termed 'propositions of psychology') in the explanatory base of economic phenomena.[184] Other catchwords have taken over the function of blowing research from the path of success.

The Explanatory Principle of Cassel's Theory

Cassel's way of posing the problem – certainly a novelty in comparison with all previous theories – presents itself as *normative*. 'We have...to see how the problem of restricting the satisfaction of wants is solved in the exchange economy.' 'In our actual economic order the demands of individuals upon the supply of goods are regulated by *putting* prices upon all goods;[185] and these must be paid before the goods can be had.' *'This restriction of the demands of consumers is...the work of the settlement of prices.'* And then the explanatory principle is immediately introduced. 'As the restriction of consumption must be all the more rigorous in proportion to the *scarcity* of goods relatively to the demands of consumers, and therefore prices are substantively determined by this scarcity, we see that the described *purpose* of the fixing of prices is an expression of the *principle of scarcity.'*[186] *'Hence...the principle of scarcity means the need to bring consumption, by the pressure of prices, into harmony with a relatively scanty supply of goods.'*[187] 'The principle of scarcity is, in fact, of fundamental importance to the theory of prices, and therefore to the whole of economic theory.'[188]

The 'principle of scarcity' and the assumption of a *given value of money* are, in Cassel's view, a sufficient foundation on which to erect the theory of prices. A theory of (subjective) value is 'at least quite unnecessary in economic science';[189] indeed, it has become 'fatal' because the concept of value is 'vague', 'elastic' and 'obscure' and lacks any arithmetical foundation.[190] Recent attempts 'to measure the economic importance of goods by the intensity of the feeling of their necessity' are mere 'fictions'. 'A common measure to express estimates of value' – which is imperative because 'men have always found it necessary to reduce them to a common measure – money' – can only lie in money, since 'the standard of valuation which is actually used in economic practice...ought to fix the limits of economic science'. 'Values are then *replaced* by prices, estimates of value by valuations in *money*. We have a *theory of prices* instead of a theory of value.'[191] 'In practical economic life...the emotional intensity of the demand is only considered insofar as it enters into money valuations', and so 'economic science can consider subjective economic elements only as they are manifested in monetary valuations'.[192] *'We merely postulate a scale of reckoning on which all valuations are effected.'*[193] 'The question how the scale of reckoning itself is settled – how prices are fixed in absolute figures – must be...reserved for the special theory of money.'[194] With such a simple stroke does Cassel succeed in eliminating the theory of value.

Within this framework, where the only task is to ensure that various types and variants of systems are useful in explaining price formation, it is not necessary to look in detail at the contradictions which are due not to the system as such but simply to the author's subjective failings. It would not be difficult to show the glaring contradiction between, on the one hand, the claim that subjective valuations are completely dispensable in economic theory and cannot be grasped in quantitative terms and, on the other hand, the use which Cassel himself makes of such 'psychological' categories in his clear and concise account of the basic economic phenomenon,

127

when the essence of economy is seen to lie in the satisfaction of various needs 'arranged according to their relative importance', when the talk is of 'weighing up the various needs', assessing their 'degrees of saturation and intensity' and regulating the use of goods 'according to the importance of the various needs' – what is that but the usual definition of subjective value? – or when 'sacrifice...takes the form of a restriction of the otherwise possible satisfaction of wants'.[195] Nor need we add anything about the 'novelty' or explanatory function of the concept of *scarcity*, if one recalls that the concept of *'quantitative economic relations'* – which has been established since Carl Menger within and far beyond the Austrian School – has exactly the same content and in some cases (e.g., Böhm-Bawerk) is used alternately with the term scarcity. But the Austrians, like all other theorists, have with good reason avoided describing *one premise* of economics as its 'principle'.

What is not so unimportant for the character and cognitive value of Cassel's whole system is the fact that he *'replaces'* value theory with price theory in the process of 'replacing' subjective want estimations with monetary valuations. Cassel holds the peculiar view that the construction of modern economic theory upon a doctrine of value is due to an untenable hypothesis about the historical evolution of social economy. 'In economic science,' he writes, 'the idea that the monetary economy was preceded by a "pure exchange economy", as an earlier and simpler economic type, has been fatal. It is scarcely possible to doubt that this idea is responsible for the fact that economic theory has felt bound to deal with the procedure of an imaginary exchange economy without money and to make this study the basis of the entire theoretical structure' – which must lead to 'immense difficulties' since the 'very vague and elastic idea of "value" was used instead' of the money-price of goods.[196] A further reason for the introduction of the concept of value into economic theory was an awareness of the 'relativity and mutability of every money scale'. With these views, which are at such extreme variance with the whole evolution of economic theory, it is not surprising that Cassel fundamentally misjudges the function of the value relation in the theory of prices. For Cassel things are extremely simple. Just as, at the level of individual economy, the economic principle ensures that more important wants take precedence over less important ones in the use of scarce goods, so in the exchange economy as a whole, although 'there is no such single will...the wants of all of the individual economies *must* be arranged according to their relative importance'. For 'a line must [!] be drawn between the wants that are to be met [!] and the rest', and 'the entire production must be regulated in this sense'. It is 'first' assumed of the exchange economy 'only [!] that it meets the requirements of the economic principle – the uniform restriction of wants and the direction of production'.[197] That is what counts for Cassel as the *empirical* presupposition of exchange economy! And to guarantee that the economic principle is applied to the whole exchange economy constitutes the 'socio-economic necessity of prices'. A certain price is 'put' [*gesetzt*] on each commodity – for Cassel prices are always 'put' or 'fixed' or 'settled' – 'so to restrict the demand for any particular article that the supply shall be adequate to the demand'.[198]

'When the prices of all goods are given, we may assume that all the factors which influence the individual in regulating his consumption are fixed'; his demand for each particular good is then determined. 'This total demand must, if there is to be equilibrium, cover the total supply..., *because, in virtue of the principle of scarcity, it is the object of prices* so to restrict the demand for any particular article that the supply shall be adequate to the demand.' 'The series of conditions we get in this way suffices, as a rule, to settle the problem of prices.'[199] Yet even Cassel cannot entirely dispense with an investigation of the law underlying changes in demand, because he needs *functional equations* for the derivation of price. In a terse account already anticipated by Cournot – which still assumes that individual demand for each good depends only on the relevant given prices – Cassel then shows that the nature and extent of the dependence of individual demand for a good can be established by *statistical observation* of changes in the price of that good. This *elasticity of demand* can only be very imperfectly ascertained, however, both because of the shortcomings of consumer statistics, and because of the difficulties that lie in the nature of the problem. For the condition that all other prices should remain constant – which must be posed if a change in the demand for a good is to be grounded upon a change in its price – can never be strictly fulfilled. Still, Cassel continues: 'It suffices for the solution of the problem of prices...if we assume that the demand for each of the articles in question is settled as soon as the prices of these goods are fixed. We need not analyse the demand further in connection with the problem of prices. The extent of demand at a given price is a tangible fact of a quantitative, arithmetical nature, and in this form it may be used directly in economic science as part of its structure. The *psychological* processes which lie behind this fact have, of course, a certain interest for the economist...; but that study clearly does not fall within the domain of economic theory proper.' 'We have to point this out particularly in opposition to what is called "the theory of marginal utility"', which is an attempt to present a 'psychology of demand'.[200]

If anyone were to think that want-values had thus been definitively removed from economic theory and replaced with a statistically ascertainable elasticity of demand, they would very soon be disappointed. For

129

Cassel next asserts that it is the essence of economics to choose from the infinite number of wants those which are to be satisfied according to their importance. 'For this purpose the *exchange economy* needs a common measure of the importance of all the different wants.[201] It finds this common standard by fixing a single price for each article of the same quality, and exacting payment of this price before the want shall be satisfied. This means that a want for which the price demanded is paid is always regarded as more important than some other want for which the price is not paid. Thus the *exchange economy* measures the importance of the various wants by the sums of money that are paid for the satisfaction of them.' Or in other words: 'Since we have, in regard to the regulation of consumption [in the whole exchange economy! HM], recognized that the amount of money that is offered for the satisfaction of various wants is the correct [!] measure of the importance of those wants, the same standard must hold good for the regulation of production. We thus come to the conclusion that the means of production must [!] be used in such ways that they will meet the demands which will pay most. The solution of the problem is, therefore, to fix [!] uniform prices for the means of production; to determine the prices of finished goods according to these prices; and to control production in such a way that those wants are met which are prepared to cover the price of satisfying them, determined in this way, and the others not.'[202] 'The fixing of uniform prices is the particular way in which the typical exchange economy applies the principle of the most "economical" use of its available goods.'[203]

Once he is under the spell of this fiction, the problem simply does not arise for Cassel whether it has any *explanatory value* for the formation of prices in the real world. All that counts is whether 'this method' – that 'a society' [!] satisfies its wants according to its ability to pay – is also the 'right one' for the realization of the economic principle. His answer is of course in the affirmative, because the objection 'that a hungry man's want of bread is much more important than a rich man's want of it for feeding his dogs' is an objection 'either to the irrational use which the wealthy make of their money...or it is, in the main, a criticism of the actual distribution of income.'[204]

After this exposition, there can no longer be any doubt what to expect of Cassel's price theory. His cognitive purpose is not to explain – or even to 'describe' – price formation in the *real world*, but to ascertain the prices which must be normatively 'established' or 'calculated' by 'the exchange economy' so that it realizes the 'economic principle' in a plan-like manner for *society as a whole* – to ascertain, then, price formation for a wholly unempirical, *fictitious* case in which the exchange economy as a whole is governed by the norm, and the price instrument steers all scarce quantities of goods available within the economy to those uses which are the 'most rational' from the point of view of the *whole society*. It is enough to clarify the normative character and the fictitious starting-point to show the complete and inevitable failure of Cassel's theory as an explanation of empirical price formation.[205]

Who is this commanding subject, the exchange economy, which attends to the realization of the economic principle in society as a whole; which thereby sets the goal for the whole economy; which 'needs' a measure for the classification of individual economic needs according to the importance of their satisfaction for the whole society, so as to select the more important ones; and which to this end 'establishes' or 'calculates' the 'right' prices of products and the means of production? Quite evidently, the figurative expression 'exchange economy', which denotes an abbreviation, has led Cassel, like many organically minded social theorists, into insinuating the reality of an individual economy into a personalizing metaphor, so that he ascribes to this fictitious subject all the functions which exist in the collectivist planned economy but not in its opposite, the exchange economy. There is thus a blatant conflict between the premises of the derivation and the logically necessary premises of the problem as it is posed; on the one hand, *price formation in exchange economy*, a form of organization with individual freedom of consumption and production *in which every individual economy complies with the 'economic principle'*; but on the other hand, *no authority which regulates that principle for the social totality*. Cassel's procedure must therefore lead to results which tell us nothing about price formation in the exchange economy of the real world.[206]

For all his occasional remarks that there is no single regulating instance in the exchange economy, Cassel still seems to assume that there is a mysterious will at work. But what if there actually were such a will, which *knew* the total quantities of goods available to a society, the total wants directed towards them, the purchasing-power behind each of these wants and hence the total demand for each good at every price, which further considered its task to be the alignment of demand and stocks of every good through the setting of prices, and which did set the 'correct' prices on the basis of this knowledge and norms? Well, there would be nothing left to explain for *that* problem of price determination; it would be 'solved' in its entirety. But that problem of normative *determination* of prices is quite different from the problem which has occupied economic theory since its inception: namely, how does the *formation* of univocal prices take place in the market?

It is certainly no accident that Cassel, like Cournot, takes prices as the independent variables which are given first, and demands as the dependent variables fluctuating along with prices. Nor is it an accident that, in his theory of money, he rejects the idea that its primary function is as means of exchange and prefers the hypothesis that money was consciously introduced by some authority as a standardization of the means of payment and an abstract scale of reckoning. Cournot, for his purpose of deriving the *monopoly* price, is quite right to identify price as the independent variable in relation to demand, because the monopolist who knows his stocks and is able to estimate changes in demand at various price levels really does have it in his gift to establish or 'standardize' a price. The premises are quite different, however, in the case of competitive prices, where the assumption of price as the independent variable *vis-à-vis* demand no longer makes any sense at all. Admittedly Cassel remains wedded to the view that, with the help of the scarcity principle, he will be able to offer a unified theory which embraces both competitive and monopoly prices, as well as the formation of prices for the numerous intermediate types of monopoly and competition. But such a 'price theory' does not move beyond the most general of generalities, and in view of the undeniable difference in the actual bases of monopoly and competitive price formation it is unable to offer anything in the way of substantive knowledge. There is even less need to discuss it as Cassel himself did not make the slightest attempt to fulfil its promise and indeed subsequently based his derivations on the premises of competitive price formation.[207]

And now for the 'replacement' of value theory by price theory! If Cassel were to say that he wanted to *eliminate* value theory from price theory, that would not be open to objection on logical grounds. Why should one not be allowed to present the latter without the former, provided that one is modest enough in one's demands on the price theory? How far someone takes their knowledge is their own affair. On this point Cassel can even appeal to the 'classical' economists. Did not Adam Smith – admittedly a century and a half ago – derive the 'normal price' without value theory, by having it consist of the combined costs of wages, rent and profit which he considered to be tangible facts according to the 'average relations of each country'? And did he not deduce the oscillations of the market price around the normal price from the tangible facts of the respective size of supply and demand? Or can one not – as Cournot did a century ago and many others since – put together a price theory out of tangible statistical data concerning changes in supply, demand and price represented in graphs or in functional equations and then, in the manner of Cassel, decree that 'further than that...economic science need not concern itself with the question'?[208] Of course one can, just as a medical man can limit his investigation of an illness to the correspondences between its manifest symptoms, without going into the aetiology or course of the actual illness.

But we should not confuse the different *cognitive purposes*. Price theory built upon a theory of value seeks to achieve something different from price theory without any ideas relating to value. Its aim is to present the *process of price formation*, which simply does not come to light if the investigation remains confined to the correspondences between already existing prices or the laws of price changes. (Cassel's talk of his theory of price *formation* is quite unfounded.) Its aim, in other words, is essentially to develop our understanding of how – that is, according to which laws – the *subjective side* (wants, stocks available to economic agents, subjective valuations) is 'objectified' in social relations and processes (exchange, prices) which do not exist unless they are borne by subjects; and to show the regularities whereby the social relations developed in this way (exchange, prices, wages, revenue, interest, etc.) react upon the subjective facts (individual demand, etc.), as not only price formation but the whole economic process unfolds in the interplay between the subjective and the social. That is quite a different cognitive purpose from that which Cassel projects in his theory of price. Its scientific legitimacy comes from the fact that its fulfilment allows us to solve questions thrown up by real economic life which the results of the more modest approach fail to address.

That Cassel himself is guilty of such confusion is most clearly expressed in his supposed 'replacement' of value theory with price theory. Once one has recognized the *instrumental* character of value for price theory, one can never call for the means of achieving a broader purpose to be 'replaced' by a narrower purpose which does not require that means.

What is supposed to be the meaning, in Cassel's 'value-free' system, of the idea that in exchange economy as a whole 'the wants of all the individual economies must be arranged according to their relative importance', so that the wants to be satisfied by the exchange economy are separated from those which are to be left unsatisfied and 'the social regulation of consumption' is made a possibility? Or what of the argument that 'the realization of the economic principle in regard to the direction of production in the economy depends upon the way in which the wants are graduated', so that the wants which have to count as more important are simply those whose satisfaction commands higher prices; and that this is the 'correct measure of the importance of those wants'?[209] Why is it that Cassel is not content – in keeping with his rejection of value theory – to note the fact of differential price bids on the demand side, but implies that demand with greater purchasing power involves wants of greater importance in terms of the exchange economy as a whole? Value theory is not here replaced with a theory of price, as Cassel wrongly interprets his own approach. Rather, in place of subjective individual valuations which have a real existence and can therefore help causally to explain the formation of

133

prices, we are presented with purely imaginary valuations of the wants of individual economies, to be carried out by a non-existent 'direction of the exchange economy', so that on the basis of this classification the 'exchange economy' can standardize the 'right' prices. This 'doctrine of value' is what Cassel puts in place of the 'unnecessary', 'psychological' theory of value! And all this just to be able to shunt aside the problem of the *process* of price formation, the central and most difficult problem of the whole theory of commercial economy which, to be sure, cannot be solved without an analysis of demand. All this just to be able to assume, on the basis of prices set by the 'exchange economy', that demand is the dependent and supply the independent variable; to narrow the task to one of deriving, not the law of price formation, but the law of change of already formed prices![210]

This fictitious valuation of the needs of individual economies through a fictitious direction of the exchange economy, for the purpose of a non-existent 'social regulation of the exchange economy' by means of 'price-fixing', is in Cassel's view applicable not only to consumer goods but also to the means of production. 'The means of production must be used in such ways that they will meet the demands [*Bedürfnisse*] which will pay most.' 'The solution to the problem is, therefore, to fix uniform prices for the means of production; to determine the prices of finished goods according to these prices; and to control production in such a way that those wants are met which are prepared to cover the price of satisfying them, determined in this way, and the others not.' 'For other means of production,[211] prices must be calculated according to their relative scarcity, so that the effective demand for each shall be small enough.'[212] 'Thus the process of fixing prices in the exchange economy embraces both the elementary means of production and all the finished products for consumption...; all the prices are then fixed, and fixed simultaneously.' According to Cassel, production costs are not the factor determining product prices; nor is it true, as 'the whole of what is called the recent subjective theory of value' would have it, that prices of the means of production are determined by prices of finished goods.[213] And since the prices of means of production flow as income to their owners, but this income in turn determines demand, this income is also determined by the general process of price formation. 'All the unknown factors of the price-fixing process depend upon each other, and they are only determined, and then determined *together*, when we solve the problem of pricing.' 'The causal connection between the different variables is not a one-sided one', 'but is in the nature of a closed chain of causes, in which each link depends upon all the others, and which may be followed in any direction.'[214]

Thus, solely from the postulated validity of the 'economic principle' for *the exchange economy as a whole*, much more simply than in Walras and

Pareto who had to struggle with the incorporation of subjective valuations into the system, a schema of *general interdependence* is obtained whose exact formulation then follows in Cassel's equations.

The Mechanism of Price Formation in Cassel

Let us take 'a self-contained exchange economy in which pricing is entirely governed by the principle of scarcity'. '*How that state of things is brought about does not matter as far as our present enquiry is concerned.*'[215] First to be considered is the case of price formation in which production is left out of account: 'the quantities of goods available to the consumer in a definite period are given'; these quantities will be called 'the supply of the goods in question, S_1, S_2....S_n. '*We first assume that the sum of money which each consumer pays during the relevant period for the satisfaction of his wants is fixed in advance. In those circumstances the demand of each consumer for various goods during the period is clearly settled as soon as prices are settled.*'[216] It is 'most appropriate', Cassel argues, to select the price of the good as the independent variable. Then individual demand and hence total demand is a function of price, 'the form of this function expressing the subjective valuation'. 'But if we look more closely into the demand-function, we shall find that it also contains, as variables, the prices of all the other goods.' 'The demand of the individual consumer for a particular article is...not determined until the prices of all articles that can be objects of his demand at all are fixed.' 'With the prices of the n goods, therefore, the demand of each individual consumer, and consequently the total demand of the whole of the consumers, for any particular article is settled. If we call the total demand for the n goods during the relevant period D_1, D_2....D_n, we can give these magnitudes as functions of the n prices, thus:

$$
\begin{aligned}
D_1 &= F_1 (p_1............................p_n) \\
D_2 &= F_2 (p_1............................p_n) \\
D_n &= F_n (p_1............................p_n)
\end{aligned}
\tag{1}
$$

'As the fixing of prices in accordance with the principle of scarcity has to restrict the demand until it can be met out of the available supply of commodities', where there is equilibrium of the exchange economy there must be: $D_1 = S_1$, $D_2 = S_2$, $D_n = S_n$. So,

$$
\begin{aligned}
F_1 (p_1............................p_n) &= S_1 \\
F_2 (p_1............................p_n) &= S_2 \\
F_n (p_1............................p_n) &= S_n
\end{aligned}
\tag{2}
$$

135

'Hence to solve the pricing problem in the simple case we are considering, we have only to regard the n prices as the unknown quantities of the problem, and take them as given in the usual mathematical way. We are then in a position to express the demand for the n goods in these prices according to the equations (1) and equations (2) that follow as a consequence of the principle of scarcity. This system contains n equations for the determination of n unknown prices; which is generally supposed to determine the n unknown quantities. *Once the prices are known, the demand of each individual consumer and the total demand for each particular commodity, can be calculated.*[217] As the demand is satisfied at the prices calculated in this way, the whole problem of the distribution of the commodities available to consumers is solved.' 'The fact that the demand for an article depends...upon the prices of all other articles...makes it necessary to express the pricing process (!) by a system of simultaneous equations like our system (2).' 'The intrinsic nature of the pricing process cannot be adequately represented in any other way.'[218]

In an analogous manner, prices are incorporated into the problem of production. If r denotes the number of means of production, $R_1, R_2.....R_r$ the available quantities of them, n the number of goods produced by them, $a1_1, a1_2.....a1_r; a2_1, a2_2.....a2_r$, etc. the given technical coefficients.[219] $q_1, q_2.....q_r$ the (unknown) prices of the r different means of production, and $p_1, p_2.....p_n$ the prices of the n finished products, then

$$a1_1 q1 + a1_2 q2 + ...a1_r q_r = p_1 \text{ etc.} \tag{3}$$

(which express the fact that production costs for each good must be equal to its price). Since the total demand for each good is expressed by the equation system

$$D_1 = F_1 (p_1.....p_n) \text{ etc.} \tag{4}$$

and since the principle of scarcity entails that

$$D_1 = S_1 \text{ etc.} \tag{5}$$

(where $S_1.....S_n$ denotes the quantities produced of the particular goods), so that the total demand for means of production 1, for example, is

$$a1_1 S_1 + a2_1 S2 +.....a_{n1} Sn \tag{6}$$

then because 'in accordance with the principle of scarcity, this demand for each means of production must be equal to the quantity of this means of production available within the unit-period considered, since (!) it is the object of pricing to restrict the demand just as much as is necessary for this purpose', then we have:[220]

$$R_1 = a1_1 S_1 + a2_1 S2 +.....a_{n1} Sn \text{ etc.} \tag{7}$$

'Here the S are, in virtue of equation-systems (5) and (4), functions of p, and therefore, in virtue of equation-system (3), functions of q. The system of equations (7) thus contains as unknown quantities the r prices of the means of production. There are also r equations, and the system therefore suffices generally to determine the unknown quantities.' Once the prices of the means of production are known, the prices of the finished goods can be calculated from equations (3), the demand for the finished goods from equations (4), and thus the distribution of the means of production among different lines from equation (5). Formula (6) allow us to calculate the claims made by the demand for various means of production which is regulated by this formation of prices. The adaptation of these claims to the available quantities of means of production is assured by equation-system (7). *Thus the pricing problem is entirely solved for the case we are considering here.* 'Our equations show the real nature of the pricing process which cannot be exactly represented in any simpler form.'[221]

From the demand for the finished goods ensues 'a struggle for the relatively scarce means of production; in the exchange economy this struggle is settled by fixing uniform prices for the means of production; these in turn fix the prices of the products, and are thus a means of restricting the demand.'

Cassel maintains that this derivation puts an end to the dispute over the *determinants* of price: 'The determining factors of the prices...are the different given coefficients of our equations...[which] may be distributed in two chief groups...the objective and the subjective determining factors of prices. The objective factors are the quantities of the means of production (R) and what we may call the technical coefficients (a). The subjective factors are the coefficients of equations (4), which represent the dependence of the demand upon prices.' 'We may say, therefore, that prices are determined by the scarcity of the means of production in proportion to the indirect demand of consumers for them. The scarcity of the means of production, in accordance with our assumptions, is a given factor of the problem. The demand, on the other hand, is itself a function of the price of finished goods, and consequently, in virtue of equation-system (3), a function of the prices of the means of production, and therefore cannot be a determining factor of them. What is on this side a given factor of the problem of prices is the way in which the demand-functions depend upon the prices of the means of production; that is to say, the form of these functions or the aggregate of their coefficients, which characterize the nature of the demand for the means of production.' The 'scarcity of the means of production and the character of the demand for them' are thus 'the two determining factors of prices', both of them 'essential in the full sense of the word'.[222]

If we now finally drop the assumption that the consumers' monetary

137

expenditure on finished goods is fixed in advance – for 'the amount of all payments of each consumer...is determined by his income', and 'the income of the individual...is determined by the prices of the means of production which he sells in the course of the production process, and neither these incomes nor the payments made in virtue of them should be regarded as questions of the pricing problem given in advance' – this 'makes no change in the outward form of the systems of equations which serve to determine prices'. But the starting-point now is the prices of the means of production, which can be provisionally assumed as known. They help us to calculate the incomes of the various individual economies, and these incomes – in connection with the prices of goods, which can also be calculated from the prices of the means of production – then determine the total expenditure on consumption of the individual economy, so that the form of equations (4) remains unchanged. 'But they no longer include the total payments, which we previously took for granted, as constants. Now, however, we have the coefficients of the functions $F_1...F_n$ as functions of the prices of the means of production. But the variables $p_1...p_n$ are themselves, in accordance with the equation-system (3), functions of the unknown quantities $q_1...q_r$. Hence functions $F_1...F_n$ now contain, besides the variables $q_1...q_r$, only constants which must be regarded as given in our problem, and represent the dependence of the demand upon prices and upon the distribution of income determined by these prices.'[223]

Summing up, Cassel once more draws attention to the 'immediate determinants of prices': 'The subjective factors of prices lie in the character of the dependence of the demand for finished goods upon prices. The objective factors are...the *technical conditions of production* and the quantities of the available *means of production*.'[224] Of course, 'in cases in which the supplementary principles of pricing also apply' (the differential principle, the principle of substitution, the principle of falling average costs, the principle of price formation of related products), these determinants are partly modified and replaced by others.

'But if all three groups of determinants must be taken into account, the theory of price formation is essentially contained in our solution to the problem, and *besides this solution there can be no other theory of price formation which describes and explains the actual processes of the exchange economy.*'[225]

Critique of Cassel's Theory of Price

Does Cassel's theory of price really fulfil the promise that it will provide deeper insight into the *process* of price formation than that which is contained in the theories of his predecessors? The first requirement for this to be true would be that the deduction had fully and correctly grasped the pricing forces operating in the real world and the manner of their combination. But it would appear that a glaring contradiction lies at the heart of Cassel's system. Whereas the first part, which is supposed to lay the basis for the derivation, has a purely *normative* character, the actual solution presented in the second part under the title 'mechanism of price formation' moves along the well-worn *functional* tracks, where a system of simultaneous equations is supposed to bathe the reciprocal dependences in the light of knowledge.

After the points we have discussed above, there can be no doubt about the normative character of the first part. Indeed in the same way that, if this is thought through logically, a standardizing will necessarily stands in the end behind each normative principle, so in Cassel's system the principle supposedly regulating the exchange economy as a whole must have lying behind it the fiction of a *supreme unified will*, a kind of central command post, which steers the whole economy in accordance with a plan and lays down its governing law. This may never be explicitly stated, but it finds expression in numerous phrases – at crucial points in the argument – which would have no meaning without this assumption. For what could it mean that the 'task' or purpose of price formation is to 'restrict the demands of consumption', if not that, since goals do not lie in things themselves but are set by a will, it is tacitly assumed that a central direction of the economy sets the task? In a free, individualist commercial economy, who has an interest and who plays a role in ensuring that 'the wants of all the individual economies are arranged according to their relative importance', that 'the entire production must be regulated in this sense', and that 'the requirements of the economic principle are met'? Which is the authority that 'needs a common measure', to 'gauge' the importance of all the different wants of all individual economies from the point of view of the economy as a whole? Who judges 'the most rational use of all goods' and 'fixes prices in conformity with it'? Who can be allocated all this deliberation and goal-determination for the economy as a whole, if not a regulatory will standing above the individual economies which makes it the job of price formation 'so to restrict the demand for any particular article that the supply shall be adequate to the demand'? This *fiction* is no mere figure of speech or permitted shorthand; it loses its non-committal character and acquires very real importance for Cassel's derivations at the moment when they enter into the strictly formulated assumptions of exact deduction. Clarification of this point is of the greatest significance for a theory like Cassel's, which sets itself the problem of securing knowledge of the price formation process – and not just of

139

describing the already formed system of prices. For the cognitive value of a theory which seeks to portray the process of price formation in an exchange economy must crucially depend upon whether it accurately grasps, and includes in its formal presuppositions, the real driving forces of that form of social economy – the forces which trigger and sustain the whole price formation process, the striving for optimum satisfaction of wants, on the one hand, and the greatest possible profit on the other; or whether instead it invents as the driving force a regulatory norm (and implicitly a norm-fixing will) which is supposed to plan the exchange economy as a whole. If it does the latter, it brings about a transformation of the problem; but it thereby rules out any way of solving the problem of price formation in an individualist commercial economy. This is so even if the final result achieved with the help of this fiction – correlation in equilibrium of prices, demand, supply of various goods, income, and so on – were in itself correctly presented. For, as is well known, the same outcome can be reached along very different paths, and once you start working with fictions there are any number that can be made to serve the same end.[226] But in the case of a problem like that of price formation in the individualist commercial economy as it empirically exists, the core of the special cognitive task is not to describe the final result of price formation (although of course that is also important) but to show *how that outcome is reached in reality* (i.e. the law of the *process*), how the interaction of already existing elements (wants, quantities of goods, etc.) gives rise to new magnitudes – prices – which were not present before. Insofar as it is the route to market equilibrium in the freely competitive economy which poses the problem – equilibrium not consciously willed by anyone involved in the price formation process, nor by 'the economy' as a whole – the researcher no longer has the freedom to invent some arbitrary path starting from premises other than those of this *form* of social economy, unless he wishes to do away with the problem itself.

But that is precisely what happens in Cassel's theory of price. The *problem* is to delineate the price formation process in a social economy with no single regulatory will, where everyone present on the market is guided only by their own interests. And the *starting-point* for Cassel is a norm which floats over the whole economy independently of the individual forces driving the formation of prices, and which assigns to prices the goal of fulfilling the economic principle for the whole of the national economy. The question was: how do prices and price correlations arise from the individualist premises of commercial economy? But this has now become a quite different question: how does the formation of prices attain its predetermined goal of fulfilling the economic principle – equalization of supply and demand – for the economy as a whole? *An unintentional goal of the process that requires explanation is thus taken as its intentional starting-point.*

In Cassel's system, then, the specific problem of the theory of price formation is eliminated from the outset by a normative definition of the starting-point. Nothing could be added to this result of critical analysis by the objection that the norm in Cassel's system – 'demand must be made equal to supply by means of price formation, because it is the object of price formation to realize the principle of scarcity' – is only a 'purely formal' affair which merely provides formulation for a *conditional equation* of the equilibrium state. For, however legitimate and necessary this formal assumption of the equality of supply and demand may be for an exact description of the *finished* system of prices – that is, of the *achieved* state of equilibrium – it is also methodologically illegitimate (because non-specific to the problem) if the cognitive task is to demonstrate the path leading to the formation of prices and of the supply-and-demand equilibrium. Cassel's procedure involves drawing up the conditional equations $S_1 = D_1$ etc. simply as an expression of the norm that there *must* be equilibrium: they do not incorporate the forces known from experience which actually tend to bring about equilibrium – that is, the variable magnitudes obtained through experience which make for a definite maximum (as is the case in Jevons, Walras or Pareto) and express the law of motion that produces equilibrium. And this means that from the very beginning Cassel gives up any attempt to solve the problem. Instead of these functions which give expression to the law of motion, what we find is a most awkward attempt to steer clear of subjective utility functions and to pose the norm of $S_1 = D_1$ as being required for the whole economy in virtue of the economic principle.

This also dissolves the ostensible contradiction between the first and the second part of Cassel's theory. Only in appearances is his derivation of the 'mechanism of price formation' a functional account. Insofar as he tries to avoid using the causal relation, he resorts to ways around a normative approach and moves towards a teleological derivation in terms of a *pre-established goal of price formation*.

Let us consider this further, remaining within the imagery suggested by Cassel's presentation. In the first part of his theoretical drama, the imaginary normative subject – 'exchange economy' – appears on the market and sets prices that will achieve equilibrium of supply and demand. In the second act, however, we are given an insight into the computation office of this price-fixing will, where he himself tries to achieve clarity about the conditions that he must fulfil in setting the price levels of various goods in order to make his norm – equalization of supply and demand – actually come into force. These conditions are then developed in the form of

141

simultaneous equations from Cournot's demand function as expanded by Walras. So this 'mechanism of price formation' also rests entirely upon normative foundations. The first premise remains: D_1 must be made equal to S_1, and it is highly characteristic that in the course of the mathematical deductions the connecting link is repeatedly inserted: 'since it is the task of price formation to fulfil the principle of scarcity'.

It still has to be investigated whether, in spite of the unreality of the (normative) driving force upon which Cassel grounds the whole of price formation, the other conditional equations (1) and (2) – just to take Cassel's elementary case which leaves out production – may not contain the factors or forces actually determining price formation within the postulated framework of an individualist commercial economy.

In principle, one of two cases is possible here. In the first, these equations do contain the forces determining price formation (individual demand functions or index functions of ophelimity or indifference, as in Walras and Pareto), so that a glaring contradiction arises between Cassel's basic normative equation ($D_1 = S_1$ etc.) and equations (1) and (2). For if Cassel's norm is the force determining prices, everything else (subjective utility functions etc.) must be only a condition or a datum. In the second case, the subjective forces and relations determine prices, so that Cassel's norm set over all economic subjects cannot hold at the same time. An equation-system which combined the two would be intrinsically – i.e., on the assumptions underlying the various equations – self-contradictory and therefore unusable. Cassel now has to remain consistent, for his programme is to offer a 'theory of price without a theory of value', to eliminate the subjective factor whose exact definition and insertion in the system presented, as we have seen, enormous difficulties to his predecessors. Thus, the equation groups (1) and (2) tell us nothing about factors *determining* price; on the contrary, they merely present the *effect* of prices (and indirectly of their regulating norm) with given conditions or data. According to equation group (1) in Cassel's system – $D_1 = F_1 (p_1.....p_n)$ etc. – demand is nothing other than a function of prices; it is the dependent variable while price is independent; it is the *passive* element, the material formed by the norm which operates through price regulation. And equation group (2) – $F_1 (p_1.....p_n) = S_1$ etc. – does not contain a relation established independently of the basic normative equation, $D_1 = S_1$, or of equation (1), but simply concludes from these two that, if the demand for a good depends upon all price and if demand must be equal to supply, then the supply of each commodity must also be dependent upon all prices. The cognitive value of the whole mathematical derivation stands or falls with the empirical or fictitious character of that norm.

If it is accepted that Cassel's normative foundation is unusable for a theory of the price formation process, there are also in the mode of derivation many substantive propositions and deductions that require explanation. First of all, the form in which Cassel introduces his norm into the mathematical derivation is simply that of an identity equation. For each kind of commodity the demand and the supply must be equal ($D_1 = S_1$ etc.); so 1000 apples = 1000 apples! Instead of placing on one side the *set of magnitudes* which make up the demand, and on the other side the *set of magnitudes* which make up the supply – which is necessary for a genuine equation, and which is what Jevons and Walras, for example, tried to do – Cassel presents us with a mere tautology. As we have seen, Cournot started from the basis that effective demand and effective supply are identical with 'turnover', and then operated only with turnover as a function of price. But Cassel uses his tautology to establish two groups of equations: one which states that the demand is a function of all prices; and one which affirms that precisely this function of all prices is equal to the supply!

Stranger still is the route to equation group (1), which alone in Cassel's equation-system contains a synthetic judgement. The drawing up of the equation $D_1 = F_1 (p_1.....p_n)$ is based upon the ever recurring proposition that given the consumers' spending fund (income), '*the demand of each consumer for various goods...is clearly settled as soon as prices are settled*'. But reflection on the whole of inner and outer experience shows that this basic proposition is completely untenable; that in fact, if the only givens are the income of the various subjects and prices, then the effective demand of individuals and hence the sum of all their demand remain completely undetermined. A hundred different subjects may, with the same income and at the same prices, develop a hundred different orders of demand for the individual goods; and moreover, their demand may respond to price changes in quite different ways. Thus, assuming that the problem is posed with already given prices, the self-evident determining magnitudes (income and prices) lack the further elements which are necessary for a real determination of demand. This is what outward experience tells us. Inner experience – self-observation of the motives which guide the individual in shaping his or her effective demand – shows that 'absolute', 'virtual' or 'psychological' demand, existing independently of prices and incomes, is the indispensable prior condition for effective demand to come into being, and that its nature and extent again depend upon wants and their structural interrelations. Income and prices join the elementary determinant, the structural law of the system of wants, as a restricting factor, and the result of their influence (the nature and size of effective demand) will vary greatly according to the shape (the nature and

143

size) of the absolute demand for the various goods. If that is the case, however, the ratios which Cassel dresses up in his first and main group of equations are unsound, insofar as he claims them to be univocal. But if their only content is supposed to be the completely vague assertion that effective demand displays *some* dependence or other – including on existing prices and incomes – then they are indeed correct, but they tell us nothing and cannot be used for the univocal derivation of prices and their correlation with demand.[227]

The conclusion that D_1, D_2 etc. stand in some *undefined* dependence on $p_1.....p_n$ says as little or as much as the formulation that all elements in the course of the world are in *some kind* of dependence upon one another. Evidently nothing is gained by way of explanation, so long as nothing more precise can be said about the particular *form* of dependence. It is not as if in Cassel's system this equation group (1), so inadequate for the determination of demand, were complemented by a supporting group through which that indeterminacy was removed. For – as we have already seen – the group of binding equations $D_1 = S_1$ etc. contains a mere tautology; and equation (2) contains no ratio established independently of these two equation groups, but only the conclusion from the two. It is thus immediately apparent that equation group (1), because it alone involves a *synthetic* judgement, really constitutes the second load-bearing pillar of the system after the normative principle. But since those equations (1) have no *determinate* content, say nothing about the *form* of the putative dependence, they are only illusory equations. They would be genuine only if, through the incorporation of constants or other variables such as $p_1.....p_n$, they exhibited quantitative relations which expressed the *law of the distribution of income among the demand* for various goods; that is, only if the subjective utility functions for the various goods were contained within them. But that is precisely what Cassel wanted to avoid. In striving for the greatest possible simplicity, he totally underestimated the indispensable role which subjective utility functions had played for his great predecessors in mathematical theory.

How could Cassel come to that completely untenable conclusion that existing prices and incomes are enough fully to determine the demand of each consumer for various goods. *Either* he tacitly assumes it as self-evident that each consumer will know without further ado, by referring to the prices, how to distribute his or her income for the acquisition of the various goods.[228] This, clearly, would evade the heart of the problem: that which has to be derived would appear as already known. In effect, the theorist would withdraw from the search for a solution, with the simple words that 'reality already solves it by itself'! *Or else* Cassel is tacitly suggesting that the precise distribution ratio of total demand at given prices is directly known from the statistically established 'elasticity' of demand – that is, from the statistically established behaviour of consumers at the respective prices. In that case, statistically established behaviour would be posed as the 'determining factor' instead of a law requiring theoretical derivation.

Cassel does both. He is not interested in developing the law by which economic subjects divide their income among demand for various goods: how that division comes about is entirely a matter for the subjects themselves. He is thus content to establish by statistics that a certain distribution always follows at given prices. It is true that this procedure becomes totally clear only at the end of Cassel's derivations, where the coefficients of equation (1) are given by the statistically established elasticity of demand, so that the former indeterminacy of this equation *appears* to be removed. But now every argument against the *replacement* of theory by statistics must be asserted against this whole procedure – as we have already partly done ourselves.[229]

To gain an understanding of the process of price formation, we need to know how the determination of demand comes about. And we are referred to the *fact* that, according to the statistical evidence, some such determination always does come about – that is, in every concrete historical situation. But even this assertion, evidently modest in its cognitive pretensions, proves on closer inspection to be of no use. For, as Cassel himself could not fail to see in the end,[230] it is technically very difficult to establish by statistics the fact and the degree of a change in demand caused by a change in certain prices. This is not only because of the poor quality of consumption statistics, which has been repeatedly used as an excuse since the time of Cournot. There is also a more essential reason. In order to establish statistically the effect (the degree) of a change in price p_1, then price p_2 etc., upon demand D_1, D_2.....D_n – that is, the coefficients of equation group (1) which are supposed to remove the indeterminacy of those equations – it is necessary to assume that price p_1 changes in *isolation* while all other prices remain constant, and to observe the effect of this on the demand for the various goods. However, this assumption (change in *one* price with all others remaining the same) stands in an irreconcilable contradiction with the basic premise of all equilibrium theories which start from the general interdependence of all prices, from their univocal, mutual relationship of correspondence. It also strikingly contradicts the whole of our experience. Thus, the figures for changes in demand which are obtained under this unrealistic assumption are equally unreal in their significance.[231] This is closely bound up with a second basic deficiency. Even if it were legitimate to assume isolated price changes for each good, so as to ascertain, from observation of their effect, the dependence of demand on changes first in price p_1, then in price p_2 etc., it would clearly be quite wrong to assume that the *isolated* and thus *alternate* changes in D_1, D_2 etc. obtained through alternate changes in p_1, p_2 etc. asserted themselves *simultaneously*. For it is obvious from experience – and needs no prior deduction here – that the change in demand is different when ten prices change simultaneously and when the same ten prices change in succession (by the same amount) and the resulting ten changes in demand are then added up. In the first case, one obtains the expression for the dependence of demand D_1 etc. on a *price totality in globo* and thus gives up ascertaining the special dependence of demand on the price of a particular kind of goods: that is to say, one does not obtain the coefficients which are indispensable for the solution of equation group (1). But in the second case, where the *alternate* dependence of demand on the prices of the various goods is taken as *simultaneously* operative by being introduced into one and the same equation, the coefficients in use are actually *incorrect*. The detour which was supposed to pass round the 'psychological processes' constituting demand and lead on to the goal thus turns out to be impassable. Nor can the required coefficients of equation (1) be obtained from the fact, obvious enough even without statistics, that all prices have to be paid out of income, and that consequently when a price changes, the proportion of purchasing power thereby released or bound must *somehow* be divided among the demand for all the goods. It is true that 'the extent of the demand at a given price is a tangible fact of a quantitative, arithmetical nature'.[232] But the conclusion which Cassel draws – namely, that this 'tangible fact' may 'be used directly in economic science as part of its structure' – is rather hasty to say the least. The coefficients of Cassel's equation (1) are simply *made out* to be given; they cannot be determined in reality. Thus, despite the attempt to give it a definite content with the help of statistics, equation (1) remains a mere illusion whose content is an undetermined ratio and which is therefore of no use in the derivation of prices.

But leaving aside this impossibility of the attempted derivation, we must pose a more fundamental question. In a theory of price formation, what is the cognitive value of starting with prices and deriving demand from them, rather than the other way around? Cassel justifies his procedure simply by arguing that it is 'most appropriate...to select the price of the good as the independent variable'. But if the process of price *formation* is taken as the problem, the theorist no longer has the arbitrary freedom to 'select' what is *given* and what is to be *derived*. The process which theory has to demonstrate – the emergence of univocally determined prices – may not be taken as the assumed point of departure, unless a wide berth is given to the whole problem. It is not avoiding the issue to assume *temporarily* that the prices in the mathematical derivations are

already known; but it is to assume that the relevant (statistically established) *demand* is shaped by already existing (temporally prior) prices.
Prices are determined by demand, and demand is determined by prices!
That would be correct if it was a question of a *genetic* process taking place
over time – though even then not in the abstract sense that 'demand'
determines 'price' in general and vice versa, but in the sense that demand
d_{t_1} (at the point or short time interval t_1) determines price p_{t_1} and this
again determines demand d_{t_2} in the following interval. But in a system of
simultaneous relations of magnitude, which is how Cassel's system sees
itself,[233] it is a truly *circular argument* – quite apart from the fact that a
system of simultaneous relations or magnitudes (none of them containing
the time factor) can never yield information about a *formative process*.
What Cassel actually strains to show is not, as he wrongly believes, the law
of the formation of univocal prices and price correlations – that is, the law-
governed emergence of definite prices out of elementary determinants not
located in the (provisional) prices – but merely the law of price change
which is intended to derive present prices with the help of the statistically
defined shaping of demand formed by past prices.[234]

It is very characteristic how Cassel, in discussing the 'factors determining price', seeks to escape from the circular argument. As determinants he
points to 'the scarcity of the means of production in proportion to the
indirect demand of consumers for them.' 'The scarcity of the means of
production...is a given factor of the problem. The demand, on the other
hand, is itself a function of the price of finished goods, and consequently,
in virtue of equation-system (3), a function of the prices of the means of
production, and therefore cannot be a determining factor of them. What is
on this side a given factor of the problem of prices is the way in which the
demand-functions depend upon the prices of the means of production;
that is to say, the form of these functions or the aggregate of their
coefficients, which characterize the nature of the demand for the means of
production.' Thus one factor d (demand) is the factor determining a result
p (price). In its concrete form, however, this determinant d is partly
determined by its own determined result p and can only be ascertained if
its dependence on p has already been established! And this all refers to a
process of formation, where there can be no talk of reversible connections!
In place of a manifestly circular argument we now have a more hidden
one. And the only purpose is to avoid 'psychological analysis' designed to
ascertain the real determinants of demand.

In analysing this breakdown of the basic components of Cassel's system,
we no longer need to go into such details as the assumption of a given
constant value of money – an assumption which in itself would certainly
obstruct any deeper insight into the process of price formation.

If the results of our critical analysis are correct, it cannot be claimed that Cassel's theory of price comes closer to solving the problem of price formation than do the functional theories of his predecessors. On the contrary, by renouncing a general comprehension of the way in which price-shaping forces actually work and by assuming the structure of demand at given prices as a (statistically established) constant, its cognitive goal and implementation mark a regression to the level of the classical theory of 'supply and demand', which also operated with an unanalysed structure of demand that was always assumed as given.

Concluding Remarks

There is no space left in this article for a full evaluation of the critical and positive results of our enquiry.[235]

The limited productivity of equilibrium theories, their unsuitability for the understanding of price formation, are in the end a result of the fact that they represent pure systems of conceptual truths or analytic judgements ('*vérités éternelles*', in the words of Leibniz); that they display not a single *general synthetic proposition* ('*vérité de fait*'), not one *general* law obtained from *experience*, as in the natural sciences. Equilibrium equations (e.g., equations B-E in Pareto's formulation) are obtained from previously established definitions and identity statements drawn explicitly or implicitly from one another. These are then used to derive, through purely logical inference, a nexus of substitution relations which can evidently give no more knowledge of reality than was already contained in the premises. This is real 'derivation' in the sense of 'proofs' in pure logic and mathematics, and not the acquisition of new knowledge about correlations in the real world. This is not to say anything against the use of mathematics in economic theory, provided that it serves the goal which Poincaré expressed so well and so accurately: the only object, he said, 'is to coordinate the physical laws with which physical experiment makes us acquainted, the enunciation of which, without the aid of mathematics, we should be unable to effect.'[236] Only at one point does the free-floating system represented by equilibrium theories seem to come into contact with reality: that is, at the point where the indispensable insertion of *demand*, the dynamic factor, takes place in equation A. If here a *general* empirical law of the correlation of individual demand for various goods were to be deployed (a law which could only be 'psychological'), the 'dynamization' of the system and its correlation with the real-world process of price formation would indeed be established, although it is true that the transition from merely functional to causal relations would come to pass at the same time. Jevons, Walras and – though he would not admit it – even Pareto attempted this with their psychological-causal foundation (utility or ophelimity functions, indifference lines, the law of marginal utility level). But they stopped half-way (at the breaks mentioned above) and were content to follow another road, which seemed to point more easily to the goal but which, in reality, led to a different, more modest goal. This is the road that Cournot and Cassel took from the beginning: they made demand, the driving force of the whole system, into 'effective demand', and effective demand into 'turnover'.[237] In this way the motive force is divested of its essence; as a dependent magnitude, it becomes a function of the other magnitudes in the system. The *de-dynamization* of the system is thus complete: causality is shut out, universal interdependence restored. The price, of course, is an utter abandonment of reclamation work, which might have allowed the system to explain real-world processes of motion and development.

But the younger scientific generation – of every age – feels ever more strongly the narrowness, the insufficiency, the lack of development of static equilibrium theory. It is not ungrateful for the propaedeutic knowledge it received, and fully appreciates its value in solving special problems with narrowly defined premises (the static theory of monopoly price, the theory of the effects of changes in taxes, cargo charges or tariffs on already existing prices, and so on). On this basis, it is increasingly aware that the *integrated forms* provided by mathematical science can carry us further only if we first draw upon extensive experience to obtain *empirical laws* about the action of the (subjective and social) forces which – with historically typical foundations of social organization – cause socio-economic connections to emerge and develop, and shape the course of the economic process. Tired of the game of constantly linking in to the chain of syllogisms, present-day theory is turning from mere 'derivation' back to *research*. This is the road on which the great system-builders of the 'older' German historical school meet up with the founders of the 'Austrian School'. And to have rebuilt it for those who come after is in no small measure the contribution of Friedrich von Wieser who, with a rare degree of both historical understanding and theoretical knowledge, discovered the laws of *being* in the laws of *becoming*. It is to him that this work is dedicated.

NOTES

1. Or exchange-value in the terminology of classical economics.
2. *Principles of Political Economy* (London, 1849), bk iii, ch. 1, sect. 1, p. 533.

3. *The Theory of Social Economy*, 1st English edn, trans. Joseph McCabe (London: T. Fisher Unwin, 1923), p. 138. Cf. 2nd English edn, trans. S. L. Barron (London, 1932), pp. 140–1.

4. Neither the fact that the historian's choice of object is guided by theoretical perspectives, nor the fact that his accounts employ concepts established by theory, means that his own work is theory. But if he goes beyond the description of concrete facts and attempts to demonstrate their underlying genetic or structural laws, he no longer does this as a historian but constructs theory with (useful or unuseful) historical material.

5. Older attempts to grasp the function of the subjective factor in the emergence of exchange relations did not, however, lead to a consistently developed theory of price, most notably in Bentham, Davanzati, Galiani, Genovesi, Turgot, Condillac, Soden, Auguste Walras, Hermann, Dupuit, Say and Senior.

6. Translated respectively as *Principles of Economics*, trans. J. Dingwall and B. F. Hoselitz (Glencoe, IL: The Free Press, 1950); and *Investigations into the Method of the Social Sciences with Special Reference to Economics*, trans. Francis J. Nock (Urbana: University of Illinois Press, 1963).

7. *Wesen und Hauptinhalt der theoretischen Nationalökonomie*. It may be concluded from numerous later works by Schumpeter, however, that he no longer holds to that brusque rejection of the causal-genetic problematic.

8. Criticizing older theory, Mill remarks that for the derivation of price 'the idea of a *ratio*, as between demand and supply, is out of place, and has no concern in the matter: the proper mathematical analogy is that of an *equation*. Demand and supply, the quantity demanded and the quantity supplied, will be made equal.' *Principles*, p. 547.

9. Auspitz's and Lieben's *Mathematische Untersuchungen über die Theorie des Preises* (1889) and Launhardt's *Mathematische Begründung der Volkswirtschaftslehre* (1885) failed to make any significant impact. As is well known, the same is true of the development of equilibrium theory in the work of Gossen, which only applied itself to functional analysis and later became celebrated more as a forerunner of the 'psychological' school. As to the major works of Léon Walras and V. Pareto, the need has still not been felt for a translation into German!

10. *Recherches sur les principes mathématiques de la théorie des richesses* (1838), quoted here from the German translation (Jena, 1924), Preface, p. xxiii.

11. Ibid., p. 17.

12. Ibid., p. 18.
13. Ibid., p. 35.
14. Value, for Cournot, here denotes *exchange-value*.
15. Ibid., p. 35. The following key remarks are mostly to be found in ch. iv, 'On the Fundamental Law of Demand'.
16. Emphases added.
17. Emphases added. Notice the glaring contradiction with this on p. 43, where it is said that '*use of a commodity is always limited*, even on the assumption that it is *absolutely free*': that is, if the price is zero. Already Adam Smith argued: "The demand for food is limited by the capacity of a man's stomach.'
18. Emphases added.
19. Emphases added. Cf. p. 43: 'The law of demand may also change in the same time period, if the state passes through a sudden movement of progress or decline.'
20. Emphasis added.
21. Ibid., pp. 40, 43.
22. Cournot's use of his function F (*p*) to derive the price at which the aggregate exchange-value of annual turnover in the whole economy is at a maximum (ibid., p. 43) has not been considered here, because it does not involve any problem of modern price theory.
23. See especially the treatment given to it in F. Y. Edgeworth, 'The Pure Theory of Monopoly', *Papers Relating to Political Economy* (London, 1925), vol. 1, pp. 111ff. Cf. my investigation into the formation of monopoly price: 'Preis, Monopolpreis', *Handwörterbuch der Staatswissenschaften*, 4th edn, vol. 6, which comes to different conclusions from Cournot's in the case of partial monopolies.
24. Ch. ix, 'On Collaboration between Producers'.
25. I did not know of these remarks of Cournot's when I was working on my investigations into the imputation problem. See the articles 'Zurechnung' [translated in this volume as 'Imputation'] and 'Verteilung', in *Handwörterbuch der Staatswissenschaften*, 4th edn, vol. 8; and 'Die Wert- und Preisbildung der Produktionsmittel', *Economia Politica Contemporanea*, vol. 2 (Padua, 1930), pp. 1–51.
26. Ch. xi, 'On Social Income'. Emphases added.
27. Emphases added. This is opposed to *reciprocal and simultaneous* determination of the elements by one another.
28. See, for example, M. Schlick, *Allgemeine Erkenntnislehre*, 2nd edn (Berlin, 1925).
29. W. C. Mitchell is not wrong to speak of the 'protean problem of supply and demand'. *Business Cycles: The Problem and Its Setting* (National Bureau of Economic Research, Inc.: New York, 1927), p. 154.

30. This will be discussed more fully below, in the analysis of Pareto's price theory.

31. One can see the difference. For the mathematician and also for the phenomenologist, the form of the (statistically established) demand curve is also its 'law', and that 'law' changes from place to place and time to time. The non-phenomenologist would like to know more and asks what determines the course of the curve. If he is not brushed off with the reply that such a question is inadmissible, he must be content with the answer: statistics.

32. Thus, when it comes to the statistically produced demand figures which correspond to the various price levels for each commodity (as well as to the value of the currency), Cournot can incorporate them into his system only in the form of 'data'. But the whole evolution of the exact sciences – as Henri Poincaré has well shown in his *Science and Hypothesis* (London, 1905) – is increasingly tending to dissolve the quantities which have previously been taken as data or 'constants', breaking them up into relations of variable factors.

33. Nevertheless, such a system-determinant is present in the background, as a kind of gate-crasher, in Cournot's book: it is the good old, empty economic principle that 'everyone seeks to draw the greatest possible value [that is, for Cournot, exchange-value] from their property or from their labour'. This would only have any content if aggregate exchange-value – that is, the price and cost relations of all commodities – were already given. But in that case it would no longer need to be deduced.

34. As I have tried to show in my article 'Monopolpreis', *Handwörterbuch der Staatswissenschaften*, 4th edn.

35. Private economic adjustment to the goal of maximizing total exchange-value is applied by Cournot to the economy as a whole (see below the interesting parallels with Cassel in this respect). 'The construction of a table from which these values [i.e., the values of p for any commodity where the product of $p \cdot Fp$ is the maximum] could be read off, would be the most original work of the most thorough practical preparation to solve the questions touching upon the theory of wealth' (p. 44).

36. Ibid., p. 48.

37. Ibid., pp. 50–2.

38. Ibid., pp. 86ff.

39. Cournot thinks he can derive a univocal solution from the following equations. If D represents the turnover or output volume of the producer or producers of commodity $(a\ b)$, D_1 and D_2 the effective demand of these producers for raw materials a and b, then:

$$p = m_1 p_1 + m_2 p_2,$$
$$D = F(p) = F(m_1 p_1 + m_2 p_2),$$
$$D_1 = m_1 F(m_1 p_1 + m_2 p_2),$$
$$D_2 = m_2 F(m_1 p_1 + m_2 p_2).$$

And the values of p_1 and p_2 are determined by the two equations

$$\frac{(dp_1 D_1)}{dp_1} = 0; \frac{d(p_2 D_2)}{dp_2} = 0,$$

which express the condition of maximum return for each of the two monopolistic owners of the raw materials. Cournot also considers – this follows from the last two equations – that each of the two monopolists, *by varying his price independently of the other's*, can and will so change the quantity of his sales of raw materials that the mathematical sum of price plus sales at this price will be a maximum. But this assumption is completely unwarranted, indeed unempirical. If A were to reduce his price p_1, it is very unlikely that B would then simultaneously lower his price p_2 with the aim that p would fall, D increase and thereby D_1 and D_2 would grow again. It is much more likely that each of the two monopolistic owners of raw materials will say to himself: 'What use is it to me if I lower the price for my raw material? It wouldn't increase my sales and therefore my proceeds; the other monopolist's share of p would simply increase at my expense.' But then numerous 'unstable equilibria' are possible. The solution to the problem remains open.

40. Ibid., p. 80 and pp. 53–5, 74ff., 98, etc.
41. Vilfredo Pareto, *Manual of Political Economy*, trans. Anne S. Schwier, chapter iii (New York: Augustus M. Kelley, 1971), p. 162.
42. *Traité d'économie rationelle* (1927), pp. 204–5. ['In fact, supply will be constituted by the quantity given rather than offered, and demand will be constituted by the quantity received rather than demanded.' The full force of this quotation is, of course, lost in English, where the French *offre* corresponds to both 'supply' and 'offer'. *Trans. note.*]
43. Auguste Walras, *De la nature de la richesse et de l'origine de la valeur* (Paris, 1832), pp. 235, 237: 'Absolute demand...is the expression of all needs grouped together; it is presented at all times – tacitly one might say, but in no less tangible a manner – for all the scarce things which can contribute to human wellbeing, by all who are able to know and appreciate the enjoyments these procure – abstracting from the means they may have of procuring them. Similarly, I understand by the word *supply*, that general and absolute supply which, in

153

all times and for all countries, is nothing other than the expression of the quantity of scarce or limited goods at the disposal of men – abstracting from the means that some of them have of procuring them, and from the necessity for the greatest number to do without them... The difference between *absolute* demand and supply, on the one hand, and *real* [i.e., effective] demand and supply, on the other, is that real demand and supply can balance or exceed each other; but the same is not true of absolute demand and supply... Absolute supply is always lower than absolute demand; it can never be equal to it and still less higher.'

44. Cournot, op. cit., pp. 123–4.
45. Ibid., p. 4. See below on Cassel's close proximity to these ideas.
46. See the preface to the second edition, W. Stanley Jevons, *The Theory of Political Economy* (London, 1879).
47. 'The laws which we are about to trace out are to be conceived as theoretically true of the individual...but the laws of the aggregate depend of course upon the laws applying to individual cases.' Ibid., p. 52.
48. In the foreword to the second edition of his book, Jevons wrote of Gossen's work which he had not known when writing the first edition: 'From this statement it is quite apparent that Gossen has completely anticipated me as regards the general principles and method of the theory of Economics.' Ibid., p. xxxviii.
49. *Theory of Political Economy*, p. vii.
50. Ibid., p. xxxi.
51. Ibid., pp. 174ff.
52. Ibid., p. 179, in the course of counterposing his own theory to that of Ricardo.
53. Ibid., p. 179.
54. Ibid., p. 15. All objections of later writers to the to the notion that utility can be measured were here already anticipated by Jevons.
55. For example, p. 34, where algebraic sums and differences of pleasure and pain are set out.
56. 'The final degree of utility is that function upon which the Theory of Economy will be found to turn.' Ibid., p. 56.
57. Ibid., p. 55.
58. It can already be found in Gossen.
59. On this aspect, see my critical article: 'Eine neue Grundlegung der theoretischen National-Ökonomie', *Zeitschrift für Volkswirtschaft, Sozialpolitik und Verwaltung* (1911).
60. Mill, *Principles*, pp. 532–3.
61. Jevons, pp. 63–6.

62. Ibid.

63. Ibid., pp. 64–5. Emphases added.

64. Ibid., p. 65. Emphases added.

65. Ibid. Emphasis added.

66. Ibid., p. 66.

67. For example, Walras, Marshall and, later, Schumpeter.

68. The detailed statistical research of recent decades to ascertain the varying 'elasticity' of demand for different goods already constitutes a *de facto* refutation of the law of marginal utility level. The statistical regularities thereby obtained, by completely overturning the basic law, evidently do not only have the function of auxiliary laws in relation to it.

69. This is very clearly expressed in Enrico Barone: 'In the allocation of his income to various possible uses, the individual acts in such a way that the final unit of income (last disposable unit of money) which is put into the consumption of each particular commodity yields the same utility in all its uses. *Otherwise it would be advantageous for that individual to invest the relevant unit of income not in the consumption of the commodity with less utility for him, but in the consumption of another commodity with greater utility.' Principi di economia politica* (Rome, 1920), pp. 4–5.

70. To avoid burdening this account still more, we shall not go here into the controversial question of the smallest (infinitesimal?) unit of the various goods which can be taken as a basis for the construction of the curves. Suffice it to say that what matters in this respect is not the technical but the economic divisibility of goods, and that the smallest unit is therefore that whose use brings about a further noticeable increment of satisfaction for the individual.

71. Carl Menger and Wieser already recognized that 'all utilities are in essence complementary', although they did not investigate matters further, as those authors who operate with indifference lines and aggregate utility functions – such as Edgeworth, Irving Fisher, Pareto, Wicksell and most recently L. Schönfeld – have attempted to do.

72. It should hardly be necessary to point out, for the avoidance of any misunderstanding, that the above points do not only refer to the well-known and, since Gossen, continually observed *'dynamic'* phenomenon of the development of the system of wants through ever-changing higher (or more sophisticated) cultural or luxury wants – on the ground of the regular satisfaction of cruder wants – through evolution, habit, imitation, practice, etc., and hence the further shaping of the system of wants or the cultivation of the capacity for enjoyment. They also refer to the *static* regularity whereby the

155

immediacy of already-formed wants is determined through prior satisfaction of other kinds of wants, to which every individual is subject in
every period of consumption, regardless of the level of development of
his system of wants. A graphic example of this would be the case
where someone who is still tormented by feelings of thirst or hunger is
not able to take in the exquisite pleasures of art.

73. Only Wieser appears to have recognized this, when he occasionally
speaks of 'different points of tension' for different wants. Friedrich
von Wieser, *Social Economics*, translated by A. Ford Hinricks (London: George Allen & Unwin, 1928), pp. 29f.

74. Some aspects of the problem are dealt with in my 'Untersuchung über
das Grundgesetz der wirtschaftlichen Wertrechnung', *Zeitschrift für
Volkswirtschaft und Sozialpolitik* (1922), and my article 'Produktion'
in the *Handwörterbuch der Staatswissenschaften*, 4th edn.

75. In his *Cours d'économie politique*. [Mayer explains that *besoins* corresponds to *Bedürfnisse* 'in the narrow sense' (that is, objective
needs), and *goûts* to *Genüsse*, which has been translated elsewhere as
'pleasures' or 'gratifications' but would here suggest 'tastes' or 'pre-
dilections'. *Trans. note.*]

76. Here too Wieser's sensitive investigations are an exception in the
literature: 'For this value which we desire with the greater intensity is
by no means the one which we would "rather" have. Generally the
most keenly desired are all those which tend to preserve life. Those
which embellish it are usually placed lower on the scale.' *Social
Economy*, p. 33.

77. *The Theory of Political Economy*, p. 101.

78. Ibid., pp. 102–3. Emphases added.

79. Ibid., pp. 124–7.

80. Ibid., p. 125. Emphases added.

81. Ibid., p. 126.

82. Ibid., p. 126.

83. Ibid., 127–8.

84. Ibid., pp. 150–1.

85. See the discussions below of Walras and Pareto.

86. This is just what is involved in modern attempts to establish demand
curves by empirical means.

87. The fundamental difference from Cournot, who also expects all progress to come from statistics, is quite clear. For Jevons the statistical
understanding of utility curves is a concretization of his laws, whereas
for Cournot the basic demand function is already a curve obtained
through statistics.

88. Ibid., p. 118.

89. See ibid., pp. 146 and 213f. respectively.

90. Ibid., p. 99.

91. For it is a 'far more easy task to lay down the conditions under which trade is completed and interchange ceases, than to attempt to ascertain at what rate trade will go on when equilibrium is not attained.' Ibid., pp. 101–2.

92. Edgeworth, and above all Alfred Marshall, *Principles of Economics* (London, 1898), pp. 414ff., 795–6 and note xii have already drawn attention to the impermissibility of the assumption that the exchange ratio is constant.

93. 'The quantity of any article purchased is a function of the price at which it is purchased.' Ibid., p. 101. Hence a shift in the starting-point to Cournot's demand function! See also the remarks below on Cassel's theory of price.

94. It is not necessary to explain that precisely the same holds for every synchronizing account which seeks to derive from *already achieved kinetic equilibrium* (cyclical repetition of the same) the *process* which leads to the *formation of that equilibrium*.

95. See Eugen V. Böhm-Bawerk, *The Positive Theory of Capital*, trans. William Smart (London: Macmillan, 1891), book iv 'Price'.

96. Curiously enough, Jevons interpreted the theoretical indeterminacy of price in a two-sided exchange as merely the special case that one of the two goods was *indivisible*. *The Theory of Political Economy*, pp. 132–3.

97. Ibid., p. 180.

98. The analogy in theoretical physics would be the famous 'three-body problem'.

99. This is clearly shown, for example, in the earlier quotation according to which the ratio in which people divide their money or income in exchange for quantities of other goods 'will partly depend upon the ratio of exchange, partly on the final degree of utility of these commodities'.

100. Cf. the excellent ideas of E. Schams, who has grasped the problem of method in all its profundity, in 'Komparative Statik', *Zeitschrift für Nationalökonomie*, vol. 2 (1930), and 'Konstanz und Variabilität ökonomischer Größenbeziehungen', *Weltwirtschaftliches Archiv*, vol. 31 (1930).

101. See *Élements d'économie politique pure ou théorie de la richesse sociale* (Lausanne, 1874) [English translation by William Jaffé: *Elements of Pure Economics* (London: George Allen & Unwin, 1954)]; and the four memoranda, summarizing the *Elements*, of which the first was submitted to the Académie des sciences morales et politiques

in Paris in August 1873, and the other three to the Société Vaudoise des sciences naturelles in Lausanne in December 1875, January–February 1876 and July 1876 respectively. (*Elements*, p. 36.) All four were subsequently published in German translation as *Mathematische Theorie der Preisbestimmung der wirtschaftlichen Güter* (Stuttgart, 1881), and the extracts below have been translated into English from this edition.

102. See the interesting correspondence between Jevons and Walras, published in the four memoranda.
103. *Mathematische Theorie der Preisbestimmung*, p. 3.
104. Ibid., p. 5.
105. Ibid., p. 24. Emphases added.
106. Ibid., pp. 33ff.
107. Ibid., p. 38.
108. Ibid., p. 8.
109. Ibid., p. 12.
110. The translation of Walras's *Elements* has been followed in its rendering of *course de besoin* as 'want curve'. *Trans. note*.
111. [The English translator of the *Elements*, like Mayer, leaves the term *rareté* in the French. See the extensive translator's note in *Elements*, pp. 506–7.]
112. Ibid., p. 17.
113. Ibid., p. 10.
114. Ibid., p. 12.
115. Ibid., p. 14.
116. Ibid., p. 14.
117. Ibid., p. 15.
118. Ibid., pp. 15ff.
119. Emphases added.
120. Walras repeatedly and explicitly refers to this analogy. For example (pp. 23–4): 'In the same way that mechanics deals with motion and velocities, so does pure economics, as we have defined it, deal with exchange and prices...prices are the inverse ratios of the exchanged quantities of commodities; these magnitudes can be expressed numerically as well as being represented diagrammatically...it is thus legitimate to apply mathematics to pure economics, as much as to mechanics and astronomy; that is, to develop pure economics in the same way as mechanics and astronomy...and if this is allowed, it should be done.'
121. The fact that Walras himself points this out makes the confusion of the two problems in the course of the derivation appear all the more disconcerting: '*Rareté* is the *cause* of value in exchange. For value in

exchange is a *dependent* fact; *rareté* is an *independent* fact.' Ibid., p. 17.

122. As A. Amonn recently argues with particular emphasis in *Objekt und Grundbegriffe der theoretischen Nationalökonomie*, 2nd edn (1927).

123. Walras, p. 16.

124. Ibid., pp. 24ff.

125. Ibid., p. 26. Emphases added.

126. As we know, one fewer equation than commodities, because prices are actually expressed in one kind of commodity (A).

127. Emphases added.

128. They corresponds to Lesson 11 in the *Elements*: 'Problem of Exchange of Several Commodities for One Another', pp. 132–42.

129. Ibid., pp. 29–40.

130. Even this last phase is dealt with incompletely. For in the above case, it cannot be the end of the matter that the holder of A, who has first ascertained his marginal utility level for commodities A, B, C on the basis of existing prices, henceforth exchanges part of his C for B in accordance with his experience of the price of B in terms of C; rather, since the satisfaction level for B and C in comparison with A has changed for him, he must now again turn to the principle of maximum utility and exchange part of the newly acquired B for A. And since all other market participants do the same, all prices will be continually set in motion. These movements will diminish slowly but surely, until complete adjustment is finally reached – *and all this on the basis of initial prices that are somehow already given.*

131. The heading of section 5, p. 33.

132. Ibid., p. 37.

133. Milan 1906. [Mayer's discussion is based upon the French edition *Manuel d'économie politique*, 2nd edn (Geneva, 1927). He remarks that 'the price theory which Pareto earlier offered in the *Cours d'économie politique*, 2 vols (Lausanne, 1896 and 1897) is repeated in essentials by the system in the *Manuel*. Of Pareto's many important articles in the *Giornale degli Economisti*, see especially "Considerazioni sui principi fondamentali" (1892 and 1893).' This translation uses the English *Manual of Political Economy*, trans. Ann S. Schwier (New York, 1971), which also derives from the French edition of 1927.]

134. *Manual of Political Economy*, pp. 2–3.

135. Ibid., pp. 4–9.

136. Ibid., p. 103.

137. Ibid., p. 104.

138. Ibid., p. 106. Within the concept of *Bedürfnis* as it is used in

German theory, Pareto distinguishes between two different categories: *besoins* [wants or needs] – that is, *Bedürfnisse* in the narrow sense – and *goûts* [tastes], that is, desires for certain pleasures. In order to avoid misunderstanding, we shall retain Pareto's expressions in this account. [Since the range of *Bedürfnis* does not correspond to that of any single word in English, an analogous problem does not present itself in English translation of Pareto's work. This translator has thus simply followed the equivalents of *besoins* and *goûts* used in the English edition of the *Manual*, rather than quoting in French as Mayer mainly does. It should also be remembered, of course, that Mayer did not have a German edition available when he was writing the present essay. *Trans. note.*]

139. Ibid., pp. 108–9.
140. Ibid., p. 110.
141. 'If this quantity [of the good] is very small (infinitely small) and if the pleasure which it gives is *divided by the quantity itself*, we have elementary ophelimity.' Ibid., p. 112. That cannot be so easy to imagine: a psychological magnitude divided by a quantity of external objects! See also the fundamental article by P. N. Rosenstein-Rodan, 'Grenznutzen', *Handwörterbuch der Staatswissenschaften*, 4th edn.
142. Ibid., p. 112. Similar points had been made before by Auspitz and Lieben, Edgeworth and Fisher. Cf. the important and acute studies by J. Neubauer, 'Grenznutzen, Indifferenz, Elastizität und Durchschnittsnutzen', *Jahrbuch für Nationalökonomie und Statistik* (1930), and 'Die Gossenschen Gesetze', ibid. (1931).
143. Ibid., pp. 118ff. If x and y are the quantities of goods X and Y which the individual holds, then $f_1(x,y) = 0$ is the equation of an indifference line, from which a certain $y_1y_2y_3$ ensues for each $x_1x_2x_3$. See ibid., Appendix, p. 391.
144. Ibid., p. 119.
145. Ibid., p. 124.
146. Ibid., p. 125.
147. Ibid., p. 130.
148. Ibid., pp. 133–46.
149. Ibid., p. 137.
150. Ibid., pp. 152ff.
151. Carl Menger already came close to this idea when he sometimes said that prices are 'purely superficial phenomena', or links in an overall economic process which originates in human wants and the scarcity of goods and ends with the satisfaction of wants through the transformation or exchange of goods.

152. Ibid., p. 162.
153. Ibid., pp. 165ff.
154. Ibid., p. 168. Pareto calls the marginal utility level equations 'the cornerstone of mathematical economics' (*Enzyklopädie der mathematischen Wissenschaften*, vol. 1, p. 1105).
155. Ibid., pp. 165–6.
156. Ibid., p. 166.
157. See ch. iv, sects 10 and 11, pp. 183–4.
158. Ibid., pp. 167–8. The question of *production* lies outside the field of this essay, which is confined to the elements of price theory. But if we were to build it into the picture, the new *unknowns* would give rise to a further 'category D' of conditional equations, which would express the fact that for each commodity the production costs must equal the selling price (admittedly on the assumption of free competition); and a 'category E' which would imply that – like the quantitative constancy of the commodities in the exchange, expressed by category C – the quantities of the means of production which are used to produce the commodities (Pareto's 'transformed' commodities) must be equal to the *quantities* of those means of production contained in the products. In other words, *the starting quantity and the final quantity are the same in production*. It is true that the numerous auxiliary materials (e.g., coal) and quantities of labour used in production – just to mention the most obvious cases – no longer exist after the production process has been completed. But remarkably, this does not seem to have troubled Pareto when he was formulating the equations. Here we see a typical example of the unthinking transference of physical laws (law of the preservation of energy) to economic realities.
159. Ibid., p. 171.
160. The reproach is even directed at Walras, on the grounds that he too looked for causes of value in exchange.
161. Ibid., p. 180.
162. We cannot go here more closely into the development of the concept of indifference and indifference lines in the economic literature. Special attention should be given to: F. Y. Edgeworth, 'Mathematical Psychics' (London, 1881), pp. 1–28; 'On the Determinateness of Economic Equilibrium' (London, 1891), pp. 313–19; *Papers Relating to Political Economy*, 2 vols (London, 1925); and Irving Fisher, *Mathematical Investigations in the Theory of Value and Prices* (reprinted, 1925), p. 32. For further elaboration, see P. Boninsegni, 'I fondamenti dell'economia pura', *Giornale degli Economisti*, February, 1902, and M. Fanno's sophisticated study: 'Die Elastizität der

161

Nachfrage nach Ersatzgütern', *Zeitschrift für Nationalökonomie*, vol. 1 (1929), pp. 51–74.

163. Ibid., p. 118.

164. Ibid., p. 406.

165. See Furlan's article, 'Wirtschaftliches Gleichgewicht', *Handwörter-buch der Staatswissenschaften*, 4th edn, vol. 8.

166. 'The difference (from the earlier solution of the exchange problem on the basis of Walrasian equations) is that we then started from the measurement of satisfaction, whereas today the starting-point is *ex-perimental* results by which the wishes of individuals are revealed to us. The functions F_a, F_b (of the differential equation of the indiffer-ence curves) are purely *empirical facts* and theoretically have no-thing undetermined or doubtful.' *Enzyklopädie der mathematischen Wissenschaften*, vol. 1, p. 1110.

167. Ch. iii, sect. 65, 'Continuous variations and discontinuous varia-tions', pp. 122–3.

168. Yet another finesse, also recommended by Schumpeter, relies on the fact that the base magnitude is supposed to be chosen only very roughly. 'I set a value on a packet of cigarettes, and in relation to my total consumption per annum this is an infinitesimal magnitude.' But this example proves nothing: first, because the quantity demanded for a single, short period of consumption is counterposed to the total quantity demanded in an 'infinitely' large number of such periods (which is the basis for the infinitesimal in the example); and second, because here it is a question of the infinitesimal divisibility of *stocks of a good*, whereas the real problem at issue is whether it is permissi-ble to assume the infinitesimal divisibility of *units* of a good – and that is not even touched upon. In *this* matter one has to agree with Valk's views against those of Schumpeter. Cf. Willem Valk, 'Zur Frage der Grenzproduktivität', in *Schmollers Jahrbuch*, 51st year, no. 4 (1927), and Schumpeter's reply in the same issue.

169. Which Pareto also considers in connection with the *variability of production coefficients*.

170. Ibid., pp. 110–38, 181–209, and at many other points in the text, especially in the Appendix.

171. Ibid., p. 182.

172. Ibid., pp. 182–3.

173. Ibid.

174. Pareto's argument is as follows. One might try to consider the whole complementary group – for example, coffee, sugar, cup, spoon – as a 'composite' or 'notional' commodity. But then the difficulties would be still greater. For where would be the boundary of this 'notional

commodity'? Why not also include 'the table, the chair, the table cloth, the building in which all these things are located, and so on *ad infinitum*'? And anyway, this would multiply the number of goods because every possible combination of *real* goods would give us as many new 'notional commodities'. It is therefore better to choose the lesser evil and – abstracting from cases where the goods 'are so closely dependent on each other that it would be very difficult to consider them separately' – to treat complementary goods according to the preceding case (first variant of A_1), that is, to leave dependence out of account. Ibid., p. 184. Translation slightly modified.

175. Ibid., p. 184.
176. Ibid., p. 185.
177. Ibid., pp. 200–1.
178. Pareto himself most accurately expressed this awareness in one of his early essays: If one denotes the ophelimities of x_a, x_b... quantities of goods by $\phi_a(x_a)$, $\phi_b(x_b)$, and the total utility or ophelimity of an aggregate consumption of different goods by the function ϕ, then 'one can proceed from the consideration of ϕ to arrive...at ϕ_a, ϕ_b, or vice versa. The latter is the simplest path, because *one may be conscious of the pleasure which* $\phi_a dx_a$, $\phi_b dx_b$...*affords, but have no awareness of the total pleasure* ϕ.' 'Anwendungen der Mathematik auf die Nationalökonomie', in *Enzyklopädie der mathematischen Wissenschaften*, vol. 1 (Leipzig), pp. 1103f.
179. On the fundamental distinction between, on the one hand, the pure type of household (consumption) economy with its multiplicity of goals and, on the other hand, the economic enterprise with its homogeneous, unstructured overall goal (maximum net profit, for which all the various goods and means of production are interchangeable according to criteria of price and technical suitability), see my article 'Untersuchung zu dem Grundgesetz der wirtschaftlichen Wertrechnung', *Zeitschrift für Volkswirtschaft und Sozialpolitik*, New Series, vol. 2 (1922).
180. Op. cit. Cassel already presented his basic ideas in 1899, in the article 'Grundriß einer elementaren Preislehre', *Zeitschrift für die geschichtlichen Staatswissenschaften*. He also provides a concise summary in *Grundgedanken der theoretischen Ökonomie* (Leipzig, 1926).
181. On the actual assertions of these grounds for rejection or 'objection', see the outstanding article by P. N. Rosenstein-Rodan, 'Grenznutzen', *Handwörterbuch der Staatswissenchaften*, 4th edn.
182. Schumpeter's cleverly written attempt to make Walras's ideas, and the mathematical presentation of economic connections, easily

understandable to the German world of learning (*Wesen und Haupt-inhalt der theoretischen Nationalökonomie*, 1908) enjoyed a success which, though neither quick nor dramatic, was all the more lasting in certain restricted circles.

183. 'Cassels theoretische Sozialökonomik', *Schmollers Jahrbuch*, vol. 51.
184. Prof. A. Amonn, for example, is still sticking to his guns. See his *Objekt und Grundbegriffe der theoretischen Nationalökonomie*, 2nd edn (Vienna, 1927), and 'Der Stand der reinen Theorie', *Festgabe für Brentano*, vol. 2 (1924).
185. Emphasis added.
186. *The Theory of Social Economy*, pp. 73–5.
187. Emphases in the original.
188. Ibid., p. 75.
189. Ibid., p. 51.
190. Ibid., p. 50.
191. Ibid., pp. 50–1. Emphases added.
192. Ibid., p. 50.
193. Ibid., p. 52. Emphases added.
194. Ibid.
195. Ibid., pp. 8, 36, 65.
196. Ibid., pp. 49–50.
197. Ibid., p. 65.
198. Ibid., p. 76.
199. Ibid., emphases added.
200. Ibid., p. 81. Apart from the charge that it is driven by psychology, the theory of marginal utility is also accused of presenting 'a considerable distortion of reality', by assuming 'an abstract estimate, expressed in any scale of reckoning whatever, of the utility of the various stages of the satisfaction of wants in all its branches'. (Ibid., p. 82.) This, Cassel argues, is impossible for *homo oeconomicus*, who needs at least the support of existing prices for such valuations. We have already referred to the glaring contradiction between this claim and the procedure of Cassel himself who, in stating the essence of economy, starts from a hierarchy of wants and uses of goods according to their relative importance – which obviously presupposes a yardstick of comparison.
201. Ibid., p. 85.
202. Ibid., pp. 87–8. A highly characteristic assertion: 'For other means of production, prices must be calculated [by whom? by "society"?] according to their relative scarcity, so that the effective demand for each...shall be small enough to be met with the existing quantity of means of production.' Ibid., p. 89.

203. Ibid., p. 86.
204. Ibid., pp. 85–6.
205. Cf. W. Kromphardt's thoughtful book *Die Systemidee im Aufbau der Casselschen Theorie* (Leipzig, 1927), p. 14: 'By employing the economic principle as the channel of selection, Cassel opposes an imaginary, not a real, price cosmos to possible and conceivable price systems.'
206. Strangely contradicting this approach is Cassel's accurate remark: 'Methods cannot be arbitrarily chosen; they are essentially determined by the inner nature of the reality in question.' *Grundgedanken*, p. 11.
207. On the programme and development of such a 'metatheory' in Cassel, see Schumpeter, *Wesen und Inhalt*, pp. 83–4.
208. Ibid., p. 82.
209. Ibid., pp. 45, 85, 87. The price reckoned in money is described as 'the value dimension'.
210. It is hardly necessary to stress the misleading play on the words 'importance of wants' which is contained in Cassel's assertion that 'the amount of money that is offered for the satisfaction of various wants is the measure of the importance of those wants'. Ibid., p. 87. Apart from the fact that 'exchange economy' does not exist as a subject measuring and comparing the wants of individual economies according to their importance, and the fact that, even if such a guiding authority of the whole social economy were present as it is in planned economy, the measurement or comparison of the wants of *different* economic subjects would be impossible for lack of a common system of reference, such statements are quite devoid of scientific value. There are two possible ways in which Cassel might understand the words 'importance of a want'. *First*, they could refer to the strong sense of the concept, importance for the subject of the want – in which case it is wrong to claim that the importance of a want is measured by the sum of money offered for its satisfaction. For everyone knows, without first having to compare the needs of different individuals, that the price which a person in a worse income bracket can offer for the satisfaction of a stronger want is lower than that which a person in a better income bracket can offer for the satisfaction of a less urgent want. But *second*, if by 'importance of a want' in exchange economy Cassel means the purchasing power which stands behind a want, then it is all a quite improper use of words which yields nothing but a tautology: a want with greater purchasing power = a demand with greater purchasing power. It is not a step forward to abandon the result of scientific analysis – the

165

knowledge that effective demand is composed of two elements, urgency of want and purchasing power – in order to make possible a simplified but very incomplete account which only takes account of one element.

211. [That is, those which do not exist in abundance. *Trans. note.*]

212. Ibid., p. 89.

213. Ibid., pp. 89–91.

214. Ibid., pp. 97–8.

215. Emphases added.

216. Ibid., pp. 135–6.

217. Emphases added.

218. Ibid., pp. 137–8.

219. The quantities $a_1.....a1_r$ are necessary for the production of a unit of good 1, the quantities $a2_1.....a2_r$ for a unit of good 2.

220. Ibid., pp. 141–2.

221. Ibid., p. 142.

222. Ibid., pp. 143–4.

223. Ibid., p. 148.

224. Ibid., p. 152.

225. [The reference of this final quotation, which has no real equivalent in the English edition of Cassel's book, is given in the footnote as p. 134 of the German edition. *Trans. note.*]

226. Laplace's mechanical world-view, for example, was based upon the fiction of a world spirit who, knowing at any given moment the position of all the solid points in the universe as well as their provisional velocity, is in possession of an immense system of differential equations by which they are linked to accelerations, so that he is able to calculate with absolute precision all the events in the past and the future. Cassel goes even beyond this, insofar as in his system that all-knowing spirit *sets the norms* which determine the content of these differential equations.

227. The indeterminate content of equation (1) has also been pointed out by A. Amonn, 'Cassels System der theoretischen Nationalökonomie', *Archiv für Sozialwissenschaft und Sozialpolitik*, vol. 51; E. Schams, 'Die Casselschen Gleichungen und die mathematische Wirtschaftstheorie', *Jahrbuch für Nationalökonomie und Staatswissenschaft*, vol. 127; and J. Neubauer, 'Die Casselsche Preistheorie', *Zeitschrift für die geschichtliche Staatswissenchaft*, vol. 89.

228. There seems no other way of interpreting the propositions: 'When the prices of all goods are given, we may assume that all the factors which influence an individual in regulating his consumption are fixed', and 'If we keep strictly to the simple facts, we can only say that men decide what they will buy when all the prices are given...;

further than that, economic science need not concern itself with the question.' Ibid., pp., 76, 82.

229. See p. 57 above. A. Löwe clearly identifies the inevitable barrenness of attempts to replace nomological knowledge with statistical-empirical material, in 'Wie ist Konjunkturtheorie überhaupt möglich?', *Weltwirtschaftliches Archiv*, October, 1926. (See also A. A. Young, 'English Political Economy', *Economica*, March, 1928.) On our knowledge of natural events, see especially the fine lecture by the creator of quantum theory, Max Planck, *Dynamische und statistische Gesetzmäßigkeit* (Leipzig, 1914).

230. See p. 129 above.

231. After our earlier discussion, we need say no more here about the legitimacy and value of operations with infinitesimal changes. On the essential question of whether fictitious device can be used to obtain continuous relations through interpolation, see E. Lohr, *Atomistik und Kontinuitätslehre in der neuzeitlichen Physik* (1926), p. 60: 'Mathematical ordinal forms must and can be simply arranged only insofar as this is appropriate to the experience which is to be ordered.'

232. *The Theory of Social Economy*, p. 80.

233. 'All the unknown factors of the price-fixing process depend upon each other, and they are only determined, and then determined *together*, when we solve the problem of pricing.' 'The causal connection between the different variables is not a one-sided one', 'but is in the nature of a closed chain of causes, in which each link depends upon all the others.' Ibid., pp. 97–8.

234. The critical analysis does not even need to be repeated in the case of Cassel's derivation incorporating production. There the unknowns are the prices of the means of production; and the equation which is essential to ascertain them – analogous to equation (1) – contains as 'subjective' coefficients the demand for means of production formed in the same way, by already existing prices ('Now, however, we have the coefficients of the functions $F_1...F_n$ as functions of the prices of the means of production'. Ibid., p. 148.) For Cassel these coefficients, along with the given quantity of the means of production and the technical coefficients, are the ultimate determining factors, and are given as constants.

235. This will shortly be done in a more extensive demonstration, where we shall look at, among other things, the cognitive significance of the 'synchronization' implicit in all equilibrium theories; the fiction of the *equal mobility* of all economic elements; and the attempts to 'dynamize' equilibrium equations by introducing a *duration* variable or temporal *indices* and *coefficients* for the movement of particular

economic magnitudes, as in the fine recent efforts of H. L. Moore, H. Schultz and their numerous followers, to obtain the law of demand from broader statistical experience and thus to pass beyond the syllogistic character of static equilibrium theory to achieve formulae for *mobile equilibrium*.

236. Henri Poincaré, *Science and Hypothesis*, trans. by W. J. G. [?] (London: Walter Scott Publishing Co., 1905), p. 211.

237. In the language of the new mathematical physics: a *vector* (a 'directional magnitude' symbolized by an arrow) is replaced by a *scalar* (a non-directional magnitude which can only be indicated on a numerical scale).

Paul Rosenstein-Rodan, 'Marginal Utility' (1927), trans. *International Economic Papers* no. 10 (London: Macmillan, 1960).

Paul Rosenstein-Rodan (1902–85) was prominent during the 1920s among the younger Austrian economists close to Hans Mayer. Years later he expressed pleasure at having maintained 'very good relations' with Mises, despite ideological differences. He also records that he did what he could to 'mitigate the coolness' between Mises and Mayer. (See Margit von Mises, *My Years With Ludwig von Mises*, 2nd edn (Cedars Fall, Iowa: Center for Futures Education, 1984), p. 208.) Rosenstein-Rodan left Vienna for London in 1931, and was later to become a Harvard-based internationally celebrated leader in post-war development economics. Originally published in the 4th (1927) edition of *Handwörterbuch der Staatswissenschaften*, vol. iv, pp. 1190–213, (under the title 'Grenznutzen') this paper is an excellent expression of the state of Austrian economics in the 1920s.

17

Marginal Utility

PAUL ROSENSTEIN-RODAN

*Translated by**

WOLFGANG F. STOLPER

Introduction

The concept of marginal utility has proved to be the most fruitful explanatory instrument of economic theory. In order to understand the function of marginal utility it is necessary to go back to the facts of the perception and satisfaction of needs and to general economic calculation.

The following remarks are intended, therefore, to develop the laws according to which man manages his resources in order to satisfy his needs to the greatest possible extent by the use of scarce means, that is, means which are insufficient for the full attainment of his ends, or 'economic goods', as they are called. In pursuit of this aim man makes a choice as to how to allocate goods to his best advantage. The complex of considerations by which he weighs and judges the expediency of his allocations is known as economic calculation. This is the basis of pure economic theory, which, building upon its main concept of (marginal) utility, attempts to explain the course and the forms of economic conduct.

Part I. *The Theoretical Bases of Economic Calculations*

A. *The System of Needs* (*the Hierarchy of Needs*)

The prime reason and driving force of all man's economic actions are his needs – as Tiburtius says, 'desires born of the sensation or illusion of a disturbance of man's inner equilibrium and aiming at its maintenance or restoration'. If the economic subject is to provide for the satisfaction of his needs during a certain period (the economic period), *i.e.*, if he is to make an economic plan, he must be able to ascertain and evaluate his needs. This he will obviously do on the basis of his personal experience. The degree of accuracy with which he succeeds is irrelevant for economic theory, in so far as only those needs which a person thinks he will experience motivate his economic behaviour. If it turns out later that he has made a mistake in evaluating the intensity of his needs, he cannot annul his prior decisions; the error can merely add to his experience and so enable him to assess the strength of these particular needs more accurately in the future.

In order to gain a picture of his needs for any given period, the individual, synchronizing the experiences of several periods, must assess the intensity of his needs and arrange them in the order of their intensity. Now, it may seem as if an important psychological fact ruled out such an assessment of needs, for we know that at any one moment only needs of one intensity can be felt. Only one layer of needs of the same, or almost the same, intensity has real existence, and less urgent needs do not assume real existence until the more urgent ones are satisfied. Is it, then, nevertheless possible to assess at one moment the intensity of all needs, that is, needs of different intensity? It can easily be shown that this is quite possible. Difficulties would arise only if we had to deal with each moment's present needs. But in the process of assessment needs which have arisen at different times are remembered and can be synchronized by assuming that at any moment the most urgent stratum of needs has already been satisfied. We can then imagine the next layer of most urgent needs, and so on, through the whole hierarchy of intensities.

By reasoning and judging the consequences for his welfare of satisfying or not satisfying particular needs of varying intensity, the individual attributes different importance to his separate desires. The psychologically determined order of intensity of his needs leads him to establish an order of their importance.

Clearly, such reflections presuppose economic experience. Without experience no economic action is thinkable at all, and neither foresight nor evaluation of anticipated needs would be possible. In such an experienceless and therefore pre-economic state desires would be purely instinctive and would not lead to premeditated action but only to disconnected impulsive acts without reference to past or future. Only experience makes it possible to foresee needs; many instinctive desires are rationally appreciated and only then become motivations for economic action.

B. *Economic Utility*

The first conceptual step in economic calculation consists of an assessment of needs; it concerns only desires, without as yet any idea of what goods may be suited to satisfy them. There is no relation between the subjective need and objective means for its satisfaction. The notion of the ability of goods to satisfy needs is introduced only in the second phase of economic calculation. With this step the individual transfers the importance which he attributes to his needs to the means of satisfying them; to the degree of importance of each need there corresponds the degree of utility of the good capable of satisfying this need. The concept of utility therefore refers to the state of imagined satisfaction of needs and is the expression of a property attributed to a good, namely its effectiveness in fulfilling the purpose of satisfaction of wants. Since only expected anticipated needs are the motive force of economic action, only the expected and not the actually realized utilities are relevant to economic theory. Owing to economic experience the two will, however, not diverge significantly from each other.

The magnitude of the utility attributed to a good is determined, together with its use, by the allocation of goods in the overall plan; once an individual has established particular utilities, these become for him indices of the optimal allocation of goods. All economic action designed to maximize utility takes its cue from these indices.

1. *The evaluation of utility*

In order to reach the ultimate aim of economic action, the maximization of utility, and in order to ascertain the degree to which this aim is attained, utilities are evaluated by methods that differ according to the purpose. Various utility concepts correspond to these different methods. If we are interested in the utility of an individual good we use the concepts of direct or indirect utility depending on whether or not the good can be replaced (substitutability). For the utility of a stock of goods as a unit, we use the concept of total utility. These utilities indicate changes in an individual's total subjective welfare. Every actual evaluation of the utility of a good or a stock of goods implies an evaluation of subjective welfare. It is only through their relation to total subjective welfare that individual utilities are comparable with each other. The subjective welfare which makes individual utilities meaningful we call, with L. Schönfeld, total economic utility.

(a) *Total economic utility*. Every economic unit strives for the greatest overall utility, that is, greatest total economic utility. Mathematicians

173

represent total economic utility as a function of all goods owned by the economic unit (*e.g.*, Wicksell's total utility function).

The individual utility of a good is in the first instance expressed by the utility of the use to which the good is put. The choice of the use to make of any one good obviously depends on what other possible uses of it are already assured by other goods. Hence the individual utility of a good depends not only on its own quantity, but also on the amounts of all other goods which are at the disposal of the individual. To every particular individual utility of one good there correspond, at the same time, particular individual utilities of all other goods. It is necessary, therefore, to reduce all individual utilities to a common denominator, as it were: all of them must be related to a common superior concept which expresses their efficiency in terms of the ultimate economic purpose. The purpose of economic action is the attainment of the maximum subjective welfare possible in given circumstances. Total economic utility expresses the level of the individual's subjective welfare. This is the superior concept which permits us to consider the interrelatedness of all utilities.

(b) *Individual utilities.* (i) *Direct utility* is the concrete usefulness of a good in a particular application, it is the increment in welfare due to a particular manner of utilizing the good. In order to assess the direct utility of a good *a* we compare the total economic utility of all goods including good *a* with the total economic utility of the same goods in the same applications, but without good *a*: the difference is the direct utility of *a*.

This comparison of two total economic utilities which leads to the determination of direct utility corresponds to the most recent formulations of economic theory which demands 'operating with complete systems'. However, this approach cannot always go unqualified. Take O. Neurath's statement that 'strict reasoning shows that even in cases where an increment in pleasure is due to the addition of units, the result is a new total pleasure which is compared with the previous total pleasure'. In actual fact experience indicates that the opposite is true, that people always act according to the individual utility of goods without ever having to evaluate total economic utility directly. Nobody is even conscious of it; it is a datum of the past, and all that is needed is to determine individual utilities, *i.e.*, changes in total economic utility. Total economic utility does not have to be determined over and over again (see II A).

(ii) *Indirect utility* (which Böhm-Bawerk calls 'dependent utility') is the increment in welfare due to a change in the use of a good when the uses of other goods are appropriately modified. In order to assess the indirect utility of good *a* we compare the total economic utility of all goods including *a* with the total economic utility of the same goods in appropriately changed applications and without good *a*. The difference is the indirect utility of a. Unlike direct utility, indirect utility is determined on the basis of altered assumptions about the total utility of all goods without a, in that we assume that the uses of all these other goods are appropriately modified. The assumed absence of good a entails a certain loss of utility and the speculating mind redresses the situation by rearranging the uses of other goods so that this loss is diminished or indeed minimized. It is easily seen that the indirect utility of a good is identical with its marginal utility.

The three utility concepts discussed under (a) and (b) suffice to explain economic activity. They alone are the foundation of modern theory and its most recent results. However, economic literature uses a number of other utility concepts, the most important of which are as follows:

(c) *Weighted utility* (*ophélimité pondérée*), according to Pareto, is the utility of a good divided by its price. Since utility is a quality (intensity) and a subjective category, and price is a quantity (extensity) and an objective category (see I B 2), such a division, taken literally, is meaningless. Only if price were defined not as the quantity of the good in which prices are expressed, let us say money, but as its utility, only then could weighted utility acquire meaning as the result of comparing two individual utilities. So understood, weighted utility would be identical with the

(d) *Consumer's rent* (*Konsumertrag*), defined by Liefmann as the difference between two utilities ('pleasure and pain, utility and cost'). It is important to remember that such a 'utility yield' is not a primary psychological magnitude but the result of a comparison between two individual utilities (of the good and money in the above sense) and that this comparison does not enable us to determine the difference of the utilities, that is, the size of the utility yield, but only tells us whether one utility is larger or smaller than the other.

If, to go even further, weighted utility is to be expressed as the ratio of two utilities in terms of a common utility unit, we arrive at

(e) *Relative utility*, according to Liefmann and Engliš. This concept is based upon an entirely unempirical and untenable view: since utilities represent intensities, there can be no such thing as a utility unit, and a utility ratio is therefore even less possible than a utility difference.

(f) *Negative utility* (cost) – see II B.

(g) *Social utility* – see II G.

2. *The comparability of utilities* (*utility 'calculus'*)

Economic action is conditioned by individual utilities. If, as we have asserted, these utilities are to be indices for the best allocation of goods, they must be determined and ascertained in some manner. We shall have to show how this can be done.

A single concrete utility cannot be directly ascertained in isolation. Nor is this necessary in practice, because there is no occasion for evaluating utility unless the advantages or otherwise of a change in allocation of goods are under consideration. We compare two utilities, that after the change in allocation and that before it, and all we have to do is to decide whether one is larger or smaller than the other or whether they are equal. This is all that is needed for economic calculation. Measurement of utility is neither necessary nor possible. Utilities are not susceptible of exact quantitative measurement, because they are not homogeneous magnitudes and cannot be reduced to one unit. They are qualities (intensities) and not quantities (extensities). It may be possible to compare utilities within a wider context and to state that the difference between two utilities is larger or smaller than, or equal to, the difference between two other utilities ($U_1 - U_2 \gtreqless U_3 - U_4$), but here, too, it is not possible to state how much larger or smaller the utility difference is. We have only 'a sense of distance as regards the size of the divergence', as Wieser says in his *Theorie der gesellschaftlichen Wirtschaft*.

In the literature we can find three opinions about the utility calculus. (1) Utility is measurable: Gossen, Menger, Jevons, Walras, Edgeworth, Marshall, J. B. Clark, Launhardt, Böhm-Bawerk, Sax, Auspitz and Lieben, Pantaleoni, Bortkiewicz, Pareto until 1900, Wicksell, Ricci, Schumpeter, Birck, and others. (2) Utilities are neither measurable nor comparable: Marx, Lexis, Hilferding. (3) Utilities are not measurable but can be compared: Voigt, Komorzynski, Cassel, Pareto after 1900, Čuhel, Neurath, Wieser (to some extent), Bilimovich, Engländer, Hans Mayer, Schönfeld, and others, and among non-economists, Kant (*Critique of Practical Reason*), J. Bertrand, H. Poincaré, P. Painlevé, Bertrand Russell, L. Couturat, and others.

The evaluation of individual utility can be illustrated by an imaginary loss. Assume the loss of the good the utility of which is to be assessed, and ask yourself what loss is implied thereby (the difference between two utilities). This imaginary loss is, of course, merely an auxiliary notion to which no real process corresponds. In reality, people part with any good only against some requital and any 'loss of utility' is compared with the corresponding gain of utility. The notion of imaginary loss is always invoked in estimating both the good which is to be acquired and the good which is to be given in exchange, that is, always twice for any one ('internal' or 'effective') exchange (see II C).

3. *Utility scales (utility curves)*
If we arrange utilities in order of size, we get utility scales. Three types are commonly found:

(a) *the utility scale of unit quantities of one type of goods in one use* (class of needs);

(b) *the utility scale of unit quantities of one type of goods in several uses*. This is the most common utility scale and it suffices for economic theory;

(c) *the utility scale of unit quantities of one type or several types of goods applied to the same need class*. (About utility scales see also I B, 5 and 6b.)

Utility scales also furnish a classificatory principle for goods, in that we can distinguish between (i) goods which can satisfy only one class of needs, corresponding to utility scale (a), and (ii) goods which can satisfy one or more classes of needs, corresponding to utility scale (b). This psychological classification principle for goods is the counterpart of the technical principle which classifies goods according to their production affinity. We could here speak of affinity by needs (or purposes).

4. *The complementarity of utilities*

The recognition of the complementarity of utilities is one of the most important insights of modern theory. Careful analysis of the system of needs does indeed show a far-reaching, though not everywhere equally close, interdependence among the various needs.

The satisfaction of one need may be the precondition for the emergence of another ('tied needs'), or it may increase or diminish the intensity of another ('complementary' and 'supplementary' needs in Pareto's terminology).

The interrelation and interdependence of needs give rise to a complementarity of the utilities of goods. This psychological complementarity is conditioned exclusively by the pattern of needs and is not to be confused with technical complementarity, which means that certain goods can only jointly serve for the satisfaction of needs.

The psychological complementarity of goods means that the manner in which each good is employed depends upon the employment of all other goods available to the economic subject. It follows that, if the mutual dependence of needs is to be taken into account, the uses of all goods must be decided upon simultaneously. Since the disposable amounts of all the various goods determine the manner of their employment, *i.e.*, which needs will and which will not be satisfied, the utility of any particular good depends not only upon its own disposable quantity, but also on the disposable quantities of all other goods.

Because utilities are complementary, individual utility scales can convey a correct picture only if we think of them as referring to the same time span, that is, as simultaneous components of the system of needs. Otherwise they would rest on different and mutually contradictory assumptions and would be meaningless for an unequivocal determination of economic action.

177

Mathematical economics has taken account of this complementarity of utility by the introduction of so-called indifference curves (Edgeworth, I. Fisher, Pareto) in the place of isolated utility curves (see also I B 6). Complementarity is the reason for the interdependence of all economic phenomena, with the exposition of which modern economic theory has, for the first time, not only asserted but also explained and proved the economy's organic interdependence and unity.

5. *Gossen's law*

If the term 'need' is used in the sense of a whole class of needs, it can be seen that every 'need' so understood is composed of a larger or smaller number of partial needs (need impulses) of varying intensity, and that it can therefore be satisfied to a greater or lesser extent, depending on the amount of disposable means of satisfaction. We speak of the divisibility of needs (need classes). We know from experience that the great majority of needs is divisible, regardless of whether a given amount of goods is applied to their satisfaction successively or all at once.

Suppose, now, that among the whole range of possible applications we choose to satisfy the needs of one class by the application of goods in successive units. We arrive at the rule that within each need period every succeeding phase of satisfaction yields a smaller increment in welfare – so that every succeeding unit of goods has a smaller utility than its predecessor – until the addition of yet one more unit results in no increase in welfare at all, *i.e.*, until satiety is reached. This rule was formulated by H. H. Gossen in 1854 in the theorem known as Gossen's first law: 'The amount of satisfaction derived from consumption decreases with each additional unit of the same commodity, until it reaches zero or the point of satiety.' This formulation was improved by Wieser in 1889 by limiting the validity of the law to a particular time section of needs, or need period. In his *Theorie der gesellschaftlichen Wirtschaft*, 1914, Wieser gave it the following definitive formulation: 'With every divisible need, the satisfaction derived in one need period from the first unit is desired with the greatest intensity; every application of succeeding units of the same kind is desired with decreasing intensity until the point of satiety is reached. Beyond this point desire turns into revulsion.' In this form the law is known in the literature as 'the law of the satisfaction of wants', or Gossen's law of satiety. It is one of the most fruitful and most important results of modern economic theory and explains why the utility deriving from a good decreases in relation to the size of the stock of the good ('law of diminishing utility').

In this formulation, Gossen's law is valid only within one need period. The economic plan, on the other hand, is always made for a period which includes several need periods. For purposes of economic calculus, Gossen's law must therefore be reformulated in such a manner that it encompasses several need periods; its validity must be extended to cover a longer period. Hans Mayer was the first to introduce the time factor with his 'law of the periodic recurrence of needs'.[1] When making his economic plan, *i.e.*, when choosing the most suitable allocations, the economic subject must indeed consider several or many need periods and evaluate the importance of his needs over a longer span of time (see I A). Even needs of one kind are then not arranged in the order of their successive emergence, but in the order of their importance. Periodically recurring needs of the same intensity are regarded as equal for all the need periods making up the economic period. Every degree of importance therefore appears several times in utility scales which encompass a longer time span, so that these scales show a series of need layers of diminishing importance.

If we now go through the range of possible applications of goods within this longer period, which alone corresponds to the empirical conditions of the economy, in such a manner that the amount of goods used to satisfy the needs of a particular class is successively increased by one unit, we again find the rule that every succeeding phase of satisfaction yields a smaller or equal increment in welfare – so that every successive unit of a good has the same utility as, or a smaller utility than, its predecessor until satiety is reached. When the stock of goods is increased by equal amounts, the utilities now decline in layers and the utility derived from a unit in the last, smallest layer of needs (that is, the smallest utility or one of the smallest) is the marginal utility.

In a very similar manner L. Schönfeld extended Gossen's law in 1924 for the purpose of its incorporation into general economic calculation; in its expanded form he called it the 'law of partial utility orders'.

Gossen's law was often criticized in the early days, mainly in an attempt to restrict its validity, but the critics frequently overlooked the fact that it applies only to one need period at a time. The best known criticism is that of A. Graziadei (1901). Like Umberto Ricci later (1905), Graziadei precisely analysed the shape of the utility curve[2] in the case of continuous satisfaction of needs of the same need class, and noted that the utility curve at first rises somewhat, reaches a maximum and declines only thereafter. Since goods are available only in limited quantities, Graziadei concluded that it is precisely the rising branch of the utility curve which is relevant for economic action, and that, in its only practically relevant part, the utility scale showed increasing rather than decreasing degrees of utility. On this issue it should be pointed out that the possibility of an initially rising utility curve had indeed been noted already by Pantaleoni (1889) and Böhm-Bawerk, and later also by professional psychologists such as O. Kraus, J. Kreibig, F. Čuhel, and others, but this did not prevent them from accepting Gossen's law as valid. In point of fact, the rising branch of the utility curve is usually constructed by assuming that any particular need class is initially satisfied by infinitely small units of goods, in which case, of course, the corresponding utility increments would also be infinitely small. (Neither assumption is exact, since in economic reality there are no indefinitely small utility increments; for technical as well as for psychological reasons all utility increments are finite.) If subsequently the amount of goods is increased enough to yield a noticeable utility increment, the utility curve rises suddenly. But if one proceeds correctly, *i.e.*, if one starts not with the technically smallest unit of a good, but with that unit which yields the first noticeable utility increment, and if the analysis does not extend beyond one need period, Gossen's law can be verified almost without exception, and indeed, if 'tied wants' are strictly considered, always. Even if sometimes the utility curve should rise initially it must be emphasized in opposition to Graziadei that this is irrelevant for empirical economic conduct, since this phenomenon concerns only a few of the upper ranges of the utility scale, which are in any case assured by a very few goods and which, as part of the basic wants, generally remain unchanged, while most of the considerations concern the lower ranges of needs. In practice it is even in that case the falling branch of the utility curve which is relevant for economic action. Most recently O. Spann has taken up this out-of-date criticism of Gossen's law, but because of his methodologically inadmissible changes in the assumptions (emergence of new needs) his objections are completely beside the point and have no relevance at all to Gossen's law.

6. *Formal and substantive laws of the structure of utility*

The subjective state of welfare or the total economic utility which man tries to achieve by his economic action is determined in a purely formal manner in modern economic theory. It encompasses everything that man desires – though obviously only to the extent that economic goods are involved in the satisfaction – regardless of whether he desires it for egotistical or altruistic, ethical or unethical motives, and of whether his needs are 'real' or only 'imagined' needs. Modern economic theory does not rest upon the concept of *homo oeconomicus* acting exclusively on the motive of 'egotistical pleasure' (the term pleasure being used here in a rather narrow sense), not even when he explicitly forms part of the assumptions, as is the case of the theorists of the Lausanne school; in actual fact all modern economists refuse to discuss the purpose of human action.

Precise observation of reality does, nevertheless, enable us to transcend merely formal definitions and to arrive at a few statements of substance concerning the nature and relationships of needs, it being understood, of course, that form and substance are not thought of as contradictory but as different degrees of increasing concreteness. These substantive statements constitute the structural laws of utility and have led to extraordinarily valuable progress in economic theory. The most important of them are as follows.

(a) *The divisibility of needs* (see I B 5), that is, the proposition that needs can be satisfied partially. This was first discovered by Gossen in 1854, and later independently and simultaneously by C. Menger and W. S. Jevons, both in 1871, L. Walras in 1874, and apparently again independently by J. B. Clark in 1881.

(b) *The discontinuity of utility scales*, that is, the proposition that utility scales are not continuous and do not contain all degrees of intensity. The protagonists of this view include Böhm-Bawerk, Wieser, Sax, Pantaleoni, Hobson, Fetter, Oswalt, Rist, Hans Mayer, Bilimovich, Verrijn Stuart, Engländer, Schönfeld, and others.

(c) *The complementarity of utilities* (see I B 4), that is, the proposition of the interdependence of individual utilities. This was upheld by Edgeworth (1881), I. Fisher (1892), Voigt (1892), Komorzynski (1893), Pareto and the Lausanne school, and also by Schumpeter, Bilimovich, Wieser (to some extent), Engländer, Hans Mayer, Schönfeld, and others.

(d) *The non-measurability of utility* (see I B 2), that is, the proposition that utilities are not measurable quantities, but intensity magnitudes. This was maintained by Voigt, Komorzynski, Cassel, Wieser (to some extent), Pareto after 1900, Čuhel, O. Kraus, Kreibig, Furlan, Fetter, Oswalt, Neurath, Bilimovich, F. X. Weiss, Mises, Amoroso, Engländer, Hans Mayer and Schönfeld.

(e) *The polynomial nature of need grades*, that is, the proposition that in the order of needs there appear as a rule several similar or different needs of equal importance. This was mentioned by Engländer, Hans Mayer and Schönfeld.

(f) *The alternativeness (counterbalancing) of needs*, that is, the proposition that certain needs arise in the system of needs as alternatives to others, so that with the satisfaction of one particular need certain others disappear. The most frequent case is that of several low-ranking needs together forming or counterbalancing one higher-ranking need, so that the lower rank of needs appears only when the counterbalancing higher-ranking need is not satisfied. Counterbalancing needs are discussed by Engländer.

(g) *The relative constancy of needs*, that is, the proposition that the majority of needs remains unchanged and that within any given period only a relatively small part of needs changes. This was stressed by Hans Mayer.[3]

181

(h) *The periodicity of needs and the time factor*, that is, the proposition that the majority of needs recurs periodically and that the unique determination of economic action demands consideration of the time factor. This was noted by Voigt, Komorzynski, Marshall, Wieser, Oswalt (emphatically), Pareto, Amoroso and Schönfeld, and consistently and systematically discussed by Hans Mayer.[4]

C. *Total Economic Allocation*

An economic plan aims at the selection of the most suitable allocation of goods. Since the allocations of all goods are closely linked by the latters' psychological and technical complementarity, the process of selection must be unitary and systematic. The entire set of allocations which appear expedient in any given economic situation is the total economic allocation.

In reality the economic subject always starts out with the economic considerations and decisions of the past, which relieve him of the necessity to think through the situation anew every time. However, reliance on the economic considerations of the past logically presupposes the assumption that the total allocation has once been determined for the first time, when all considerations had to be thought through *ab ovo* and without the help of past allocations. We must, therefore, trace the logical scheme of such a 'first' total allocation, without implying at all that it has in reality ever been established in this form by any economic subject (see II A). It will be convenient to treat the allocation of consumer goods and of producer goods separately.

1. *The determination of the overall consumption combination*

Consumption goods must be assigned to their appropriate uses *i.e.*, their employment has to be determined. The genesis of the final allocation could be described as the successive assignment of goods to the satisfaction of needs of the highest order (= greatest importance), then of the next highest and so forth, until the stock of goods is exhausted. If two or more kinds of goods are equally suitable for satisfying one need, the possibilities of satisfying the needs of the next order are considered, and the first need is assigned that good which in another use would yield the smallest utility, *i.e.*, that good which, if used for the first need, would leave unsatisfied another need of the relatively lowest rank. Reflections of this kind imply the consideration of combinations of possible uses, the simplest type of which may here be mentioned.

Suppose an economic subject has three goods, a_1, a_2, a_3, of the same kind, which can be used in two ways, I and II. There are four combinations:

182

(1)	I	—			II	a_1	a_2	a_3
(2)	I	a_1			II	a_2	a_3	
(3)	I	a_1	a_2		II	a_3		
(4)	I	a_1	a_2	a_3	II	—		

The formulation of the total allocation plan can be theoretically developed by assuming that each combination is successively examined for the individual utilities of all goods in all uses, preference always being given to the greater utility, *i.e.*, that which creates the greatest increment in total economic utility. In this manner one arrives at an overall combination such that no change in allocation can increase total economic utility.

In reality, these combinations are not all considered simultaneously. The majority is taken over unchanged from the past and only a fraction is thought through anew.

2. *The determination of the overall production combination*

Producer goods must be allocated to their most efficient uses, *i.e.*, their employment has to be determined. A given stock of producer goods, or goods of higher order, is capable of yielding varying quantities and kinds of consumer goods, or goods of the first order, depending on the known technical data and in particular on the variability of the technical coefficients. A quantitative limitation is of course given by the disposable amount of producers goods. The economic subject therefore has the choice among different combinations of consumer goods, and he will aim at choosing that combination which yields the highest total economic utility. While the determination of the total consumption combination involves a direct assignment of goods to their most profitable uses, the transformation of a given stock of producer goods into consumer goods is preceded by a choice among different combinations of consumer goods, that combination being selected which, by virtue of its judicious allocation, yields the highest total economic utility. The allocation of producer goods therefore presupposes the allocation of consumer goods. The first step is to see what combinations of consumer goods could be produced with the given stock of producer goods. Then goods are allocated within each of these combinations, that is, their total economic utility is established. Finally that combination of goods is chosen which yields the highest total economic utility.

Here, too, not all the combinations are considered simultaneously, but experience of the past enables the most efficient combination to be determined by an abbreviated procedure.[5]

3. *The time factor in economic calculation (the economic period)*

The kind, number, importance and capacity of an individual's needs, the given stock of goods of all kinds, and the technical and psychological relationships known from experience are the determinants of his optimal total economic allocation. To every system of needs, given for a particular period, and to every given stock of goods at the disposal of an economic subject, there corresponds a uniquely determined total set of economic actions. During a given period certain needs are given and certain goods are available; during a longer or shorter period, more or less needs and goods are given. Every change in the period to which the plan is to apply (the economic period) entails a change in the optimal total allocation. Hence the plan period, *i.e.*, the period for which the satisfaction of currently emerging needs is to be systematically planned, must also be uniquely determined. The economic period must be determined if the economic calculus is to lead to a uniquely determined result.

The determinants of the length of the economic period which underlies the economic calculus are both of a technical ('objective') and of a psychological ('subjective') nature. They can only be briefly mentioned here. To some extent, the limits of the period are determined by the mere fact that some goods become available at discrete intervals governed by the laws of nature – crops which are the basic food supply, and the raw materials needed for the production of most consumer goods. However, this delimitation is incomplete, since goods which are available at such technically conditioned intervals are only one part of the total supply of all kinds of goods, and since these time intervals themselves can within certain limits be lengthened or shortened by economic action. In the market economy, the counterpart of the discontinuous supply of goods is the discontinuous supply of money incomes, which may well be connected with the naturally conditioned discontinuity of the increases in the supply of goods. Furthermore, the technical laws of production determine the minimum length of time required to produce certain consumer goods from the available producer goods. Thus we have an objective determination of the minimum length of the economic period. Its psychological determinants are the 'horizon, imagination and strength of mind of individuals', as Hans Mayer says. If we could say for how long ahead individuals assess their needs, this would be a substantive statement about the system of needs and as such, like the other structural laws of utility (I B 6), of the greatest importance. Careful analysis of the system of needs shows that as a rule the most important needs are assessed for the longest period, and less important ones for shorter periods. A certain complex of very important needs is considered *en bloc* for the longest period (lifetime or even longer). This is the reason why people strive to maintain intact from one economic period to the next the stock of producer goods from which a great variety of products can be made. A detailed investigation of household budgets would no doubt produce valuable material for the explanation of the time factor. But it is no explanation merely to distinguish three types of economies, with growing, stable and declining supply.

The role of time in evaluating 'present' and 'future' goods is only part of the economic problem of time, which, as Marshall and Edgeworth emphasized long ago in another context, is probably the most difficult of all economic problems.

Part II. *Marginal Utility and Economic Calculus*

A. *The Function of Marginal Utility in the Economy*

Once all goods are allocated to optimal use, their marginal applications, or marginal utilities, in a given economy can be determined. It follows that the marginal utility of any good is the result of total economic allocation, which in turn is not a *uno actu* creation but the outcome of an historical development. But once the marginal utilities of goods in an economy are established, they become indispensable starting points for such further economic allocations as a changed situation may require and all subsequent economic considerations are based upon them. Their function is to provide a link with the existing economic situation and its marginal results and so to obviate the enormous task of recreating a new system of overall allocations every time an economically relevant change occurs.

In empirical reality it hardly ever happens that an individual is forced to make his economic plan from scratch. he does not suddenly assume economic behaviour after a pre-economic period, but he always acts according to economic experience. He always starts out with his present stock of goods and the uses which experience has shown to be best. Many of the past's economic data, and in particular the bulk of needs and of productive resources, remain the same throughout the course of successive economic periods, and only a fraction of the data changes, though always a different one. It follows that the bulk of optimal allocations also remains unchanged and new allocations have to be made only to take care of those conditions which have changed. In these circumstances the individual does not, as a rule, have to determine the whole set of his economic actions anew. He does not need to worry about the formation of his total allocation plan, but only about the changes therein.

It might be supposed that because of psychological complementarity even a relatively small change in the economic data would necessitate a complete revision of the whole economic plan. If all allocations are interdependent in the sense that each use of one good is conditioned by quite

185

specific uses of other goods, then one single change in utilization is bound to entail a great number of other changes in utilization. In theory, the whole chain of individual utility comparisons would then have to be repeated. In practice, however, certain empirical facts enable anyone possessed of economic experience to omit most of the individual utility comparisons and to employ an abbreviated procedure which yields the same result, namely the determination of the most expedient changes in the existing total economic allocation. Notwithstanding its limitation to only a few specific utility comparisons, this abbreviated and simplified procedure is neither incomplete not approximate, but is complete and establishes the correct result with precision. The reason why this short-cut is possible is that certain psychological principles yield premises for conclusions which obviate the necessity of very many utility comparisons because these latter are implicitly included in the few specific ones which are performed. In the remaining comparisons marginal utility plays the dominant part. Before we explain this function of marginal utility more precisely we must, however, briefly discuss the empirical facts which permit an abbreviation of the allocation procedure.

Like all economic determinants they are of a technical and psychological nature. Careful observation shows that during an economic period the majority of needs, and particularly those of a higher order, *i.e.*, the more important needs, usually remain constant, so that most changes concern only wants of a lower order, the marginal layers. This relative constancy of needs is explained by the mere fact that certain needs, particularly those of a physiological nature, always remain more or less the same and always occupy the highest ranks. Barring sudden and large economic disturbances, the supply of productive resources is, in its turn, even and continuous, *i.e.*, it does not change very much from one economic period to another and thus assures the satisfaction of most existing needs. This is another reason why new decisions (changes in allocation) generally have to be made only with respect to marginal uses. Furthermore, it so happens that the complementarity of utilities is very weak in these marginal layers and its effect the smaller for being concerned with the smallest utilities. Hence a change in marginal uses will frequently have no further repercussions, and at the margin direct and indirect utility are usually equal.

The marginal layers of needs are also the most extensive and, by virtue of their diversification, they absorb relatively many uses of goods. Hence even changes in a comparatively large part of the data need not require reallocations which transcend the marginal layers. There is, thus, a fairly wide area within which the abbreviated procedure can be applied and, so long as the allocation changes do not go beyond the marginal layers, the static method[6] is in order. In this sense statics encompasses not only a strictly stationary economy but also one which changes gradually.

For all these reasons and in these conditions, the marginal utilities remembered from the past suffice for the determination of the most expedient choice of new uses (change in allocation). The utilities of the new uses which are contemplated are compared with past marginal utilities in these uses; if they are larger, the new ones are expedient, if smaller, the new ones are not expedient. The marginal utility in different need classes (kinds of uses) thus fulfils a watch-dog function with respect to consumption and, as Wieser says in his *Theorie der gesellschaftlichen Wirtschaft*, makes possible a great 'simplification in the evaluation of the economic means used to satisfy needs of a certain magnitude. The entire surplus utility of needs beyond marginal utility is neglected; it is not necessary to establish in each case the full value, which it is so difficult to do, but only to determine the marginal value . . .' This is how, under the assumptions mentioned, the evaluation of marginal utility renders possible that abbreviated economic calculus which is used in practice and fulfils within the framework of the economic calculus an abbreviating function[7] without which there simply could be no rational economic conduct at all, since nobody could possibly have a complete picture of the whole range of data.

It remains to state the psychological reason why individuals remember marginal utility in all need classes while neglecting all other individual utilities, all intra-marginal differences. This is due to a well-known peculiarity of human nature. Man easily forgets experiences which encounter no obstacles, but is deeply impressed by those which meet with strong obstacles. An event is all the more vividly remembered for the frictions and difficulties which attend it. Now, the satisfaction of needs proceeds smoothly as long as the stock of goods is not exhausted, and since, of course, the most important needs are satisfied first, no particular difficulties are encountered. But when the limits of the stock of goods are approached, that is, when it is the turn of marginal needs, then obstacles appear, and the satisfaction of marginal needs has to be broken off. Therefore marginal utilities become apparent in circumstances which are apt to make a particularly deep impression on people.

Economic calculus as found in practice naturally presupposes economic experience. Modern economic theory, which sets out to explain empirical economic life, therefore must 'fully explore the content of common economic experience and interpret it scientifically', as Wieser says in *Theorie der gesellschaftlichen Wirtschaft*. It would, however, be methodologically inadmissible to consider economic experience as the final explanation of economic action, since experience concerning the utility of goods itself presupposes those self-made laws of utility which are to be explained.

Economic experience is merely an epistemological instrument for arriving at the final explanation of economic action, and not the final explanation itself. If we are to avoid circular reasoning, we must therefore first describe economic action as if man were without experience, and so explain the formation of that experience which in practice permits man to take for granted all those interrelationships which, in theoretical deduction, appear as the 'logical completion of the economic subject's actual train of thoughts'.[8]

B. *Marginal Utility and Cost (Wieser's Law)*

The scarcity of goods precludes the satisfaction of all needs and the application of a good to one use precludes its use in another manner. It follows that the decision to realize some particular utility always implies forgoing the realization of another. The utility of the uses which are forgone must therefore always be evaluated precisely, lest a smaller utility be realized at the expense of a larger one. This would miss the whole purpose of economic action, namely the maximization of total economic utility. By taking account of all utilities and by always preferring the larger to the smaller (see I C 1 and 2), the larger is assured at the cost of the smaller. *'Cost' is therefore nothing but the utility of uses which cannot be realized; cost is forgone or, as it were, 'negative' utility.* Valuation according to cost means to compare the utility of a good in one use with its utility in alternative uses, and so provides a full picture of the whole set of possible utilities and a key to correct choice among them.

If utility is to determine all economic decisions, *i.e.*, not only the plans of households but also the general economic plan, which includes the production plan, then it must be shown that all economic goods including producer goods are allocated according to their utility valuations. A good is assigned utility in accordance with the need it satisfies. But needs are directly satisfied only by consumer goods; producer goods satisfy only indirectly through their products. Hence producer goods derive their utility from the consumer goods which they produce. Their 'utility' is not original but derived.

Since a producer good produces a final good only in particular combinations with others (technical complementarity), it is in the first instance only the entire productive group which acquires the utility of its products. How this utility is split up among the individual means of production forming the group is shown by the theory of imputation, to which we must refer.[9]

We have seen that knowledge of individual utilities is essential for a choice among all the possible uses even of consumer goods. In the case of producer goods, which can be employed in many, and sometimes very many, ways, it is more necessary than ever to weigh all the possible utilities carefully so as to maximize total economic utility. It follows that all derived utilities of producer goods must also be evaluated and compared. Every kind of producer good enters into the production of many kinds of consumer goods which, because of their common origin, have a 'production affinity'. A few (primary) means of production yield, through many processes of transformation, all the different consumer goods. It would, of course, be completely impossible to get a simultaneous comprehensive picture of the enormous number of possible combinations of means of production and to evaluate them. A single-valued utilization of producer goods would be impossible if we could not, in their case too, use an abbreviated procedure based on the experience of past allocations, the same short-cut which is the very essence of the function of marginal utility. Indeed, the 'abbreviating' principle of marginal utility applies also to the means of production where it finds its most important application.[10] The overall production combination of the past determines the allocation of producer goods and with it the marginal utilization of each class of producer goods, that is, the production of its least important product, the marginal product. The use of producer goods is determined by the marginal utility of the marginal product, that is, the utility of the least important consumer good that can be made from each unit of each class of producer goods.

Once the marginal utility of every class of producer goods is known, the relative constancy of economic data makes it unnecessary to think through anew all possible combinations whenever the existing data change. It is quite sufficient to compare the utility of the contemplated new use of the producer good with the marginal utility of its class and then to put the good to the new use or not according as its utility is larger or smaller than this marginal utility. The valuation of the marginal utilities of producer goods gives us a completely sufficient means of achieving optimal production results.

Given the relative constancy of the existing stock of means of production characteristic of a smoothly running economy, any consumer good produced from a particular class of producer goods can be replaced at the cost of the marginal product of this class of producer goods. Hence the utility of any consumer good is valued according to the marginal utility of the marginal product of the relevant class of producer goods, *i.e.*, according to its cost of production. The law of cost in this sense was first formulated by Friedrich von Wieser in 1884. Pantaleoni suggested calling it Wieser's law.

Valuation according to cost of production means to compare the utility of a producer good in one use with its utility in alternative uses and so provides, by an abbreviated and simplified procedure, a full picture of the whole set of possible utilities and a key to the achievement of maximum total economic utility by a correct choice among them. The extension of the principle of marginal utility to producer goods, that is, valuation according to cost of production, is a further abbreviation and simplification of the economic calculus already abbreviated by marginal utility valuation of consumer goods.

The proposition that cost is nothing but unrealized utility, the magnitude of which is determined by the general laws of economic utility, brings to light the organic connection of all the economic actions of an economic unit. The principle of marginal utility has proved itself a unitary principle of explanation.

Cost is either the (forgone) utility of the next best use given up in favour of the better ('opportunity cost' according to D. J. Green) or the pain of work entailed by some use ('pain cost' according to D. J. Green). Since the pain of work can be understood also as 'utility of leisure' (see below), 'pain cost' is the forgone utility of leisure. An analogous distinction was recently made by O. Engländer with the concepts of genuine and false cost, corresponding to direct and indirect utility respectively.

A group of theorists considers not only marginal utility, but also marginal sacrifice or marginal disutility of labour as independent determinants of the choice of the utilization of goods. While utility is a 'feeling of pleasure', disutility is a 'feeling of displeasure'[11] which, together with utility, determines the optimal total allocation. We do not deny, of course, that in primary psychical experience feelings of pleasure and displeasure may coexist, and that pleasure and displeasure intensities may not always offset each other. But once these primary psychical phenomena are rationalized, the displeasure of work, of the disutility of labour, can nevertheless be understood as a desire for leisure and the two scales of intensity can then be reduced to one common order of importance[12] which reflects both the feelings of pleasure and displeasure.

Interpreted in this manner, the disutility theory also furnishes a unitary principle of explanation, since, like pure marginal theory, it regards psychological (subjective) marginal magnitudes as the determinants of economic action and drops the old classical notion of the determination of the value of goods through objectively determined cost. Since this view is professed by all modern theorists either expressly or in a more or less veiled form, the basic idea of marginal utility theory is the foundation of all modern economic theories.

C. *The Evaluation of Utility*

We have shown that in the economic calculus we always compare two utilities – the utility of a good in one use with the utility of the same good in an alternative use (the case of 'internal exchange' according to Schumpeter and Engländer), or the utility of one good with that of another (the case of 'effective exchange'). In effective exchange we compare the utilities of the good which is to be acquired with that of the good which is to be given up for it.

Since all individual utilities are either direct or indirect, we must first decide which (direct or indirect) utilities of the two goods are to be compared with each other. Consider the exchange of good a against good b. Four pairs of utility comparisons are possible:

(1) The direct utility of a and the direct utility of b.
(2) The indirect utility of a and the indirect utility of b.
(3) The direct utility of a and the indirect utility of b.
(4) The indirect utility of a and the direct utility of b.

Only one of these comparisons actually underlies the economic calculus. A simple consideration unequivocally determines the most suitable type of utility comparison. The acquisition of good b at the expense of good a is profitable only if

I. The total economic utility (TEU) of all goods (q) including a but excluding b, with unchanged total allocation (UTA) is smaller than the total economic utility of all goods without a but including b, with changed total allocation (CTA).

In reality, as we have shown above under II A, we never compare total economic utilities, but only their respective changes, and this is done by means of individual utility comparisons. In the case of exchange we need a comparison of individual utilities which implicitly includes a comparison of the relevant total economic utilities (I). Only a comparison of type (3) fulfils this condition [direct utility of a (II) compared to indirect utility of b (III)], which looks as follows when written out:

II. direct utility of a $= \begin{cases} \text{(1) TEU of } q \text{ including } a \text{ and excluding } b \text{ (UTA)} \\ \text{(2) TEU of } q \text{ excluding } a \text{ and excluding } b \text{ (UTA)} \end{cases}$

III. indirect utility of b $= \begin{cases} \text{(3) TEU of } q \text{ excluding } a \text{ and excluding } b \text{ (UTA)} \\ \text{(4) TEU of } q \text{ excluding } a \text{ and including } b \text{ (CTA).} \end{cases}$

When II and III are confronted it turns out that the two middle terms (2 and 3) are identical so that they can be cancelled. The result is the comparison I, which we have mentioned as relevant for deciding on an exchange. Thus we get the rule that when an exchange is contemplated, we always have to compare the indirect utility of the good to be acquired with

191

the direct utility of the good to be sacrificed. Since the indirect utility of good *a* is identical with the marginal utility of the whole class of goods *a*, it turns out that *in an exchange the marginal utility of a certain quantity of the class of goods to be acquired is always compared with the concrete usefulness (direct utility) of a certain quantity of the class of goods to be sacrificed.*[13] It follows that in the case of exchange we do not compare two (indirect) marginal utilities. Marginal utility is valued only once on the occasion of a change in allocation. Given the relative constancy of economic data, the direct utility of the good to be given in exchange is frequently identical with the marginal utility of its class of goods, since changes relate only to the marginal utilizations, where complementarity is generally weak. Evaluation with relative constancy of conditions is only a special case, albeit the practically most important one, of the principle which we have developed. This principle does, however, also cover cases in which a larger part of the data changes and permits even then an abbreviation of the economic calculus while taking strict account of the complementarity of all utilities.

D. *'The Equalization of the Level of Marginal Utilities'*

Goods are assigned to their optimal uses by applying them successively to the most important needs in each class until the supply of goods is exhausted. In every separate utility scale the highest utilities are successively assured in descending order. The greatest total economic utility is achieved when needs are satisfied in such wise that no more important want is left unsatisfied at the cost of satisfying a less important one. The simplicity of the unrealistic assumption that all needs and all goods are infinitely divisible has induced some theorists to formulate a 'law of the equalization of the marginal utility level'. This goes back to Gossen's second law, which states that the limitation of the (labour) time available to man prevents him from satisfying all his needs fully, and that maximum satisfaction is achieved by discontinuing the satisfaction of different needs at the point at which their intensity has become equal. This law was later accepted by many theorists in one formulation or another; it says, in effect, that optimal allocation of goods leads to equal marginal utilities of all units of all classes of goods and thus to 'equalization of the level of marginal utilities'. The conclusion is then drawn that all units of all classes of goods should be so used that they yield the same marginal utility in all uses.

This law rests on an impermissible simplification of empirically observed facts, in that it assumes continuously falling utility curves and complete divisibility of all kinds of goods. The possibility of applying infinitesimal calculus to continuously decreasing utility curves may have tempted the followers of the mathematical school of economics to make this unrealistic assumption. In empirical reality utility curves are as a rule discontinuous. Not all degrees of intensity occur in all utility scales, since some needs appear only intermittently in conjunction with others, and some have only a few intensities and either no further ones at all or much lower ones at greater intervals. We can observe that with rising income the satisfaction of different needs is expanded to a different degree, that in fact the increase in income is used to satisfy only particular additional kinds of needs. This confirms the discontinuous nature of utility curves. Furthermore, goods are not infinitely divisible. Quality differences of goods of the same kind can modify but not overcome the limitations of indivisibility. The law of equalization of marginal utility levels rests on two unrealistic assumptions and is illusory. Wieser emphasized this as long ago as 1889: 'The principle of the economic use of goods with multiple usefulness is not to get the same marginal utility in all uses, but to achieve in every use the smallest possible marginal utility without thereby forgoing a higher utility in another use.'[14] Or, put positively, the same principle reads: 'Every economic resource should be used for the greatest utility increment it can still add when marginal utility is already achieved in all other uses.'[15] The assumption of proportionality between price and utility led, on the basis of the law of equalization of marginal utility levels, to the further proposition that the exchange ratio of every pair of goods equals the reciprocal value of the ratio of their marginal utilities. Accordingly, it was argued that not 'simple' marginal utilities, but marginal utilities divided by price *i.e.*, weighted marginal utilities, are equal in all needs. The result was the 'law of equalization of weighted marginal utility levels'. This law was accepted by all the followers of the Lausanne school; it means that every unit of money is spent so as to yield the same marginal utility in all uses. Since, however, as we have shown above (I B 1 c-e), it is meaningless to divide marginal utility by price, all that this law can really tell us is that the surplus of marginal utility over marginal cost is always the same, or that at the utilization margin consumer rents are equal. So interpreted this law is actually identical with Liefmann's later 'law of equalization of marginal consumer rent'. It is indeed logically conceivable that the differences between two utilities (between the last utility still realized and the first not realized) are equal in the basic uses, but in empirical reality this need not be so, for two reasons.

(1) Utility and disutility are not always continuous, as this law illegitimately assumes;

(2) It is not the purpose of economic action to achieve equal utility

differences, which are not primary psychological magnitudes, but people are solely intent on achieving the greatest possible utility as such, regardless of whether the surplus over 'cost' (other utilities) is large or not.

Frequent attempts were made to maintain the law of equalization of marginal utility levels in an attenuated from, by emphasizing that it merely expresses a tendency. But even this would be an imprecise statement, while Wieser's formulation – no smaller utility at the expense of a larger one – represents the facts more precisely and more correctly. When no change in allocation can achieve a higher total economic utility for an economic subject, he has reached his state of equilibrium.

E. *The Determinants of Marginal Utility*

The determinants of marginal utility are, as we have already stated, of two kinds. There is a psychological (subjective) and a technical (objective) component: on the one hand, the needs determined by number, kind, importance and capacity, that is, the system of needs and its psychological relationships; and on the other hand, the number and kinds of goods and their technical interrelationships (laws of production). Marginal utility is the resultant of these two components, it is the organic and synthetic expression of objective and subjective factors.

F. *Marginal Productivity*

The output of a particular amount of some consumer goods depends on the inputs of particular amounts of producer goods. The quantity of a consumer good which is economically attributable to the marginal utilization of a class of producer goods is the latter's physical (natural) marginal productivity, as opposed to its economic marginal productivity, which is the utility of the relevant amount of consumer goods produced. The economic marginal productivity of a class of producer goods is therefore identical with its marginal utility.

The product which is to be economically imputed to a class of producer goods as a whole represents its (physical or economic) total productivity. It is evaluated only in exceptional cases, owing to the divisibility of needs and of goods, decisions are in reality generally required only with respect to limited quantities of goods.

A number of economists, especially in England, America and Italy (J. B. Clark, Marshall and others) developed the so-called marginal productivity theory, which is in all essentials identical with marginal utility theory and which can be found in rudimentary form already in Thünen's work. Most modern theorists have accepted this doctrine, particularly in the theory of income formation. Terminological prodigality (marginal productivity, marginal efficiency, specific productivity, effective productivity, specific efficiency, and other terms) and an insufficiently clear distinction between the concepts of physical and economic total and marginal productivity unnecessarily complicated the exposition of marginal productive theory. The above conceptual distinction, identically, was very clearly worked out by A. Aftalion in 1911.

G. Derived Applications of the Concept of Marginal Utility

The concepts of social marginal utility and of stratified marginal utility are derived applications.

1. Social marginal utility

In the opinion of several theorists (J. B. Clark, Seligman, I. Fisher, Seager, B. M. Anderson Jr., Alessio and others) it is social rather than individual marginal utility which determines the valuation of goods. 'Society as a whole, not the individual' attributes utility to goods; society determines the direction and extent of human needs. Hence, social marginal utility (or social marginal disutility of labour) is decisive for people's economic behaviour. This doctrine must be sharply contradicted. It rests upon a logically impermissible assumption and a hypostasis in social philosophy. The concept of utility always presupposes subjective valuation and only persons can be subjects in this sense; society does not exist as a subject, and can therefore neither perceive nor evaluate utility. 'Social utility' can only be the result of individual utility valuations, although no-one denies, of course, that this social result, once formed, reacts back on the individual in a modificatory and unifying manner. But this reaction influences only the content of their needs, their actual formation and their concrete composition; it dies not alter in the least the logical and formal laws of the structure of needs. In any case, whether individuals or society determine the content of needs, the question about the origin of needs is irrelevant for economic theory, for, as Schumpeter says, this is not an epistemological question, which would indeed be valuable for theoretical economics, but a methodological one. Unlike, say, economic or cultural history modern economic theory does not presuppose knowledge of the actual content of needs; it merely seeks to create a tool of explanation which is practically applicable to empirical reality. In reality, needs can be ascertained only with respect to persons and not with respect to society,

195

which is an abstract concept. Every explanation must start with the individual.

In the Anglo-American literature the concept of welfare is frequently found in the sense of social total economic utility (Edgeworth, Marshall, Pigou, Patten, Fetter and others). This concept presupposes the solution of a problem in social philosophy to determine the content of welfare. This question of social philosophy is answered differently depending on people's general convictions (the Cambridge school, for example, answers it in the sense of utilitarianism, as 'the greatest good of the greatest number'), but not scientifically solved. It can play a part in economic policy, but not in economic theory.

2. *Stratified marginal utility*

According to Wieser, stratified marginal utility is the marginal utility of those classes (strata) whose price willingness determines price formation.

H. *The Quantification of Utility*

Value and price theory have to show how the individual utilities of goods (that is, intensive magnitudes which cannot be expressed numerically) determine their prices (that is, extensive magnitudes which can be expressed numerically). The main problem is the translation of qualities into quantities, *i.e.*, the quantification of utility. We can merely sketch the problem here.

The economic subject is prepared to give up certain goods in exchange for a good of particular utility. The upper limit to which he is prepared to go, *i.e.*, the greatest amount of goods which he is willing to give up in order to acquire another good, is his highest offer, his price willingness ('subjective valuation'): it is the quantified utility of this good. Once the highest offers of all economic subjects are established, the price can be determined without difficulty by the law of marginal pairs.

So long as all desires are purely instinctive and therefore not rationalized, an individual actually feels at any one moment only needs of equal – and indeed the highest – intensity (see I A). To acquire a good capable of satisfying these needs, the individual would be prepared to offer all the other goods at his disposal. Since the available stock of goods and the system of needs are given, the goods which an individual is ready to offer in exchange for another good are also determined and they represent the highest offer, the quantified utility of that good. At any one moment an individual can make only one maximum offer (or, for several goods, several alternative maximum offers of equal magnitude); the poorest

196

(marginal) stratum always determines the price of a kind of goods and is then eliminated from the demand for other goods. The prices of different goods are thus determined by different strata of purchasing power at different moments.

Although in a rational assessment needs of different intensity are evaluated simultaneously, the individual still proceeds on the basis of his experience of instinctive desires. The quantification of utility is more complicated because of the existence of alternative needs and counterbalancing needs, but utility is still determined essentially in the same manner as in the case of instinctive desires.

The prices of different goods are therefore not reciprocal values of their marginal utility ratios – taken literally, this is impossible since there can be no such thing as a utility ratio – and there is no 'conformity of price and utility'; nevertheless, the marginal utilities of goods determine their prices in a unique manner.

J. *The Principle of Marginal Analysis*

The essential function of marginal utility is to abbreviate economic calculations in a procedure which, given the relative constancy of economic data, permits allocations to be made on the basis of past marginal results without having to think through all considerations anew each time. It suffices to establish partial changes in order to determine the total course of economic action.

This abbreviating function of marginal utility rests on a psychological principle which is completely analogous to a basic idea of higher mathematics, the principle of marginal analysis. With variable quantities, the extent of the variation is itself retained as a new magnitude, and this makes it possible to compare the different stages of change in the given magnitudes. In economic calculus marginal utility is a similar magnitude which allows us to compare the changes in the data of several economic periods.

The individual economic units whose interactions form the economy as a whole always start with marginal utilities: the whole economic process is determined by the marginal utility valuations of individual economic units. Since prices are determined by only a fraction of all individual economic units, namely the marginal strata, and since these do not change for all goods so long as the data remain relatively constant, it is sufficient to consider simply the valuation of these marginal strata in order to explain price changes and (on the basis of the preceding economic period) the whole course of the economic process. The principle of marginal analysis amounts therefore to an abbreviation and simplification of the necessary

197

considerations also for the market economy; provided the data remain relatively constant, it can be applied to all economic phenomena.

The principle of marginal analysis is not identical with Hobson's 'marginalism', which would establish only the limits within which prices can form. It represents an abbreviated procedure which gives a uniquely and not merely approximately determined result.

Part III. *The Literature and Critique of Marginal Utility Theory*

A. *The Literature of Marginal Utility Theory*

Gossen's work, which was the first to apply the laws of utility valuation to the explanation of all economic activity, was published in 1854, but it remained unknown for a long time and could therefore not exert any influence. Modern economic theory really begins with the doctrines, enunciated independently of Gossen, by Carl Menger (1871), William Stanley Jevons (1871, and to some extent even in 1862), and Léon Walras (1874). All three independently established the concept of marginal utility as the explanatory principle of economic phenomena. It penetrated the whole world in less than twenty years, and is today not only the dominant theory but, except for differences of detail, the only theory which systematically and uniformly encompasses all economic phenomena.

In later years we can distinguish two schools which both use the basic principle of marginal utility, but which differ to some extent in the manner of its application. One school uses the data and, as far as possible, empirical facts to describe the whole sequence of the economic process and its final result, namely economic equilibrium. This is the 'Austrian' or 'psychological' school, the marginal utility theory in the narrower sense. The other school seeks to determine and explain the final result, economic equilibrium, directly from the data, without tracing the course of the economic process in all its phases in more detail. This is the 'mathematical'[16] theory, the 'Lausanne school'.

The *psychological approach* was at first further developed primarily in Austria by Wieser, Böhm-Bawerk and Sax, whence its name of *Austrian school*. Amongst its many representatives we may mention the following: (a) in the *German* language: Friedrich von Wieser, Eugen von Böhm-Bawerk, Emil Sax, Robert Zuckerkandl, Robert Mayer, Julius Lehr, G. Sulzer, Eugen Philippovich, Henry Oswalt, Richard Schüller, Hans Mayer, Ludwig von Mises, F. X. Weiss, R. Broda, Oskar Engländer, Carl Landauer, Richard Strigl, Leo Schönfeld, W. Vleugels, F. A. von Hayek, Gottfried von Haberler, and to a considerable extent also Emil Lederer,

Otto Zwiedineck von Südenhorst, A. Amonn, and others; (b) in *England* and the *United States*: P. Wicksteed, James Bonar, W. Smart, D. J. Green, S. N. Patten, Frank A. Fetter, and others; (c) in *Italy*: Maffeo Pantaleoni, Ugo Mazzola, Giuseppe Ricca-Salerno, Augusto Graziani, A. Montanari, C. Conigliani, G. Valenti, R. Benini, D. Berardi, R. Dalla Volta, and others; (d) in *France*: Charles Gide, H. S. Marc, Charles Rist, Adolphe Landry, Albert Aftalion, Bernard Lavergne, H. Truchy, C. Bodin, P. Reboud, M. Roche-Agussol, and others; (e) in the *Netherlands*: N. G. Pierson, C. A. Verrijn Stuart, De Vries, H. W. C. Bordewijk, R. Van Genechten, and others; (f) in *Denmark*: L. V. Birck; (g) in *Norway*: T. H. Aschehoug, H. B. Morgenstierne, O Jäger, T. Aarum; (h) in *Sweden*: Knut Wicksell, Erik Lindahl, and others; (i) in *Russia*: M. Buniatian, A. Bilimovich.

As a variant of this school, the *disutility theory*, which postulates the concept of social utility, was established in America by J. B. Clark in 1881. Apart from J. B. Clark himself, its representatives include T. N. Carver, R. Seager, J. Hobson, H. J. Davenport, A. S. Johnson, A. T. Hadley, F. B. Hawley, E. R. A. Seligman, F. W. Taussig, and others. In Germany Liefmann adheres to this theory to some extent, at any rate so far as disutility is concerned. In England this variant is represented by the Cambridge school, which is already a transition to the mathematical school: Alfred Marshall, Francis Ysidro Edgeworth, A. C. Pigou, A. W. Flux and others; and in France it is represented by C. Colson.

The *mathematical school* began with W. S. Jevons and L. Walras and was later perfected and developed especially by Vilfredo Pareto. Its best known representatives are: (a) in the *Latin languages*: Léon Walras, G. B. Antonelli, Vilfredo Pareto, Enrico Barone, Umberto Ricci, P. Boninsegni, R. A. Murray, A. Graziadei, A. Osorio, Marco Fanno, Enrico Leone, A. Pietri-Tonelli, Luigi Amoroso, E. Cesari, Gustavo del Vecchio, G. Sensini, L. Moret, and others; (b) in *English*: W. S. Jevons, F. Y. Edgeworth, P. Wicksteed, Irving Fisher, A. L. Bowley, and others; (c) in *German*: R. Auspitz, R. Lieben, Ladislaus von Bortkiewicz, Joseph A. Schumpeter, V. Furlan, as well as W. G. Waffenschmidt, O. Kühne and O. Weinberger; (e) in *Denmark*: H. Westergaard; (f) in *Sweden*: Knut Wicksell and Gustav Cassel; (g) in *Russia*: W. K. Dimitriev, N. N. Shaposhnikov, B. Samsonov, E. Slutsky; (h) in *Poland*: W. Zawadzki, Z. Strashewich.

The precursors of modern economic theory or in any event of some features of it include Bernoulli, Laplace, Buffon, Quetelet, Bentham, Davanzati, Galiani, Genovesi, Montanari, Beccaria, Ortes, Le Trosne, Turgot, Condillac, Fulda (1805), Jakob (1805), Sartorius (1806), Soden (1806), Hufeland (1807), Lotz (1811), Storch (1815), Rooke (1824), W.

Thompson (1824), Thünen (1826), Auguste Walras (1831), Hermann (1832), W. F. Lloyd (1833), N. Longfield (1834), Cournot (1838), Thomas (1841), Dupuit (1844 and 1849), B. Hildebrandt (1848), Friedländer (1852), Knies (1855) and Mangoldt, and, among the classical economists, chiefly J. B. Say, Nassau Senior and McLeod.

B. *The Critique of Marginal Utility Theory*

Marginal utility theory provoked a spirited and often sharply critical discussion. The critics either attacked the theory's methodological principles in general or pointed to specific supposed gaps or mistakes in the structure of its system. Most of the objections were raised already before 1900 and continue to be brought forward, often in identical form, although they have long been refuted. In the light of these criticisms it might appear as if marginal utility theory were a conglomeration of all possible kinds of mistakes. The following is a sample catalogue of objections, several of which were often raised by one and the same author.

1. (a) Life and empirical reality are too complicated to be formulated in exact laws (the historical school);

(b) marginal utility theory is much too complicated for a correct understanding of life, which in reality is much simpler (among others Leroy-Beaulieu and Oppenheimer);

2. (a) marginal utility theory is based on psychology (among others Amonn and Diehl);

(b) marginal utility theory is not based upon scientific psychology (among others Amonn and Diehl);

3. (a) it is a bourgeois-liberal-capitalist theory (among others Hohoff, Kautsky, Oppenheimer, Veblen);

(b) it explains only a barter economy such as a socialist economy, but not the modern market economy (among others Eckstein and Hohoff);

4. (a) it is too strictly separated from economic policy, so that it is useless in the fight against social evils (Brentano and others);

(b) it mixes up economic theory and policy (*e.g.* Diehl);

5. (a) it deals with causal relationships instead of functional ones, as it should (Pareto, Schumpeter and the Lausanne school, Amonn);

(b) it is not strictly causal, in that it indicates only a sufficient, but not the effective cause of economic activity (Veblen);

6. (a) it errs in assuming that producers evaluate commodities (Oppenheimer, Turgeon and many others);

(b) it neglects the point of view of the producer and considers only the valuation of goods by the consumer (Stolzmann, Turgeon, Bucharin and many others).

This enumeration could easily be continued. It is obvious that of any two so contradictory objections, both cannot be valid at the same time. We will briefly discuss the most important ones to see whether and to what extent they hit the mark.

1. *The objection of historicism*

As a pure economic theory, marginal utility seeks to describe the immanent principles of economic behaviour in all its conceivable forms. To this end it concentrates on the common features of the economic phenomena and initially abstracts from the peculiarities of any particular economic form. Wherever and whenever people strive to satisfy their needs with scarce means, their actions follow a certain pattern of successive and simultaneous behaviour, which brings to light what is common to all economies. In this manner a basic stock of knowledge is gained which applies to all conceivable economies and which alone enables us to compare these various economies and some of their separate phenomena. The principles thus found enable us to explain all actual economic phenomena by allowing for the peculiarities of specific economies through a process of diminishing abstraction.

The general validity of these economic laws seemed to contradict the principle of historical relativity, the 'uniqueness' of all social phenomena. The view that all forms of civilization are products of historical development seemed to justify the conclusion that there could be no 'universal' principles independent of specific contexts of space and time. But, although economic phenomena as such are historically conditioned and subject to change, the existence of supra-historical phenomenological principles is not in contradiction with the fact of historical development. In trying to establish these generally valid principles, pure theory does not overlook the role of historical development; on the contrary, it is only once two economic stages have been precisely explained that they can be compared and that the direction and extent of development can thereby be gauged. By regarding yesterday's prices and incomes as the determinants of today's, and today's prices and incomes as the determinants of tomorrow's (Wieser's 'principle of the continuity of the economy'), marginal utility theory expresses the historical idea of 'organic growth' much more exactly than the 'historians' themselves.

The economists who deny the general validity of economic laws voice further objections according to the particular school to which they belong.

(a) The *historical school* (B. Hildebrandt, Rau, Roscher, Knies) originally objected against the 'universalism' (general validity), 'perpetualism' (validity for all times) and 'cosmopolitanism' (validity for all peoples) of the economic laws of classical theory. The younger historical school (Schmoller and his disciples, Cliffe Leslie, Ashley, Levasseur) usually overlooks the distinction between classical and modern (marginal utility) theory, fights both and, in addition to the general objection of historicism, also accuses marginal utility theory of individualism, atomism and mechanistic views (see below under 2, 2b and 7, respectively) – objections which have nothing to do with the historical approach as such. Furthermore, the historical school insists on the right of economics to make moral value judgements and hence on that blend of ethical and economic points of view which the works of theorists such as Max Weber, Benedetto Croce, F. Simiand (E. Durckheim) and E. Sella independently and in complete agreement showed to be inconsistent with scientific procedure.

(b) The *social-organic school* (R. Stolzmann, and on largely similar lines Amonn on the one hand and O. Spann on the other), which in the last analysis is the end product of the historical school, emphasizes primarily the influence of the 'social category' and accuses marginal utility theory of failure to consider existing social reality. This school argues that the structure of social power determines distribution (income formation) and that it eludes formulation in exact universal laws.

Against this view it must be stressed that the social power structure finds its expression in the size of the stock of goods (purchasing power) and in the manner in which they can be used. It is therefore already included in the data of marginal utility theory and the peculiarities of any particular set of social circumstances can be taken into account within the framework of that theory by successive concretization. Since social phenomena are included in the data, the introduction of a special social category is superfluous. It would merely involve double counting. Just to mention the social power structure would, of course, furnish no general theoretical explanation, but would merely replace one unknown by another. In modern theory the effects of social power deploy themselves within general economic laws.[17] As to the objections (also raised by Stolzmann) of individualism see 2, of atomism see 2b, of mechanistic views see 7, and of causality see 9b.

The integration of 'subjectivism' and objectivism' is also achieved by marginal utility theory (see above II E and below 4 and 5).

(c) The *socio-legal school* (Stammler, Diehl) emphasizes with Stolzmann the role of social circumstances and in particular the influence of the legal framework. Here, too, we have to reply that this influence is already included in the data of marginal utility theory. It is expressed in the concept of the right and power of disposal over goods.

(d) *Institutionalism* (Veblen, Mitchell, Tugwell), which is the American

202

representative of the ideas of the historical school, attacks in particular the supposedly hedonistic foundation of modern theory, without differentiating between classical and modern economics. Instead of looking for a formal principle for the explanation of economic action, the institutionalists try to enumerate its motivations, and in so doing often retain mere special cases (R. B. Perry, A. P. Usher, G. B. Dibblee and others), and fail to investigate the general role of motivations and their real scope, as A. Wagner, for example, has done in his theory of motivation. The institutionalists' creed of the 'statistification' of economics is not in contradiction with marginal utility theory, but in fact corresponds to the latter's principle of diminishing abstraction. It would be wrong, however, to believe that this makes pure theory redundant. Theory assigns statistical work its field and tasks.[18]

2. *The objection of individualism*

Marginal utility theory starts with the needs of the individual in order to explain the course of the whole economic process. This does not mean that the individuals determine the direction and kinds of their needs 'autarkically' and independently of the social context. We recall Max Weber's early emphasis on the fact that such 'methodological individualism' has nothing whatever to do with philosophical or historical, let alone political, individualism. Nevertheless, marginal utility theory is often accused of an individualistic approach and it is argued that in the relations between society and individuals the primacy belongs to society, and that society determines the pattern of individual needs (Rümelin, Schäffle, Schmoller, Stammler, Stolzmann, Spann). As we have stated above (II G 1) this way of posing the problem owes more to social philosophy than to economics. The objection of individualism rests on a misunderstanding of the tasks of economic theory.

(a) In social philosophy the rival concepts of individualism and collectivism do indeed claim attention (K. Pribram, Scheler, Litt, Max Adler, Spann), but, no matter how this problem is solved, the outcome can change nothing in the laws of marginal utility theory.

(b) The charge of individualism is often coupled with that of *atomism*, or the confusion of the general economic point of view with the private one. This confusion allegedly arises because marginal utility theory does not consider economic phenomena in the context of all phenomena. As early as 1883, Menger proved this to be a misunderstanding of the nature of economic theory.[19]

(c) A misconception about the methodological task of the idealizing and isolating procedure has frequently led to the objection that marginal utility theory deals with Robinson Crusoe economics (Schäffle, Amonn, Diehl,

Lifschitz, Stolzmann, and others). Laws derived from the consideration of an isolated economy supposedly cannot explain socio-economic phenomena. The examples of the desert traveller and others are often cited with the remark that such a simple situation cannot explain the complicated phenomena of a modern economy. But the critics overlook the fact that marginal utility theory investigates the isolated economy not for its own sake, but for the sake of studying in this simplest of all cases the immanent problems of all economic action.

3. *The objection of psychologism*
(a) In order to explain man's economic behaviour, marginal utility theory must go back to human needs as the motive forces of all economic action and must seek to understand the principles which govern human needs. For this reason the theory must be founded on psychological facts. Some authors consider this an improper transgression beyond the limits of economics and speak of the 'confusion of psychology and economics' – a slogan which is as cheap as it is ill-conceived. The fact of scientific division of labour is taken as an epistemological postulate, while actually the very unity of all knowledge justifies 'transgressions' into all special disciplines. Economics draws on psychological facts for different purposes than does psychology, and the objection of psychologism uncovers a serious misunderstanding, as indeed Max Weber has shown with all necessary clarity. Many authors actually attack not the fact but only the manner of the psychological foundation of marginal utility theory. Thus

(b) the objection of *hedonism* (utilitarianism, eudaemonism) is raised by many authors, including Davenport, I. Fisher, Fetter, Veblen, Mitchell, Boucke, McDougall and others. Human activity, they say, is not – or not only – determined by a pleasure-pain calculus.

The mere fact that some followers of modern theory, like I. Fisher and Davenport and others, were pioneers in the fight against hedonism and that Böhm-Bawerk himself also pronounced against it, proves that hedonism is by no means intrinsic to a marginal utility theory. Even where self-interest is isolated as the motive force of economic action (Pantaleoni, Pareto), this isolation is consciously only a methodological means. The truth is that marginal utility theorists do not use a hedonistically and sensualistically limited concept of pleasure, as is proved by the inclusion of 'altruistic' needs in the concept. Davenport was right with his well-known statement that all pronouncements of a hedonistic complexion could be omitted from marginal utility theory without changing a single one of its laws.

(c) Individual psychology rather than social psychology underlies marginal utility theory, so Tarde, Simiand and Lifschitz maintain and regard this as fatal one-sidedness. We may point out that at present social psychology hardly exists as an established science. Social relationships find their expression in economics in the needs of the individuals. Modern theory does not preclude recourse to social psychology, as is shown by the work of Roche-Agussel, whose advocacy of marginal utility theory was in no way inconsistent with the findings of his teacher Tarde, the man who accused the Austrian school of neglect of 'inter-psychology'.

The results of modern economic theory are indeed confirmed and strikingly verified by the various psychological schools (Ehrenfels, O. Kraus, Kreibig, Meinong and others). Pantaleoni for example, reached the laws of marginal utility theory on the basis of hedonism, and the same laws were reached by Davenport and Fetter on the basis of voluntarism and in part behaviourism, by Roche-Agussol on the basis of Tarde's psychology, by Engländer on the basis of Brentano's psychology, and by Jurovski on the basis of Bergson's psychology.

4. *The objection of subjectivism*
Some theorists, who believe it to be an advantage that their own theory is 'objective', accuse marginal utility theory of subjectivism. It is quite clear that they confuse 'objectivism' with 'objectivity' and that they equate 'subjective' with 'uncertain' or 'fluctuating'. However, 'subjective'[20] in the sense in which this word is used in economics, does not mean arbitrary; the subjectively interpreted meaning of action follows strict ('objective') laws. Subjectivism in economics has nothing to do with philosophical subjectivism or relativism. Allowance for subjective (psychic) facts is by no means equivalent with a subjective manner of viewing facts.

For the rest, marginal utility theory is based not merely upon psychological (subjective) but also upon technical (objective) determinants (see above II E). For this reason the objection of (economic) subjectivism is unjustified.

5. *The objection of objectivism*
Equally unjustified is Liefmann's charge of objectivism. The extent of this misunderstanding has been shown most clearly by Amonn's proof that both the 'purely subjective' theory of Liefmann and the 'purely objective' theory of Oppenheimer are equally based upon 'subjective' and 'objective' factors.

6. *The objection of materialism (quantitativism)*
This, too, is raised by Liefmann and it overlaps in part with the above charge of objectivism. Marginal utility theory is accused of dealing with the quantitative relationships of goods, which is said to be a 'materialistic'

205

approach proper to the 'natural sciences', while it should consider merely psychological relationships. It is obvious that marginal utility theory draws on psychological relationships in its explanation of the quantitative relationships of goods, about which, after all, decisions have to be taken; the very concept of 'goods' implies a psychological relationship with the economic subject. It would be impossible for economic theory to proceed otherwise.

Materialism (also positivism and empiricism) of economic theory was supposed to be implied also in the assumptions of egotism and of *homo oeconomicus*. We have already shown that neither of these assumptions underlie modern theory (see above I B 6 and III B 3b). This objection is relevant to the psychology of scientists, but not to science. About this subject, as about 'big words' generally, see Schumpeter in *Wirtschaftstheorie der Gegenwart*.[21]

7. *The objection of mechanistic views*

Schäffle, Stolzmann, Spann and others accuse marginal utility theory of looking upon the economy as a mechanism rather than as an organism. This objection was refuted by Menger as long ago as 1883.[22] How much this is a quarrel about words rather than about problems can be seen by the fact that the word 'organism' can be substituted for 'mechanism' throughout the writings of marginal utility theorists without having to change anything else at all. The use of slogans such as mechanism vs. organism has had no other result than that today the word 'organic' has come to mean 'obscure' or 'vague'.

8. *Universalism*

(a) The objection of universalism was levelled against marginal utility theory in more than one sense and by more than one critic.

(i) The historical school objected to universalism in the sense of 'general validity', 'perpetualism' and 'cosmopolitanism'.

(ii) P. Struve, from his point of view of 'singularism', objected against marginal utility theory (as against the classics) that it personifies unreal magnitudes such as national income, distribution, social product, etc., which in reality merely consist of a multiplicity of individual acts. Marginal utility theory, however, fights just as much against such 'personification' – a fact which in the mind of some critics contributed to the misunderstanding of atomism. We have already shown above (III B 1d) that the postulate of the statistification of economics, to which Struve is led by Lotz's concept of the 'singular fact', does not contradict the methodological postulates of modern theory.

(b) Struve's concept of universalism has nothing to do with the universalism of O. Spann (in further development of Adam Müller). To all the misunderstandings in our list – there are eleven of them – Spann recently added an indeed entirely new one, namely that of 'equal importance' or 'equipollence'. Spann's procedure is methodologically somewhat reminiscent of Marx's elimination of the concept of utility; he abstracts from everything that is economically relevant and is then able to give 'equal importance' to what is economically irrelevant.

9. *The objection of causality*

(a) 'Functional, not causal relationships' should, in the view of some theorists (Pareto, Schumpeter and the mathematical school) form the basis of the marginal utility theory's explanation of economic phenomena. This objection also rests upon a misunderstanding. Functional and causal dependence are not in contradiction. A causal view does not exclude mutual efforts. If A causes B and B in turn has an effect on A, the functional dependence is written $F(A,B)$, while in the causal approach the same dependence is expressed more precisely and clearly by writing $A_1 \rightarrow B_1 \rightarrow A_2$.

(b) 'Teleological, not causal explanation' is called for in the view of other theorists, such as Schäffle, Stolzmann and Spann. There is another misconception here, for the causal chain includes the teleological one.

10. *The 'Dying Value' theory*

A number of theorists would banish the concept of value from economics. Some of them, like Schumpeter in 1908, Liefmann and Pareto, object only against the word value, others against the concept itself. The latter include Cassel, Gottl, Dietzel, Aupetit, Briot, Brouilhet, Zorli, Gobbi and Friday. Nevertheless they themselves operate implicitly with the concept of value only they give it another name, such as index function, economic dimension or economic convenience. It is perfectly obvious that nothing of substance is thereby gained for economic theory.

11. *The political objection*

(a) Marginal utility theory is described as 'bourgeois-capitalist' by such authors as Hohoff, Eckstein, Kautsky, Oppenheimer, Veblen and Bucharin. Although even a number of socialists have pointed out that marginal utility theory pursues purely scientific and not political ends, this objection is raised by many socialists. Since marginal utility theory, as pure theory, seeks only to know and explain reality and is not concerned with political postulates, this objection is a severe misunderstanding.

(b) Marginal utility theory is described as liberal by others, who reach this conclusion from the fact that the theory, for purely methodological reasons, assumes free competition. It may also be a contributory reason for this charge that several marginal utility theorists are liberals in private life. In fact, there are marginal utility theorists of all political persuasions. In the early days, Gossen and Walras were agrarian socialists; nowadays modern theory has among its representatives fascists, conservatives, liberals, socialists, syndicalists and communists – surely the best proof that it is not wedded to any political doctrine.

(c) Marginal utility theory is essentially un-German, in the view of Spann and Suranyi-Unger. Is it really necessary in our days to point out that there is no German, French or English truth, but only one truth recognized by Germans, Frenchmen and Englishmen?

12 *The objection of incompleteness*

Many authors accuse marginal utility theory of being incomplete, in that it allegedly explains only

(a) consumption but not distribution (Stolzmann, Turgeon, Cornélissen, Tugan-Baranovskii and others);

(b) distribution but not production (Veblen);

(c) consumption and production, but not circulation (G. Sorel, Lederer);

(d) the socialist barter economy but not the capitalist economy (the Marxists);

(e) the capitalist but not the socialist economy (Veblen);

(f) the value of unique goods but not that of reproducible goods (Dietzel and others);

(g) the value of goods but not the value of money (Helfferich and others, to some extent also Amonn).

The refutation of these diverse objections of incompleteness can readily be found in any systematic treatment of economics based upon marginal utility theory.

13. *Non-methodological objections*

(a) Marginal utility theory supposedly explains only utility, not cost, it 'considers only the viewpoint of the consumer, not of the producer', and therefore explains only demand, not supply (Dietzel, Scharling, MacVane, Diehl, Turgeon, Pirou and others). However, it is precisely modern theory which devotes most attention to the explanation of cost phenomena and it is one of its greatest merits to have explained the nature of costs and the determinants of their level.[23]

(b) Marginal utility theory is said to start out from a given stock of goods, while the basic question of any economic unit is: 'how many goods should be provided'? (Dietzel, Liefmann, Stolzmann). This serious misunderstanding was refuted long ago by Zuckerkandl (1893) and Böhm-

Bawerk. The 'given stock of goods' includes not only consumer goods but also factors of production, especially labour. These are always given at the moment when the economic plan is formulated for a certain period. On the basis of a given stock of (producer) goods and the known technical possibilities of use (technical data) it will be decided how many (consumer) goods are to be provided.

(c) Marginal utility theory is said to be unable to define the commodity unit which is evaluated (Dietzel, Stolzmann). The smallest economic unit of a good is the technically smallest amount which yields a noticeable increase in utility.

(d) The objection of circular reasoning:

(i) Circular reasoning in the assessment of exchange value (Stolzmann, Oppenheimer and others). Marginal utility theory explains prices from subjective valuations. It is true that in practice a good is often valued according to its price, but this short-cut by no means signifies that the assessment of exchange value is the ultimate determinant of price. The ultimate determinant of price is always the assessment of utility.

Because of the complementarity of utilities the highest offer for a particular good depends on the prices of other goods. This has led to the conclusion that marginal utility theory explains prices not solely on the basis of utility valuations, but also on the basis of prices (of other goods) and that it is therefore guilty of circular reasoning. *De facto*, price formation does not take place simultaneously for all kinds of goods. Only utility valuation and purchasing power are relevant for the quantification of the utility of any one class of goods (see above II H).

(ii) *Regressus ad infinitum* in the process of substitution (Oppenheimer). According to the 'law of cost' the utility of a good with multiple uses depends on its 'cost', *i.e.*, on the forgone utility of other uses. Oppenheimer objects that the marginal utility theory's solution of the cost problem merely shifts the problem by explaining every utility in terms of another, a procedure which he describes as *regressus ad infinitum*. But he overlooks that the given stock of goods constitutes the limit of substitution.

(iii) Marginal utility is the consequence, not the cause of the choice of goods, so argues Stolzmann, and hence explanation on the basis of marginal utility is circular reasoning. But precisely marginal utility theory shows that marginal utility results from economic calculation; Böhm-Bawerk explicitly stated that marginal utility is only an intermediate cause of value, albeit a very characteristic one. Even though marginal utility emerges only at the end of economic calculation, it is nevertheless decisive for economic action, as has been explained in detail above (II A).

(e) Marginal utility theory, according to Oppenheimer, explains only the nature, not the level of the value of the goods. It is methodologically

209

not permissible to separate the explanation of the nature and of the level of the value of goods, since it is not possible to imagine value at all without some level of value. The explanation of the nature of value necessarily includes the explanation of its level.

(f) Marginal utility theory assumes the measurability of utility, so F. J. Neumann, Lexis and others object, whereas in fact utility is not measurable. We have already stated that marginal utility theory makes no such assumption (see I B 2). This objection is therefore as unjustified as

(g) the objection of the complementarity of utilities (I B 4).

(h) As to the objections against Gossen's law, see I B 5.

In most disciplines professional criticism, by pointing out deficiencies or inconsistencies, contributes to the development of theory. But the critique of marginal utility theory has so far mostly failed to understand it and has remained sterile. As often as not the critics construct a caricature of marginal utility theory and then proceed to shoot it down, or else they attribute to marginal utility theory some special pet theories of individual marginal utility theorists. The edifice of modern economics has been completed without any contribution by its critics. Its followers alone are responsible for the three great stages of progress; the principle of complementarity, the principle of non-measurability of utility, and the introduction of the time factor. Most of the theorems of marginal utility theory have now become common property, so much so that discussion no longer turns on fundamentals but on minor differences of detail.

NOTES

* 'Grenznutzen', *Handwörterbuch der Staatswissenschaften*, 4th edn (Jena, 1927), vol. iv, pp 1190–213. The extensive bibliography annexed to the original has been omitted with the author's approval.

After having left the International Bank for Reconstruction and Development, where he served from 1947 to 1953 as Assistant Director of the Economic Department and Head of the Economic Advisory Service, Paul Rosenstein-Rodan joined the Massachusetts Institute of Technology as Professor of Economics.

1. Hans Mayer, 'Untersuchungen zu dem Grundgesetz der wirtschaftlichen Wertrechnung', *Zeitschrift für Volkswirtschaft und Sozialpolitik*, New Series, vol. ii, p. 16.

2. A. Graziani (in *Istitituzioni di economia politica*, 4th edn (Turin,

1925), pp. 69–72) sharply objected to the statement of the problem in psychological rather than in economic terms.

3. See entry 'Produktion', *Handwörterbuch der Staatswissenschaften*, 4th edn, vol. vi, especially pp. 1110–16.
4. *Zeitschrift für Volkswirtschaft und Sozialpolitik*, New Series, vol. i, pp. 431–58, and vol. ii, pp, 1–23.
5. For details see below, II A and B, and also the entry 'Produktion', *Handwörterbuch der Staatswissenschaften,* op. cit., pp. 1112–14.
6. This reference is, of course, not intended as a definition of statics.
7. This extremely important point together with the recognition that marginal utility is found only at the end of the total allocation, was first explicitly stressed by Hans Mayer (*Zeitschrift für Volkswirtschaft und Sozialpolitik*, New Series, vol. ii, p. 13). L. Schönfeld (in *Grenznutzen und Wirtschaftsrechnung* (Vienna, 1924) discussed it later in detail.
8. Schönfeld, op. cit., p. 107.
9. See entry 'Zurechnung' [Imputation], *Handwörterbuch der Staatswissenschaften,* op. cit., vol. viii.
10. See entry 'Produktion', loc. cit., p. 1108 et seq.
11. The content of 'feelings of pleasure and displeasure' is not defined; they signify anything the fulfilment or avoidance of which is desired.
12. Since every desire refers either to the achievement of a feeling of pleasure or to the avoidance of a feeling of displeasure, any desire can rationally be described either as a feeling of pleasure or as a negative feeling of displeasure, and *vice versa*. In the first case, economic action aims at a minimum of displeasure, in the second case at a maximum of pleasure. Both views are permissible.
13. The quantity to be given up will, of course, always be taken from marginal uses. However, the marginal utilization of a class of goods is not always valued with the latter's marginal utility. If there are substitutes for these goods and if substitution is expedient in case of loss, marginal uses are valued only according to the 'pseudo-marginal utility' of the class, as Böhm-Bawerk calls it.
14. Wieser, *Natürlicher Wert*, p. 14.
15. Wieser, *Theorie der gesellschaftlichen Wirtschaft*, p. 41.
16. Its peculiarity consists not in the use of mathematical symbols, which is merely a particular way of expression that could be applied to all theories. Classical theory, for example, was mathematically formulated by Whewell. What is peculiar to this theory is rather its attempt to determine the economic equilibrium system directly from simultaneous assumptions. So understood, there exist also followers of the mathematical school who do not use mathematical symbols, such as Montemartini.

17. See Böhm-Bawerk, 'Macht oder ökonomisches Gesetz?', *Zeitschrift für Volkswirtschaft* (1914).
18. Concerning the institutionalists, see F. A. Fetter in *Wirtschaftstheorie der Gegenwart*, edited by Hans Mayer, vol. i (Vienna, 1927).
19. See C. Menger, *Untersuchungen über die Methode der Sozialwissenschaften* (Leipzig, 1883), pp. 82–93.
20. The abbreviated phrase 'subjective value theory' instead of 'theory of subjective value' may have contributed to this misunderstanding.
21. Op. cit., pp. 9–12.
22. *Untersuchungen* etc., op. cit., pp. 139–86.
23. See above II B, and also the entry 'Wert' in *Handwörterbuch der Staatswissenschaften,* op. cit., suppl. vol. viii, p. 1007 et seq.

A10

Gottfried Haberler, 'Die Nationalökonomie als exakte Wissenschaft', *Zeitschrift fur Nationalökonomie*, band iii, 1923–4, pp. 771–81.

Gottfried Haberler (1900–) has been a prominent twentieth-century economist specializing in business cycle theory and the theory of international trade and finance. He was a member of Mises's seminar during the 1920s. (For Haberler's reminiscences of those years see 'A Vienna Seminarian Remembers: Letter from Gottfried Haberler', in John K. Andrews, Jr., ed., *Homage to Mises: The First Hundred Years* (Hillsdale College Press, 1981), pp. 49–52. This paper, a review essay of Richard von Strigl's 1923 book referred to in the editorial note introducing paper no. 14, p. 2, has been translated into English especially for this volume.

18

Economics as an Exact Science

GOTTFRIED HABERLER

Translated by

PATRICK CAMILLER

I. Introduction. – II. Definition of the problem. – III. Economic theory and economic history. – IV. The economic categories. – V. Organization of the economy. – VI. The economic system. Value and price. – VII. Critical remarks on the definition of the problem. – VIII. Critical remarks on the construction of the economic system.

I

The classical economists wrote their theory on two assumptions, without being clearly aware of them or at least without plainly expressing them. These two assumptions are: a static economy and specifically 'economic' behaviour by individuals. Their opponents did not find it difficult to demonstrate the incorrectness of Ricardo's laws – or rather, their discordance with reality; for the assumptions, which include those laws, seldom or never hold true.

The marginal utility school has dropped the assumption of a static economy – or, where it needs it, has explicitly stated it and thus drawn the sting of many objections. The other assumption, of a specifically economic form of behaviour, has been explicitly or tacitly retained.

Amonn, among others, has taken offence at this concept of a special economic principle. And in fact it cannot be denied that this concept does not fit into pure economic theory, which is supposed to hold for any conceivable economy. Recently, in reference to Cassel's system, Amonn has convincingly shown that theorists who include this concept in the 'foundations' have to drop it silently at a later stage.[1] Admittedly he draws from this correct perception a conclusion which in our view is false: namely, that economics is a social science (in the methodological sense) and has nothing to do with theoretical economics (roughly what is otherwise called the theory of a simple or single-root economy), which is indissolubly linked with the forbidden concept of an economic principle.

More recently, Strigl has attempted to establish economics as an empirical science of laws, without giving up all claim to deal with simple or individual economy.[2] It turns out that the concept of an economic principle, of specifically economic behaviour, can also be avoided in the theory of the simple economy. Let us now look in detail at this work of Strigl's.

II

'The object of my investigation is the forms of economic thought, and the problem is drawn up in such a way that it coincides with the question of the facts of economic events, with the question of the place of historical relativity in the economy' (p. v). The writer has avoided close dependence upon an epistemological system, on the one hand because he lacks the necessary dogmatism to appropriate one of the dominant systems, and on the other hand because he sees in such dependence a great danger for economics in its currently immature form. If a science does not fit in with an epistemological system, he points out, it is by no means certain that the science is therefore bad; philosophy too, like any specialist subject, is the work of human beings. That is certainly true. But in that case it is the duty of specialists to correct the theory of knowledge. For a theory of knowledge is implicit in any methodological investigation, whether the author is aware of it or not. Since knowledge of the correctness of a theory of knowledge cannot, or cannot simply, arise out of specialist considerations, the author of a methodological enquiry must be aware of its underlying theory of knowledge, either by relying on an existing system or by working out one of his own. If he does not do this, he runs the risk that the epistemological consequences of his system will be inconsistent without his being aware of this, so that his whole structure collapses. There is thus a serious defect in the refusal to take an explicit position on the problem of the theory of knowledge. For the reader, however, it is not all that difficult to reconstruct the author's own philosophical attitude.

Strigl sets out to construct theoretical economics as an empirical science of laws. Early on he takes up a quotation from Cassirer: 'There is no empirical law which does not involve the combination of given groups of facts, and the development of others which are not given; while on the other hand, every fact is established by reference to a hypothetical law and only acquires its determinateness through such considerations' (p. 4).[3] Theoretical economics cannot therefore take over the empirical material which it at least partly shares with many other sciences as it presents itself in pre-scientific thought or in other sciences; rather, it must grasp that material with specifically economic means (or forms) of thought established with regard to hypothetical economic laws. These forms of thought are the economic categories. 'Economic research finds its material in a peculiarly tainted condition... Elements dissimilar in nature, discovered side by side, at one moment become the presupposition of economics, and the next reassert their own laws in the economy... it consists of a huge number of component parts, each of which is for itself the object of a particular science... People appear with mental and physical qualities, with certain abilities and needs; goods appear which are subject to natural law; legal and social phenomena appear, conditions of climate and soil, technological achievements, religious and national ideals – all this and much else besides is somehow the economy or operates within it' (pp. 3–4). Here indeed an example from other sciences would be appropriate. For this is not at all peculiar to economics. The empirical material of any science is heterogeneous; it only becomes homogeneous because the respective science grasps the material with its specific forms of thought, contemplating it, as it were, from a particular side. Mechanics, for example, only deals with masses in which motion inheres and which have a position in space. These are its forms of thought, its categories. It does not see colours or material composition: it is blind to them. Chemistry again abstracts from mass and motion. It knows only material composition, in the same empirical objects in which mechanics sees only mass and motion. The situation is quite similar in the case of economics. The point is to show from what point of view economics contemplates the complex empirical material. In other words, it is necessary to deduce the specifically economic forms of thought, the economic categories. But more of this later.

The economic categories fully encompass the facts of the economy; they grasp everything of relevance, everything that one calls economic facts. They stand, as it were, at the threshold of the system, denying entry to elements which are alien to it. Pre-scientific concepts must take the form of an economic category in order to find a place in the system of theoretical economics.

III

The economic categories thus embrace the complex, heterogeneous material of experience and make it useable by theory. The facts, on the other hand, constitute the content, the concrete form, the realization of the economic categories. Everything meta-economic is referred to the facts. Only through the facts does the way open up from outside for any force to exert an influence on economic phenomena. The relationship between economic theory and economic history will now also be clear. The task of theory is to establish economic laws by inflecting the four economic categories. These laws are, so to speak, formulae with four independent variables. Economic history, however, gives a description of the concrete form of the economic categories. These quantities discovered by economic history are then inserted into the formulae established by theory. The 'calculation' of economic events down to the last detail now depends entirely on the accuracy with which the concrete form of the economic categories has been described.

The historical school denies the possibility of a general theory. What does the economy of a primitive people have in common with that of high capitalism? A specific theory, comes the answer, must be developed for each period. However, one wonders what is the meaning of economy in the two cases. If this expression is to have any meaning, there must be something common to every economy. And to identify that something common is precisely the task of pure theory. One can, of course, limit its area of validity by making historically relative assumptions. Then there will be a special theory which does not apply to any economy but only where the postulated form of the economic categories is present. Amonn, for example, sets out a special theory insofar as he limits it to 'the social'.

IV

The second part of the book presents the derivation of the economic categories. The starting-point is the concept of the right of disposal over goods. Every economy presupposes a distribution of this right of disposal, a distribution of goods; this is true even of a communist economy, where the right belongs precisely to the collective. The concept of the distribution of goods is imprecise. It is not always the case that whole goods are allocated to economic subjects. One speaks rather of possibilities of using goods, which are determined not only by technical factors but also by social, ethical or religious conditions. Exchange opportunities, for example, will increase them, while religious food taboos will reduce them. Often different possibilities of using a good are cumulatively possible at the same time; often they are alternatives which exclude one another. 'Thus the possible uses join together again in new units. Such alternative groups of feasible use possibilities are described as goods.' It is not a question here only of actual goods, but also of rights and relationships. Even labour appears in pure theory as a 'group of alternative use possibilities', which are admittedly determined by all manner of physiological and psychological, social and ethical conditions. But that is of no concern to economic theory, for which potential uses are given as such. This is how Strigl deduces the first two categories; possibilities of using a good, and right of disposal over goods.

The subject which is assigned the right of disposal is an economic subject. This is the third category. Economic subject and natural person do not coincide. There are natural persons who are not economic subjects (children), and not all economic subjects are natural persons (impersonal economic subjects). In the end the use possibilities must be graded according to their importance: a grading of use possibilities or a scale of values (not to be confused with economic value) is the fourth category.

'With the discovery of the four economic categories we have found the concepts which demarcate the terrain of pure theory. If an economic subject disposes of goods for which it has certain use possibilities, and if these use possibilities are ranged in a scale of values, the uses of the goods are unambiguously determined and the law-like regularity of these uses can be investigated by theoretical economics' (pp. 68–9). We find a very similar determination of the concept in Spann, for whom the economic subject disposes of means (goods) as the bearer of powers (use possibilities) for goals which he has brought into a system (scale).

According to certain theories, the field of economic theory is the field of economic behaviour: that is, there is an economic goal (purpose) alongside many others. But if – as is the case here – one considers the goal of the economy to be the achievement of several purposes, it is no longer possible to separate out one purpose as economic. There is no economic motive in addition to non-economic ones! 'In the empirical economy all uses of goods are "correct": that is, they correspond to economic law' (p. 77). For irrationality can only express itself in deficient knowledge of means. Then, for the person lacking knowledge, they are actually not means. Or else the error shows itself in the weighing up of goals; then the goals will be irrational but remain goals nonetheless. There is no non-economic behaviour! Economic laws are absolute laws, like those of mechanics; they hold always and everywhere. But how is a law-based science possible in relation to freely acting men and women? There is only one solution and it is offered here: namely, what is not economic law must be included among the facts and thus eliminated from theory. The question is not 'How do people behave in a particular situation?', but rather 'How are the uses of

219

goods determined by the given facts?' What is true of the concept of economic behaviour is also applicable to the concept of productivity. It too has no place in the system of theoretical economics.

V

'Let us call organization of the economy the principles which give us the form of the economic categories in a concrete situation. The organization of the economy embraces the historically relative' (p. 16). To economic history falls the task of describing the organization of the economy. It will never be possible here to reach into the smallest details. A choice has to be made. Only the general features of the economic organization can be indicated; the less important and the self-explanatory have to be left out. In order that the basic facts of an economy can be recognized, economic history must start from economic behaviour and interpret it accordingly. Yet this is a difficult path which is not always passable. Other methods must therefore be chosen to reach the goal. The state acts upon the economy, becoming involved in the shaping of certain economic categories. In particular, the concretization of the category of economic subject will largely depend upon national law. Since it can be assumed that national laws are by and large observed, economic history may closely follow the history of law. Technology too 'forms one of the meta-economic elements which decisively affect the economy because human behaviour must take its bearings from them' (p. 106). The use possibilities constitute the true realm of technology. Psychology, physiology and ethics work together to explain the grading of use possibilities. Changes in the facts can only partly be clarified by economics, insofar as they result from the uses of goods. Other factual changes – those due to natural phenomena, for example – cannot be explained by economics.

VI

In the next section we shall attempt to show how the economic system can be constructed out of the four categories. The law-like regularity in the use of goods has to be explained. The facts of the economy are only ever real in an individual economic subject; that is what theory must start from.

The theory of the use of goods has been almost completely elaborated by the marginal utility school. The school makes its focus the concept of value, which it understands as a psychological quantity experienced as want avoidance. But in Strigl's work the psychological apparel is cast off.

The concept of value becomes an aid to clarify the use of goods. Value is the measure which indicates the replaceability of one quantity of goods with another. There is no longer any talk of absolute value in the sense of a psychological reality. But this does not give rise to a material dispute with the marginal utility school. In any case, Spann has already reproached the marginal utility doctrine for its limitation of theory to the question of value, which in fact must be preceded by a theory of performance.

The prices of goods constitute data for the individual economy, but they are data of a particular kind. For theory does not simply accept prices – as it does other data – by assuming their free formation; it also explains them. The situation is different if prices are established under the influence of 'power', if, for example, wages are fixed by the collective agreement of two tightly knit professional associations. 'Such price-setting is not part of the economic process, but is a fixing of data which lies outside that process and even determines it' (p. 149).

One can hardly accept this division of price phenomena into a part which can be handled by economic theory and another part which is 'completely free'. The question is whether the despotic power holds complete sway. Often that will not be the case: often power will only influence prices without determining them. Such price-formation is no different from that which takes place under the influence of 'extra-economic motives' and which, as Strigl himself says, underlies the general law of prices. Quite fluid transitions are imaginable here, and it is not apparent why theory should call a halt at a certain point. Nor is that at all necessary. Price-formation under the influence of power is in principle the same as 'free' formation of prices. The price derives from subjective evaluations, which are in turn based upon the scales of values and use possibilities of individuals. These scales of values are influenced by all manner of motives, including 'extra-economic' ones. Nothing forbids us – on the contrary, purity of method requires us – to include 'power' among the forces which jointly establish the scales of values. By threats and promises, fear and hope, 'power' influences or determines use possibilities and scales of values. Thus, price-formation under the influence of power also comes under the general law of prices.

VII

We have already pointed out what a shortcoming it is on the author's part that he takes no position on problems of the theory of knowledge. We referred to the fact that an epistemological system must underlie every methodological investigation and that it should not be all that difficult to reconstruct this system. It is now time to prove this assertion.

To this end let us make absolutely clear how Strigl poses the problem. His programmatic question is: 'Which elements can be extracted from the (prescientifically understood) fact of vital need and have to be conceived as *a necessary prerequisite of the possibility of economic laws*, in such a way that an economic law is unthinkable without the positing of these elements, while at the same time the positing of all these elements means that the correlation described in economic laws necessarily occurs? These elements, the economic categories... therefore define the facts of the economy with the... necessary precision' (p. 14). In other words, the existence of economic laws is assumed and their conditions of possibility are then considered. The Kantian demarcation of theory has thus become quite evident. In Kant the question concerns the conditions of possibility of pure mathematics and pure natural science. Here the search is for the conditions of possibility of economic laws.

It is now clear how we must proceed in the deduction, or more accurately the hunting, of the categories. If one wishes to examine the conditions of possibility of economic laws, one must know what an economic law is. Just as Kant defined the problem more precisely by showing that pure mathematics and pure natural science consist in synthetic a priori judgements, so the point here is to define more accurately what is human economy. For example, economy is the utilization of goods. And then it can be asked under what conditions the use of goods is determined univocally (that is, in accordance with laws). Strigl proceeds in a different way. He does not place his definition of the concept of economy at the front, but presents it after the deduction of the categories. His deduction therefore makes an unsystematic impression; it lacks a guiding principle. The categories appear to have been merely collected rather than deduced. Let us look at this more closely. In Strigl's question that we quoted above, two points need to be distinguished: first, the categories should be extracted from the fact of vital need; and second, they should constitute the conditions of possibility of economic laws. Concerning the first point, an essay by Dr Kaufmann on the basic concepts of economics has already objected that the fact of vital need is the material basis of human economy but does not constitute its essence.[4] There is a confusion between the ground of being and the ground of knowledge. In fact, this does not escape Strigl's notice. On p. 157 he says that the fact of vital need is only the 'external hoist' for the economy. The first point is thus not sufficient for the deduction of the categories. From the fact of vital need all possible 'elements' can be deduced, even ones having nothing to do with economy, precisely because the fact of vital need is not congruent with economy, as

Strigl himself says elsewhere. As to his second point, we have already seen that he does not stick to it; or at least it does not follow from his presentation. Perhaps his concept of economy hovered before him in the deduction of the categories; perhaps he mentally checked whether his categories were the necessary conditions for a definite use of goods – as certain turns of phrase suggest. At any event, he has not expressed things clearly.

VIII

The second point on which our critique must focus concerns a sin of omission. To be blunt: the author has failed to work out properly the transition from 'pure' to special theory.

Let us recall what is the relationship between pure and special theory. 'We have identified as the content of pure theory the deduction of the laws governing admissibility which are given with the economic categories' (p. 20). Since the categories describe the facts of the economy as such, the laws of pure theory, which have to do only with these four basic concepts, are valid everywhere, in any economy. 'But this does not exhaust everything which can be ascertained with regard to law in the realm of the economic; economic theory with a narrower validity is also possible' (p. 20). That is, one can conceive of economic laws valid not for any economy but only with a particular mode of organization, a particular arrangement of the economic categories.

Thus, in order to develop a special theory, one proceeds in such a way as to construct types of economy distinguished by their organization, and then one seeks the laws which are valid for all these types. 'It is possible to construct these types of economic organization more or less far removed from reality, so that between the incalculable diversity of experience on the one hand, and the system of pure economic categories encompassing every conceivable economy... on the other hand, we preserve a structure of different economies each with a typical organization' (pp. 20–1). Through the incorporation of ever more historically relative determinants, these special theories move further and further away from pure theories.

The static economy is one example of such an ideal type. A certain arrangement of the economic categories is required to make an economy static: the data must be constant, and the scales of values must have a special form. Present and future needs must be equally highly valued – otherwise it is not possible that the same economic sequence will repeat itself year in year out. Another example would be the way in which Wieser has composed his theory of the social economy. Incorporating various historical-relative presuppositions, he advances from the theory of the simple economy (which is not 'pure' theory, however!) to the theory of the national and world economy.

The structure of theoretical economics thus takes the form of a pyramid, whose apex is made up of pure theory. Making our way down towards the base, we reach ever more special theories with an ever broader content and an ever smaller field of application.

In Section IV of Strigl's book, entitled 'The Economic System', this absolutely must find expression. The first step is to establish the laws of pure theory. Where pure theory ends and special theory begins, cannot be seen in Strigl. Coming down from the apex of this pyramid towards its base, the first specialization of theory is to be carried out through the incorporation of a series of technical facts. That is roughly what Strigl calls data theory but criticizes elsewhere. Certain technical distinctions have to be drawn between goods of different kinds – for example, between consumer goods and producer goods. Now the imputation problem presents itself for the first time. These technical determinations of data are also of significance in the so-called technical laws of economics – for example, the law of declining crop yield or the greater productivity of indirect production. So far theory corresponds to what Spann calls the theory of the single-root economy. But it does not completely coincide with Wieser's theory of the simple economy, because Wieser further presupposes a special economic mode of behaviour.

The next step along the path is of decisive importance. It is to find, by assuming appropriate preconditions, the transition from the theory of simple economy to the theory of national economy or, to use Spann's terms, from the single-root to the multiple-root economy. In this way, theory enters the area of the problems to which Amonn would like to see economics restricted. As is well known, Amonn reproaches the dominant teaching for its failure to draw a sharp distinction between economic theory and economics. In his view, the latter has nothing to do with the former: its object of knowledge is completely different; the theory of the simple economy can at most clarify the real basis of the price phenomenon. By contrast, Strigl stresses that the facts of the economy are only ever present in individuals, independently of their social relations. He makes his own, Spann's objection to Amonn: that 'all elements of the commercial economy can be brought down to the basic relations of a Robinsonade, because every commercial relation is nothing other than individual economic behaviour'.[5] This objection can easily be reduced *ad absurdum*. The argument could also support the assertion that economics is a part of psychology, because all commercial economic relations can also be conceptualized as psychological phenomena. Furthermore, Strigl's relationship to Amonn is different from that of most other theorists. His system does not contain the concept of an economic principle to which Amonn rightly objects, because it does not fit into theoretical science. And Strigl avoids the psychological apparel which Amonn considers essential to the theory of the simple economy, and in particular to the concept of subjective value.

Let us repeat that the transition from the theory of simply economy to the theory of social economy has not been adequately worked out. It would be in order here to show that a series of economic laws also belong to special theories, insofar as they presuppose specifically economic behaviour. A general law of prices is unthinkable without such an assumption, as Strigl rightly emphasizes. The same is true of most of the propositions of monetary theory. Finally the same kind of attention should be given, at least in passing, to the theory of interest and crises.

One might draw a parallel between Strigl's work and Kaufmann's book *Logik und Rechtswissenschaft* [Logic and Jurisprudence]. At any event, it marks a great step forward on the road to a logical underpinning of economic science.

NOTES

1. See *Archiv für Sozialwissenschaft*, vol. 51, p. 1.
2. Dr Richard Strigl, *Die ökonomischen Kategorien und die Organisation der Wirtschaft* (Jena: Gustav Fischer Verlag, 1923).
3. Quoted from Cassirer, *Substanz und Funktionsbegriff* (1910), p. 313.
4. See Felix Kaufmann, 'Die ökonomischen Grundbegriffe. Eine Studie über die Theorie der Wirtschaftswissenschaft', *Zeitschrift für Volkswirtschaft und Sozialpolitik*, vol. 4, pp. 31ff.
5. Spann, *Fundament der Volkswirtschaftslehre* (1918), pp. 10ff.

Leo Schönfeld, 'Über Joseph Schumpeters Lösung des ökonomischen Zurechnungsproblem', *Zeitschrift für Volkswirtschaft und Sozialpolitik*, band iv, 1924–5, pp. 432–77.

Leo Schönfeld (1888–1952) was a leading member of the interwar Austrian School, who continued to teach and write in Vienna until after World War II. Like Strigl he had been a member of Böhm-Bawerk's seminar prior to World War I, and was a link between that generation of Austrian economists and the subsequent one. His work on utility theory was cited favourably during the 1930s by Lionel Robbins and by John Hicks. His 1924 book *Grenznutzen und Wirtschaftsrechnung* (recently republished by the Philosophia Verlag, Munich) explored the implications of the time dimension for utility theory. After the 1930s he is often referred to as L. Illy. Emil Kauder, in his *A History of Marginal Utility Theory* (Princeton: Princeton University Press, 1965, p. 73) writes that his name was originally Leo Schönfeld but that the Nazis compelled him to change his name to Illy. This paper has been translated into English especially for this volume.

19

On Joseph Schumpeter's Solution
of the Problem of Economic Imputation

LEO SCHÖNFELD

Translated by

PATRICK CAMILLER

I. Let us begin with a very general introductory remark about the theme of this essay, which in both content and terminology remains within the present-day economic theory of the Austrian School.

Carl Menger's theory that the economic value of commodities is determined by their satisfaction of wants – their utility – led in its most consistent sequel to the realization that the value of productive goods (i.e. those which originate utility not in a direct sense but only indirectly by producing useful products) has its measure in the utility of the product: in other words, that the value of the production yield is to be imputed to the relevant productive goods. Since, however, several productive goods act together to bring about each product, the theory is faced with an extremely difficult problem of imputation (as Friedrich Wieser first called it): namely, *how is the value of definite quantities of each productive good active in production to be ascertained by reference to the known value of the joint product?* The same problem that concerns productive goods also arises for those which directly furnish utility ('consumption goods') but either generally do so in complementary association with other useful goods or are more useful within such an association than outside it. In this conception, therefore, any economic organization of productive activity and any economic decision about the use of complementary goods proceed on the basis of questions as to the imputation of value. The answer to such questions must be of decisive importance for the theory as well as the practice of all economic activity, given that the economic disposition of goods is governed by estimates of their value.

227

For many years I had the opportunity, especially in managing large enterprises, to observe the principles which underlie practical economic measures. And this impelled me, within the framework of other studies and of research into exact economic theory, to try to find for the problem and its solution some explanation of the kind which is also not offered in otherwise quite well-covered areas of the practical economic sciences – for example, in the theory of agricultural and commercial management or of taxation and bookkeeping. I thus came to the conclusion that in current theoretical research, both the presentation and the solution of the problem of economic imputation are still a thoroughly controversial matter. The striving for complete clarity about my own experience and opinions regarding the available theorems of value imputation first required that I should first subject them to critical examination. As part of this project, I shall concisely set out here my view of Joseph Schumpeter's theory of imputation.

The present work is purely critical in intent, but it does adopt a definite point of view. The little criticism that has so far been produced of Schumpeter's theory of imputation may perhaps be most succinctly described as a nonsuit. Essentially all it does is either reject the fundamentals of Schumpeter's whole system on general epistemological or economic-theoretical grounds, or dismiss his whole theory of value and other partial questions, so that any closer examination of his imputation theory built upon those foundations is held to be superfluous.[1] It may be because of this critical procedure that no advance has yet been made in the requisite testing of Schumpeter's solution of the problem of economic imputation. Even the author who had the most reason to do this, Böhm-Bawerk, refrained from any detailed analysis of Schumpeter's attempted solution despite his own recognition of the crucial importance of the imputation problem, on the grounds that Schumpeter's account was 'not lucid enough' for a reliable judgement to be made.[2] To a considerable extent this may indeed refer to the way in which Schumpeter presents his positive theory of imputation – which is not easy to understand at every point and is certainly not altogether clear. But the deeper reason why Böhm-Bawerk essentially confined himself to a defence of his own theory against Schumpeter's objections must, in my view, also be sought in the differences between the two authors concerning the general theoretical system of economics and most of its associated problems, which were such that from Böhm-Bawerk's basic standpoint there must have seemed no hope of reaching a satisfactory balance. We shall come back to this point, both here and elsewhere.

As far as we can see, however, none of Schumpeter's critics has done his imputation theorems the justice that is surely due to a theoretician of his standing and which Schumpeter himself, in his critique of Wieser's theory of imputation, so strikingly expressed with the question: 'Does the author achieve *his* purpose with *his* means?' Let us try to do the same in formulating our own critique of Schumpeter's theory of imputation. We shall try to form a judgement about the correctness of the solution which he provides to the problem of economic imputation; and purely for the purposes of this critique, we shall accept his theoretical economic system together with its general brief and hence his theory of value and so forth. Naturally such a way of proceeding can at first yield no more than a judgement about the correctness or usefulness of Schumpeter's solution to the problem of economic imputation within the framework of his economic system. Only if that judgement proves favourable will it be necessary for us critically to examine the system itself and its whole detailed brief. The reverse procedure – that is, to begin with so-called a priori analysis – is therefore in our view precisely the wrong way around. If it is generally employed in theoretical discussions, it inevitably involves dismissing out of hand much that is useful in the special theorems to be tested in each case; it is completely unable to do justice to a demand which Schumpeter himself fulfilled with the most commendable impartiality in relation to many theorems of other theoreticians: 'Every properly considered process of thought has a right to be itself considered in all its details.'

What we would add to this should go without saying: namely, that the arguments set out in our critical investigation are in no case to be understood as representing our own positive view of the matters under investigation. That cannot be alleged if we carry out our intention of *evaluating Schumpeter's solution to the problem of economic imputation from the standpoint of his theoretical economic system.*

II. In any problem the following points are essential: the *formulation* of the problem, its unknowns and – directly associated with them – the purposes for which they are ascertained and a solution is attempted; the *process* of working out a solution; and finally the *results* of the solution. Thus to solve correctly any special economic problem, including the problem of imputation, *from the standpoint of a particular theoretical system of economics* means, first, accurately to define the *terms* and the *data* of the problem from the basic principles contained within the system, and then, by applying a logically faultless *procedure* consistent with the system, to achieve *results* which answer the questions posed, determining the unknowns relevant to the purpose for which the solution has been undertaken. These results, like the question itself, must therefore be in complete harmony with the basic principles and the whole brief of the system – which already gives us a general picture of what our investigation has to cover.

229

The first question that we have to clarify is the following. How is the question of the imputation of value *formulated* in Schumpeter's economic system? That is, *which unknowns* does it seek to determine and *for what purposes* should they be used if they are found to be the result of the solution of the problem? And *what data* are available for the solution of the problem? Furthermore: how should we assess the formulation and the data that Schumpeter provides for the problem of imputation, from the point of view of his own economic system?

As is well known, Schumpeter's economic system culminates in the univocal determinateness and univocal determination of the static *problem of price*. The author describes this problem as follows.[3] (Here and wherever possible in our analysis we shall quote the author's own account, so as not to introduce by indirect presentation something that he did not mean to express.) 'The problem of price theory, in general terms, is the following. Given: m individuals A, B, C,... and their *value functions*[4] for n goods I, II,..., and so their ownership of these goods q_{a_1}, q_{a_2},...q_{b_1}, q_{b_2},... Find:[5] The value ratios p_1, p_2,..., at which exchange takes place and the (positive or negative) increases dq_{a_1}, dq_{a_2},...dq_{b_1}, dq_{b_2},..., which take place in the given ownership of the goods. That is the basic problem which allows of numerous variations and elaborations and which is of quite fundamental significance. Its formulation and the discussion of its results comprise, properly understood, the whole of pure economics.' Let us hold on to the following thematic points in Schumpeter's exposition of the imputation problem: 'And here lies the truly fundamental idea in the new, as opposed to the classical, system of economics. It lies in the fact that, *starting from the value of consumption goods, we base the theory of price formation upon it; that we obtain the value of the production goods – which we also need in this procedure – by deriving it from the value of the consumption goods*.'[6] Moreover, 'one need only "enquire" of individuals the value functions of the consumption goods, and one thereby obtains everything else.'[7] Finally there is his formulation of the imputation problem itself: 'Our problem is directly this: we must derive the *value functions of the individual production goods* from those of the individual products.'[8]

It would appear unnecessary to amass further quotations of similar import, as we shall content ourselves in what follows too with citing only those of the author's points which form the cornerstone of Schumpeter's argument. From these few propositions we can already see as plainly as possible the main features of his account. Thus the *unknowns*, whose determination Schumpeter defines as the task of imputation, are the *value functions of the individual production goods*, and *the purpose of ascertaining them is to introduce them as data into the price problem*.

Thus far everything is in perfect order as far as Schumpeter's system is concerned: the value functions of production goods, like those of all other goods, are needed as indispensable data for a complete solution of the general problem of price,[9] which is the crux of the whole system. Such a way of posing the question of value imputation does not only perfectly fit the basic principles of the system but is a vital necessity to it. Without that problem and its satisfactory resolution, the system would remain a torso and would fail the purpose for which it was established.[10]

So much for Schumpeter's way of *formulating* the problem of imputation. The *data* of the problem, as we can readily see from what has been said, are the value functions of the products ('consumption goods'), since it is from them that the value functions of the individual production goods are to be derived by imputation. Of these data too, which the author introduces, we should add that they are present and assimilable within his system; we will simply discover, in 'querying' the value functions of the products (or 'consumption goods'), that a certain connection is established among 'elements of the system', among different quantities of goods exchangeable for one another, which, in accordance with the aims of this critique, will be accepted together with the system. (A discussion of the practical limits of such querying would go beyond the framework of this investigation.)

We can thus turn straight to the other two major points – the procedure and the results of Schumpeter's proposed solution to the imputation problem. And here again it would seem that the quickest way of reaching our desired judgement is to start by directly considering what is most important: the *results* of that solution. We might thus perhaps pass over the procedural details of the solution and leave until later all those related disputes which, as is well known, range very widely but are not all that stimulating. We would then have to keep directly before us the results of Schumpeter's recommended procedure of imputation (i.e., the *value functions of the individual production goods*) which he describes in detail in his solution,[11] and to verify whether they can be *usefully incorporated into his formulation of the price problem*. Let us try to do this.

The place which Schumpeter actually ascribes to the value functions of production goods in the problem of prices cannot be deduced from his mathematical formulations of the problem which encompass the whole system, because these formulations – which we shall have occasion to discuss further – do not describe or complete anything lying between the data and the results of the process of price determination.[12] However, we must try to deduce it from the account he gives of particular phases of the solution to the price problem – that is, from his account of the nature and action of the demand and supply curves – which is intended to explain

231

the details of price formation but actually raises a claim to universal validity.[13]

These two 'curves', representing value functions geometrically, are the terms in which the values of the goods are combined and directly serve the solution of the problem of price. The demand curve of any good, and thus especially of any product, is nothing other than its value function (or its geometric expression – an alternative which, like Schumpeter, we shall not mention each time): 'The demand curve is simply the value function.'[14] The supply curve is the expression of costs. In Wieser's fundamental analysis, however,[15] costs are also values – of goods which must be given up to procure the demanded good; that is (where the product is obtained through production), the values of its production goods.

Accordingly, Schumpeter says on this point: 'We shall therefore conceive of the supply curve as an inverted demand curve, as a value curve of the production goods.'[16] Each demand curve is a downward curve; as geometric expression of the value function, it exhibits smaller ordinates (value magnitudes) for larger abscissae (quantities of goods).[17] Each supply curve, as 'inverted' value function, displays the opposite formal character: 'If the supply or asking price of a good rises, so does the supply quantity under otherwise unchanged conditions. Or: if the supply quantity increases, so does the supply price.'[18] By comparing the demand and supply curves on the same abscissae and thus ascertaining their point of intersection, it is possible to *solve the price problem* for each good (without exception and in fundamentally the same way) – which, in the case of economic comparison of a product and its means of production, means *ascertaining the point of intersection of the product's value function and the 'inverted' value function of its production goods*. At that point of intersection – which is the point of static economic equilibrium, of the static 'margin of production'[19] – 'demand' is equal to 'supply'. The 'demand price' and 'supply price' become equal in the 'equilibrium price'[20] – which, as we shall see later in more detail, Schumpeter expressed by saying that 'the marginal return equals the marginal cost'.[21]

We have thus reached a point, however, where the critique of Schumpeter's theory already appears to have a weighty objection to deploy. For in our view, Schumpeter's account of the products' supply curve contains the following defect. According to his more general analysis,[22] a certain value function only refers to the values and quantities of one good. But now he introduces, as the supply function of any product, the value function which must contain in itself the values and quantities of *several* production goods which are required to complement that product. Without providing the necessary clarity in this regard, he places before the reader, as the individual product's supply function, '*a value function of the production goods'*. 'The supply curve of a good,' he says, 'gives us, indeed is, the value function of the production goods.'[23] In principle there can be no objection to the construction of such a value function: a particular group of complementary production goods, like one individual good, certainly has a value which in a way depends upon its quantity – and at least in principle, this makes it possible to establish a value function for the whole group of production goods. Schumpeter presents the supply of the product in the form of one such value function referring to the whole group of production goods in question. But the result of the imputation is *'the value functions of the individual production goods'*. Thus, somehow or other, *the imputed value functions of the individual production goods* which combine to produce the demanded product in question within a complementary group *must be translated into the form of a supply curve* – into the 'inverted demand curve', the 'value curve of the production goods', the inverted value function of the 'mix of participating means of production'[24] – that is, *into a process which is logically opposed to that of imputation*. For imputation ascertains the value functions of the individual members of a complementary group of production goods, but in the employment of the results of imputation, in the solution of the price problem, these value functions of the individual production goods within the requisite combinations must somehow be recombined[25] so that, in accordance with Schumpeter's instructions, they are contrasted to the demand curve of a given product as its supply curve, as a value function of the particular production goods which produce this product. *Of this process, however, Schumpeter gives us no elucidation.*

We must leave it open whether the author *accounted to himself* for this extremely important point which has to be explained by his theory of imputation – that is, whether he ever tried to do what we have attempted here: to check the results of his proposed solution of the imputation problem by looking further at its useability in individual cases, at its suitability for the systemic purpose which it and the whole imputation problematic are supposed to serve. At any event the objection remains that Schumpeter *does not give his readers sufficient information about the matter*, that the whole of a crucial part of his account is incomplete or imprecise, that there is a yawning gap or a logical jump in the exposition of his system. For if the value functions of the production goods are indispensable data for the basic problem of this system – the price problem encompassing all goods – if the imputation problem is duly thrown up as a consequence of such knowledge, and if it is demonstrated how the value functions are determined through the solution of that problem, then it would naturally also have to be shown and proven how the value functions can be usefully combined, and thus employed as data of the price problem

233

in the course of its solution. The relevant statements by Schumpeter on this matter, to which we shall return below, cannot reasonably be considered as proof of this; they do not go beyond a mere assurance that everything is in order.

This failing on Schumpeter's part means that we cannot tell how the addition of the value functions for production goods – functions derived from his solution to the imputation problem – is supposed to take place in detail in what he regards as the typical solution to the price problem. And if we are in the dark about *how* this is conceived, then any attempt to answer, in the direct way initially adopted here, the question of whether it is *useful* to insert the value functions must remain pure conjecture – to say nothing of the fact that we have no right to complete Schumpeter's construction, and no intention of attempting it here.

III. We are thus forced to give a different direction to our enquiry. We shall have to look more closely at the nature of the results delivered by Schumpeter's proposed solution of the imputation problem, and thus at the properties of the value functions of individual production goods. The assessment we have to make can, of course, be reached only by analysing the author's own proposed *method of solving* the imputation problem, because only that is able to give us more precise information about the nature of the value functions. We thus come to the last of the major components of Schumpeter's imputation theory which we have to test.

If our critique is not to run into the sand, however, we must at all costs avoid falling into the kind of situation, as embarrassing for the author's theory as for its critics, which arose in the just failed investigation – it would be too complicated and not very profitable to show that this might happen[26] – and we must believe that we have in what follows a sure and simple, methodologically well-grounded path of advance. If we are afraid of obtaining from the author's own statements too little precise information about what we have to analyse, we will *restrict the material* of our enquiry – not in the sense of completely eliminating even one of its objects, but in that of initially focusing upon a quite definite, substantively well-defined area of one of these objects, which is given a precise definition by the author himself. What does this mean for the value functions of the individual production goods, as they are given in our author's procedure for solving the imputation problem? It means that initially we do not include them *as a whole* in our investigation – that is, not over their whole course or their full extent. Rather, we concentrate upon one quite definite *point* of those value functions concerning which we receive precise information from the cohesive set of basic theorems in Schumpeter's system: the point where, in rough geometric terms, the abscissae of those value functions represent the *equilibrium* quantities of the goods to which the functions apply, and the ordinates represent their equilibrium prices. The following investigation will therefore be conducted *on the assumption of the equilibrium state* in Schumpeter's economic system, and initially we shall – of necessity, in our view - focus upon precisely this limited investigation, because we have for that assumption, and not otherwise, it would seem, a series of statements by Schumpeter regarding the links in his system which have to do with imputation.

It is also necessary to go somewhat further afield. But let us stress at once that here too we shall remain completely consistent with the opening intention of this critique. Although the next part of our investigation might perhaps have a more positive face, all the relevant arguments – if they are to be useful for this immanent critique – must be exactly and narrowly fitted into Schumpeter's theoretical system, and they must be strictly and directly built up on its own premises.

We shall start from the problem of price, as Schumpeter himself does with his theory of imputation, and take up the assumption of our immediate investigation – that is, the assumption of equilibrium in Schumpeter's economic system which, in terms of the price problem, denotes nothing other than that systemic condition where the price problem is solved all along the line and everything is 'adjusted' to this solution throughout the system. The solution to Schumpeter's problem of price, as we have already briefly mentioned, is characterized by the equation of economic equilibrium – 'marginal return = marginal cost' – for every product and each of its means of production without exception. Let us consider more closely what these two magnitudes represent. According to Schumpeter, we must here assume a common measure of price: money.[27] Then the *'marginal return'* appears as that sum of money which is realized for the 'last-produced quantity of the product':[28] that is, the unit price of the product multiplied by the number of units contained in this last-produced quantity of the product. In the state of equilibrium, the unit price of the product is by definition its equilibrium price; for the sake of simplicity let us call the product A, its equilibrium price P_a, and the magnitude (i.e. the number of units) of its last-produced quantity M_a.[29] Therefore the *marginal return* $= M_a P_a$. The *marginal costs* – 'the monetary measure of the production goods, the "equivalent" on the right side of our equation'[30] – are the 'sum of money' that must be expended for those quantities of the production goods which serve to produce the last quantity of product M_a: that is, for the requisite quantity of each one of those production goods. These sums of money are again, for each of the production goods, the unit price of the individual production goods multiplied by the quantity of it that must be employed to produce M_a in a complementary association with the other means of production. The unit price of each production good is – without exception in the state of equilibrium – its equilibrium price.[31] Let us now term B, C, D etc. the production goods which serve in complementary association to produce A; P_b, P_c, P_d etc. their equilibrium prices; and M_b, M_c, M_d the magnitudes required for joint production of the last quantity of product M_a. The marginal costs then come to: $M_b P_b + M_c P_c + M_d P_d + \ldots$ *The equation of economic equilibrium – marginal return = marginal costs* – thus reads with the terms we have introduced for product A and its complementary means of production B, C, D:[32]

$$M_a P_a = M_b P_b + M_c P_c + M_d P_d + \ldots$$

Schumpeter himself provides us with the interpretation of this equilibrium equation for each product and its means of production. For example: 'Let us now take a producer in a commercial economy and follow the observations and modes of expression of everyday life. When will there be "no tendency" for the man to undertake changes – that is, to produce? When the return he can expect from selling more products no longer shows any surplus over the costs incurred by this further production – that is, when the marginal return equals the marginal costs.'[33]

Now, the equation

$$M_a P_a = M_b P_b + M_c P_c + M_d P_d + \ldots$$

...expresses a relation between the *equilibrium prices* of the complementary means of production and their common *product*; but it can be of use to us only with a relation between the *value functions* of those goods for the purpose of their assessment. Thus, if we want the equation to be useful for that purpose, we must first link it up with a relation between the *marginal values* or marginal utilities of the goods in question. From a relation between marginal values, a certain ratio between the *value functions* of those goods must directly result by virtue of the general relations that hold between marginal value and value function within Schumpeter's system.

Our next task, then, in linking the relation between equilibrium prices to one between marginal values, is *to establish what is the relation in Schumpeter's system between equilibrium price and marginal value or marginal utility*. On this matter Schumpeter gives us no clear indications. He expresses the 'law of the marginal utility level'[34] – the condition for that 'point at which the acquisition of each good ceases for each economic subject'[35] – by means of equations which hold for each economic subject and for any two goods A and B:[36]

$$\frac{marginal\ utility\ of\ good\ A}{marginal\ utility\ of\ good\ B} = \frac{1}{exchange\ ratio\ or\ price\ of\ B\ in\ terms\ of\ A}$$

'These equations state that equilibrium prevails within the system if the exchange ratio of each good to each other equals the reciprocal value of their marginal utility relation.'[37] In order to give this formula of Schumpeter's too the simplest possible algebraic expression, let us denote the marginal utility or value of his good B by Y_b, the marginal utility or value of his price-measure good A by Y_p, and the 'price of B in terms of A' – which, as the price resulting from the conditional equation of equilibrium, is by definition the equilibrium price of good B expressed in A as the measure of price – as P_b. Then we must write the general conditional equation of economic equilibrium in Schumpeter's system as:

$$\frac{Y_p}{Y_b} = \frac{1}{P_b}$$

or as: $Y_b = P_b Y_p$. The same relation holds, of course, in Schumpeter's thinking, not just for the particular good B but for any good whatever; we may therefore, by omitting the b index, write it quite generally as: $Y = PY_p$, that is: *in the equilibrium state of this economic system, the marginal value of each good equals its equilibrium price multiplied by the marginal value of the price-good*, where price-good, in conformity with what Schumpeter has earlier said, should be understood as the good in which the equilibrium price of the good in question is expressed or measured.

Let us now return to our product A and its complementary means of production B, C, D,... As for any good in general, so for each of *these goods* in equilibrium, its marginal value equals its equilibrium price multiplied by the marginal value of the price-good (that is, for Schumpeter, money). Call the marginal values of these A, B, C, D... goods in the state of equilibrium Y_a, Y_b, Y_c, Y_d etc., their equilibrium prices P_a, P_b, P_c, P_d..., and the marginal value of money in the state of equilibrium Y_p. We then have the above relation between marginal value and equilibrium price for A, B, C, D..., written as: $Y_a = P_a Y_p$; $Y_b = P_b Y_p$; $Y_c = P_c Y_p$; $Y_d = P_d Y_p$, and so on.[38] Let us then represent the equilibrium prices out of these expressions for the marginal values:

$$P_a = \frac{Y_a}{Y_p}; \ P_b = \frac{Y_b}{Y_p}; \ P_c = \frac{Y_c}{Y_p}; \ P_d = \frac{Y_d}{Y_p} \ etc.$$

and let us finally insert these magnitudes into the equation for the equilibrium prices of the product and its production goods that is, in the formula for the equation: marginal return = marginal costs, $M_a P_a = M_b P_b + M_c P_c + M_d P_d + ...$, so that we have:

$$M_a \frac{Y_a}{Y_p} = M_b \frac{Y_b}{Y_p} + M_c \frac{Y_c}{Y_p} + M_d \frac{Y_d}{Y_p} + ...,$$

and after multiplication of both sides by Y_p: $M_a Y_a = M_b Y_b + M_c Y_c + M_d Y_d + ...$[39] Converted accordingly, this equation reads:

$$Y_a = \frac{Y_b}{M_a/M_b} + \frac{Y_c}{M_a/M_c} + \frac{Y_d}{M_a/M_d} + ...$$

This means, expressed in words, that *in the state of equilibrium in Schumpeter's system, the marginal value of each product produced by a group of complementary production goods* (i.e., in our notation: Y_a) *is equal to the sum of the marginal values of these individual production goods* (i.e., Y_b, Y_c, Y_d, etc.) – *if each of these marginal production-good values is applied to the relation between the last-produced quantity of the product and the quantity of production goods required to produce it, that is, respectively, to the ratio*

$$\frac{M_a}{M_b}; \frac{M_a}{M_c}; \frac{M_a}{M_d} \; etc.$$

This ratio, and thus the postscript referring to it, need to be considered if one follows Schumpeter's general rule for the value functions of the individual production goods: that is, 'to take into account that for the abscissae[40] of the value curves of the production goods, it is necessary to choose units corresponding to the quantity of goods which are required to produce a unit of product. Of that too this will be the one and only mention.'[41] This rule, in other words, states that the quantity of each means of production which is required to produce one unit quantity of the product is itself a unit quantity. For the production of one unit quantity of the product, then, one unit quantity of each of its means of production is employed: for M_a unit quantities of our product A will be employed M_a unit quantities of production good B, M_a units of C, of D, and so on. But this simply means that each of the magnitudes we have so far called M_b, M_c, M_d,..., which represent precisely the quantities of production goods B, C, D etc. used to produce M_a, the last quantity of the product, contains exactly the same number of units (i.e., is equal to M_a); and that therefore, in algebraic terms, $M_b = M_a$, $M_c = M_a$, $M_d = M_a$, etc. It follows, however, that the quotients

$$\frac{M_a}{M_b}, \frac{M_a}{M_c}, \frac{M_a}{M_d}, ... = \frac{1}{1} = 1$$

and cease to apply as divisors of the marginal values in the above formula:

$$Y_a = \frac{Y_b}{M_a/M_b} + \frac{Y_c}{M_a/M_c} + \frac{Y_d}{M_a/M_d} + \ldots$$

.[42] Thus, based directly upon the main theorems of Schumpeter's system, this reduces to a simple *formula for addition of the marginal values of the complementary production goods in the state of equilibrium*:[43]

$$Y_a = Y_b + Y_c + Y_d + \ldots$$

In this formula we now have before us a relation between the *marginal values* of the complementary means of production and their common product – a relation which applies universally to the state of equilibrium in Schumpeter's system. Now for the last step in our immediate enquiry. What does this relation between marginal values signify as a relation between the *value functions* of those goods?

The general connection between value function and marginal value in the state of equilibrium directly results from the essence or definition of the value function. Fully in line with Schumpeter's thinking, we may most briefly characterize the content of the value function as the compiled statements[44] of all possible subjective marginal values for all possible quantities of a good in the possession of an economic subject.[45] Even at equilibrium within an economic system, the value function remains what it is. It reacts to the introduction of the postulate of economic equilibrium in no other way than as a table: we put a finger on one of its columns in order to read off what corresponds to that place in another column. At equilibrium the quantity of each good owned by each economic subject is its equilibrium quantity, and the value function of each good indicates the marginal value for that equilibrium quantity – or, more concisely, the marginal value of the good at equilibrium.

Let us now combine this fact, universally applicable and quite self-evident in Schumpeter's system, with that formula for addition of the marginal values at equilibrium which also applies universally in the system. This tells us the following.

In the state of equilibrium within Schumpeter's economic system, the value functions of the individual complementary production goods must – quite generally, as a matter of principle – exhibit for each production good marginal values whose sum is equal to the marginal value of the joint product – that is, to the marginal value which the value function of the joint product displays in the state of equilibrium.

We have thus identified an essential and universal property of the value functions of the complementary production goods in Schumpeter's system. It can now serve us as a lever to appraise the value functions which Schumpeter's proffered solution to the imputation problem furnishes for these goods – only a potential criterion, it is true, but one which, on the assumption of equilibrium, hardens into a clear and dominant feature directly resting upon, or contained in a different form within, the basic principles of Schumpeter's system. *If it is claimed of any value functions that they are proper value terms for the complementary production goods, then we must verify whether the marginal values of these production goods which the value functions give us for the state of equilibrium correspond or not to the additional relation in question. Only if they do so correspond can they be correct*: that is, in this context, only then can they be assimilable to the most important theorems of Schumpeter's theory of price and compatible with the doctrinal foundations of his system.

IV. Let us then examine the value functions for complementary goods which are furnished by Schumpeter's solution to the imputation problem. Without having for the present to go into details, we will find a generally applicable image of their character if we focus on the first *'fundamental principle'* of Schumpeter's solution – that is, *the basic procedure of deriving the value functions of the individual production goods, upon which his proposed solution is principally constructed*. At the crucial point he explains: 'We suggest the following path. *In principle each production good should have imputed to it the values of all those products in whose production it participates; or rather, the value functions of all those products should appear in the value functions of the production goods*. This has the result, certainly, that the latter's scales of value cannot be added. But what does that matter? For what purpose would such an addition be required?.... We find something similar with the value functions of consumption goods. If several consumption goods combine in a particular useful effect, so that all are necessary for it to be achieved, this useful effect must appear in the value functions of *them all*.... In the case of complementary consumption goods, it may again seem that we are operating a perverse double accounting, that we are entering the same value several times. And we are doing that...'[46]

The basic claim of this principle may be understood – although admittedly it is a purely formal matter – from two points of view. *From the point of view of the individual production good*, it stresses the necessity that the values of all the products to which that good contributes should be expressed in its value function. The other point of view seems clearer to us, however: namely, that of *the individual product*. In this regard, Schumpeter's propositions quoted above contain the fundamental postulate – which is most insistently expounded with the help of detailed examples – that *the value of the joint product* should appear in the value function of each of its means of production: that is, *should be imputed to each of these means of production*. We prefer the latter classification in presenting the relevant connections, because it is clearer and congruent with the ordering of the data which Schumpeter as well as other authors, including ourselves in this essay, have employed for the definition of the imputation problem,[47] such that the comparison is not between a given production good and all its products but between a given product and all its means of production. Of course, the author's explanation should not be misunderstood: the *whole* value of the product does not always have to be imputed to each of its contributing means of production. In most practical cases it is a question of an 'overlapping'[48] imputation (i.e. operating in favour of all or at least several of the participating production goods) of 'that value surplus which we measure here with money and call the net return – the surplus over and above the value of the individual means of production, in other uses than the one just now under consideration'.[49]

Be this as it may, there remains the basic claim that certain parts of the product value which are actually present only once should be included in the value functions of several or all of the production goods contributing to the product – that is, 'that the production goods together are worth more than their product'.[50]

Application of this principle of 'overlapping' imputation has the inescapable consequence (as Schumpeter himself is immediately obliged to add as a general rule) that the value functions which his solution to the imputation problem provides for the complementary production goods 'are not addable'; or, to be more precise, that the marginal values contained in those value functions – in geometric terms, the ordinates of the value curves of the complementary production goods – cannot be added up. Thus, *as regards the marginal values displayed by the value functions of the complementary production goods* (as well as the complementary consumption goods) *ascertained through Schumpeter's procedure for a solution*, we can say that *in general, and especially in the state of equilibrium, their sum must be* greater *than the marginal value of their joint product* or (in the case of the complementary consumption goods) of their joint useful effect. *But we have thus acquired, as a result of our preceding exposition, a most compelling reason to reject Schumpeter's solution altogether.*

The formula for addition of the marginal values showed us that the possibility of such 'addition' must be present, at least in the state of equilibrium, for otherwise, after the value functions of the production goods have been inserted into the price problem, the solution to that problem could never lead to the basic equation: marginal return = marginal costs, upon which the formula for addition of the marginal values directly rests. With the value functions supplied by Schumpeter's proposed solution to the imputation problem, such addition is impossible in principle because the resulting sum of marginal values of the individual production goods to which a certain part of the product value is several times imputed, is in principle *greater* than the marginal value of the joint product – and so *the production-good value functions which Schumpeter gives as the result of his solution of the imputation problem are fundamentally incompatible with the last and most important results of his theory of price*. It is an objection to Schumpeter's imputation theory *which becomes so strong as completely to destroy it, precisely because*, according to his own statements, the only role which falls to the solution of the imputation problem is to secure the results of the price theory, and those results constitute the very essence of his entire system.

We consider that this argument, which at every point takes Schumpeter's own words as its basis, is so self-evident and irrefutable that it requires no further demonstration. Everything else that we will think it necessary to say will mainly involve an absolutely necessary total explanation of this cardinal point of our critique: it should show the erroneous views which lie at the root of Schumpeter's theory of imputation which is so crucial to his system; but it should thereby also indicate the direction in which we shall have elsewhere to undertake a positive evaluation of the critical results of the present investigation.[51]

V. Now, the proposed refutation of the bases of Schumpeter's theory of imputation contains a major error; it is, to be brief, suspiciously simple. Could an author like Schumpeter fail to notice such a blatant contradiction, in his own theoretical system to boot, with whose structure he must have been intimate in all its last consequences? Ought a principle to be inapplicable in solving a problem if it seems so evident to the author that he gives only a few examples (which we shall explore below) by way of illustration and considers virtually no justification to be needed for it? In fact, all we find among his positive statements are the following two propositions: 'And these value curves will offer us correct laws of exchange: Whenever an element necessary for a certain productive combination has to be given up, the owner will look at the whole result which thereby becomes impossible and not just at one part of it.' And: 'It [i.e., our approach] expresses the fact that each of the complementary goods must be granted that economic attention which is due to the joint useful effect, since that effect is dependent upon each one of them. Particularly in the exchange of a good belonging to such a combination, the whole useful effect always comes into consideration.'[52] Furthermore, Schumpeter feels entitled to be brief at a point which he confesses to be vital to his whole theory, evidently on the assumption that his solving principle is known and accepted by his readers because it is already found in its early stages in Carl Menger's theory of value and is employed with explicit justification in Böhm-Bawerk's theory of imputation – the latter even including the bases for the solution to the problem. In fact, that which seems even more questionable in our critique – the principle of 'overlapping' imputation – is closely and amicably associated in Böhm-Bawerk with a basic idea which, when translated out of his imagery and terminology, precisely corresponds to the principle of addition contained in the formula for summation of the marginal values that was derived above for Schumpeter's system.[53]

All these points require full elucidation if our critique is to meet the resulting objections and to reveal its innermost core.

Schumpeter's basic principle of imputation, as identified above, is nothing other than the 'idea of loss' used by Böhm-Bawerk,[54] the principle of calculating value from the 'decrease in the total return' or 'the decrease in return which ensues in the case of loss'.[55] And it ultimately goes back to Carl Menger's declaration: 'If we summarize these three cases, we obtain a general law of the determination of value of a concrete quantity of a good of higher order:[56]...[namely, that it] is equal to the difference in importance between the satisfactions that can be attributed when we have command of the given quantity of the good of higher order whose value we wish to determine and the satisfactions that would be attributed if we did not have this quantity at our command.'[57] We find the same procedure for the determination of value in Böhm-Bawerk's famous 'master-key', only now it is valid for goods of every order: 'But practical economic life brings out a great many complications which the practical man treats with easy assurance, but the theorist finds considerable difficulty in explaining. To understand these everything depends on the correctness of our casuistical decision as to that amount of utility which, in the given circumstances, is the marginal utility. For this purpose the following general direction may serve as master-key to all the more difficult problems of value. We must look at the economic position of the person who is estimating the value of a good from two points of view. First, we must in thought add the good to his stock, and consider what further and lesser concrete wants can *now* be satisfied. Second, we must in thought *deduct* the good from his stock, and consider again what concrete wants will *still* be satisfied. In the latter case, of course, it becomes manifest that a certain layer of wants, viz. the lowest layer, has lost its former provision; this lowest layer indicates the marginal utility that determines the valuation.'[58] The result of applying this general procedure to the case of complementary production goods can be gathered from Böhm-Bawerk's following statement of principle: 'Both Menger and I, in our conception of the problem, come to the conclusion that the full decrease in return that would ensue from its loss should be imputed to each of several complementary elements as the basis for its valuation.'[59]

In this way, however – and we too believe this is fully in line with Menger's thinking – Böhm-Bawerk quite fundamentally limits the applicability of the principle contained in the above procedure to his own theory of imputation: 'overlapping judgements of imputation' can for him only ever have *'alternate'* validity.[60] This means that the imperative requirement for actual application of the principle in determining the value of the individual complementary good is that the same procedure is *not* applied in valuating the *other* goods of the same complementary group; but especially not if the value expressions of all members of the complementary group are to be jointly introduced in *one* calculation. Böhm-Bawerk has developed this basic principle at considerable length in his counter-critique of Wieser. We refer the reader to the 'Exkurs' (pp. 180–201), from which we can reproduce here only the author's own résumé: 'Nor is it a matter of drawing from such imaginary numerical sums [the author is referring to the cumulative addition of only alternately valid overlapping appraisals of value, "numerical addition of alternate individual values" – LS] – if one wishes to construct them at all, even arithmetically – some substantive conclusions in the field in which the "together" really does have to be taken seriously.' *Such a field, however, by its whole conception and innermost essence, is Schumpeter's problem of price.* We have no need at all here to invoke his general brief and the formulae for addition of the marginal values and equilibrium prices. We have just to consider the point at which Schumpeter's economic subject – who, according to his whole conception, must be the most far-seeing, subtly calculating and judicious ever to have existed in an economic system – is faced with the task of reaching decisions about the price and use of all elements in his overall individual economy, as a result of the general interdependence among the economies of all other subjects. In that situation, the mere idea is completely implausible that in the very process of imputation the subject should be content with one-sided evaluation of *'one* element required for a certain productive combination' and lend his 'economic attention' just to the 'exchange of *one* good', instead of calculating with precision and – which is what matters here and is the core of the Walras-Schumpeter problem of the exact price – calculating *everything*.

We can now see what this all amounts to. The exact equation-system in the Walras-Schumpeter problem of price requires as data the 'value functions and quantities of all goods'.[61] These useable value functions of *all* the production goods to be obtained individually from the solution to the imputation problem must be *determined without any equivocality and be suitable for simultaneous insertion in a complete, univocally determined equation-system*. At no event can they *collide with one another*; *alternate* values, resulting from an only alternately applicable solution of the imputation problem, *are of absolutely no use for this purpose*, and their introduction cannot but land the general problem of exact prices in a state of serious confusion. Being himself fully aware of this fact, Schumpeter banished from his positive explanation any reference to the possibility of a merely alternate solution of the imputation problem.[62] That he nevertheless adopted a solving principle which, seen correctly, can only provide alternately valid results was due to a misconception. Schumpeter's attempt inevitably failed to use these results to consolidate his system and his price problem, which requires the value functions and quantities of all goods as univocal data.

Nothing is changed in this respect by the fact that Schumpeter, in denying the possibility and necessity of adding the results of imputation,[63] also adopted Böhm-Bawerk's restricted application of the principle of overlapping imputation. For such addition, as we have seen, is actually essential if the results of imputation are to fit at all into Schumpeter's price problem. Schumpeter failed to see this, nor did he take into account a more far-reaching fact which underlies the main error of his theory of imputation: namely, that the solving principle which seemed to him useful for Böhm-Bawerk's imputation problem *could not for that reason* be used for his own imputation problem, since *the two are quite different in the respects that are relevant here*. Moreover, as we shall have occasion to repeat, this divergence in their conception of the imputation problem stems from a *fundamental difference in their formulation of the price problem itself*. If Schumpeter had paid heed to this, he would certainly have realized that the imputation principle at issue, which served as an instrument for Böhm-Bawerk's ends, was of no use for his. But instead, the standpoint for the whole construction is that general static problem of price upon which he tried to base his whole theoretical system. So, as he followed through in detail the necessary connections within his system, he overlooked its difference with that of Böhm-Bawerk – and without further ado transferred from Böhm-Bawerk's circle of ideas things which had no possibility of surviving in his own system.

The reader is referred here to the discussion in the next section of one of Schumpeter's examples. We also hope on another occasion to look more closely at Böhm-Bawerk's theory of imputation – but for the moment we will just say a few words about it to clarify the contrast with Schumpeter's theory and to make what follows easier to understand.

In the passage quoted above, Menger calls what has been known since Wieser as the imputation problem, the 'general law of the determination of value of a concrete quantity of a good of higher order'. And Böhm-Bawerk in his own theory has well and truly stressed that it is a question of *one* good; indeed it is hard to imagine a firmer expression than that which he uses for this limited purpose of his imputation of value. Thus, he quite explicitly narrows the problem down to the value magnitudes of *one* of the complementary goods, for which he coins the term 'final piece' of the complementary group; consequently he vindicates only one alternate value in his solution of the imputation problem,[64] and can operate with a solving principle which delivers only alternately valid results. There can only ever be *one* member of the 'final piece' group: *which one* is a question of the concrete 'circumstance'. We think we can add that this circumstance is nothing other than the complex of conditions which fixes the actual object of price determination and value imputation; if this changes, the circumstance becomes different and another member of the group becomes the 'final piece'. In that case Böhm-Bawerk's rules for imputation can be applied to this other member only if the procedure for ascertaining the value of the first member is *completely abandoned* – indeed, only if this latter magnitude which was previously the *unknown quantity* in the problem becomes one of its data instead. This is easy to see if Böhm-Bawerk's formulation of the problem is expressed in mathematical terms. And the same thing would be represented if the value of the joint useful effect (product) is equated with the sum of values of the complementary goods (production goods),[65] all members of which sum (except for one – the value of the 'final piece') must be given[66] in order to ascertain this one unknown by allocation of the residual value which remains from the known value of the joint useful effect (product) after deduction of the known values of the other members of the group. In Schumpeter's imputation problem, however, the number of unknowns in each complementary group is generally higher than one, and it is rigorously excluded that a value magnitude should move from the realm of unknowns to that of the data in the imputation problem and so adapt to the alternation built into the principle of its solution. The solution to Schumpeter's price problem must in principle follow at once all along the line – that is, for all economic subjects and all goods. It employs univocal, cumulative value functions of all individual production goods, valid simultaneously and alongside one another: that is, the solution to the imputation problem, which is also supposed to provide these value functions, must follow at once all along the line – for all economic subjects and all goods, and in particular for all production goods, all members of each individual complementary group.

VI. We have already said that Schumpeter refrained from giving a detailed justification for the principle underlying his solution. On the other hand, he placed special weight upon two examples which he introduced before the principle itself in order to make it clearer – and so we too must give them a certain amount of attention. Let us select the first and more precisely elaborated of these; the second is analogous. First of all, it is necessary to reproduce the passage in question: 'I wish to make a business trip which will bring in, say, 1,000 marks. I therefore whistle a cab to go to the railway station. If I cannot get to the station in any other way because no other cab is available, so that my business completely depends on this one cabby and his willingness to take me to the station, what is the most I will be prepared to pay him? Naturally the difference must compensate me not only for my other monetary expenses (railway ticket, etc.) but also for my labour: that is, it must bring in as much as my activity would otherwise have earned me in the same time and with the same expenditure of energy. Let us say 500 marks. But if necessary, I will be prone to hand over the other 500 marks – assuming I am driven purely by economic motives – until I reach the minimum that must remain to induce me to choose this particular activity. There is nothing paradoxical in this. If 500 marks really is adequate compensation for expenses, labour, the inconvenience of travel and of the transaction, and the other 500 marks is a kind of "net profit", then the journey is truly "worth" 500 marks to me. But in reality I will only pay the man his "fare" plus a generous or not so generous tip, and in general he too will be content with a very small part, roughly a hundredth, of that sum. Does this mean I have "exploited" him?' After a not strictly relevant digression against the meaninglessness of such moral questions within pure economics, the author continues: 'But here we are interested in other questions. Above all, is our example not rather pointless? What does it mean to say that the cabby performs a service worth 500 marks, if he neither receives nor should receive so much and if there is no intention of paying it to him? In fact, no pleasure would be cheaper than that of poking fun at our story. Exactly the same could be said of all the other expenses involved in my business trip. Would it not turn out that together they were worth far more than its result? And yet the example is not at all pointless. If the cabby were alive to his own interests, he could actually make much more than his fare – at the most 500 marks. Of course, one can say the same of everyone else whose cooperation I need for my business, and together they could not all receive more than that sum. But at the outset each has the same claim to it, and everyone's maximum gain as well as the value to me of everyone's perform-ance is measured by the 500 marks.'[67]

We think we can quite justifiably say the same about this example that we did about the basic principle of Schumpeter's solution: that precisely insofar as it is unsuitable as a support for Schumpeter's theory of imputa-tion, it can be applied without hesitation to Böhm-Bawerk's. Let us first test the relevant features of Schumpeter's example in terms of the schema we used at the end of the last section to define *Böhm-Bawerk's* theory of imputation.

The *data* of the problem comprise, in addition to the joint useful effect (the 1,000 marks that the trip 'will bring in'), the 'other expenses' of 500 marks: railway ticket, compensation for labour, etc. Thus, expressed in terms of the sum of their monetary values, certain magnitudes are fixed for all the 'production factors' combining in the realization of the business trip, with the single exception of the cab ride. The *unknown quantity* to be discovered through imputation is the value of this cab ride, of the 'final piece' in the complementary group. This quantity is ascertained as the difference between the 'product value' (i.e., the value of the trip: M1,000) and the known sum of values of the other members of the complementary group (M500): M1,000 − M500 = M500. 'So the ride is actually worth 500 marks to me.' This result is perfectly satisfactory from the standpoint of *Böhm-Bawerk's* theory: the traveller knows what the cab ride is worth to him, because in the given circumstances (that is, on Schumpeter's assumptions for the sake of the argument) he has to act in a business-like manner in acquiring this productive element. But this economic indicator, like the validity of the whole value imputation in question, is only of an alternate character. If the traveller asks himself about the value of another indispensable and irreplaceable productive element – the railway journey, for example – he will arrive at Schumpeter's conclusion: 'the value to me of everyone's performance is measured by the 500 marks'. Thus, calculation by imputation of the 'net return'[68] can lead to the analogous value (500 marks) for the railway journey only if, apart from the problem itself – the fact or object of price determination and value imputation – its data also change; if, that is, the first alternate solution (value of the cab ride = M500) is dropped and the ride is included in 'total expenses' not with the M500 value resulting from that solution but with another *known* and fixed quantity such as the standard fare, which is deducted from the return on the trip. The traveller can only be *prepared* to give up the whole profit from his trip *either* for the cab ride *or* for the railway journey,[69] but never for both at once.

We must confess that we would be rather at a loss if faced with the task of discussing Schumpeter's example with his advocated means of value imputation: not because, as Schumpeter fears, the field of his chosen example is too crude, but on the contrary – the simpler the better! – because its construction by no means appears to us to be as 'inherently faultless' as it does to its author. Actually, what kind of values are the 500 marks which the cabby can be given 'at the most', or the values of the other 'production factors' to be ascertained in a similar manner? Are they total values of those production factors? Schumpeter can have no truck with such an interpretation – just read his categorical warning a few pages after he introduces the example: 'Nor must it be forgotten that by means of the theory of imputation we derive only value functions and not total values.'[70] Are they value functions, then? Hardly. Their role is to provide different quantities of goods and different magnitudes of value, but there has been no talk at all of any possible variation in quantities. We are forced to assume – if the formal structure of the example can be accommodated at all to the author's approach – that it refers to a certain point of the value functions. Thus, the 500 marks would be the marginal value of the cab ride in the case of economic equilibrium: if the traveller pays all the other 'expenses' of the trip with the 500 marks allocated for them and the cab ride too with the 'at the most' 500 marks, then the 'margin of acquisition' is reached for him and a state of economic equilibrium obtains. For 'equilibrium is the state where the tendencies toward further acquisition of a good – whether "money" or some other – counterbalance those working in the opposite direction.'[71] But even so things are not quite right. Since the declarations of value apply to greater than infinitesimal quantitative intervals, it cannot, as we said earlier, be a question of just one point of the value function; a whole line of points must be involved. The marginal values are not true marginal values – that is, ordinates of value functions – but partial integrals of the same and thus, to be precise, total values after all. Once again Schumpeter does the same as – or more than – Böhm-Bawerk, whom he nevertheless reprimands: 'Strictly speaking, Böhm-Bawerk's enquiry also concerns total values, but total values of very small quantities of goods.'[72]

The agreement with Böhm-Bawerk has major implications not only for this perhaps less significant point, but also for what is of most importance in the example. The 'other monetary expenses', 500 marks, appear as *data*: if they were not given, there would be no means of calculating 'the other 500 marks' that the cabby can receive. Why does the author build in pre-determined value magnitudes for all but one productive element? What kind of amounts are those which he simply calls 'expenses'? They are anyway not prices. For in Schumpeter's theory, the price problem is as yet completely unresolved: imputation is supposed to provide certain data for a solution in the shape of the value functions or – we should rather say in this context – the values of the productive elements. There are no values of those productive elements in other uses, since these cannot be their true values in Schumpeter's theory. And yet, he sees the 'main difference' between Böhm-Bawerk's solution and his own in the fact 'that in establishing the value function of a productive good, we must always attend to all the products it helps to produce and have no right to exclude from it the value of one or another of them'.[73] Compare this with his statement: 'If a new and advantageous use of a good becomes possible, its value increases for two reasons: above all because a smaller amount is now left for the former uses; but also because its value function is altered.'[74] In the end, the only explanation why the value magnitudes are introduced as data is that they are values with regard to the use in question. But even that assumption is impossible, since in Schumpeter such values cannot be *data* of the problem but only *unknowns* whose result will be given by the solution. For what is the imputation problem? 'We may define it a little more closely as the problem of deriving the value functions of goods which only produce a useful effect together, *from the value function of that useful effect*.'[75] Thus, in our example, the values also of the other 'production factors' are first *derived* from the value of the trip (1,000 marks). The information this gives does not seem adequate.

But let us now pass over such inconsistency and turn to the question of whether the results of Schumpeter's value calculation in this example are useful for his other theoretical purposes. The value of the cab ride (500 marks) may become the price: 'if necessary, I will be prone to hand over the other 500 marks.... If the cabby were alive to his own interests, he could actually make much more than his fare – at the most 500 marks.' This value – if, like Schumpeter, we disregard all other considerations – is certainly suitable to be introduced into his price problem. But the other, similarly calculable values for other productive elements of the same group *are not so suited*. If, in accordance with Schumpeter's solution – 'Of course, one can say the same of everyone else whose cooperation I need for my business' – they are each valued at roughly 500 marks, then these are *values which can never become prices*, because 'together they could not all receive more than that sum'; the traveller would have a very bad trip indeed if he was really prepared to offer some 500 marks for each of his expenses. And such value magnitudes are not suited to be introduced into Schumpeter's price problem, which applies to all goods. Any calculation which refers to all productive elements (unquestionably the framework of Schumpeter's price problem), but which is based in reality upon only alternately valid appraisals, must of necessity lead to false conclusions. In Schumpeter's otherwise not quite exact mode of expression which we have to adopt for the moment, we could say that *if the values for the productive elements in the calculation of the price problem are to serve at all their purpose of price determination, they must potentially contain in them the price*; each one of them must 'in the extreme case', simultaneously with the value magnitudes of all other participating productive elements, be capable to its full amount of becoming the price. And the sum of potential prices of the production goods may never – if the economy is in equilibrium – exceed the value and price of their total economic product. However one turns the thing around, one cannot elude this principle which constitutes the ultimate practical meaning of the formula for addition of the marginal values.

If, however, the values for the productive elements which are yielded by Schumpeter's imputation method cannot become prices in their full amount, even though this is what provides the solution to the price problem, then it still has to be determined, for a genuine, workable solution to this problem, in what amount the 'values' of the individual productive elements can be realized as prices – and thus in what amount everyone's claim to the 'maximum gain' can actually become a reality, or how much the economic subject may really be prepared to offer or give up for each productive element. *But this means that the solution to the imputation problem which Schumpeter sets himself, and which is set in his system, lies before rather than behind us.*

VII. So far we have only gone into the most essential point of Schumpeter's theory of imputation. We would now like to show, on the basis of his casuistical solution and a series of passing remarks, that there is much else besides with which one can find fault. Here we cannot refrain from reproducing Schumpeter's casuistical rules of imputation, and for the sake of clarity we will number the author's cases successively.[76]

Case 1: 'If a good has only one use, if, for example, a means of production can produce only one consumption good for which there is no substitute, then its value function is simply that of its use, of the consumption good. Its supply function is then this value curve, only "inverted". We shall not keep repeating this here but shall be content to derive the value functions of the means of production, although the same applies to consumption goods with several uses.'

This case contains two distinct possibilities. Either other production goods as well as this one are necessary to produce the consumption good, or they are not. If we assume the former, then this case is contained in any other of Schumpeter's compilation of rules in which such a production good, both otherwise unuseable and irreplaceable in this use, is found in a complementary group (cases 2, 5, 8 – such conjunctions of cases appearing more than once in Schumpeter's casuistic rules for the solution). This unfortunate circumstance, which does not assist clarity, would be avoided if the author had not classified the cases now from the standpoint of the product, now from that of the means of production.[77] What we have to say about the first possibility in case 1 (several production goods) is thus encompassed in other cases, especially case 2. As regards the second possibility in case 1 (one product with a single irreplaceable and otherwise unuseable means of production), two points should be noted. First, in reality there is no such case, because there are no means of production which operate alone. But if there were, one could for example – whether rightly or wrongly is here irrelevant – try to arrange the resulting increase in return simply by augmenting one of several complementary means of production. And then, by definition, there would be no imputation problem. At any event, for Schumpeter it was at least unnecessary to give this case one any separate importance.

Case 2: 'A consumption good has several production goods, which cannot be used for anything else and cannot be replaced. Their value functions, taken separately, are then identical with the value function of the consumption good, so that we only have to take into account that for the abscissae of the value curves of the production goods, it is necessary to choose units which correspond to the quantity of the goods needed to produce the unit of product. This will be the only time we mention this point.'

The solution of this case contains the most extreme application of the principle of 'overlapping' imputation to which we have refused a place in his system. Not only must a definite part of the product value be cumulatively imputed to each of the complementary means of production, but this must happen with the product value in its full amount. To make this review more intelligible, we shall very briefly repeat what we argued above against Schumpeter's system. If it were true, as Schumpeter believes, that the value function of a product A is identical with the value function of *any* of its otherwise unuseable and irreplaceable means of production B, C, D...etc., then the marginal values which each of these value functions displays in equilibrium – that is, for the equilibrium quantity – would also have to be identical, equally large; that is, to use our earlier algebraic notation, $Y_a = Y_b = Y_c = Y_d = ...$; and since in this case $Y_b = Y_a$, $Y_c = Y_a$, $Y_d = Y_a$ etc., the ratio of marginal value addition applicable to the state of equilibrium in Schumpeter's system, $Y_a = Y_b + Y_c + Y_d + ...$, would have to be expressed by the evidently inaccurate equation: $Y_a = Y_a + Y_a + Y_a + ...$[78]

Similarly, though with relatively smaller amounts, the value functions of production goods derived through Schumpeter's method of imputation clash with one another if the overlapping imputation does not, as in this case, extend to the whole product value but only to a certain part of it, which is cumulatively imputed to each production good of the complementary group. It is unnecessary to repeat this explicitly in the following cases of a solution.

Grave doubts also arise concerning Schumpeter's recommended mode of construction by calculating the abscissae for the value functions of the production goods. With regard to the abscissae (quantitative expressions) of the value curves of the production goods, we are told always to choose units which correspond to the quantity of the goods needed to produce a unit of product. This procedure can certainly be followed at *one* (random) point of the value functions, since the first and only choice of the unit quantities is left to the whim of the person doing the calculation.[79] But once unit quantities have been established for one point of the value function, they must be maintained for its *whole length*. And here one obviously runs into the difficulty that in very many cases the quantities of production goods 'needed to produce a unit of product' – and thus the unit quantities of one and the same production good with reference to one and the same product – are not equal but *differ* according to the technical results of production for various levels of expenditure on the production goods. Here we shall simply draw attention to this fact, which is a problem in itself and probably a major obstacle to Schumpeter's intended construction of the value curves of the production goods from which the product is constituted;[80] to investigate this more closely would take us too far from our present theme. What does directly concern the question of imputation is the fact that in the choice of the abscissa units, and even more in the changes which must result from the above-mentioned difficulty in constructing the value curves of the production goods, we find the factor by which the technical proportions of production are introduced as decisive ratios in the calculation of its value and thus also, for example – insofar as it applies – the technical law of 'diminishing returns' in production. It is a purely terminological matter whether one concludes from this that, in the concrete process of imputation, that law impinges as a direct link between the value of the product and that of its means of production through their quantitative relation;[81] or whether one agrees with Schumpeter, who would probably count this as well as other effects of the law among extra-economic data. At least that is what one suspects from his final verdict on the law in *Wesen und Hauptinhalt*: '...so we have absolutely no use for it – it no longer has a role to play in the modern system of economics.'[82] But the remark which he makes in discussing the price problem, immediately after the development of his theory of imputation, is by no means adequate: 'Secondly, however, we would note that the opportunity arises here for a major enlargement of our equation-system. Nothing prevents us from introducing into it the production coefficients of the separate products – that is, from taking into account the quantities of production goods technically necessary for them to be produced.'[83] One need only consider Schumpeter's proposal or any other for establishing the abscissae of the value curves of the production goods in their relation to those of the products, in order to accept at once that it is not a question here of a mere *opportunity* for enlargement of an equation-system; rather, the introduction of the technical coefficients of production as a simple quantitative

253

relation is an absolute *necessity*, in both the imputation and the price problem, for any calculation of the value of the means of production relative to the product value.

A further note is called for about an expression in Schumpeter's rules for imputation in the case under consideration. 'Their value functions,' he writes, 'taken separately, are then identical with the value function of the consumption good...' The inconspicuous little words 'taken separately' – on the meaning and implications of which the author has so little to say – are in our view the Achilles heel of Schumpeter's proposed solution to the imputation problem, perhaps even of his whole exact system and not only his. Whether they mean 'alternately' or 'cumulatively', there is no satisfactory way out: a system of economics such as Schumpeter's cannot make do with value functions for the production goods that are only alternately applicable; but if they are supposed to apply cumulatively, those value functions are false because it is inevitable within the system that they will actually conflict with one another.

The next case, no. 3, is considered by Schumpeter in special detail. 'Let a product have a production good which is "irreplaceable" but also be able to be used in another way. The latter's value function is a kind of value function of the group of goods for whose production it is necessary. This function is composed of the parts of these goods' value functions which at that time have the largest ordinates. Let us express this in the language of psychology. The first use to be adopted will be the one which supplies the greatest utility. So long as one keeps to this, the value curve of that use will apply to the part of the abscissa axis which represents the quantity of the good devoted to this use. If the relevant economic subject only had this quantity of the relevant good, the other uses would not come into consideration and only the value function of this use would apply to our good. But if the economic subject has more of it and puts this "more" first to another, then to a third use, and so on, the value functions of these uses will apply to the quantities of our means of production devoted to the single use, but it is in the nature of the case that the individual pieces making up the value function of the means of production join on to one another. For at the place of transition from one use to the other, the value function of the one must affect that of the other, since the former falls from above to a place below the latter. It may thus happen that the value function of one use, once it has fallen below that of others, later becomes crucial again as a result of the others' faster rate of fall: that is, that a use already abandoned in favour of others may be adopted again at a later time. This alters nothing in the principle, which we may express as follows. For the individual parts of the value function of a good which, while suitable for various uses, is indispensable for this one, the value

functions which come into consideration are always those which correspond to the actual uses of the individual quantities of the good.'

It is impossible to give an account of this value function in terms of
Schumpeter's basic conception of marginal utility theory. Compare the
following words of the author with the ones we have just quoted: '... we
must start from the point where the individual is not yet clear about the
choice between the existing possibilities of employment. Then he will first
employ his means of production in the production of those goods which
satisfy his most pressing needs, and thereafter proceed to produce for
continually less urgently felt needs.'[84] That is precisely the situation, then,
in case 3 that we are presently discussing. But how are the means of
production here assigned to the various uses? Schumpeter continues:
'Moreover, at every step he will consider what other feelings of want must
go unsatisfied in consequence of the employment of production goods for
the wants preferred at the moment. Each step thus involves a choice and,
if necessary, also a renunciation.[85] Each step may only be taken economically provided that the satisfaction of more intensive wants is not thereby
made impossible.... The fundamental condition that a given want will not
be satisfied before more intensive wants have been satisfied leads finally to
the result that all goods should be so *divided* amongst their different
possible uses that *the marginal utility of each good is equal in all its uses*.'[86]
'If I divide a good among different uses, must the marginal utility not be
the same in all? must its units not bestow the same marginal utility in all,
if my possession is to afford me maximum utility?'[87] The picture this gives
of the composition of the relevant value function is different from Schumpeter's account in case 3 of his imputation rules. For here one use is not
adopted *after* another; rather, all possible uses must apply *alongside* one
another, so long as they provide a marginal utility which exceeds the
lowest still achievable with the first use; the existing stocks of the production good (or the means for its economically justified production) must be
'distributed' among all uses, and in such a way that the lowest marginal
utilities are always the same for each use. The decision about such distribution has to be repeated 'at each step' – that is, at intervals in the
quantitative series of the production goods where their marginal value
changes in any one of the possible kinds of use. Since, however, according
to the calculus of Schumpeter's theory, this is always the case with quantitative changes of an infinitesimal amount, the quantities assigned to the
individual uses do not follow one another in closed 'pieces' – as the account
of Schumpeter's that we have so far been discussing would suggest – but
must alternate with one another in the most varied sequence, in principle
distributed among infinitesimal magnitudes. Indeed, if a value curve is to
be constructed which includes all the uses of the production good, the

theoretically infinitesimal quantities of it must not be added to the abscissa axis without regard to particular use, but must be ordered in sequence according to the appropriate magnitude of the marginal utility. Thus, the case of which Schumpeter says that it can happen – 'a use already abandoned in favour of others may be adopted again at a later time' – is in principle the normal, regular case. Nor is this all. If, in the state of equilibrium, 'the marginal utility of each good is equal in all its uses', then all these equal marginal utilities resulting from different uses must be contained together in Schumpeter's value function which embraces all the uses of the production good. But this conjures up a value function quite different from Schumpeter's general picture of constantly falling value functions: it is not a succession of constantly decreasing marginal utilities, but necessarily also contains within itself *equally high* marginal utilities. Now, a major complication of this divergent formal character suggests that it is by no means established from the start at what point equilibrium will be established in the value function referring to all uses of the production good. In principle, marginal values for all its uses – if they are high enough – must stand alongside one another as equal utility or value magnitudes at every point in this value function. If one thinks this through a little, it will be clear that the value function presented here by Schumpeter *does not ever have the formal character which he postulates in his 'basic outline' for value functions in general*: 'It now appears that only one property is necessary for our curves and otherwise they can behave as they wish: namely, that in the relevant interval for us *they are negative everywhere on the abscissa axis*.'[88] For 'to be negative everywhere on the abscissa' means that the value curve only contains within it constantly declining, but never equally large, value magnitudes. Not for one moment does the author take into account this result of his construction which – to express ourselves cautiously – cannot be entirely without consequences for application of those value functions of multiple-use production goods which he ascertains through his imputation procedure – all the more since in practice these production goods constitute an especially important case. But we cannot go into this here in greater detail.[89]

This suspicion is strengthened by a further consequence of our objection to Schumpeter's proposal to select the (quantitative) abscissa units of the production goods by deriving their value function from that of their products. In general, if the unit quantities of a particular production good – that is, the quantities 'necessary to produce a unit of product' – are not equal for all stages in the production of *one* product, how could one possibly give congruent expression to those unit quantities of the production goods which, for unified construction of the value function relating to its various uses, must be derived from the *several* products produced in the different uses of the production good?

Case 4: 'If a production good is suited to several uses and replaceable in all of them, it has a value function constructed in accordance with a similar principle, except that for parts of it the functions of its replacement come into consideration in those uses which would have to be forgone if the replacement were brought in. This is the second basic principle of our solution to the problem.'

As this value function is constructed 'in accordance with a similar principle', the objections to it are analogous to those which we developed for the one in case 3. But the author also introduces something new here – the 'second basic principle' of his solution to the problem. (By the first is understood the principle of overlapping imputation which we examined on p. 241 above.) This second basic principle is the principle of substitution. The laconic form in which it is introduced must appear extremely odd. As is well known, Böhm-Bawerk made the substitution principle one of the bases of his account of value formation in complementary goods. Thus, for the many members of a complementary group of production goods which 'are replaceable by other specimens of their kind',[90] he took from other uses the value magnitude determined by those other uses (the 'substitution value'[91]) and introduced it into the value calculation of that group as a datum for the solution of the imputation problem. Schumpeter objected to this procedure in a detailed critique,[92] of which the most important argument is that the marginal utility of a production good must be equally high if it is rationally distributed among all its uses, so that 'it is impossible for anything to be gained' by replacing one such value magnitude with another.[93] He then draws the following conclusion about Böhm-Bawerk's 'concept of substitution': 'It is only this way of giving it validity that we reject; the concept itself, however, must be taken into account in the solution to the imputation problem.'[94] And he adds the remark: 'The question of how it should be taken into account cannot be answered here. On this see my earlier quoted book.' But there too – in the book under discussion here, *Wesen und Hauptinhalt der theoretischen Nationalökonomie* – all we find apart from the very meagre text already quoted are purely negative, critical reflections on the principle of substitution. The author does not provide the necessary explanation and justification in the form he would like to remember, nor therefore the opportunity to form a judgement on this point. Two things can be established, however. First, Schumpeter's term 'replacement' is too broad if he is not also referring to goods of a different kind from the production good in question, but only to 'replacement specimens' of the same kind in Böhm-Bawerk's sense. Second, to employ substitution in the usual sense is incompatible with Schumpeter's above-quoted definition of the imputation problem: 'We may define it a little more closely as the problem of deriving the value functions of goods which only produce a useful effect together, from the value function of that useful effect.'[95] For: if the value function of a production good is derived by substitution from another use – that is, from another useful effect – than the one whose imputation is at issue here, then it is evidently not derived from 'that useful effect'.[96] For the rest, given the sparseness of his own positive statements, we cannot consider here whether the substitution principle can have any place at all in a system such as Schumpeter's; we must leave further clarification of this whole matter, which concerns marginal utility theory right down to its last foundations, for investigations that we shall be presenting elsewhere.

As to the remaining cases of Schumpeter's proposed solution, everything of significance has already been said in our previous accounts. They are as follows.

Case 5: 'Let a product have two production goods, one of which is useable elsewhere and the other not. Neither of the two can be replaced. Only for the one which can be used elsewhere do the previous rules apply; for the other it must be taken into account that if we wish to realize its value, we must do without another value, which is that of the other uses of the means of production useable elsewhere. The value function of the latter cannot therefore be that of the product, but its ordinates must be shortened by an amount corresponding to that circumstance. It should be stressed once more, however, that the value function of the otherwise useable factor is not composed simply of its other uses but also contains that of our product.'

Case 6: 'If a product has several production goods which are irreplaceable but can be used in another way, then each of them has the value function resulting as shown from its uses, but their ordinates must be shortened in accordance with the values of the other production goods in their other uses.'

Cases 7 and 8: 'No new principle is necessary if these production goods are also replaceable, and the case in which they combine with irreplaceable and not otherwise useable production goods can be dealt with in the same way.'

We reproduced these last cases verbatim to make it easier for the reader to check that our earlier objections are also valid here. Schumpeter himself stipulates that the 'previous rules' apply to case 5 and the derivation of the value functions 'as shown' to case 6. Of case 7 he says that 'no new principle is necessary', and of case 8 that it should be dealt with 'in the same way'.

VIII. Schumpeter adds the following points to the above summary of his theory of imputation: 'All that has to be established is that in principle it is possible to solve the imputation problem. This has already been demonstrated by the fact that we assign definite values to production goods with the same assurance that we have in relation to consumption goods.' Clearly, for Schumpeter the solubility of the imputation problem must be maintained in any event. He knows this better than anyone. On the possibility of solving the imputation problem – *his* imputation problem, we should add – directly depends the solubility of his price problem and hence the *raison d'être* of his whole static system. Whether this or some other – for Schumpeter there must be a solution to the imputation problem, because economic practice actually does solve it.

The reader will already know what is our reply to this. But what if Schumpeter's imputation problem is not the same as the one which 'every practical calculator, whether an Australoid or the manager of a trust, solves every day and every hour',[97] if it is as different from it as the Walras-Schumpeter price problem is from the one which presents itself in practice? Must we not assume that a different problem requires different data for its solution and thus – because the purpose of imputation is to obtain such data – different services from value imputation: that is, *a different imputation problem*? Here and now I can only say that that distinction does exist, and reserve a more detailed account for another place.

And now, in conclusion, let us ask what this investigation has achieved. One would be doing us an injustice if one thought us so petty-minded as to be capable of seeing the achievement merely in the refutation of Schumpeter's theory of imputation. Nor is it satisfying to have merely negative knowledge that the imputation problem is a cornerstone of Schumpeter's whole economic system and of any other with similar foundations, and that once it has been established that the imputation problem is not solved in his system, the inner unity and survival of that system – and of all others with similar foundations – is placed in question. What we feel is almost the opposite of satisfaction. Whoever has learnt to appreciate through careful study the grand scheme of the system as a whole will not bring himself to rejoice at such critical knowledge: it is all a great pity.

What we think has really been gained from this investigation is much more the following. Our examination of the account given by one of our most prominent theoreticians has fully demonstrated to us the deplorable consequences, for one central problem, of the systematic discrepancies existing within economic theory today, and hence the evil from which it undeniably suffers and which threatens to leave it at the mercy of a hopeless number of passing atomistic disputes and to neglect any synthetic, truly great achievement. A common approach is lacking in pure economic theory as a whole – one that would be both theoretically and practically useful and could be accepted on all sides without any victory. In positive terms, this means that such an approach must be found. Once it is found, everything else – the whole construction of economic theory, in relation to each and every problem and not just imputation – will follow almost automatically in a useful and generally acceptable way, as a pure matter of formal logic and ever verifiable empirical facts.[98]

NOTES

1. Typical in its way – and we mention only this example – is Broda's rebuff ('Die Lösungen des Zurechnungsproblems', *Zeitschrift für Volkswirtschaft, Sozialpolitik und Verwaltung*, vol. xx (1911), pp. 387f.): 'I could demonstrate many more absurd directions in which Schumpeter's whole conception of value leads, especially in its practical application. This is only natural, because as soon as a system is seen to suffer from a defect of principle, each one of its consequences must logically lead at some point to a contradiction. It is not even necessary to comment in detail on Schumpeter's casuistry on pp. 256–9 of his work, once we have seen that most of the foundations of his reasoning are fallacious...'

2. 'Exkurs VII', in *Positive Theorie des Kapitals*, 3rd edn (Innsbruck, 1912), p. 219.

3. Joseph Schumpeter, *Das Wesen und der Hauptinhalt der theoretischen Nationalökonomie* (Leipzig, 1908), p. 261.

4. Emphases added.

5. Emphasis in the original.

6. Joseph Schumpeter, 'Bemerkungen über das Zurechnungsproblem', *Zeitschrift für Volkswirtschaft, Sozialpolitik und Verwaltung* (1909), p. 83.

7. *Das Wesen und der Hauptinhalt*, p. 227. Emphases partly added.

8. Ibid., p. 241. Emphases added.

9. See, for example, ibid., p. 53: 'For us value is simply an explanatory principle which helps us to demonstrate the univocal character of our system and to indicate the conditions of equilibrium more completely than the older theory did.'

10. We think we may assume that the reader is familiar with 'Gossen scales of utility' and 'value functions'. But to avoid any misunderstanding and fully to clarify certain quotations below, we shall add a brief note on Schumpeter's views on this matter.

    The *value function*, which is Schumpeter's most important tool in his theory of value, is an equation – or, in geometric terms, the connecting line (curve) representing this equation in a right-angled system of coordinates – which indicates for a good the connection between its value for a particular economic subject and the quantity of the good which that subject possesses. In other words, it represents the value of the good as a function of its quantity, and of course vice versa. Corresponding to the presence of different subjective magnitudes of value, which can be linked to the quantity of the good, there are also different kinds of value functions. These are: (1) the total value function, which indicates how the total value of a good varies with changes in its quantity, and thus the different total values of the good for different quantities of the same; and (2) the marginal value function – which Schumpeter generally calls simply the value function and with which we shall be exclusively concerned in examining his theory of imputation – a function which, apart from some minor differences, is otherwise denoted as the Gossen scale of utility. In mathematical terms, this is the first derivative of the total value function and indicates the different 'marginal values' or 'marginal utilities' for various quantities of the good, and thus what in Schumpeter's view marks the 'usual definition of marginal utility' as the 'value of the last part'. (See above all ibid., pp. 106f. By the way, in this context the expression *marginal value*, as used by Schumpeter, seems to us more consistent than *marginal utility* for what these '*value*' functions indicate, although the matter is of no consequence since Schumpeter explicitly states that for him there is no difference between the concepts value and utility.)

Schumpeter describes as follows how the value function is to be ascertained as the 'scale of demand prices': 'If one were now to ask the individual economic subjects what they are prepared to give for a certain quantity of any good, they would as always provide a definite answer rather than refuse. For every economic subject and for every quantity of a good, it is always possible to identify a quantity of some other good which he is prepared to give, while at even a slightly higher "price" the exchange no longer takes place.... Let us now, for each economic subject, set the various quantities on the abscissa of a right-angled system of coordinates, and the prices which he has indicated to us on the ordinate. And finally, let us join up the resulting points by interpolation into a continuous curve... The function depicted by means of this curve is then everything we need, and at the same time everything that economists really grasp when they pursue a psychology of value.... But why is this function called the value function [*Wertfunktion*]? That is not difficult to explain. The economic subjects, when questioned, will say that a certain quantity of a good is at most "worth" [*wert*] so much to them and no more.... This everyday

261

expression induces us call our function the value function.... We could do nothing with our function if we were unable to say anything about its shape.... It turns out that only one property of our curves is required – to be everywhere negative on the abscissa during the interval which comes into consideration for us – and that they may otherwise behave as they wish. That is the exact form of Gossen's Law, the "law of satiable wants", which is usually roughly expressed as follows: The intensity of want impulses declines with the rise in satiation.'

In this way, then, the value functions of the products (consumption goods) are 'asked' of the economic subjects, but the value functions of the production goods are derived from these value functions of the products precisely through the process of imputation.

In order fully to grasp all the questions connected with Schumpeter's theory of value, it is important to establish why it is not the same to ascertain the marginal value or utility of a good and its value function – a fact to which Schumpeter attaches the greatest importance through repeated emphasis. To ascertain a certain marginal value always presupposes that a certain quantity of the good is in the possession of the subject in question. By drawing up the value function, however – theoretically in endless repetition of the process in ascertaining the individual marginal value – one obtains *the marginal values for all possible quantities*. It directly follows that in economic calculations or analyses, knowledge of a good's value function is incomparably more advantageous than knowledge of an individual marginal value.

11. Ibid., pp. 256–8.
12. See in this regard 'Grenznutzen und Wirtschaftsrechnung', afterword to parts i and ii (and cf. note 98 below).
13. See *Wesen und Hauptinhalt*, pp. 219ff., etc.
14. Ibid., p. 219 etc. See also above note 10.
15. Friedrich von Wieser, *Natural Value*, trans. Christian A. Malloch (London: Macmillan, 1893), pp. 173ff.
16. *Wesen und Hauptinhalt*, p. 236.
17. See note 10 above.
18. *Wesen und Hauptinhalt*, pp. 227f.
19. Schumpeter, *Theorie der wirtschaftlichen Entwicklung*, 1st edn (Leipzig, 1912), p. 45 and elsewhere. [*The Theory of Economic Development*, trans. Redvers Opie (Cambridge, Mass.: Harvard University Press, 1951), p. 29. It will not always be possible to give an equivalent reference from the English edition, which is translated from the partly rewritten and partly reorganized second German edition of 1926.]

20. See Schumpeter's well-known and repeated figure of two intersecting curves, and his explanation of them: 'If we draw on the ordinate axis of a right-angled system of coordinates all the possible prices of a good, and on the abscissa axis all the quantities of the good which are offered and demanded at those prices, there results a "demand curve" shaped MN and a "supply curve" shaped PS. The point of intersection R gives the state of equilibrium, RQ represents the equilibrium price, and Q the quantity turned over at that price.' (*Wesen und Hauptinhalt*, p. 225.) No further references are required for what is repeated here; it contains the common knowledge not only of Schumpeter's theory but of what is generally asserted by economic theory (and by other theory besides) briefed with the above analysis.

21. *Wesen und Hauptinhalt*, p. 216; *Theorie der wirtschaftlichen Entwicklung*, p. 46 and elsewhere.

22. See, for example, *Wesen und Hauptinhalt*, pp. 70ff., 105ff., and 'Bemerkungen', pp. 109ff.; as well as note 10 above.

23. *Wesen und Hauptinhalt*, p. 238. Cf. ibid., p. 226: '...a value curve ...of the goods...the [value function] of the production goods to be employed in the production [of the good to be acquired]', and other such statements. The explicit use of the plural rules out the explanation that here too the value function of the production goods is supposed to mean the value function of one good. It also shows that Schumpeter cannot here be talking of *identical* value functions for each individual production good used in creating the product in question, because for Schumpeter too these value functions are in general by no means the same.

24. *Theorie der wirtschaftlichen Entwicklung*, p. 43. [Cf. *Theory of Economic Development*, p. 29.]

25. See, for instance, *Wesen und Hauptinhalt*, p. 240: '...of a supply of means of production which, of course, *combine* differently in each good.' Emphasis added.

26. See note 80 below.

27. 'If, as is necessary, one measures both sides of our equation with a common yardstick, money...' Or: '...the sums of money on the left-hand side of our equation.... The sums of money which are on the right side of our equation...' *Wesen und Hauptinhalt*, pp. 217–19.

28. Cf. *Theorie der wirtschaftlichen Entwicklung*, p. 46.

29. In Schumpeter's use of infinitesimal calculus, this quantity is an infinitesimal magnitude, a differential of the stock of goods which he writes as dq_a in his formulations in *Wesen und Hauptinhalt*, pp. 180f. and elsewhere. We think, however, that we can with complete justification – that is, in this context, without deviating in the slightest from

the precise meaning of Schumpeter's formulations – refrain from using his own mode of description, although this might be adopted without causing any difficulty and, in particular, without altering in any way the results of the investigation. We omit it simply because we are convinced that this makes both Schumpeter's theory of imputation and our own critique more readily comprehensible. Our whole account is based on the aim of allowing anyone who reads with only average attentiveness and prior training to follow and check it in full, and thus in an exact manner.

30. Ibid., p. 227.

31. In the price problem, the production goods do not merely serve as links for ascertaining the price and quantity of the consumption goods or products, and the solution to the general problem must lead in their case also to definite equilibrium prices and a definite distribution. This is already evident from the whole structure of Schumpeter's system, with its inclusion of all goods. And if it were not so, one would have to exclude from the solution of the price problem not only all consumption goods which for Schumpeter are covered by imputation, but the majority of goods in general and, on closer inspection, perhaps every single one. In this connection we can refer to Schumpeter's explicit statements. For example, in *Wesen und Hauptinhalt*, p. 237: 'This conception helps us to apply the moment of exchange to the derivation of the "prices" of the production goods, which yield the static divisions of income...' Or on p. 239: '...the values and prices of the production goods...' And on p. 243: '...the theory of income formation: that is, the formation of the values and prices of production goods...'

32. This equation is nothing other than the (separately derived and differently written) section for a certain product and its means of production – the section, that is, of the second conditional equation encompassing all goods for the ascertainment of economic equilibrium: $p_a \, dq_a + p_b \, dq_b + p_c \, dq_c + \dots = 0$, which Schumpeter introduces in *Wesen und Hauptinhalt* (p. 130) as the expression of the fact that 'the sum of prices of the "sold" goods and the sum of prices of the "bought" goods must be the same'. In that equation, then, a part of the stocks differential dq has an essentially *negative* sign: namely, the 'sold' marginal quantities which are represented as 'negative additions' (p. 261, and see p. 230 above). These correspond to the marginal quantities of the production goods which have to be given up in the production of the last quantity of the product and which, in our above notation, lie with a plus sign on the *other*, right-hand side of the equation.

33. Ibid., p. 216.
34. Ibid., p. 131.
35. Ibid., p. 129.
36. Ibid., p. 213.
37. It is unnecessary to reproduce here the mathematical basis that Schumpeter gives for these equations. A simple test confirms the correctness of these formulae, if one accepts, as we must do here, the assumptions they use and the form in which they are presented. Let us then think of the prices of the two goods A and B as expressed in terms of any third good, the price measure, and rewrite the above equation as follows:

$$\frac{marginal\ utility\ of\ good\ A}{marginal\ utility\ of\ good\ B} = \frac{price\ of\ A}{price\ of\ B}$$

or:

$$\frac{marginal\ utility\ of\ good\ A}{price\ of\ A} = \frac{marginal\ utility\ of\ good\ B}{price\ of\ B}$$

If we then call 'priceworthiness' the quotient: marginal utility divided by unit price, we obtain: priceworthiness of good A = priceworthiness of good B. The following quotation from Launhardt (*Mathematische Begründung der Volkswirtschaftslehre*, 1885, pp. 17f.) refers to this mode of expression: 'The goods in the owners' possession must achieve the same priceworthiness through exchange. The correctness of this proposition can also be grasped without any mathematical proof, by a simple process of thought. The priceworthiness of a good denotes the measure of the utility or pleasure which is offered for the unit of price. If this measure were less for one of the goods than for the other, then one would gain in pleasure by continuing to exchange the good which affords less utility per unit of price for the other good which assures greater pleasure per unit of price. The limit for the continuation of exchange is reached as soon as no more utility is obtained for the unit of price of the one good than for the other.'

The equation quoted above is nothing other than a section from the third equation encompassing all goods in the whole system – the equation which the author (*Wesen und Hauptinhalt*, p. 131) writes up as the analytic expression of the law of marginal utility level:

$$\frac{1}{p_a}\frac{d\phi}{dq_a} = \frac{1}{p_b}\frac{d\phi}{dq_b} = \frac{1}{p_c}\frac{d\phi}{dq_c} = \dots$$

If we, like Schumpeter, take any two goods – e.g., the first two members of this 'belt of equations':

$$\frac{1}{p_a}\frac{d\phi}{dq_a} = \frac{1}{p_b}\frac{d\phi}{dq_b},$$

then we obtain:

$$\left(\frac{d\phi}{dq_a} : \frac{d\phi}{dq_b}\right) = \left(1 : \frac{p_b}{p_a}\right),$$

that is, precisely: (marginal utility of good A : marginal utility of good B) = (1 : exchange ratio or price of B in terms of A); and therefore directly the binominal equation: (marginal utility of good A : price of A) = (marginal utility of good B : price of B), or: priceworthiness of A = priceworthiness of B.

38. That Y_p – i.e., the marginal value of money at equilibrium – must be the same in all its uses as 'means of exchange' and thus also as 'measure of value' for the same economic subject, directly follows from the consideration that the utility maximum characterizing the state of equilibrium cannot be attained so long as a difference remains between the marginal value of money in all its uses, simply because it is then always possible to improve the economy by exploiting this tension, by shifting quantities of money from uses with less marginal value to ones with a higher marginal value – which contradicts the postulate of equilibrium. This fact, which Schumpeter explicitly states several times and which in his view holds for every good, also directly follows from his own formulations. On this point, one need only write down his equation expressing the law of marginal utility level (*Wesen und Hauptinhalt*, p. 131 – and see our previous note 37), and do so at sufficient length for the price-good also to appear, as the last member, for example. It then reads as follows:

$$\frac{1}{p_a}\frac{d\phi}{dq_a} = \frac{1}{p_b}\frac{d\phi}{dq_b} = \frac{1}{p_c}\frac{d\phi}{dq_c} = \dots = \frac{1}{p_p}\frac{d\phi}{dq_p};$$

where p_p, as the price of the price-good, is by definition equal to 1;

$$\frac{d\phi}{dq_p}$$

is nothing other than the marginal utility or marginal value of the price-good which, in analogy with Y_a, Y_b etc., we shall simply denote as Y_p. With these notational additions, Schumpeter's equation then reads:

$$\frac{1}{P_a}Y_a = \frac{1}{P_b}Y_b = \frac{1}{P_c}Y_c = \ldots = \frac{1}{1}Y_p.$$

From the consistency of each member of the series with the last one, and thus from the individual equations:

$$\frac{1}{P_a}Y_a = Y_p; \frac{1}{P_b}Y_b = Y_p; \frac{1}{P_c}Y_c = Y_p \text{ etc.}$$

the equations in the main text above: $Y_a = P_a Y_p$ etc. directly follow. (Only in them is Y_p – as had to be shown here – one and the same magnitude.)

39. The sense of this equation, in respect of goods A, B, C, D..., is identical with that of equation 1 which appears on p. 130 of *Wesen und Hauptinhalt*:

$$\frac{d\phi}{dq_a}dq_a + \frac{d\phi}{dq_b}dq_b + \frac{d\phi}{dq_c}dq_c + \ldots = 0$$

See also notes 37 and 33 above.

40. That is, for the terms referring to stocks. See note 10 above.

41. *Wesen und Hauptinhalt*, p. 256. There can be no objection to pursuing this instruction of Schumpeter's to one specific point in production, since the first and only choice of the stock units is essentially arbitrary; nor, therefore, to pursuing it for the sake of our immediate investigation, which is limited to one such specific point – the point of economic equilibrium or the margin of production. Besides, if this justification is quite inconsequential for our immanent critique, we could simply refer to the fact that Schumpeter actually did draw up that instruction, and with an explicit claim to universal validity. We shall return to this matter below.

42. We could also argue as follows. The first and only choice of the units for each of the goods in question is in principle arbitrary; we can therefore regard the last-produced quantity of each product, here M_a, as the unit and make it $= 1$ – in which case, for Schumpeter, the M_b, M_c, M_d... quantities of production goods used to produce M_a also become units and thus $= 1$. Similarly, this yields the magnitude

$$\frac{1}{1} = 1$$

for the quotients at issue:

$$\frac{M_a}{M_b}, \frac{M_a}{M_c}, \frac{M_a}{M_d} \text{ etc.}$$

43. Of course, the previous equation for the equilibrium prices of the product and its means of production is simplified in an analogous manner: that is, $M_a P_a = M_b P_b + M_c P_c + M_d P_d + ...$, because $M_a = M_b = M_c = M_d = ...$, becomes $P_a = P_b + P_c + P_d + ...$

It must be explicitly noted that this *marginal value* formula says nothing about distribution of the *total* value of the product or about the *total sums of prices* falling to the share of the owners of the individual production goods, and still less, of course, about any identification of these two magnitudes. There can be no question of blaming Schumpeter for some conflation of the imputation and distribution problems. Such an objection (cf. Schumpeter's polemic against Wieser on this matter, note 104 and elsewhere) affects Schumpeter's own arrangement of his system no more than it does the above presentation, which is and wishes to be nothing other than a clear and concise account of connections established in the foundations of Schumpeter's system.

To avoid repetition, let us also consider here the question as to how things stand with this formula for the addition of marginal values, if for each production good it presents not just one value function referring to all its uses, but a separate value function for each of its uses – a case which, according to Schumpeter (*Wesen und Hauptinhalt*, p. 255), occurs where it is a matter of 'establishing the economic significance of one type of use'. But even so the formula would not be altered, since both in Schumpeter's general thinking and in his explicit formulations, the marginal values of each good in the state of equilibrium must be the same for all its uses, so that in equilibrium only one identical marginal value exists in all uses, and thus in all the individual value functions of the product. See also p. 237 above; 'Bemerkungen über das Zurechnungsproblem', p. 128; and *Theorie der wirtschaftlichen Entwicklung*, p. 39 and elsewhere.

44. That is, in the shape of a functional equation for the algebraic compilation, and of a 'value curve' for the geometric.

45. Cf. note 10 above.

46. Ibid., p. 248. Emphases in the original.

47. On Schumpeter's inconsistency here in his *solution* of the problem, see p. 252 above.

48. See Böhm-Bawerk, 'Exkurs VIII' to the German edition of *Positive Theorie des Kapitals*, p. 213.

49. *Wesen und Hauptinhalt*, p. 248.

50. 'Bemerkungen...', p. 104.
51. In his *Theorie der wirtschaftlichen Entwicklung* (p. 43) Schumpeter says in relation to the margin of production, the point of economic equilibrium, that 'the costs rise to the height of the marginal utility of the product, therefore also of the mix of participating means of production'. [Cf. *Theory of Economic Development*, p. 29.] Does this not clearly express that in the state of equilibrium the marginal utility of the product is equal to that of the mix of participating means of production: that is – in the terminology Schumpeter uses elsewhere – of the complementary production goods which serve to produce the product? It is easy to see that, in terms of content, this amounts to the formula for addition of the marginal values and is not in the best accord with the principle of Schumpeter's theory of imputation, 'that the production goods together are worth more than their product'. However, we would think it a petty, lightweight and unproductive exercise to forge counterarguments from these and other of the author's statements. We do not wish to quibble over words, but to get to the bottom of the matter itself. Blind demolition, without knowledge of the basis of the error, can do little by itself to foster reconstruction.
52. *Wesen und Hauptinhalt*, pp. 248–50.
53. In all the rules and examples that Böhm-Bawerk's uses for the solution of the imputation problem (see *Positive Theorie des Kapitals*, pp. 276–86 and 'Exkurs' pp. 173–220), the sum of values of the complementary goods is equal to the value of the joint product or useful effect. Schumpeter himself writes of Böhm-Bawerk in this connection: 'It is true that in his view the sum of values of these [i.e. complementary] goods may never be greater than that of their joint product.' 'Bemerkungen...', p. 119.
54. Schumpeter himself says in his critique of Böhm-Bawerk's theory of imputation: '...so let us keep still more firmly with the idea of loss, which is really of fundamental importance.' 'Bemerkungen...', p. 131.
55. Wieser, *Natural Value*, pp. 81, 83.
56. That is, in Menger's terminology: a production good.
57. Carl Menger, *Principles of Economics*, trans. James Dingwall and Bert F. Hoselitz (New York: New York University Press, 1981), pp. 164–5.
58. Eugen von Böhm-Bawerk, *The Positive Theory of Capital*, trans. William Smart (London: Macmillan, 1871), p. 154.
59. 'Exkurs VII', p. 180.
60. Ibid., p. 213.
61. *Wesen und Hauptinhalt*, p. 239.

62. See, for example, ibid., p. 240: 'With regard to all production within any given state of the economy, there is a univocally determined supply for each of those means of production which contain all decisive factors.' And again on p. 251: 'Otherwise too, their [the production goods'] value functions remain in our view completely fixed.'

63. See *Wesen und Hauptinhalt*, p. 248 (as quoted on p. 241 above) as well as, for example, ibid., p. 250. Cf. 'Bemerkungen...', p. 104: 'Menger's result is thus not wrong, and the striking conclusion that the production goods are together worth more than their product is only seemingly a mistake. Their values may not be added up in such a straightforward manner.'

64. See, for example, 'Exkurs VII', p. 204: 'The fact that my formula allows for twofold valuation does not make it indeterminate or uncertain. For it does not permit two divergent valuations for one and the same circumstance, but only one particular valuation for each of two different circumstances.'

65. Schumpeter, however, assumes an inequality between these magnitudes – on the grounds of the claim, arising from combination of the alternate values, that 'the production goods are together worth more than their product'.

66. The assumption of zero in certain cases (see *Positive Theorie*, p. 278) does not constitute an exception, because even zero is a definite number.

67. *Wesen und Hauptinhalt*, pp. 245ff.

68. See p. 241 above.

69. We have stressed these words to point up the difference from Schumpeter's conception. For Schumpeter allows for alternatives only in distribution (in the possibility of *really giving something up*); but there is also an alternative in the appraisal of value – that is, already in the *preparedness* to give something up.

70. Ibid., p. 246.

71. Ibid., p. 216.

72. 'Bemerkungen...', p. 117.

73. Ibid., p. 253.

74. Ibid., pp. 252f.

75. Ibid., p. 249. In the original the whole definition is emphasized.

76. Ibid., pp. 256–8.

77. Cf. note 47 above.

78. This faulty conclusion can be avoided in three ways, which we can only briefly mention here as this falls outside the framework of the present critique.

    1. The relevant case of imputation is declared to be *insoluble*. (This

is Wieser's position in, for example, *Natural Value*, p. 86: 'Taken singly, on the other hand, there is no means of calculating the value of each [of the complementary goods]. They are unknown quantities for which there is only one equation. Let us call them x and y, and put the successful result at 100; all that can be said as to their value lies in the equation: $x + y = 100$.')

2. Alternatively one makes $Y_a = Y_b$ and at the same time $Y_c = 0$, $Y_d = 0$, and so on; or $Y_a = Y_d$ and $Y_b = 0$, $Y_c = 0$ ... etc.. Thus, on the right side of the equation $Y_a = Y_b + Y_c + Y_d + ...$, *only one of the summands ever* $= Y_a$ and *all the others* $= 0$, so that the equation balances. (This path of alternate application corresponds in principle to Böhm-Bawerk's solution. See *Positive Theorie*, p. 278: 'If none of the members allows of a use other than the common one, and if none can be replaced in the effect it produces for the common utility, then a single piece already has the full total value of the group, while the other pieces are completely lacking in value.')

3. Or each of the production goods B, C, D, ... is allocated a marginal value b between zero and Y_a such that the condition $Y_a = Y_b + Y_c + Y_d + ...$ is maintained. (For this see Karl Landauer, 'Der Meinungsstreit zwischen Böhm-Bawerk und Wieser über die Grundsätze der Zurechnungstheorie', *Archiv für Sozialwissenschaft und Sozialpolitik*, vol. 46, and *Grundprobleme der funktionellen Verteilung des wirtschaftlichen Wertes*, Jena 1923.)

We cannot discuss here whether or to what extent the first and the third solution or even all three are basically the same, and thus only casuistical variations of one principle.

79. See note 41 above.
80. This is one of the reasons why our derivation of the marginal value ratios has been restricted to the point of equilibrium.
81. Schumpeter himself says of the 'fact' of the law of diminishing returns: 'It is one of the factors affecting the available quantity, and therefore value and price.' 'Das Rentenprinzip in der Verteilungslehre', *Schmollers Jahrbuch 1907*, p. 162; see also, for example, p. 172.
82. *Wesen und Hauptinhalt*, p. 231.
83. Ibid., pp. 262f., where much of the passage is italicized.
84. *Theorie der wirtschaftlichen Entwicklung*, pp. 38f; *Theory of Economic Development*, p. 26.
85. This sentence does not appear in the English edition.
86. Ibid.
87. 'Bemerkungen...', p. 128.
88. *Wesen und Hauptinhalt*, p. 74. Cf. above, note 10 and elsewhere.

89. I refer the reader to my positive investigations, and in particular to the development of the 'ordering law of partial utility', in my book *Grenznutzen und Wirtschaftsrechnung*.

90. *Positive Theorie des Kapitals*, p. 279.

91. Ibid., p. 277.

92. 'Bemerkungen...', pp. 124–31.

93. Ibid., p. 128.

94. Ibid., p. 131.

95. *Wesen und Hauptinhalt*, p. 249.

96. Our last few points are a special application of the argument used above (p. 250) concerning the substitution principle. What Schumpeter describes, admittedly in a different context, as a 'closer' definition is probably too narrow in the present connection. Böhm-Bawerk was much more cautious: it cannot be fortuitous but must be quite intentional that he never gives anything like Schumpeter's definition of the imputation problem; we read only of 'value formation' of complementary goods (*Positive Theorie*, p. 276).

97. This is also the concluding point in Schumpeter's other work on the imputation problem which, as we have seen, also takes the solubility of the problem in practice as the *ultima ratio*. 'Bemerkungen...', p. 138.

98. The present author has tried from the very beginning to follow the positive path merely indicated here. The reader is referred to his *Grenznutzen und Wirtschaftsrechnung*, published in Mainz and Vienna, as well as to the article 'Nutzen und Wirtschaftsrechnung' in the previous volume of this journal, which contains the first, introductory part of that book.

D24   274 – 315
        [1935]

Fritz Machlup, 'Professor Knight and the "Period of Production"', *Journal of Political Economy*, vol. 43 (1935), pp. 577–624.

Fritz Machlup (1902–1983) was a brilliant young Viennese economist during the 1920s. A disciple of Mises, he emigrated in the 1930s to the U.S. where his reputation as a world-famous economist was established. While Machlup firmly believed that what was valuable and important in the economics of the Austrian School had, by the 1930s, come to be successfully absorbed into the mainstream of the profession, he remained fully and gratefully aware of the value of his Austrian training.

20

Professor Knight and the 'Period of Production'

FRITZ MACHLUP

The past few years have been prolific of contributions about 'capital and the period of production.'[1] Any increase in the output of such contributions certainly takes place under increasing cost (because it is necessary for the writer to study all his predecessors' products), and, probably, under decreasing return. Nevertheless, there seems to be good reason for submitting another unit of product. In a series of ingenious articles[2] Professor Knight has proposed to discard as worthless some tools of economic analysis which I consider indispensable for successful handling of certain problems. The tools he wants to scrap are those concepts which have been used in capital theory under different names, such as 'length of the production process,' 'roundaboutness of production,' 'period of waiting,' 'period of production,' 'period of investment,' 'time structure of production,' 'period of maturing,' and similar terms. Professor Knight's opinion has great weight with every serious student of economics; if the disputed concepts are to be rehabilitated, Professor Knight's criticism must be answered. This will be attempted here, partly with explicit reference to the contentions of Professor Knight, partly by way of general discussion of the concepts and the problems involved. An effort will be made, upon this occasion, to clear up a number of obscurities and ambiguities connected with the theory of capital 'promulgated by Böhm-Bawerk and his followers and generally accepted and taught in the past generation.'[3]

I. *Is Capital Perpetual?*

I. *Stationary, growing, or retrograde economy*. – The usefulness, or even necessity, for economic theory of the conception of a 'stationary economy'

275

cannot be seriously questioned. This conception is inseparably bound up with the application of the method of variation in economics. One cannot arrive at any conclusion about the effects of any change if the 'other' (independent) things (or conditions) are not set 'invariant' or assumed to be unchanged. Thus, in a discussion of the effects of a certain 'shift in demand,' or of a changed supply of money, or of better crops, or of any other 'substantive' change, one conveniently starts out with the assumption that the supply of 'capital' does not change independently at the came time. One of the greatest difficulties in our theory, the problem of 'maintaining capital intact,' is, of course, evaded by assuming a stationary economy, but this can be considered permissible for certain problems. There is, however, one problem in the discussion of which the simple assumption of the stationary state is not permissible, namely, the problem of the capital stock or capital structure itself. To assume perfect maintenance of capital where one should discuss the conditions of such maintenance is a case of begging the question, or, at least, of avoiding the problem which is to be solved.

A statement such as 'all capital is inherently perpetual'[4] is of doubtful value. If it is limited to the case of an economy which is assumed to maintain, or to add to, its capital, it is but a repetition of the assumption. If it is stated as a fact, it is wrong. If we define a stationary economy as one which (perhaps among other things) maintains its capital, and if we call capital 'perpetual' when it is (at least) maintained, then the assertion that for a stationary economy all capital is inherently perpetual obviously means no more than that an economy which maintains its capital maintains its capital. Much more important is the question whether economies always maintain their capital, and under what conditions they do so.

Professor Knight thinks he is warranted in asserting 'the *fact* of perpetuity.'[5] He adds, however: 'Unless society as a whole becomes decadent with respect to its stock of capital, no increment of capital viewed as a quantity ever is disinvested.'[6] This 'unless' qualification reduces the 'fact' again to tautology. (Unless society acts differently it acts in the asserted way.) In other places the 'fact of perpetuity' is stated in a less safe – because less tautological – formulation.[7] There was and is always the choice between maintaining, increasing, or consuming capital. And past and 'present' experience tells us that the decision in favour of consumption of capital is far from being impossible or improbable.[8] Capital is not necessarily perpetual.

2. *Individual disinvestment, social disinvestment.* – In a 'capitalistic society,' in which property is owned privately, the process of capital disinvestment is the result of action or inaction of individuals, under the influence of their personal preferences or of certain institutional forces or

276

of state interference.[9] It must be clear that at any moment of time the alternatives are open to change in either direction, or to leave unchanged the relation between the current stream of consumption income and the future stream of consumption income, the latter partly being represented in the existing capital (which is the 'capitalized' value of future income). The conditions under which such alternatives can be realized are dependent on the given production structure of the whole community and on the simultaneous choices on the part of the other individuals within the community. Dissaving and disinvesting by one individual can be offset by saving and investing by another individual, in which case the individual disinvestment does not become social disinvestment. That 'in a stationary or growing society disinvestment by an individual owner in no wise involves actual reconversion of "capital" into income'[10] is again nothing but a tautology. It is just the relation of the total amounts of capital individually disinvested to the total amounts of capital individually invested at any moment of time which makes society stationary, growing, or retrograde.

The problem of social 'net' investment or 'net' disinvestment is important, and its discussion calls for consideration of certain 'time relations.' Since investment is a conversion of present income into future income (i.e., capital) by abstaining 'for a certain interval' from a 'strip' of the present consumption stream; and since disinvestment is a 'reconversion of "capital," i.e., of [future] income, into income for a short period at a correspondingly higher time rate,'[11] it is an economic problem of major importance to find out about the time distance between those present and future incomes, about the mentioned 'interval,' and about the mentioned 'period.' These 'periods' are important for the main problems of capital theory which is the theory of actual or potential changes in the quantity relationship between present and future services – or, in other words, the theory of distribution of services over time.

3. *Are production and consumption simultaneous?* – The assertion that all capital (in terms of value of anticipated future income) is always maintained and, therefore, 'perpetual' was made to support the view that the notion of a period between production and consumption is meaningless. The assertion to the contrary that capital need not, and, in fact, is not, always maintained ought to support the view that the notion of the mentioned period has meaning and significance. Professor Knight is prepared to admit that 'the notion of a lapse of time between production and consumption has practical meaning where society has to meet *unanticipated* changes in conditions.'[12] Apart from the theoretical and practical importance of unanticipated changes in conditions – it is not far from correct to call reality a continuous series of unanticipated changes – it is

clear to me and many others that the 'potentiality' of change is always present and that the choice between alternatives (only one of which is to abstain from changing, and hence to repeat, former choices) is a category in economics.

For the picture of a stationary state, from which change is absent, simultaneity of production and consumption can be a useful fiction. With the aid of a 'cross-section' view of production and with the element of time abstracted, certain relations in the economic system become more readily perceptible. Hence, propositions such as 'production and consumption are simultaneous,'[13] or 'the production period for consumed services....is zero,'[14] are useful and admissible (fictitious) assumptions for the discussion of certain problems of the stationary economy. But the 'as if' character of such heuristic suppositions must never be forgotten. And for discussion of problems other than those of an absolutely stationary state, especially of problems of capital, or investment,[15] of changes in demand, and similar ones, the assumption of 'simultaneity of production and consumption' is misleading and inadmissible and has to be dropped. Only for problems of the first type may maintenance of capital, including replacement of particular items of 'plant,' be conceived as a part of the production of the output consumed at the same time.[16] But any theory of economic change and any theory of capital has to regard the time element as its integrant part. The production of a definite quantity of output can be done with or without full maintenance of the instruments necessary for its production. Therefore, the output of consumable services is not dependent upon the simultaneous input of productive services used for maintenance or replacement of plant; the productive services used for maintenance or replacement of plant are not a part of the production of services consumable at the same time, but at later moments of time; there is a time interval between the input of services and the 'dependent' output of services,[17] and this interval may conveniently be called 'period of production' or 'period of investment.'

4. *Capitalization of perpetual or of time-limited income*. – That the cost of production of any 'capital good' is equal to its capitalized future return is a well-established condition of equilibrium. How the rate of interest enters into both sides of the equation was shown by Professor Knight with utmost clarity.[18] On the cost-of-production side of the equation interest is calculated (as 'carrying charges') on the services successively invested during the 'period of construction.' On the capitalized-income side of the equation interest is calculated on the series of future yields to reduce it to the 'present value.' There are two methods of capitalization. The one simply capitalizes the series of gross returns expected during the service life of the capital good; the other method reduces first the time-limited

series of gross returns by way of deducting all maintenance and replacement costs to a perpetual series of net returns and then capitalizes this perpetual series. However, 'it happens to be somewhat simpler algebraically not to make this conversion formally, but to express the present worth of the time-limited income stream directly.'[19]

In practical life capitalization of a limited series of returns is more usual than that of an infinite series, not only on account of mathematical simplicity but on account of the character of the capital items. Cases of perpetual annuities are rare. The valuation of plants, buildings, machines, etc., fixes attention upon a limited service life of the particular object valued. The valuation of bonds takes into account the maturity of all payments for interest as well as for the 'principal.' How complicated capitalization would be if the 'perpetual income method' were to be used is easily seen when one again faces the fact that we live in a changing world. With 'bygones forever bygones,' the cost of production of existing items does not count for their valuation. There is now no 'actual' capital value to start with, and replacement quotas could be known only with respect to the 'historical value' but not to the 'present value.' With replacement quotas unknown there is no way of knowing the net yield. There is, then, nothing but a limited series of gross returns, and this is what is capitalized. Only afterward, when the calculation of the present value has been finished, could a 'perpetual-income series' be constructed. Take the case of finding the capital value of a plant in an industry which is experiencing bad times. Maintenance of the plant [20] would mean negative net returns. But this does not at all mean that the value of the plant is negative. If there are positive gross returns, for a limited period of time, of course, there will be a positive capital value.

These few illustrations, I hope, make it sufficiently clear that practice does not make things obscure by supposing 'perpetuity' of income or of capital. Theory should not do so either.

II. *The Length of the Production Period*

5. *The concept and its name.* – It has been stated, in the preceding discussion, that the time interval between the input of (productive) services and the 'dependent' output of (consumable) services is significant for a number of economic problems. This time interval was called, by Böhm-Bawerk, the 'degree of roundaboutness of production,' or the 'length of the production process,' or the 'period of production.' The last two names, which Böhm and most of his followers continued to use in spite of the protests of Wicksell and others, contributed much to the confusion about

the concept. The words convey a meaning which is not that of the concept: one thinks of the duration of the process of production proper, which is by some writers called '*direct* production period' (as distinguished from the duration of *indirect* production) and by others 'duration of the technical process' (as distinguished from direct and indirect *durability*).

A number of different sorts of durations or periods are embraced by Böhm's concept. If one had to find out what time would elapse from the moments at which certain services, say a number of labour hours employed in a machine shop, are being 'put in' (invested) until the moments at which the dependent consumable services mature, the following durations would have to be considered: (*a*) the duration of producing the machine; (*b*) the duration of the production of the goods made with the help of the machine, and the duration of the production of the succeeding products made with the help of the mentioned goods, etc., all the way up to the final stage; (*c*) the durability of the machine, (*d*) the durability of the goods made with the help of the machine, and the durability of the products made with the help of the mentioned goods, etc., all the way up to the final services which are to be had. All these four sorts of durations have to be considered, but this does not at all mean that they have to be added. We shall speak about this presently. First it should frankly be stated that all objections to 'period of production' as a name for that composite period meant by Böhm's concept are fully justified. Terminological magnanimity may tolerantly pass over the misnomer and continue to use it. But it certainly would be better to return, according to Professor Hayek's recent suggestion, to Jevons' and Wicksell's practice and speak of the 'period of investment.'[21]

6. *Absolute versus average length of the period.* – We warned against the fallacy of adding up all the 'durations' of direct and indirect production and direct and indirect service life. It is easily understood that, under the technique of our times, such adding-up would arrive at an infinite period. Production is continuous – not only in the sense that at any moment of time 'past services' are consumed and 'future services' provided, but also in the sense that durable instruments constructed in the past are used in the construction of durable instruments for future use. In this sense 'the production period has no beginning and no end unless. . . . the date of the end of the world is known from the beginning.'[22] Or, more correctly, only 'the beginning and end of social economic life'[23] would mark the boundaries of that 'period of production.' And 'it would never be possible to give any sensible answer to the question' when (to repeat Professor Knight's examples) the production of a certain glass of milk 'began,' or when the process of consuming the result of productive activity such as feeding a cow would 'end.'[24]

Has the *naïveté* or absurdity of the whole conception employed by

Böhm-Bawerk now been revealed and sufficiently ridiculed? Let Böhm himself give the answer:

Where I have spoken [above] of extension or prolongation of the roundabout process of production. . . . I must be understood in the sense [just] explained. The length or the shortness of the process, its extension or its curtailment, is not measured by the absolute duration of the period that lies between the expenditure of the first atom of labour and the last – otherwise the cracking of nuts with a hammer which might chance to be made of iron brought from a mine opened by the Romans would perhaps be the most 'capitalistic' kind of production.[25]

Can one warn more expressly against the pitfall of taking the absolute period of production for the significant time interval? Böhm's concept was 'the *average* period which lies between the successive expenditure in labour and uses of land and the obtaining of the final good.'[26] The fact that some of the services reach into the indefinite future represents no difficulty for averaging the time dimensions. The bulk of the services mature in the near future and fewer in the more distant future, while the number of services maturing after infinite intervals is infinitesimally small.

In the well-known diagrams used by Jevons, Böhm, Hayek, and others – be it the ring diagram or the triangle diagram – the absolute period of investment is assumed to be finite. This assumption would imply that there is one stage of production at which no tools and no instruments, but only the 'original' services of land and labour, are employed. If to this entirely unrealistic assumption another one is added, namely, that the further input of 'original' services takes place continuously at a uniform rate during the whole absolute period, then the average period of investment is half of the absolute.[27] The fiction of a finite absolute production period facilitates the exposition of certain relations but has to be dropped in the course of any further analysis. It is to be regretted that it has contributed to so many serious misunderstandings.

7. *Average period versus shape of the investment function.* – It might be well to familiarize ourselves somewhat further with the meaning of the average investment period, before we deal with a more complicated concept. Imagine for a moment that labour is the only kind of productive service and is homogeneous in quality. At any point of time all labour being invested at that instant is planned and expected to yield (to contribute to) consumable services at some future time. (Most of the input of labour of that instant is planned to be combined with additional labour which is to be invested at successive moments of time, and the final product will be, of course, a joint product of services invested at different points of time.) The labour invested today includes a certain amount which is to yield services consumable today, another amount which is to yield services

281

consumable tomorrow, another the day after tomorrow, etc. Smaller amounts of labour invested today in some durable instrument of production will get very high 'futurity indices' and an infinitesimal amount will get the futurity-index (or time-dimension) infinity. The average of all these indices, weighted according to the respective number of labour units, is the average period of investment.

The 'average period' as an expression for the distribution of services over time is serviceable only for certain purposes and only if this distribution scheme is rather simple. Imagine changing our plans, one day, simply by switching some units of labour to activities of later maturing yield. This switching may be expressed by saying that the average period of investment has been lengthened. But take another type of rearrangement, where some productive services are transferred from uses with quick maturity to uses with later maturity, but also some other productive services are transferred from uses with very late maturity to uses with medium-high futurity indices.[28] Such a change in the distribution of services over time would be possible without any change in the 'average.' This shows that not only the average of all time dimensions but also their dispersion may be significant. The 'shape of the investment function' would tell what the simple 'average investment period' conceals.

There are other reasons for not accepting the 'average period of investment' as an adequate expression for, or measure of, the time structure of investment. Professor Hayek reminds us that the time intervals of waiting are, as to their economic significance, not homogeneous magnitudes which can be averaged.[29] Another argument advanced by Professor Hayek is concerned with the relationship between the interest rate and the investment function. The investment function, he explains, is rather complicated because of the 'investment in compound interest'; this makes it not only impracticable to represent it in terms of averages but also to represent it in one-dimensional diagrams.[30] But this need not frighten us too much. For most analytical purposes it will be quite sufficient to bear in mind that one cannot do everything with the average period without reference to the 'shape of the investment function.' But one can use it for first approximations to the solution of a number of important problems in the theory of capital and, I believe, in the theory of fluctuations.

8. *'Time' per unit of output versus 'time' per unit of input.* – Two more sources of confusion must be disclosed and blocked. The one originated from a careless use of the word 'time' to measure both the input of productive services (labour hours, service hours, land-use years) and the interval elapsing between input and the dependent final output. The second confusion came from erroneous averaging of those intervals per unit of output rather than per unit of input.

A simple numerical example (Table I) will illustrate clearly this type of error. Under unchanged technical knowledge, unchanged length of the working day, homogeneous labour, and homogeneous product, three cases will be considered in one of which the average period of investment will be lengthened (Case II), and in another the number of workers will be increased (Case III). Both variations (support of workers through longer period, and support of more workers through unchanged period, respectively) are assumed to be rendered possible through the provisions of more 'subsistence fund.'

TABLE I

	Case I	Case II (Labour Constant; Subsistence Fund Increased)	Case III (Labour Increased; Subsistence Fund Increased Proportionately)
Number of workers	100 men	100 men	120 men
Length of working day	10 hours	10 hours	10 hours
Average period of investment*	100 days	120 days	100 days
Labour input during this period	100,000 hours	120,000 hours	120,000 hours
Output during this period	1,000,000 units	1,320,000 units†	1,200,000 units
Labour input per day	1,000 hours	1,000 hours	1,200 hours
Output per day	10,000 units	11,000 units	12,000 units
Output per hour	1,000 units	1,100 units	1,200 units
Output per man hour (i.e., per unit of labour input)	10 units	11 units	10 units
Labour input per unit of output	$\frac{1}{10}$ hour	$\frac{1}{11}$ hour	$\frac{1}{10}$ hour

* The length of the investment period is assumed (not calculated from the other data). In Case II production is assumed to be more roundabout through the use of an intermediate tool which is entirely used up at the end of the 120 days. In Case III the same production method as in Case I is applied.

† This figure does not show increasing returns. It has to be more than in proportion to the increase of the average period of investment, i.e., 100:120, even to show decreasing returns. A figure of less than 1,200,000 units of output over the longer period would imply negative return to the added 20 days of investment. The total 'waiting' is increased not simply by the lapse of time, but by time multiplied by the amount invested at any moment.

Comparing Case I with Case II we see that the increase in length of the investment period leads to a less than proportional increase in output per labour hour. Now 'critics' would say: 'The production of one unit of output needs in Case II not more but less time than in Case I; namely, one-eleventh rather than one-tenth hour.' The 'time' of which they speak obviously means 'labour,' which is, of course, measured by time. The saving of 'time' in this sense, i.e., the saving of labour services per unit of output, is the very objective of the lengthening of the investment period. The increment in product per labour hour constitutes the 'productivity' of the extension of the investment period. The measurement of the amount of services invested in terms of time units must not be confused with the 'time dimension' of the investment in the sense of its 'time distance' from consumption.

But other 'critics' would say: 'Not only "labour time" but also "waiting time" per unit of output is less in Case II. In Case I we had to wait 100 days for 1,000,000 units of output; in Case II we have to wait 120 days for 1,320,000 units of output. Therefore, average unit waiting time in Case I was one-ten-thousandth of a day; in Case II only one-eleven-thousandth of a day.' This 'waiting time per unit of output' is an embarrassing confusion. The 100 and 120 days, respectively, were already averages per unit of labour input, and there is absolutely no sense in dividing these figures by the amount of output. That it does not make sense is shown by a comparison between Cases I and III, both of which include an equal and unchanged production period. In Case III, 1,200,000 units are produced in 100 days. The absolute increase in output, due to the increase in men and the proportional increase in 'subsistence fund,' with the unchanged period of production would give a shorter 'period of production per unit of output'[31] if this had any meaning. The production period is the average number of waiting hours applied to the labour hour; it is an average period only in term of input (of services other than waiting). If the average investment period is to be set in relation to output, not the absolute amount of output but average output per unit of labour input is the adequate magnitude for comparison. An 'average period in terms of total output' is meaningless.

9. *Construction period and utilization period.* – The misconceptions dealt with in the last sections are of very old acquaintance – Böhm-Bawerk himself was concerned with them in his 'excursus.'[32] A novel method of arriving at erroneous averages is applied by Professor Knight. He divides the sum of the periods of construction and utilization of different plants by the number or value of plants, and states then, correctly of course, that an addition to the existing equipment may well 'involve an increase in the capital, while *shortening* the average cycle.'[33] He thinks of the replacement cycle of durable capital goods. This cycle consists of the period of construction of the equipment plus its durability. Imagine that there are three plants, one with a period of construction plus utilization of 5 years, another with such a period of 10 years, and a third with one of 15 years. Now, additional investment is made by creating a fourth plant with a 6-year period. (The productive services engaged in constructing and maintaining the fourth plant must have been employed formerly in other lines,

say, in farming.) In the case of three plants Professor Knight's 'average period' was 10 years (5+10+15 divided by 3), while in the case of four plants (more capital!) the 'average period' is only 9 years (5+6+10+15 divided by 4). This 'average per unit of plant,' or, weighted with the value of plant, the 'average per capital invested,' he erroneously took as the average investment period and, of course, found that it did not bear the well-known relation to the quantity of capital, viz., that it failed to increase with the increase in investment. The 'average period of construction' plus the 'average period of utilization' (both averages per unit of plant value) is by no means equal to the average period of investment (which is an average per unit of productive service inclusive of those not engaged in the construction and replacement of durable goods).

Making goods which need a longer time of construction and making goods which last longer are perhaps only 'two details which are of the same significance as any of an infinity of other details,' and are certainly only two 'among an infinite number'[34] of ways in investing more capital. But 'the two together' do certainly not constitute, as Professor Knight so strongly believes,[35] Böhm-Bawerk's period of production. It is inexplicable how Professor Knight could arrive at such an extremely narrow definition of the production period. Böhm-Bawerk, who is now accused of 'simply selecting these two details' and giving them 'the false designation of length of the production process,'[36] wrote the following sentence about investment in increased durability:

It represents but one of the many special forms of using labour for obtaining consumption goods by those roundabout processes which make it possible to get out more goods per unit of original factors of production but at points of time which on the average are more remote from the time of input of those factors.[37]

Hence there is no conflict of opinion between the critic and the criticized that 'average durability of the goods' and, similarly, the 'average construction period for such goods'[38] need not be increased if total investment increases.

10. *Average durability*. – In spite of the fact that it was quite foreign to the theorists who reason in terms of investment periods to identify this concept with average construction periods plus average durability of goods, it should be noted that the relationship between 'average durability' and 'capital supply' is much closer than Professor Knight seems to allow for. An increase in 'capital supply,' in a money-enterprise economy, leads to increased investment through a lower rate of interest. (The supply of other services is assumed to be unchanged.) A reduction of the interest rate decreases construction cost as far as 'carrying charges' are concerned and increases the present value of durable goods because of the lower

discount of future returns. The latter phenomenon is of major significance. The increase in present value is the stronger the more durable the instruments are.

Let us compare this effect on the value of instruments of different durability. An instrument with a service life of one year and a gross return of $1,000 would have a present value of $940, if the interest rate is 6 per cent, and a present value of $970 if the interest rate is only 3 per cent. An instrument with a service life of two years and a gross return of $1,000 in each year would have under simple interest of 6 per cent a present value of (940+880=) $1,820, and under simple interest[39] of 3 per cent a present value of (970+940=) $1,910. A fall of the interest rate from 6 to 3 per cent raises the value of the short-lived instrument from $940 to $970, i.e., by 3.2 per cent, while it raises the value of the long-lived instrument from $1,820 to $1,910, i.e., by 4.9 per cent. Cost of construction (aside from interest) being unchanged – the case is still stronger if the more durable instrument requires a longer time for construction and, hence, becomes now relatively cheaper in construction – it will be much more profitable to construct the more durable instrument.

The differences in the price increases of goods of different durability become the sharper the greater the expected service life is. Let the rate of interest drop only from 5 to 4 per cent and there results an increase in present value of a good with ten years' service life by about 5 per cent whereas the increase is more than 9 per cent for a good with twenty years' service life. (Compound interest was calculated here.)

There is, hence, a very strong presumption for the belief that increased supply of liquid capital leads to increased investment in durability, even in the sense of 'average durability of goods,' the concept emphasized by Professor Knight.

11. *'More durable' goods versus more 'durable goods.'* – In his criticism of the production period Professor Knight concentrates his forces against the alleged increase in the durability of goods. Again and again he asserts that increased investment need not involve increased durability and 'therefore' need not involve increased 'time between production and consumption,'[40] i.e., a longer investment period. The crux of the whole argument is the idea that making goods 'more durable' is, but making more 'durable goods' need not be, a lengthening of the investment period, according to Professor Knight's interpretation of the 'Austrian' theory of capital.

Investment means, for the 'Austrians' at least, using productive services for future consumable services. Increased investment means using the productive services on the average for consumable outputs in a more remote future. This lengthening of the period of maturing can be done in many ways, one of which is the making of goods and instruments of higher durability, another is the making of a greater amount of durable goods and instruments. If the primitive inhabitants of the famous isolated island, where fishing is the only line of production, and nets are the only type of durable instruments, abstain temporarily from some portions of consumption and add one more net to their stock, they certainly lengthen their investment period. (Labour is withdrawn from fishing and employed for making the net. Total labour supply remains constant, of course.) 'Average durability' per unit of stock, per net, would remain equal. But even if they make the new net of lower durability, and decrease thereby the 'average durability' of nets, the investment period would still be lengthened. Or if our good old Robinson Crusoe adds to his stock of tools, which last 'on the average' one year, a new knife which lasts only two weeks, he still lengthens his production period. By refraining from direct consumptive use of some labour hours and using them for making the knife (and, later on, for maintaining or replacing the knife), he changes the average time distance between input and dependent output.

That, with a given amount of productive services employed, the making of a greater amount of durable goods per se would not involve any greater length of the investment period is a unique interpretation of the concept. The emphasis placed on this point by Professor Knight is striking. 'More goods of the same kind,' he says, 'would mean no permanent change in either investment function or output function, as defined by Professor Hayek.'[41] This should be contrasted with Professor Hayek's statement about the possibility of 'changing the investment function for industry in general without changing it for any one industry.'[42] The proportions *within* any one industry may be rigid and remain unchanged (the durability of their equipment, of course, too), but the proportions *between* industries may change. The investment function of society as a whole changes not only if goods are made 'more or less durable' but also if more or less 'durable goods' are made.

III. *Difficulties and Complications*

12. *The view backward and the view forward.* – In the few places where we, thus far, had to define the production period we tried to avoid one dilemma which probably has not been seen clearly by Böhm and some of his immediate followers. The question how far into the future the output that depends on present activities is expected to reach, on the average, is different from the question how far back into the past reach, on the average, the activities on which the present output depends.[43] Under the assumption of a stationary economy in an unchanging world, the 'historical'

production period and the 'anticipated' production period may be equal. But how are the two 'production periods' related to each other in a changing world with changing men of changing mood? If people decide to change the time distribution of their current service input, how does this affect the 'age distribution' of the output of today, tomorrow, and the immediate future? Is there not a considerable lag of the 'real' time structure of production behind the 'anticipated' one? And if the 'anticipated' period undergoes heavy fluctuations, is it likely or possible that the 'real' production structure varies concomitantly? And if this is found to be impossible, is it then not illicit to theorize about fluctuations in the production structure in the short run?

When Mr Hill raised all these doubts he did not suggest the scrapping of the concepts altogether but a reconsideration, or the discontinuance, of their use in business cycle theory. The reconsideration may lead to a number of distinctions, refinements, qualifications of the concept, and what has been stated about it. So much seems to be clear: (1) that the significant hypotheses about the investment period and its changes refer exclusively to the so-called anticipated period, i.e., to the time distribution of the current input of services; (2) that the 'historical'[44] production structure undoubtedly offers resistance to quick changes or even to fluctuations, a resistance which is the very substance of the explanation of cyclical and other disturbances; (3) that a production period between past input and present output[45] seems to be of no heuristic value for economic theory other than as a historical account of some 'given data.'

The 'view forward' determines the employment of services available. That 'it is by its nature hypothetical, representing an average of anticipations which may not be realized'[46] is not in contradiction with the fact that it is very real in its effects on what is being done at any one moment of time.

13. *Current investment versus total investment.* – The clean distinction between the 'anticipated' investment period and the 'historical' period is more or less the distinction between an economic problem and the data given for its solution. The economic problem is the problem of choice, in this case the problem of distributing the available productive services among purposes of different time index. The data include the total equipment available which is the result of history. The historical time distributions are materialized in the stock of 'capital goods,' the quantity, composition, and quality (including durability) of which are, of course, of influence upon the present choices as to the distribution of services over time. In other words, 'past' investment, through the man-made equipment available 'at present,' influences (together with other factors) the 'present' or current investment for 'future' output. The investment function (the only

significant one as an economic problem) refers wholly to the current investment. Hence it does not contain what one could call 'total investment,' i.e., the current investment plus the existing capital goods (durable and non-durable), which are the result of past investments.[47] To mix existing capital goods with current investment and to make out of both one investment function is to mix historical data with economic problems. Past investments, so far as they are materialized in existing equipment (capital goods), certainly influence the shape of the current investment function (the investment period), but they are not contained in it with respect to the productive services which they will yield in the future. Only the productive services rendered at the moment of investment[48] constitute (with their consumption distances) the investment function.

14. *Investment of services of 'original' factors versus services in general.* – At this point in the present discussion it is high time to dispense with the idea that only 'original' factors of production should be considered. It was undoubtedly a mistake to look only at the services of 'labour' and 'land,' as Böhm-Bawerk did throughout his discussion. Whether it was an inappropriate use of the stationary-state fiction, or whether it was the fear of reasoning in a circle, which led to the exclusion of the services of existing equipment from the investment account, it was a mistake to assume that the services which can be had from capital goods are, apart from their history, different in principle from the services of land and labour. (That there is no homogeneity within these categories should be clear.)[49] At any moment of time the services available from any sources of any kind – 'free gifts' of nature as well as human labour-capacity as well as the results of past investment – are 'given' for the economic choice. Labour services, land services, machine services, are institutionally, biologically, and historically different, but there is no difference with regard to their economic position in the time structure of investment.

The resources that yield the productive services may be permanent or durable or perishable. The services are perishable altogether because they are related to the single moment of time. The labour hours, land-use hours, machine hours, become, in being employed, the items which constitute the current investment.

15. *The 'unit' of investment.* – Labour is not homogeneous in kind, in quality, in efficiency; nor is land or capital goods. There is not much more sense in trying to compare in 'physical units' the floor-space hour in a factory with the water-power hour from a river (both in some way related to 'nature' or 'land') than in comparing them with the labour hour of a bricklayer, or with that of a stockbroker, or with the hourly service from a steel hammer or that from a paper machine. And yet, should all of those services and their time dimensions be 'averaged' in an investment period

or, at least, brought into one investment function? (An additional complication consists in the circumstance that the special form of employment of transferable and versatile factors sometimes depends on the length of the investment period.)[50]

Is there a way out of the dilemma? Is it fair to 'assume' homogeneity of services, to theorize on that basis, and be satisfied with conclusions *per analogiam*? Or is it better to take 'value' as the only possible *tertium comparationis*? There may be an impenetrable series of implications in adopting value as the 'unit' of input. If it is done, the time dimensions of the productive services being invested at a moment of time would have to be weighted with the values of these services.[51]

16. *Investment period and the amount of capital goods.* – The correlation between the investment period and the amount of capital goods has sometimes been held to be true 'by definition,' sometimes rejected as meaningless or wrong. The customary proofs for the existence of the correlation run again in terms of a stationary state. The assumption of the stationary state implies that the investment function does not change but remains the same through time. The investment function of 'today' would look exactly like that of any time in the past, and exactly like that of any time in the future. In this case the amount of capital goods in existence at any moment of time would be a certain function[52] of the investment function. It goes without saying, then, that the investment function and the amount of capital goods in existence are correlative.

Imagine now a change in the system; people start saving and investing; this involves a change in the investment function through a switch of services from lower to higher consumption distances. Assume, furthermore, that the new investment function is being maintained from then on and that the mobility and transformability of capital goods was sufficient to make the change take place without any losses. The changed investment function would tell that the physical quantity of capital goods of any type will be greater in the future than it is at the moment of change.[53] One could hold, however, that, although the physical quantity of capital goods is still unchanged at the very moment of the change of the investment function, there may be an immediate increase in stock value because of the lower capitalization rate of future income. In other words, the same 'causes' which change the investment function change at once the rate of capitalization and, therefore, the value of existing equipment.

Another approach seems to be better adapted to the concepts as we have used them in this discussion. The relationship between the amount of capital goods and the investment period shows itself in both directions. First, the greater the amount of serviceable capital goods in existence, the greater is the part of the current productive services from resources of any kind which can be invested for a more distant future. Thus, the amount of capital goods in existence represents, so to speak, a potentiality of investing more for longer periods. It is a potentiality which has not necessarily to be made use of. (And, indeed, capital goods may lose in value if and when, through a change in time preferences, given 'specific' equipment cannot be utilized fully.) But, generally speaking, the investment period tends to be longer the greater the amount of capital goods in existence. Second, if we use an increased part of the given productive services for things of greater time distance, the amount of capital goods in existence will increase. This means that, other things remaining equal, a lengthening of the investment period gradually increases the amount of capital goods in existence.

17. *Investment period and the supply of free capital disposal.* – In a single-plan economy, from the simple economy of the Crusoe type up to a communistic economy, the change in time preference (in the plan-makers' taste) and the change in the investment function are analytically the same. The time preference expresses itself in the distribution over time of the use which is made of the productive services currently available.

In an exchange-enterprise economy the time distribution of productive services is not *uno actu* changed with the time preferences on the part of certain individuals. Individuals who save transfer their disposal over services to other individuals who invest. Increased supply of 'free capital disposal'[54] tends to reduce the exchange ratio of present to future income, which in turn leads to increased investment of productive services for longer periods. Individuals who disinvest, so far as they cannot draw upon the disposal over services released from individuals who save, withdraw the disposal over services from entrepreneurs. Decreased supply of 'free capital disposal' tends to increase the exchange ratio of present to future income, which in turn leads to decreased investment of productive services for longer periods.

In a money-enterprise economy 'free capital disposal' is supplied and demanded in the form of 'money capital.' Insight into the functioning of this system is much impeded by the fact that goods in process are passed over from firm to firm by way of exchange against money, whereby money appears to be free capital disposal for the individual without being so for the community as a whole. This is why the unreal assumption of production vertically integrated in a single firm is so convenient; and why under more realistic assumptions problems of great complexity emerge from monetary changes. So much seems to be clear that an increase in the supply of money capital tends (other things, including the amount of services, being equal) to lengthen the investment period; and, vice versa, a decrease in the supply of money capital tends to shorten the investment period. And this is so, whether disposal over services really is released by savers or withdrawn by dissavers, respectively, or whether only the 'elasticity' of the money system does the trick. Thus changes in the investment structure are inseparably linked with the credit cycle.

18. *'At' a point of time versus 'within' a period of time versus 'for' a period of time*. – Discussions of 'capital' and 'investment' suffer not only from ambiguous meanings of these terms but also from confusion with respect to their time quality. The terms suggested by Jevons were not striking enough to be accepted by later writers. The 'amount of investment of capital' was to mean something different from the 'amount of capital invested,'[55] but neither of them was the 'amount of capital being invested.' The first was to be a product of a multiplication (more correctly, integration) of the amount that has been invested by the time for which it has been invested. The second, the 'capital invested,' was the amount that has been (and continues to be) invested up to a certain point of time, but without consideration of 'the length of time during which it remains invested.'[56] In other words, it was the inventory at a point of time. The third is the amount that is being invested within a (very small) interval of time.

'Capital invested' in the sense of capital that has been invested can, in a changing world, apart from setting up a profit-and-loss account, be significantly expressed, not in terms of its (historical) cost – i.e., in terms of the value it had at the time when the investments were made – but only in terms of the present value of the goods or resources which exist as result of those past investments. The present value is, of course, the capitalized income which is expected to accrue from the services from these goods or resources. Since the present value of these goods or resources has not much to do with the historical amounts invested, the term 'capital invested' had better not be used for them. 'Capital equipment' or 'capital goods' are adequate terms.

'Capital invested' in the sense of capital that is being invested within a small interval of time can be expressed in terms of cost or value, both being the same under the assumptions of equilibrium theory. Can this 'capital being currently invested' be expressed without time dimension? It certainly needs a reference to the unit of time chosen, since it is a time rate (such as per hour, per day, per week). Is it necessary to add to the time within which it is being invested, also the time for which the investment is to be? The answer to this becomes clear if we recall what is being invested. If we think of capital disposal or of money capital, it can be expressed as a mere quantity without reference to the duration of investment. But if we think of the 'real' investment, of productive services, we immediately see that the time dimensions become necessary because almost all productive services employed – except the personal services of servants, actors, etc. – are 'invested' and the question is only one of their distribution over time. Under full employment no increase in investment would be conceivable if it were not for the investment of services for periods longer than those for which they were hitherto invested.

This circumstance is, I think, rather significant. The money capital which is being invested need not, and cannot, be assigned to any certain period of investment. Even if the individuals who supply it were quite determined as to the length of time for which they would like to tie it up, or even if the individuals were determined to invest it for eternity, the services which are invested by means of the money capital are invested for a period which is independent of the will of the particular saver. And the single new investment makes, *ceteris paribus* (hence, with the amount of services unchanged), the average period of investment just a little longer than it was before. If there is full employment, the increase in the amount of money capital being invested per unit of time increases the periods for which the services are being invested on the average.

19. *Capital per capita.* – Productive services are distributed among uses of different consumption distance. To distribute a given amount of services is one problem. To distribute the services from a given amount of resources and men is another problem, because the capacity of resources and men may not be utilized fully. To distribute the services from a changing amount of resources and men is a third problem. It goes without saying that these distinctions are highly relevant for the problem of the average period of investment or, more correctly, for the problem of comparing investment structures.

A greater amount of services distributed over time (over consumption distances) in the same proportions as a smaller amount of services means, of course, an unchanged average period. Should there be an increase in the number of men employed, the amount of other resources would have to increase too, if a change in time distribution is to be avoided. This is often expressed by saying that changes in the average period of investment can be seen by changes in the amount of 'capital per head.' If population grows more quickly than capital equipment, with the result that less 'capital per head' is available, shorter periods of investment become necessary. On the other hand, increased investment permits lengthened investment periods only so far as it is not accompanied by a proportional increase in men.

This interrelation (which I chose to formulate as a statement of tendencies) is sometimes suggested in the form of an analytical statement. If a cumulative investment function is drawn in the customary way (representing cumulatively the amounts of services applied at successive moments of time in the course of one process of producing the output finished at one moment of time),[57] the area under this investment curve is defined as capital (more correctly, capital goods in terms of incorporated services). The average period of investment is measured by dividing the area under the curve by the final output (i.e., by the income measured in terms of input or incorporated services.) This division represents, by definition, the ratio between capital and income.[58] If only labour income, rather than total income, is considered, and if it is (according to the ordinates of these diagrams) expressed in terms of service input, the analogous division gives the ratio between capital and labour services, or, if labour hours per labourer are fixed, capital per head.[59]

An increased supply of money capital with unemployed labour services available would lead to an absorption into the production process of more labour services rather than – or in addition to – a redistribution over longer investment periods of the hitherto employed services. (Without increase in the supply of money capital, such absorption would be practicable only by a shortening of the investment period with lower returns to labour services.) There would, however, be a different sequence of events if the additional money capital is supplied by an expansion of bank credit from what it would be if it were supplied by voluntary saving, i.e., under voluntary abstinence from consumption.

20. *The proportion between the factors employed*. – The reflections upon 'capital per head' above suggest the coherence between the concepts of the 'investment period' and the 'proportion between the factors employed.' So far as changes in the investment period are connected with changes in methods of production within single industries or even single firms, reasoning in terms of proportion between factors becomes necessary. A single firm which, under the influence of lower interest rates, buys new machines to substitute them for less efficient ones or for labour services, certainly does not calculate investment periods. The firm makes cost comparisons, and the elasticity of substitution[60] will, among other conditions, be decisive for the firm's choice. The result is, for the particular section of the economic system, to be stated only in terms of the proportions in which the factors are employed by the single firm or industry.

An average investment period or a certain investment function becomes significant only for the community as a whole. In a total system analysis it will sometimes be more convenient to theorize in terms of the proportion between the factors employed, sometimes in terms of the investment period. The use of the latter conception recommends itself in all problems where explanations of changes through time are essential. The 'analytical correlation,' mentioned in the preceding paragraph, is, of course, without significance for causal relations. What are really significant are questions as to the probable effect upon the investment period of an increased supply of money capital, and as to the effect upon the quantity of capital goods (producers' goods) of a lengthening of the investment period. Lags and friction in the realization of such sequences are not unimportant; the appreciation (increase in present value) of the bulk of existing capital goods in the case of a lengthening is not less relevant than the differentials for longer-lived and shorter-lived goods and (in the case of a sudden increase in voluntary saving) the depreciation of some specific instruments adapted for the production of consumers' goods.

The chances for a statistical measurement of the investment period are not too good,[61] for reasons which have been sufficiently indicated in the discussion of the difficulties and complications. Of these difficulties the greatest is the problem of comparability – which is present throughout the field of economic statistics and is comprehensible to anybody who has a clear understanding of subjective value theory. The chief working hypothesis of every statistical attempt at measuring the investment period seems to be its approximate correlation with the proportions in which the factors are employed.[62]

IV. *Special Problems*

21. *Width of income stream versus length of investment period.* – A great many economists substitute for the concept of the 'length of the investment period' the concept of the 'width of the income stream.' The latter concept does not encounter so many complications as the former and has the advantage of not only suggesting a picture readily grasped but also of easily fitting into any analysis of economic dynamics, i.e., of fluctuating, progressive, or declining economies. Saving is pictured as a narrowing of the income stream, which later becomes wider again, wider than it was before the narrowing; dissaving is pictured as a widening of the stream, which later becomes narrower again, narrower that it was before the widening. There are possibilities of continuous and of discontinuous changes in the width – in short, the concept is useful and adaptable.

Yet, it is a mistake to believe that one could dispose of the investment-period concept without disposing of one of its most significant purposes: to solve the time problem. Of course the 'income stream' is a function of time, but one which remains unknown as long as the 'investment period' is not introduced. It is certainly true that the income stream becomes wider again after having been narrowed by voluntary saving – but only after a while. After how long a while? How long a time does it take before the widening of the income stream occurs, and how long before the 'abstinence' is fully offset? The answer may be sought by using a concept like the 'investment period,' or it may not be sought at all. What relates the changes in width of the income stream with one another is the investment period which has been thought to have been thrown overboard. That these intervals have meaning and significance is admitted by almost every economist – even by Professor Knight.[63]

22. *Investment period and the 'stages of production.'* – In discussions of the length of the investment period one ordinarily meets also propositions about the 'stages of production.' It would, however, be too optimistic to believe that these terms have a clear and unambiguous meaning. Although there is much overlapping, one can distinguish 'stages' of production in terms of (a) units of technical acts or divisions of the process (different acts), (b) locational units (different plants, buildings), (c) vocational units (different crafts, professions), (d) financial units (different firms), (e) time units (different consumption distances). Only the last of these concepts is inherently connected with the concept of the investment period, while the others are sometimes merely phases of the underlying technical conditions, sometimes among the more or less probable accompanying phenomena, but sometimes entirely unconnected.

In the attempt at illustrating an abstract exposition by concrete examples many authors pictured the lengthening of the investment period by pointing to the introduction of certain technical or financial stages of production. Readers – indeed, sometimes the authors themselves – then took the technical or financial properties of the process for the essential factors. In the discussion of production processes without durable instruments, the divergence of the technical stages from those in terms of 'time distance from consumption' is not too disturbing; but when durable instruments are introduced into the scheme, the divergence between the two concepts becomes considerable. The steel plant and the machine shop, two definitive stages, of course, in the technical process, represent by no means two stages in the sense of consumption distance but an infinite number of such stages. One has to keep in mind that services employed for the making of a machine are, as to their consumption distances, distributed over a great range of time. Unless one goes through the procedure of averaging these time distributions for any single unit of equipment, or unit of plant – which is neither necessary nor possible – one must not consider a certain technical stage of production as a certain time stage of production.

The divergence between financial stages and time stages is not much less remarkable. This was not made clear enough by Professor Hayek in his *Prices and Production*, and led to much confusion. His diagrams are devised to show the money stream between the financial units engaged in the production process. That the lengthening of the investment period (i.e., the increase in the time stages of production) would involve an increase in money transactions to be performed because of an increase in the number of financial stages of production was an assumption of Professor Hayek's which he certainly did not state clearly enough and which was justly criticized by Professor Ellis.[64] In anticipation of the confusion, Böhm-Bawerk had expressly given warning that the length 'of the process, its extension or its curtailment . . . is not measured by the number of independent intermediate members which the production process embraces.'[65]

23. *The investment period during new capital construction.* – 'In a sense, *all* work done in a stationary society is replacement work.'[66] This mode of approach has perhaps much more justification than the crude division of the production system into producers' goods and consumers' goods production, whereby the 'early stages' of production are assumed to be engaged in the one, the 'later stages' in the other part of that process. According to this last view, the number or the work of the earlier stages is imagined to be increased if society becomes progressive. The question then arises whether lengthening of the investment period is not confined to the period of capital accumulation, while shortening occurs when the process of accumulation comes to an end and a stationary state sets in.

This is Professor Knight's view. If more capital goods are constructed, he says, 'there will be, *temporarily* (while the expansion is taking place, but not after it is completed), a slight increase in the proportion of goods in the earlier stages of processing operations, in comparison with later stages.'[67] It will be shown, nevertheless, that a society which stops constructing new capital and confines itself to maintaining capital does stop lengthening its investment period; it need not shorten it if the transition is not too sudden.

The essential point in the argument is the gradual transition from a state of new capital formation to a state of pure capital maintenance. It is easy to see that there is a rate at which new saving and investing may slow down, and finally dwindle, without necessitating a shortening of the investment period (and difficulties in the construction-goods industry). Any increment of capital involves an increment in replacement funds necessary for full maintenance. If society is 'progressive' but at a decreasing rate, the funds supplied for maintenance still continue to increase. The decrease in the supply of new savings may, therefore, be compensated by the increase in the supply of replacement fund, so that the total supply of free capital disposal remains equal.[68] In other words, the increase in construction of equipment for replacement purposes may offset the decrease in construction of new capital equipment. If the rate at which saving and investing falls off does not surpass these limits,[69] no shortening of the investment period need ensue.

297

On the other hand, it should be noted that if the increase in capital takes place within too short an interval, it will not be sufficient to maintain the lengthened investment period. If in an economy which has been stationary hitherto one single investment is made and not followed by any further complementary investments, the single investment is, generally, bound to be wasted.[70] The lengthening of the production process is itself a process which needs time to be completed and, hence, to become definitive. But if after a sufficiently long phase of capital formation the transition from this phase to a phase of pure maintenance of capital is gradual enough to 'permit the processes which have already been started to be completed,'[71] the lengthening of the investment period will have been not temporary but definitive.

24. *Changes in demand.* – Changes in the investment period are not always caused by changes in time preferences. Purely qualitative changes in demand of intentionally equal time index may cause changes in the investment function. For a single-plan economy, however, this is not true, since the omniscient plan-makers will see whether or not the changed tastes can be satisfied without any different, or more or less, equipment and, hence, without any changes in the time distribution of services. If changed tastes could be satisfied only by a changed time structure of production, the plan-makers would immediately have to balance the displaced alternatives, which in this case would be alternatives of different time index. In a money-enterprise economy the situation is different, because of the lag of cost reactions behind consumers' choices. The prices of consumers' goods between which the individuals choose may be, at the time of the choice, different from what they would be after all rearrangements of productive services necessary for the provision of the goods demanded had been performed or calculated. The change in investment periods comes about by way of interactions of entrepreneurs, and it is only through consecutive changes in prices that consumers find their changed tastes to be incompatible with unchanged time preferences.

Using less abstract language, we may say that the consumers' choices between goods made from different materials or made in different types might cause major adaptations in the productive equipment. If the specificity of equipment does not permit technical adaptation, the change can be made only out of replacement funds. The quasi-rent in the still under-equipped line of production becomes apparent in higher rates of interest offered for free capital disposal. In this way replacement funds not only from the overequipped line of production (overequipped relative to the changed demand) but also from quite different industries are attracted by the more profitable production. Resulting price increases in other products force the consumer to reconsider the distribution of his budget.

(This redistribution may include the item 'saving' because it is not only prices of commodities but also the rate of interest which undergo change.)

The adaptation in the productive apparatus to a change in demand may lead either to merely temporary or to definitive changes in the investment structure. This depends on two circumstances: first, a change in demand so sudden and sharp that the producers of the product that fell into disfavour cannot earn any replacement quotas (definitive loss of the sunk investment) will tend to definitive shortening of the investment period; second, the quasi-rents of the producers of the favoured product, if saved and invested, might counteract the first tendency.

There is another point calling for attention. Apart from the losses and gains of transition, differences in the 'capital intensity' of the goods between which the demand has shifted may be important. The favoured product may not only need different equipment but more or less equipment than the product in disfavour has needed for its production. The shift in demand may, for instance, finally be 'capital saving.' (Crude examples: tents preferred to houses; services of stage actors preferred to services of automobiles.) Whether or not such changes lead to shorter investment periods depends on many questions, e.g., whether consumers use all the money diverted from capital-intensive products for purchases of less capital-needing products (or what else they use it for); whether the sunk capital can be extracted from the industries in disfavour; whether the capital extracted from these industries is used for reinvestment elsewhere (probably under reduced interest rates), etc.

In an economy in which new savings are continually forthcoming, a part of the new savings will be used for financing the adaptations of equipment to changed demand. Since the presumption that net losses of capital are connected with these adaptations is very great, it is fair to assume that an economy can be stationary in respect to its capital base only if it provides new savings to rebuild its equipment needed for changed tastes. An economy which is stationary in terms of new savings (i.e., savings are zero) is declining in respect to its capital base, if changes in demand occur. Or, to put it in another way, 'quick change in the objects of consumption without the emergence of new savings is itself a form of consuming capital.'[72] Changes in demand represent, therefore, one of the qualifications of the proposition that any increase in the supply of capital disposal leads to a lengthening of the investment period. Changes in demand represent, furthermore, one of the important, but neglected, points in the theory of the natural rate of interest. Changes in demand tend to raise the equilibrium rate of interest[73] and may involve a sufficient impulse for an (inflationary) expansion of bank credit.

25. Changes in technical knowledge (inventions). – The invention case

299

was the basis of the very first critical discussions following publication of Böhm-Bawerk's *Positive Theory*. The greatest part of these discussions was occupied by repetitions of simple misunderstandings. The misnomer 'period of production' led critics to look at the duration of the direct technical production process proper, and then to believe that almost all inventions shorten this period. Sewing by hand is a much slower method of making dresses than sewing by machine. Hence, thought the critics, the production period was shortened by the invention of the sewing machine. Böhm-Bawerk had a hard time to explain that sewing of the dress was only the last part of the process, while in the process as a whole services were invested in iron production and machine shops and in the sewing machine and only finally in the dressmaking.[74]

In his ardour to refute the assertion that the production period is shortened by such inventions, Böhm went so far as to assure us of the contrary, which is not true either. The invention neither shortens nor lengthens the investment period. All it does is to make investment opportunities more or less profitable. If and when new capital disposal is supplied (e.g., by new savings), then the investment period can be lengthened. But if these new savings would have come forth in any case, then the investment period would have been lengthened in any case. The new invention, if it was of the mentioned type, merely made the interest rate higher than it would have been otherwise.

If there is no increase in the supply of money capital above the current supply of replacement funds, then there is generally no possibility of a lengthening of the investment period. But if the new invention is connected with some especially durable instruments, will not substitution of new instruments of itself involve a lengthening of the investment period? If exploitation of the invention appears to be profitable in spite of its taking so much capital away from other industries (under a sharp rise of the interest rate), so many other investments which would otherwise have been made are omitted that the investment period is left unchanged. The high rate of interest might, of course, induce people to save or to dissave, and in this way lead to a change in the investment period.

New inventions may suggest new sorts of equipment which compete with, and render obsolete, existing equipment. This may cause major losses of sunk investment; the investment period may be shortened (in case replacement funds have to be attracted from other industries) or may be left unchanged (in case new savings are just sufficient to finance the new investment) or lengthened in a smaller degree than would otherwise have been possible. But it would be quite unwarranted to consider this a social loss. If an undiminished or even increased product can be provided with less capital or in a shorter investment period, there is no reason for resenting such a development. (Of course, if the inventions had been known many years earlier, many past investments would have been made differently and their obsolescence saved.) Obsolescence occurs if the new equipment is relatively more efficient or if it is cheaper. The latter is a case of a 'capital-saving' invention. The old equipment is depreciated to the lower value of the new, because the price of the products of this equipment would no longer cover replacement of the former value. What the consumer had to contribute to this replacement now becomes his increased purchasing power, which may be spent for increased consumption or which may be saved. The capital loss through obsolescence is capital consumption in the sense that it is accompanied by increased consumption, but it is not capital consumption in the sense that it renders impossible permanent maintenance of consumption on the higher level.

In substance, the effect of inventions, capital-needing or capital-saving, upon the investment period is per se neither lengthening nor shortening; their indirect effects depend on the incidental losses of transition and on the incidental changes in saving and dissaving.

26. *Investment period and disinvestment period.* – Changes in technique, it has just been shown, need not involve changes in the investment period. But neither need changes in the investment period involve changes in the technical methods employed. In an economy where no durable goods exist and where no technical substitutability exists, so that the proportions between the factors in the production of any one product are fixed, shortening of the investment period would be possible through changes in the relative proportions of different industries. There are two ways of shortening the investment period without changing the technique of production in an economy which employs durable goods. One way is changing the proportions between industries; the other is neglecting temporarily the replacement of durable goods. To say this is not to assert that these are the only or the most likely procedures in disinvesting societies; but it is necessary to warn against the belief that an unchanged technique of production offers any evidence for an unchanged investment structure.

Consideration of the 'disinvestment period' is necessary for the analysis of a number of problems connected with capital disinvestment either as a phase of the business cycle or as a general trend,[75] as well as of problems connected with the adaptation of specific capital equipments to changing conditions. It is nevertheless not true that immobility or specificity of equipment are the only factors that matter. Even if every good were perfectly transformable into any other good, if we, therefore, could eat up machines and buildings directly rather than through a lengthy process of undermaintenance, even then the disinvestment period would remain significant for the questions how long 'overconsumption' can be continued, and after what interval the consecutive shrinkage in width of the consumption stream will come about.

The statement that 'in equilibrium the period of investment for the total volume of capital. . . . is equal to the period of disinvestment'[76] is liable to misinterpretation. Within what time the total capital of society can be disinvested is not the point in question. The notion of the investment period, being an 'average' of an infinite number of time indices, would not help to answer such a question. To put the question for the length of the disinvestment period in terms of an individual investment would be still less sensible. The individual investor can exchange his property rights against present consumption income (of course not at a fixed ratio) at any time, whether they are taken over out of new savings or, in want of new savings, out of some replacement funds. And the marginal investment at one moment of time will hardly concern the same lines of production as the marginal disinvestment at another moment.

The use of replacement funds for 'taking over' property rights of disinvesting individuals, hence the use of replacement funds for the disinvestors' consumption,[77] is the essential point. The speed or rate of supply of replacement funds, on the one hand, the consequences of withdrawing parts of them from reinvestment, on the other hand, are dependent on the time structure of investment. The average time interval from investment to consumption is also the average time interval from investment to the forthcoming of the capital disposal free for reinvestment, because it is the receipts from the sales of the consumption goods which provide the replacement quotas for all the earlier stages of production.[78]

Imagine a barter-enterprise economy with vertically integrated production. The entrepreneur exchanges the final products of his production, or other consumption goods which he received in exchange for his, against productive services, if he wants to continue the enterprise, i.e., if he wants to reinvest. But he eats them himself if he does not want to reinvest. In a money-enterprise economy the money receipts for the final consumption goods are the funds available for reinvestment or disinvestment. The industry where a disinvestment takes place – i.e., where reinvestment is omitted – need by no means be the same as, or be closely connected with, the industry which received for its products the money that 'financed' the disinvestment, first, because replacement, though continuous in the economy as a whole, is not continuous in single lines of production; second, because the money capital circulating in an economy with vertically differentiated production (i.e., not integrated in one firm) is a multiple of the 'real' replacement funds. This monetary phenomenon is partly responsible for the difficulties, in practice as well as in theory, which result from the fact that the money capital *de facto* available for disinvestment exceeds in so large a degree the money capital 'genuinely' released from production through the final sale of consumption goods. The meaning of these phrases is more readily apparent if one imagines the money funds which would be available for reinvestment or disinvestment in an economy with vertically integrated production.

V. *The Credit Cycle*

27. *Credit expansion and investment period.* – Analysis of the consequences of an increase in the amount of money capital given to entrepreneurs has to cover a number of possibilities. Apart from an increase in the holdings of cash reserves (hoarding), and from an increase in the money work to be done on account of a possible increase in 'interfirm transactions,' the increment in money capital may be used (1) for employing a given amount of services for other work than that for which they were hitherto employed; (2) for paying higher rates per unit of service; (3) for employing a greater amount of services from the factors hitherto employed (longer labour week); (4) for employing a greater amount of services from factors hitherto unemployed.

An analysis that begins with full employment and given supply of services has to take into consideration only the possibilities (1) and (2). But these two will have to go together under almost all assumptions. If the increase in the amount of money capital given to producers is due to voluntary saving, hence to a decrease in the amount of money spent directly on consumers' goods, the tendency toward a rise in the prices of productive services will be smallest. But there will still be a tendency for such a rise, because marginal-value productivity of labour services should be assumed to rise in those employments which are made profitable by the interest-rate reduction that accompanies the increased supply of money capital. The rise in wage rates will, of course, be sharper if not voluntary saving (abstinence from consumption), but credit expansion is the source of the increased supply of money capital. But in both cases the first of the mentioned possibilities is rather certain to come true, and, according to what has been said above (see especially secs. 17 and 18), the work that will be favoured at the expense of some other work will be of a type that yields consumable services at, on the average, more distant points of time.

The sequences of events characterized as lengthening of the investment period have mostly been described for the case of a fixed supply of productive services. Increased employment of services – i.e., the possibilities (3) and (4) above – have been ruled out. This was correct as a first approximation, but a further step is to analyze the sequences without the assumption of fixed supply of productive services.

The inclusion of the possibility (3) – i.e., of employing more services from an unchanged number of men – is theoretically fascinating (because of the interesting complications in assuming various shapes of labour supply curves), but it has less practical significance than the possibility (4) – i.e., employing formerly unemployed factors of production. The absorption into the productive process of unemployed factors has been regarded by many writers as the realistic case where the irrelevance of an investment-period theory for the analysis of credit expansion would become apparent. And this for two reasons: first, it has been said that if sufficient productive capacity is available no services have to be withdrawn from consumption-goods industries as, owing to an expansion of credit, the production of investment-goods industries is extended; second, the amount of service input being increased, the increased investment need not involve any lengthening of the investment period. There is more investment, but there are also more productive services, hence no change in proportion and no 'distortion of the investment structure' will ensue.

The correctness of this view and the applicability of an investment-cycle theory are not incompatible. One has to bear in mind that, according to the capital theory under consideration, an increased amount of services can be employed, without additional voluntary abstinence from consumption, only if the investment period is shortened[79] and the earnings per unit of service are reduced. By employing more services, through credit expansion, at unreduced rates of earnings without voluntary saving, the investment period, absolutely unchanged, becomes longer than it would be without credit expansion.

The case of credit expansion with full employment and that without full employment are, therefore, equivalent in respect to the fact that the investment period becomes longer than it would be if the supply of money capital were confined to its 'natural'[80] sources: namely, replacement funds and voluntary savings.

28. *Investment period and inevitableness of the breakdown.* – Absolute or relative overlengthening of the investment period is the probable result of expansion of producers' credit. The length is excessive in the sense that without any 'outside' influences (without change in data) internal forces will lead to a reshortening of the investment period, sooner or later. The 'internal forces' consist in a divergence between the individual time preferences (as expressed in the proportions in which the money incomes are saved and invested or spent for consumers' goods) and the time structure of production. The divergence is concealed so long as the credit system continues to subsidize successfully the employment of productive services

for work of great consumption distance – work which would not be done if the voluntary distribution of the existing money funds alone were decisive for production.

A discussion of the details of business-cycle theory and monetary management cannot be embarked upon here. But all that is needed here is to point to the essential connection between investment period and credit cycle. While some writers find the causes of the breakdown of prosperity in the imperfections of monetary institutions or in lack of skill of monetary authorities, the investment-cycle theory suggests that there is no money system and no credit management conceivable which could permanently maintain a production structure (i.e., time distribution of productive services) which does not correspond to the structure of expenditures (i.e., time distribution of purchasing power). Though monetary forces help to bring about 'prosperity,' and lead to the excessive length of the investment period, monetary forces do not seem to be capable of maintaining it permanently.

Why the boom is doomed is explained by the investment-cycle theory. This theory does not make the pretense of being the only explanation of all cycles and crises that have ever occurred, nor does it pretend that it states unconditional necessities. The gist of the theory is that there is a high chance that increased bank credit,[81] unless offset by hoarding or similar phenomena, makes for investment periods different from what they would be otherwise; that there is, furthermore, almost no chance that the distribution of expenditures in consecutive phases will adapt itself to the investment structure;[82] and that, therefore, the investment structure will be forced to undergo a process of readjustment.

29. *Liquidation for consumption versus liquidation for liquidity*. – The 'liquidation mania' commonly observed during crises and depression, the urgent attempts to exchange capital goods and property rights for liquid funds, are not motivated by the wish to use the liquid funds for buying consumption goods but by the wish to keep the liquid funds on reserve. These rather obvious facts are taken by some writers for the whole substance behind the notion of depression. The struggle for liquidity alone is held to account for the disinvestment after prosperity. Hence, the breakdown is considered either as the result of psychic (or psychopathic) phenomena or as the result of the failure of the credit system to supply the money necessary to satisfy this increased demand for liquidity.

Nobody can seriously question the fact or the significance of this 'liquidation for liquidity.' But this clearly visible fact should not lead us to forget that it is as a rule preceded and, in a sense, 'caused' by 'liquidation for consumption.' This 'liquidation for consumption' is the discontinuance of activities of great consumption distance forced upon, or suggested to, the entrepreneurs through lack of capital disposal or through cost increases which are but the expression of the comparatively more urgent demand for consumption goods. That the use of productive services ceases to be profitable for a certain kind of work is the expression of the buyers' preference for other products, e.g., for 'present' consumption goods. The first attempts at disinvesting – i.e., the failure to reinvest in work of great consumption distance – may easily, and actually did mostly, start a general flight from investment into greater holdings of cash. Although in reality the two types of liquidation are ordinarily combined, they should be distinguished in theoretical analysis. Complete absence of the liquidity rush would not imply elimination of the business cycle or of depression; only the depth of the trough, the amplitude of the cycle, would be much smaller.

30. *Deflation and shortening of the investment period*. – How much of the difficulties and frictions would be taken away from society if deflationary liquidation did not accompany and aggravate consumptive liquidation cannot be known. But that the shortening of the investment period is connected with difficulties and frictions of its own seems to be certain. They may result from several circumstances: (1) Many capital goods are specific, i.e., not capable of being used for other purposes than those they were originally planned for; major losses follow then from the change in production structure. (2) Capital values in general – i.e., anticipated values of future income – are reduced by higher rates of capitalization; the owners of capital goods and property rights experience, therefore, serious losses. (3) Specific capital goods serviceable as 'complementary' equipment for those lines of production which would correspond to the consumers' demand are probably not ready; employment in these lines is, therefore, smaller than it could be otherwise. (4) Marginal-value productivity of labour in shorter investment periods is lower; wage rates are, therefore, depressed. (5) Under inflexible wage rates unemployment ensues from the decreased demand prices for labour.

That capital loss, wage cuts, and unemployment can be explained apart from any deflation does not mean that in reality they are not entangled with deflation. We said before, and repeat here, that deflation, though sometimes 'caused' by the process of shortening the investment period, aggravates this process considerably.[83]

31. *Immobility of factors and rigidity of costs*. – The immobility and specificity of capital goods – strengthening the resistance to adaptation and adjustment – has something to do with the durability of instruments and thereby with the investment period. But, as Professor Knight points out correctly, there is no definite relation between durability and the lack of adaptability.[84] And there is certainly not the least economic connection

between investment period and the main force of resistance to adjustment: cost rigidity. Hence, with immobility of factors (human and produced) and rigidity of costs (labour and material) as the essential factors of the trouble, the period of investment would have no place in the analysis of depression.

If capital goods were mobile and perfectly adaptable there would be no unused plant capacity. And 'if labour were mobile and wages flexible, no fixity in the capital structure would give rise to unemployment.'[85] And yet, to explain unemployment (through wage stickiness) is one thing; to explain the business cycle is another. If wages were perfectly flexible there would perhaps be no sharp fluctuations in employment, but there would be fluctuations in wage rates instead. Why the perfectly flexible wages rates go up through some length of time and why they fall most heavily through some succeeding length of time – in other words, why there is boom and depression, and whether and why depression must follow the boom – would still remain open questions. For a theory of the business cycle, with no unemployment but wage fluctuations instead, the concept of the investment period would be as valuable a tool as it is for the theory of the business cycle with little wage flexibility and unemployment.

NOTES

1. Frank H. Knight, 'Capitalistic Production, Time, and the Rate of Return,' *Economic Essays in Honour of Gustav Cassel* (London, 1933); 'Capital, Time, and the Interest Rate,' *Economica*, August, 1934; 'Professor Hayek and the Theory of Investment,' *Economic Journal*, March, 1935; F. A. von Hayek, 'Capital and Industrial Fluctuations,' *Econometrica*, April, 1934; 'On the Relationship between Investment and Output,' *Economic Journal*, June, 1934; Martin Hill, 'The Period of Production and Industrial Fluctuations,' ibid., December, 1933; C. H. P. Gifford 'The Concept of the Length of the Period of Production,' ibid.; 'The Period of Production under Continuous Input and Point Output in an Unprogressive Community,' *Econometrica*, April, 1935; J. Marschak, 'A Note on the Period of Production,' *Economic Journal*, March, 1934; K. E. Boulding, 'The Application of the Pure Theory of Population Change to the Theory of Capital,' *Quarterly Journal of Economics*, August, 1934; Wassily Leontief, 'Interest on Capital and Distribution: A Problem in the Theory of Marginal Productivity,' *Quarterly Journal of Economics*, November, 1934; R. F. Fowler, *The Depreciation of Capital, Analytically Considered* (London, 1934); Erich Schiff, *Kapitalbildung und*

Kapitalaufzehrung im Konjunkturverlauf (Vienna, 1933); Richard von Strigl, 'Lohnfonds und Geldkapital,' *Zeitschrift für National-ökonomie*, January, 1934; *Kapital und Produktion* (Vienna, 1934); Walter Eucken, *Kapitaltheoretische Untersuchungen* (Jena, 1934); Karl H. Stephans, 'Zur neueren Kapitaltheorie,' *Weltwirtschaftliches Archiv*, January, 1935. The following articles came to my attention too late to be taken account of in the present analysis: Howard S. Ellis, 'Die Bedeutung der Produktionsperiode für die Krisentheorie,' *Zeitschrift für Nationalökonomie*, June, 1935; M. Joseph and K. Bode, 'Bemerkungen zur Kapital- und Zinstheorie,' *Zeitschrift für Nationalökonomie*, June 1935; Oskar Morgenstern, 'Zur Theorie der Produktionsperiode,' *Zeitschrift für Nationalökonomie*, June 1935; Richard von Strigl, 'Zeit und Produktion,' *Zeitschrift für National-ökonomie*, June, 1935; Ragnar Nurkse, 'The Schematic Representation of the Structure of Production,' *Review of Economic Studies* June, 1935. Besides the published material, manuscripts by F. A. von Hayek and an unpublished discussion in correspondence between G. von Haberler, F. A. von Hayek, J. Marschak, L. von Mises, and myself were drawn upon in writing this article.

2. Besides the three articles by Professor Knight listed in the last footnote, see also his paper,'The Ricardian Theory of Production and Distribution,' in the *Canadian Journal of Economics and Political Science*, February, 1935.

3. Knight, *Economic Journal*, xlv, March, 1935, p. 79.

4. Knight, *Economica*, August, 1934, p. 264.

5. *Canadian Journal*, February, 1935, p. 15 (italics are his).

6. Ibid., p. 15.

7. 'Capital is perpetual in so far as economic principles obtain and economic reasoning is applicable' (*Economica*, August, 1934, p. 277); or, 'in a society which is not planning for the end of all things, all property income is perpetual' (ibid., p. 268). Neither of the two contentions seems to be correct. Economic reasoning can be perfectly well applied to an economy which consumes parts of its capital. Nor is it necessary that such a society plan for 'the end of the world.'

8. For an illustration of a case of capital consumption see my article, 'The Consumption of Capital in Austria,' *Review of Economic Statistics*, January, 1935.

9. Ibid.

10. Knight, *Economica*, August, 1934, p. 273.

11. Ibid. In the original, 'perpetual' income stands for 'future' income.

12. Ibid., p. 276.

13. Ibid., p. 275.

14. Knight, *Economic Journal*, March, 1935, p. 88.

15. Note the following concession of Professor Knight's: 'In the act of growth, "waiting" can be said to be involved, both during the interval of construction itself and at least for such time thereafter as is required for the new capital to yield a total of consumption equal to that which was sacrificed in creating it' (*Economic Essays in Honour of Gustav Cassel*, p. 339).

16. Knight, *Economic Journal*, March, 1935, pp. 84–5.

17. It is absolutely incomprehensible to me that Professor Knight, as one of the rare economists who understands, holds, and teaches 'the only theory which makes sense at all' (ibid., p. 82), namely, the theory which explains 'cost' as 'displaced alternative,' should not see this point. Consumable services available at different, more or less distant, future points of time are the 'alternative' uses of the productive services available at any one moment of time. The simultaneous output is not – or only for an infinitesimally small part – among the alternatives.

18. *Economica*, August, 1934, pp. 265–6; *Canadian Journal*, February, 1935, pp. 14–15.

19. *Canadian Journal*, February, 1935, p. 14.

20. It is fair to note that Professor Knight does not assume maintenance of particular capital items, but only of their actual value.

21. Professor Eucken, in his *Kapitaltheoretische Untersuchungen*, coined the word *Ausreifungszeit*, i.e., 'period of maturing.' The choice of the name is, however, a matter of indifference compared with the importance of using the concept in an appropriate way. In the rest of the discussion the terms period of production and period of investment will be used interchangeably.

22. Knight, *Economic Essays in Honour of Gustav Cassel*, p. 338.

23. Knight, *Economica*, August, 1934, p. 275.

24. Ibid.

25. *The Positive Theory of Capital* (London, 1891), p. 90.

26. Ibid. On the limitation to 'labour' and 'land,' see below (sect. 14).

27. There is another concept which is sometimes confused with the average period of production, namely, the 'average period of waiting,' which is dependent, apart from the other time dimensions, upon whether production is arranged in simultaneously operating stages, i.e., upon whether output becomes available continuously or with intervals (e.g., crop output). See Böhm-Bawerk, op. cit., pp. 327–8. The subsistence-fund theory refers directly to the 'waiting period' and through it to the production period.

28. Changes of this type play a rôle in the business-cycle analysis of

Professor Strigl (See *Kapital und Produktion* (Vienna, 1934), pp. 192–5).

29. Hayek, unpublished manuscript.

30. Hayek, 'On the Relationship between Investment and Output,' *Economic Journal*, June, 1934, p. 217. Three principal kinds of investment functions should be distinguished. The most usual may be called the 'cumulative investment function.' It represents either the cumulative amount of services applied at any successive moment of time in the course of the process of producing the output finished at one moment of time or the cumulative amount of services (simultaneously) applied at successive stages (i.e., consumption distances) of production up to the final output. A second kind may be called the 'service-application function,' since it shows the application of services in the process of production at successive moments of time or successive stages of production. It is simply the slope (first derivative) of the cumulative investment function. The third kind, investment function proper, represents the distribution of all productive services rendered at a moment (small interval) of time among the uses of different consumption distances. It is but the inverted service-application function. Services applied to the earliest stage of production are, for the inverted figure, services applied for uses of greatest consumption distance. Services applied to latest stages of production are, for the inverted figure, services applied for uses of smallest consumption distances.

Professor Hayek drew a figure of the cumulative investment function and inverted it instead of its first derivative (ibid., p. 210). Unfortunately, he interpreted the inverted figure as though it were the inverted service-application function. I am afraid that this error may have confused some readers. It should be noted that for changing conditions only the third sort of investment function is significant, though it is for certain purposes too sensitive with regard to discontinuous outputs.

31. The erroneous reasoning would be: 'We have to wait 100 days for 1,200,000 units; average waiting time per unit of output is therefore one-twelve-thousandth of a day; this is less than the one-ten-thousandth in Case I.' It should be noted that in Case III more workers are employed in an unchanged production period, hence with a constant amount of 'capital per head.' This will be discussed later. It was on purpose that I assumed here the subsistence fund to be increased proportionately with the number of men at work, in order to avoid the complications of shortening the investment period necessary when less 'capital per head' is available. This is also reserved for later discussion.

32. See the third or fourth German edition of his *Positive Theorie des Kapitales*.
33. *Economic Journal*, March, 1935, p. 81 (italics are his).
34. Knight, *Economica*, August, 1934, p. 268.
35. Ibid., pp. 268–70; *Economic Journal*, March, 1935, pp. 78, 81, 88, etc.
36. Knight, *Economica*, August, 1934, p. 268.
37. Op. cit. (3d edn, 1909), p. 170; ibid. (4th edn, 1921), p. 127.
38. Knight, *Economic Journal* p. 78.
39. A simple example was preferred here. Compound interest should be calculated for almost all practical (and theoretically important) cases.
40. *Economica*, August, 1934, p. 269.
41. *Economic Journal*, March, 1935, p. 78.
42. 'The Relationship between Investment and Output,' ibid., June, 1934, p. 224.
43. Hill, 'The Period of Production and Industrial Fluctuations,' ibid., December, 1933, p. 601. In drawing the distinction Hill followed F. Burkhart, 'Die Schemata des stationären Kreislaufs bei Böhm-Bawerk und Marx,' *Weltwirtschaftliches Archiv*, vol. xxxiv (1931).
44. Mr Hill speaks (op. cit., p. 603) of the 'completed' period rather than of a 'historical.' It is better to reserve the term 'completed' for the discussion of other phenomena in the process of lengthening or shortening the period.
45. Mr Hill writes (op. cit., p. 605): 'Owing to the existence of fixed capital the structure of production will not contract as rapidly as the anticipated production period. The average time in which existing specific capital-goods ... pass into consumers' goods is not likely to change appreciably over a short period.' One should not forget that the fact that less or no services are currently employed to construct or reconstruct such fixed capital is quite an 'appreciable change,' even in the shortest run. Moreover, the 'contraction' of the structure of production may be very rapid indeed, if value changes rather than physical changes are considered
46. Ibid., p. 610.
47. It should be noted that this does not fit into Jevons' terminology. Our 'total investment' would correspond to his 'amount of capital invested' but not to his 'amount of investment of capital.' See his *Theory of Political Economy*, ch. vii (esp. p. 229 in the 4th edn).
48. To make it indubitably clear: The durability of existing equipment influences the current decisions about current investment and through it the investment period, but it does not enter as an item into the investment function.

49. See Knight, *Economica*, August, 1934, p. 279. Professor Knight forcefully criticizes the fallacy of distinguishing 'primary' from 'produced' factors. I also owe much to an unpublished manuscript by Professor Hayek.

50. Much emphasis was placed on this point by Franz X. Weiss, 'Produktionsumwege und Kapitalzins', *Zeitschrift für Volkswirtschaft und Sozialpolitik*, N.F., i (1921), pp. 568–72.

51. This raises a number of the most serious theoretical problems. The value of productive services is dependent on the value of their future consumable services. Both are dependent on the length of the investment period, since an increase in that period yields an increase in future output. It is not only a matter of space when I abstain from entering into so trying a discussion. I may recall to the reader that Pigou withdrew the 'Pound Sterling worth of resources' from his last editions of the *Economics of Welfare* and substituted physical units for it. The issue was a different one but similar considerations are likely to be relevant in our problem. (Cf. the recent remarks by Howard S. Ellis, *Zeitschrift für Nationalökonomie*, June, 1935, pp. 158–9.)

52. The investment function, as we defined it, represents the distribution of all services invested at a moment (small interval) of time among uses of different consumption distance. If such an investment function is (for a stationary state) drawn only for the services of original factors, then inverted and transformed to a cumulative function (now looking like Hayek's Fig. 1*b*, in his article in *Economic Journal*, June, 1934, p. 210), then the area under the cumulative investment function represents the stock of produced production goods. (About the simple and the cumulative investment function see also *supra*, note 30.) The statement in the text about the constancy through time of the investment function must be qualified by the further assumption that output is continuous. While cumulative investment functions are insensitive to discontinuities of output, and are therefore constant for a stationary state, the investment function as we defined it would vary according to the crop-distance. This is a technical defect. Better technicians may find an improved mode of expressing the investment function.

53. If all productive services are consumed simultaneously, no 'intermediate good' can exist. If production takes time, goods in process, and perhaps tools, are likely to be on the 'inventory' at any moment of time. If production is arranged in stages which work continuously, the more goods must be on the inventory the longer the production period which is chosen. With a given input (per time) of productive services the inventory, at any moment of time, must be greater the greater the average time interval is until output is consumed.

54. I follow Cassel in using the term 'capital disposal.' It is better to avoid the term 'capital' *simpliciter*. The terms 'capital goods,' 'capital disposal,' 'capital value,' 'money capital,' convey more definite meaning than the ambiguous word 'capital.'
55. Jevons, op. cit. (4th edn), p. 229.
56. Ibid.
57. See, among recent publications, the diagram in Marschak's article, *Economic Journal*, March, 1934, p. 147, or Fig 1a in Hayek's article, ibid., June, 1934, p. 210. For a short explanation see above, note 30.
58. Professor Knight (*Economic Journal*, p. 88) considers this ratio 'one of the least meaningful.'
59. Which of the two rations is more significant for capital theory is still an open question. The discussion in the following paragraph places more emphasis on the second ratio. I owe much to Dr Marschak's previously cited article and to his unpublished contribution to our private 'round-letter' discussion.
60. See J. R. Hicks, *The Theory of Wages* (London, 1932), p. 117; Joan Robinson, *The Economics of Imperfect Competition* (London, 1933), pp. 256–60; C. H. P. Gifford, *Econometrica*, April, 1935, pp. 208–10; Fritz Machlup, 'The Commonsense of the Elasticity of Substitution,' *Review of Economic Studies*, vol. ii (June, 1935).
61. See Marschak, 'Economic Parameters in a Stationary Society with Monetary Circulation,' *Econometrica*, January, 1934; and Gifford, *Econometrica*, April, 1935.
62. Lack of statistical 'verification,' or even theoretical impossibility of measurement, is no evidence whatsoever against the usefulness of a concept. As Professor Knight has said, absolutely to the point, clear and indispensable notions often 'cannot be given exact definition; but this limitation applies to all quantitative analysis in economics' (*Economic Journal*, March, 1935, p. 90 n.).
63. See *Economica*, August, 1934, p. 273: 'In reality most investments not only begin *at a fairly early date* to yield their income in consumable services ... but in addition they begin *fairly soon* to yield more than interest on cost in this form, and entirely liquidate themselves *in a moderate period of time*' (italics are mine). Or, on p. 278: 'Any net saving and investment naturally means reduction in consumption somewhere and subsequent increase somewhere, raising the total rate of consumption in the system above that obtaining before saving started, the increase measuring the rate of return. In terms of *income* sacrificed for an interval and ultimately more than made up, the notions of roundaboutness and waiting have some meaning ...'

(italics are Professor Knight's). Any investment is displaced earlier consumption income; this is the very point of the theory of the investment period.

64. Howard S. Ellis *German Monetary Theory, 1905–1933*, ('Harvard Economic Studies,' vol. xliv), p. 354. 'A given increment of capital has nothing to do with the number of independent productive stages through which the intermediate products pass.'

65. *Positive Theory*, p. 91

66. Marschak, *Economic Journal*, March, 1934, p. 151.

67. Knight, *Economic Journal*, March, 1935, p. 78 (italics are his).

68. Suppose a current replacement fund of 300 units and new capital formation of 40. In the next interval the replacement fund will have to be (if the replacement quota is 10 per cent) 304 so that new capital formation can fall to 36 without causing a reduction in the supply of capital disposal (see Fritz Machlup, *Börsenkredit, Industriekredit und Kapitalbildung* (Vienna, 1931), p. 106).

69. These limits are determined, as shown by Fowler (*The Depreciation of Capital* (London, 1934), pp. 36–54), by the average durability and its relation to the average construction period of capital goods. Here is the place where these concepts used by Professor Knight (see above, sec. 9) adequately come in.

70. For detailed explanations, see my book, op. cit., pp. 103–11; and Hayek, *Econometrica*, April, 1934, pp. 153–8.

71. Hayek, ibid., p. 157.

72. Machlup, 'The Consumption of Capital in Austria,' *Review of Economic Statistics*, xvii (January, 1935), p. 14.

73. The effect upon the equilibrium rate of interest of changes in demand can be the result of several opportunities of investment, e.g.: (*a*) financing technical adaptations; (*b*) financing quick construction of the *different* equipment needed for the newly favoured product; (*c*) financing construction of the *increased* equipment if the newly favoured product is capital-intensive; (*d*) financing construction of different and increased equipment which was, due to lumpiness, hitherto not to be used profitably but becomes so if the demand for the newly favoured product reaches a certain minimum.

74. See especially Böhm-Bawerk's 'Exkurse,' e.g., 'Exkurs II,' in *Positive Theories des Kapitales*, ii (4th edn), p. 44.

75. See Machlup, 'The Consumption of Capital in Austria,' *Review of Economic Statistics*, xvii (January, 1935).

76. Fowler, *The Depreciation of Capital*, p. 35.

77. Not necessarily the disinventors' personal consumption; if they disinvest, say, in order to pay taxes, state employees might be the persons

who do the consuming. Disinvestment for the sake of financial liquidity is to be discussed later.

78. On this point see my *Börsenkredit, Industriekredit und Kapitalbildung*, pp. 15–16; and Strigl, *Kapital und Produktion*, pp. 30–7.

79. Less capital per head is available. See above, p. 283, and also p. 293. It need not be explained that the return to labour is smaller the shorter the period of investment. In terms of cost theory one would speak of decreasing returns of increased application of labour, or of increasing marginal cost of production. A qualification should be made with reference to the unused capacity argument. If unused capacity of equipment of all sorts is available in all stages of production, and if materials, goods in process, and finished goods of all kinds are on stock in sufficient quantities, synchronized production (and consumption) could set in at a stroke all at once. No additional waiting for intermediate or finished goods would be needed. (Why there should be unemployment, under such circumstances, is, however, hardly intelligible.)

80. No value judgment is implied in using the word 'natural' as distinguished from 'artificial.' The 'natural' sources refer to the concept of the 'natural' rate of interest, which is simply that rate which equalizes the demand for money capital to the amount supplied out of replacement funds and voluntary savings.

81. Increased utilization of bank balances may take the place of increased amounts of bank balances. (Increase in V' rather than increase in M', i.e., 'dishoarding.')

82. The adaptation of the expenditure distribution to an excessive period of investment would consist in providing increased savings to take the place of infusions of new bank credit.

83. To state this is by no means to advocate reflationary measures. Although they may offset hoarding and mitigate the difficulties connected with it, they may also interfere with, and actually delay, the necessary adaptations in the production structure.

84. *Economic Journal*, March, 1935, p. 93; *Canadian Journal*, February, 1935, p. 21.

85. Knight, *Economic Journal*, March, 1935, p. 94.

Oskar Morgenstern, 'The Time Moment in Value Theory', Andrew
Schotter, (ed.), *Selected Writings of Oskar Morgenstern* (New York: New
York University Press, 1976), pp. 151–67.

Oskar Morgenstern (1902–77) was another of the gifted young
Viennese economists who were drawn to Mises's seminar (after
studying under Wieser). He was, of course, to pursue a brilliant
research and teaching career in economics in the U.S., cooperating
with John von Neumann in the writing of *The Theory of Games and
Economic Behavior* (1944). His 1972 paper 'Thirteen Critical
Points in Contemporary Economic Theory: An Interpretation',
Journal of Economic Literature, vol. 10: pp. 805–16, is evidence of
the Austrian concerns which shaped his research agenda throughout his career. This paper originally appeared in German as 'Das
Zeitmoment in der Wertlehre', in the *Zeitschrift für Nationalökonomie*, vol. v, no. 5, (September, 1935) pp. 433–58.

21

The Time Moment in Value Theory*

OSKAR MORGENSTERN

A. *Introduction*

1. *The point of departure of the investigation*

In the following expository[1] the element in its most important aspects will be introduced very briefly into the currently accepted system of modern value theory. This treatment will take into consideration management over time periods which must be determined more closely. The procedure will be to extend the present system of value theory disregarding the possible expansion beyond the framework of the value theory that may result from the introduction of the time element. Clearly, it is conceivable that one might even question the usefulness of the prevailing value theory. In that case a critique would be immanent which would be quite different from hitherto existing and invalid objections as formulated e.g. by G. Cassel. In the present essay, however, a contribution to these questions will only be made in connection with the necessary sharpening of the principle of marginal utility.

It should be mentioned, further, that I will not enter into any dogma-historic discussion since the following arguments will move in quite a different direction from that taken by the discussions in the various writings concerning the time moment. The first author who clearly recognized the significance of the time element in value theory and therefore in the basis of economic theory was Hans Mayer who put this understanding into precise formulation on which just everything depends, since mere generalities do not permit tenable theoretical assertions. In his second 'Untersuchung zu dem Grundgesetz der wirtschaftlichen Wertrechnung'[1] he introduced explicitly planning by the individual into the theory. In what follows I shall proceed primarily from the findings put forth in that essay and I shall attempt to make further rigorously formalized deductions along the lines drawn by Hans Mayer.

1. The basic problems will be developed below on the same assumptions on which the theory has rested until now, i.e. a state of want in relation to scarce amounts of goods with multiple applicability of each single commodity, an economic householder who allocates and makes arrangements, either isolated with a natural income, or, as an individual household with money income and an inflow of commodities through buying activities on the market (based on this money income). For the sake of simplicity we will assume a uniform stock of goods (e.g. money.) To the usual assumption we will merely add that the process of want satisfaction extends over time in a very peculiar manner. The resulting variations will then have to be examined closely, taking as given the usual properties on the part of needs which have been attributed to them on the grounds of observations (e.g. continuity, discontinuity and Entspannungspunkte)

2. The alleged tautology of the doctrine of wants.

Since in the following pages we will frequently talk about 'wants' and even proceed from them, we must consider the question, occasionally discussed in the recent literature, whether the choice of this particular way of exposition does not involve a tautological process. The objection is based on the assertion that the individual satisfies his most urgent needs first and that this is revealed by his behaviour which shows an ordering of choices. This formulation actually has the appearance of a tautology. However, it really is not, although a number of theoretical economists (perhaps lacking the required rigor) have for a long time accused it of being one. That no tautology is involved can be shown by reference to the complete analogy of the so-called motivational law for which it has been proven recently[2] that the latter is not of a tautological nature. When an assertion about the empirical world is made, an exception to this statement must be conceivable without being absurd at the same time. For the theorems of logic and mathematics which are in essence analytical this is not possible. Contrary to this, the claim that statements concerning need or want were tautological collapses immediately upon closer scrutiny. For it is quite conceivable and even a common fact that an economizing individual, after having resolved upon a certain ordering of choices, does not act according to it but gives himself to mood or chance, thus ending up with choices which are quite different from those planned originally and different from those he might make if the same situation should reoccur later. The individual may also act not according to the most dominating pleasure motive but he may be motivated by the strongest impulse of displeasure (as K. Menger and M. Schlick have pointed out in complete agreement in their works). There is, in fact, nothing paradoxical in such assumptions. Besides, they can continuously be observed in reality by the use of very simple methods. Thus, statements concerning the present doctrine of wants as well as those contradicting them are in this matter compatible with the principles of logic. Therefore, the opinion that the doctrine of wants is of a tautological nature and incapable of providing us with an understanding about the world is false and must be rejected from the body of criticism of modern economics.

Should the claim which has just been proved to be erroneous be formulated as an objection to operating with 'acts of choice' of which the 'Ophelimitätsindex' is an example, then the above observations mutatis mutandis are also valid. I have already proved on another occasion that statements about value theory are synonymous when made in different languages and with the use of different nomenclature or if they are pronounced by means of mathematical methods.

The desire to do honour to the genius loci is not the least of reasons why we use the doctrine wants as the most familiar way of expression. Besides, we have here before us a scheme which has been analyzed most accurately. The emergence of this reproach concerning the tautology shows incontestably that no one is really fully aware of the relationship between 'logic and economics' and that the 'interpretation of subjective value theory according to the writings of the Austrian economists' loses itself completely when guided by methodologists unacquainted with the subject, instead of being made in accordance to logic or to the field itself. It may also be observed that it is exceedingly simple to refute the argument of the alleged tautology, although the literature already threatens to swell up painfully about this.

The ease with which this objection can be refuted is a measure of the magnitude of the errors by those refuted and what applies here specially: *simplex sigillum veri*, a fact that must unfortunately be noted in economic treatises.

The point of departure for any kind of general statement concerning economic phenomena and processes under any condition is the fact that individuals decide upon and order the acts of choice. It is generally quite immaterial at the same time what the motives are, and whether a once accepted ordering is permanent or not. Instead of inspecting tables of orderings as has been done until now, as for example in C. Menger, we now proceed on the indispensable assumption that for the completion of every choice a definite time index is included from the very beginning. From this addition which agrees with the usual laws of value theory it must be possible to deduce a series of important assertions about the time element if the principle of marginal utility is sharpened (cf. below). This is the main task of the present essay. We remain, therefore, within the domain of the rigorous theory, although the starting point is an extended empirical fact.

319

3. The possible ways of introducing the time element.
The time element can be introduced into economic theory in many ways. The current fashion is to attach to the various magnitudes of processes so-called 'time-indices' or 'time parameters' and to weave these also into the various systems of equations. However, such uses frequently lead to serious blunders and often nothing but complete nonsense may come out. This kind of treatment, apart from these mistakes, is actually, not fruitful and cannot be recommended because the problem of time is so far reaching in the economy, that it has to be generally determined in the first place. It would be quite permissible to introduce the time element into the developed economy immediately, something which, also, no one has undertaken yet. What has been tried in this line until now is characterized by a number of shortcomings, a detailed discussion of which would lead too far. These shortcomings are essentially of a general type, as one can see, for example in H. L. Moore, when he introduces 'trend coefficients' into the Walrasian equations in order to obtain a moving equilibrium.

As unsuccessful as such a process would be, for which the reasons are apparent, would be the method which is based on time parameters attached almost at any economic quantity.

If, in what would be the first systematic method, one wanted to introduce the time element immediately into the economy a very appropriate procedure would be to investigate first which assumptions about time are implicit in the most complete version of the theory of economic processes. It can easily be shown, then, that e.g. Walras assumed a reaction velocity of infinite magnitude which is apparently proportional in all processes. This does not even approach reality. We would therefore have to drop this condition of abstraction and introduce a reduced reaction velocity. For the sake of convenience one would let the variations occur not evenly in all classes but in various modifications. Doubtless, this method which because of its difficulties has not been tried yet, should give good results. All results derived from the introduction of the time element must in the end be identical. This would be the test. Since no method has been fully applied, yet, we are still far away from this condition.

In whatever manner the time moment is introduced, one will ultimately always run into the problems of time in connection with the householder and the entrepreneur. One could also start here, to begin with. This would be the second systematic approach. Even if one should be able to proceed only very slowly in the subject of value theory, which is concerned with management by the single individual, there is, at least, the guarantee that one is moving on a track the pursuit of which has already led to far-reaching understanding. Besides, more so, even, than in the first case, one is better equipped against those dark, almost mystical thought processes which in connection with the time moment are now unfortunately appearing rather frequently in the latest literature because we command great precision of present day statements in value theory.

4. The conception of time in the economy.

Before we investigate the process of allocation and arrangement by the individual in time, it seems to be necessary to clarify the concept of time itself. For the present purpose, however, this is not so necessary, since, unless otherwise strictly mentioned, time should be understood purely in the sense of the clock. The consumer merely sees himself faced with the fact that his income allows only a limited number of repetitions of his e.g. daily satisfaction of a given permitted state of need; i.e. certain uses of the goods, and, further, that his income reaches him in some sort of rhythmical intervals. That we also account for time in the sense as it has been used already in the theory of the utility of work or as it appears in interest theory is self-evident, although the forms of this kind of calculation with time periods are by no means explored yet, since posing questions concerning these theories have hitherto led investigation on side tracks. Similarly, attempts to contemplate special 'time values' of the various economic goods did not lead further either, although at least some striking observations have been made. Here one should mention e.g. the names of S. Bailey, F. A. Fetter, Irving Fisher and Frank H. Knight. In general, the following observations would have to be made: Progress in the sciences seems to occur overwhelmingly in a way where useless concepts are eliminated, a constant attempt to do with fewer and fewer elements. The introduction of the time element into the economy would indicate just an opposite trend. However, this would only be the case if statements concerning the time element could be transformed into hitherto conventional assertions. Thus, it suffices to determine by means of the apparatus of supply and demand that strawberries are more expensive in the winter than in the summer. Here a special time analysis is not necessary, as some might believe. It would only add an extra weight if time were introduced as an apparently independent factor. Until now a large proportion of the introduction of time factors has been of this kind. On the contrary, the task must be, that time elements are to be explored where they are contained (implicitly as a rule) but where they cannot be transformed into other expressions about their behaviour.

To give an example of the necessity to determine the implication of known value theorems which are usually considered without regard to the time element, one may cite the theory of imputation. The so-called first case of Böhm-Bawerk reads, that a product comes into existence through the interaction of three factors each of which would be completely useless in itself. In the imputation literature the solution to the problem of evaluation as put forth by Böhm-Bawerk has been accepted generally insofar as the whole value of the combination is attributed to the part which is added last, as well as the thesis about the absolute worthlessness of a splinter of this combination, which follows from that. Evidently, the latter statement is true only, if the entrepreneur does not expect to receive the missing piece within a reasonable period of time which is in accord with his other plans. Only then will he discard the splinter. If, on the other hand, he somehow expects to receive the end piece (or if two factors are involved, these two factors) with a later income, his behaviour will differ substantially from what value theory prescribes. He will give this splinter attention by saving it, for example, in spite of its temporary worthlessness.

It is clear that an entrepreneur who owns nothing but end pieces could perform, among other things, exchanges, in which he leaves these splinters to those for whom they can act as end pieces. Disregarding the possible productiveness of the foreign combination, which may be unknown to him, what he will demand in return will depend on 4 factors:

1. on the extent of his expectation as to the attainment of the end piece which he himself needs,

2. on his economic condition at that future time,

3. as well as on his economic condition at the present time,

4. on the circumstance, whether he owns two or only one end piece. The kind of contradictory or better, onesided assumption that can be made can best be seen if we examine Böhm-Bawerk's own method. In asking what a person who owns 2 splinters will give for the third splinter he neglects to consider that the behaviour of the other contractor must also be investigated in this exchange. As has just been shown, this can be done only by means of his particular manner of expectation, which is a special manifestation of the moment of time. Case I just considered is by no means an irrelevant special case of the theory, since, as H. Mayer has shown,[3] one can reduce the entire theory of imputation of Böhm-Bawerk's doctrine to just this case. A distinction of other cases is recommended for various reasons, however all of them presuppose the solution of case I. Hence deviations from this case are much more significant than appears at first glance. This example, which can be analyzed further, shall suffice for the moment. It should be made clear, though, that the time moment should be analyzed in detail wherever it cannot be transformed into other magnitudes.

The pertinent and conceptual difficulties of the time moment appear wherever it happens that chronologically simultaneous phenomena are not economically 'simultaneous.' Thus showing different time qualities, as I have shown first, in the simple as well as in the social economy. In the framework of this essay these relationships can be considered only in passing, even in connection with the simple household. Generally speaking, there is little use to burden the beginning of an enquiry with conceptual questions, since these could easily lead one to suggest the fateful question concerning the 'essence' of the phenomena which are only described by the concept. Such a mistake would imply some painful consequences, especially in the case of time. We shall, therefore, adhere to the simple convention, that time is to be understood in the usual sense of the clock.

B. *Management over time*

5. *Income Period and Exchange Period*

As a first approach some statement concerning the contemplated time space is necessary. For the sake of simplicity it would be best to presuppose mutually constant income periods. The individual will have at his disposal incomes E_1, E_2, E_3, ... in regular time intervals t_1, t_2, t_3 ... These income periods are not necessarily identical with the 'economic or household' periods. The latter periods must be at least as long as the smallest units of income periods, but they can also be substantially larger and cover several income periods. If the consumer receives constant amounts of goods or money in regular time intervals this process would imply an infinite number of other processes in such a way that he might have to contemplate an activity of a certain kind which in turn must be geared exactly to the other activities, etc. All these extensions, as for example the question of whether the cause of income regularity is of a natural or social character, will at first not be discussed. These questions can only be understood after the formal aspects of the process have been thoroughly made clear.

According to the preceeding assumptions, the income period is therefore an objective parameter which is practically independent from the individual, while with the economic or household period this is not entirely the case. The consumer has it in his power to decide which chronological division of income he will undertake. He determines his household period according to the nature and quality of his permissible wants or according to the different possible ways of using his money. He orders his desires which depend on innumerable factors on some scale and thus determines the value or utility and the chronological ordering of his needs and their satisfaction, which contrary to prevailing opinion do not have to coincide at all. Whatever his decisions are, there are certain principles which can be induced from his behaviour.

6. Congruent division of an income period

If we consider, first, a single income period, the individual will be able to behave in various ways. He can spend all his money (which is his income) on the first day. Then, not long thereafter he will have to starve and freeze to death. Generally such behaviour does not correspond to empirical observations. Rather, the consumer usually makes the observation that after a period of certain duration following a satisfaction process several needs (wants) begin to reappear again. H. Mayer, in his two exemplary discussions, cited above, has already pointed this out, with regard to his investigation of the evaluation of commodity stocks.

A description of the consumer's behaviour can best be given by reciting a decisive passage by Mayer: The individual manages, and arranges, 'in such a way that he first satisfies the wants with the highest degree of intensity in the present consumption period. Then, however, before he proceeds to satisfy less intense requirements in the same (the present) consumption period he wishes the satisfaction of the same needs in future consumption periods up to a point at which he can expect further access to goods (in the form of new proceeds or income). Only after securing the uppermost layer of needs within a certain period by allocating some determined amount of goods does he move to cover the want layer of the next lower degree of intensity. Again, he divides out his ration of goods evenly among the present and several future consumption periods. Thus, by an even allocation of all the goods at his disposal to the needs within a time space which includes several or many micro-consumption periods (want period), he arrives at want layers of constantly lowering degree of intensity. Finally, he reaches a certain marginal layer of satisfaction.'[4] Under conditions of empirical reality the management of goods must extend over a time space for two reasons: First, because the target system of empirically observed consumers, the subjective pre-requisite for the disposal of goods, involves the duration of time. And, second, because the technical, causal relationships of the means of exchange which are the objective conditions of the disposal of goods can only become effective in time.

Mayer mentioned a 'law of the periodic reoccurence of wants.' Without testing the applicability of this statement to all wants, and disregarding first the fact that the above cited analysis by Mayer marks the situation discussed in 7, the theoretical possibility arises that all wants allowed by the consumer are of the same rhythmical nature. This permits the division of income periods into a number of equal elements (e.g. days). If this is the case, then it can seen that this involves merely identical periods in tandem arrangement. None of these offer anything new with regard to the present make-up of value theory. The individual only has to divide his initial income into as many parts as there are identical periods, and to adhere to his apportionment, in order to obtain the same maximal total utility for each interval of the income period.

To adhere rigorously to this summation until the next income payment may lay great stress on the will power of the individual, but this does not cause any difficulty for the explanation of the process. There is no special management over time; hence, also within its limited framework one can in a certain sense speak only of a pseudo introduction of time into value theory. The utility calculus would proceed for every sub-interval exactly according to the prevalent theorems of value theory. It is clear that in this most general case it is quite immaterial whether the income period changes or not. One can say that the earlier marginal utility theorists worked with a degree of simplification which was marked by the following characteristic. They considered only the lowest indivisible interval of an income period which was always identical with regard to all sub-periods, but which was subject to arbitrary extensions and continuations. Therefore they were quite correct in neglecting the summations of these intervals and in identifying chronologically the income periods themselves with these last intervals of the want period. When the various authors nevertheless commented occasionally on broader relationships between the structure of wants and income periods, it happened without a systematic investigation of all the implications of the changed assumptions, which applies especially for the case of the estimation of future needs. In any case, from what has been said, it is clear that a linking up of identical income and consumption periods is an irrelevant matter for economic practice as well as for theory, with one single hitherto unnoticed exception discussed in 10, which is fundamental for all of value theory.

7. Indivisible, mutually congruent periods

The first variation which leads already to genuine management over time, consists of the additional assumption that the rhythms of wants are mutually unequal, such that some needs A, B, C reoccur, say, daily, while other A^1, B^1, C^1, ... reappear only in greater intervals, and others still in even greater intervals. In spite of the differences among these intervals, the needs shall be constructed in such a way, that they do not permit division of income periods into several identical time intervals, but that they merely leave the income periods congruent among each other, just as it was the case formerly with the sub periods. In case the individual wishes an equalization of his want satisfaction in the sense of an achievement of a uniform satisfaction during each single period, he must arrange his economic plan for this period at the beginning of the period such that the amount of goods (money units) will be preallocated according to his

325

accepted wants. Here also, everything depends on the consumer's adherence to the plan to which he agreed at the beginning of the period, and a decision beyond it is not necessary. From this it follows, that the case discussed in 6 is only a special variation of the general type just formulated above, on which H. Mayer based his enquiry. Apparently the decisive factor is the possibility to construct congruent income periods. In the simplest case this depends merely on the structure of wants, since by definition income periods are assumed to be uniform in kind and in magnitude. It is clear that completely different constellations will result if, while the needs still agree with the conditions set above and in 6, all incomes deviate from each other. The solutions to such a system would produce those kinds of constellations that have yet to be treated in the following sections:

The deviation of the case now to be considered from the former lies in the difference that we no longer do observe the fact that within an income period all sub-intervals are identical where exactly the same state of satisfaction is maintained. Rather, now we must ascertain that, because of the irregular reoccurrence of wants during the single subperiods (e.g. days) dissimilar utilizations (applications) of goods are required. Thus, the consumer can only then adhere to his original plan if he does not divide his total income into equal parts for each day, but if, instead, he uses smaller portions than implied by equal divisions, on some days in order to enjoy a higher consumption standard in another period, as for example on a Sunday excursion or for the theater. According to the assumptions it is essential that the individual can always cover the income periods and that he confines his management over time merely to the current income period without worrying beyond it in any way. At the beginning and therefore in this whole essay it is more appropriate to refrain from any graphic description of these relationships since such an enquiry could easily fix itself on curves instead of leading to the relevant relationships and their logical connections. However, it may be pointed out here that the theorems advanced here and those that will follow qualify very well for a quite rigorous presentation with mathematical tools. They might, for reasons not to be given here, make even better material for the application of mathematics to economic theory than was evident until now in an unfortunately large number of cases of mathematical economics.

Further, we can also refrain from investigating the various sub-species of possible divisibilities of the income period. No particularly interesting result would be achieved by dividing the period into 2, 3, 4 sections which, then, some are congruent while others are not. As long as only short durations of the income period are involved the consumer is not at all confronted with a problem that differs from those elaborated above, or which is not also presented by a possible division into many dissimilar intervals. If, however, the income periods move farther apart, new situations for the consumers and for the theory appear, which in this enquiry must unfortunately be disregarded. These new problems, caused by the duration of the time interval[5] to be assessed, lead to questions which can in similar ways be deduced from the variations introduced in the following paragraphs. However, a pursuit of these matters would extend beyond the framework of the present treatise.

8. Congruent groups of several income periods

The second variation which already approximates actually observed behaviour much more, and which is not treated in Mayer's enquiry should now move into the centre of attention. It consists of the assumption that the course of the reoccurrences of wants even if still dominated by a strong rhythm is so irregular, that the income periods are no longer mutually congruent. Should the individual totally use up his income in each income period, the income periods would show very dissimilar states of satisfaction or very different total welfare. In the extreme case it would also be conceivable that in the nth income period an urgent need arises and is admitted, the satisfaction of which requires a greater amount than the total income of that period. Without some management which allocates the goods over time the household would not be able to make ends meet. Therefore, *in each income period, already decisions have to be made which extend over this period.* Thus, there is a deviation from the assumption about the later period made in earlier cases, in that in the current period actions for later periods are already decided upon. *Herein lies the actual meaning of management over time.* The process which reaches its conclusion through this management must now be examined in all directions. It seems that one must differentiate between the mere expectation of some future events and the action in the present with regard to the future.

Here appears the difficulty as to what is to be considered to be the present in the economy, since time, in our sense, describes a steady, undiminished flow thus negating a present in the sense of duration. This is neither superfluous sophistry nor an inappropriate physical analogy, but a fact which is very significant for the theory, since the latter has to take it into account.[6] The solution is again made possible by the income periods. Only, it has to be established that in the sense of management the currently passing income period is to be regarded as 'present,' while the restriction with regard to the duration of time mentioned at the end of the previous paragraph will remain valid. The justification for this provision follows immediately from what has been said above, where it has been shown that in the beginning of the period, i.e., at the point of time when additional income is made available, the plan for the whole period, until the occurrence of the next income is laid out (with the simplification of using regular intervals). Now it is completely clear that expectations about the future can still play a role if arrangements are made over a single, i.e., the present income period. However, as a consequence of expectations the actual management in time leaves the consumer capable to decide already now, in the present, upon equalizing actions for later income periods. From the fact that sometimes the consumer manages, as we may call his behaviour with regard to future income periods, we can derive the result that the complete clarification of the problem of the so-called 'inferiority' of future needs is made possible. This is a problem which until now has remained in the dark, filled with contradictions in spite of many penetrating investigations. Under the condition that the individual wishes for himself the most homogeneous state of welfare possible he must, in the case of noncongruence of the various periods, combine several of them which together, will form a congruent group consisting of a multitude of income periods. Thus the first 1–6 periods may form a group which is congruent with the second group of 7–12 periods. This case differs from that discussed in 7 in that the income for the 6 periods is made available to the consumer not all at once, but in rhythmical impulses. Also, each period has a want structure that deviates from any other. In this lies a significant difference. And this arrangement, which by no means is the least possible one, contains all the elements of management and of the so-called inferiority (of future goods) whose analysis is the subject of the theory. The exchange period now stretches over the current income period until the end of the last one for which arrangements had been made in the first group. In contrast to other impermissible uses of the concept of the exchange period (especially in its current extension as 'production period' where an absolute chaos rules and where often the most elementary demand for clear thinking remains unfulfilled) beginning and end are exactly determined. However, this does not exclude situations in which the use of the concept is impermissible and senseless because of the impossibility to specify the two end points. Besides, it should be noted that the time space which still remains in the current period for which arrangements are made get constantly shorter since the limiting point keeps moving closer. As soon as it has been reached, a new period of the length of the previous period commences. It is by all means permissible to distinguish between the whole period and that interval which has yet to pass. This is necessary for a series of problems as may be mentioned here in parenthesis.

9. Management versus mere foresight

Pre-arranging and managing consists of the use of parts of the income of those income periods which precede the contemplated expenditure itself chronologically if the particular way of application has to be unequivocally pre-determined when those parts were held in reserve. *This pre-determination of the expenditure distinguishes management from saving which has an anonymous purpose only.* Saving also implies a possible later use. However the specific time and the kind of expenditure are left open at the time when the act of saving takes place. An application may not necessarily be intended at all as, for example, in case of a simple build up of reserves or 'iron stores,' etc. With management it becomes clear that before the expenditures take place a certain point of time or length of time is attached to the execution of an exchange act through an act of choice (or several acts of choices belonging to various income periods, which have been completed already). All this does not at all imply a change of the terminology, but, on the contrary, a necessary sharpening of it, if the word 'saving' is to be limited exclusively to the reservation of economic goods, including money, for which the purpose is anonymous. It is essential that for a later application of these means not even an approximately exact point of time has been determined, whereas in the case of management this is a necessary condition, even if the particulars of the future expenditure begin to go out of focus because of the fact that the point of time is far removed, and if the zone of freedom surrounding the act of choice is incorporated. The general statement that everything that happens in the future becomes less distinguishable and more uncertain is, taken by itself, a mere triviality and as such not qualified to explain the relationships between time and value, as seems to be the opinion of those authors who speak of a tendency of consumer management to combine more and more wants into groups, the later in time these needs make their appearance. In this, there is some truth, but the evaluation of the fact is insufficient. For a simple consideration will show that also within a single income period (even according to the case in 7) the wants at the end of the period cannot be made concrete (realized) at the beginning of it, if all the necessary arrangements have already been made for them and if 'global' management is involved. An example: I appropriate a sum of x dollars for my daily dinners during a whole month; however, where and what I will eat a fortnight from now I leave completely open. Today I will also merely know the place where I will dine, but the meal itself and, indeed, the amount of expenditure will be determined only during the act of consumption. Yet I always know, disregarding a freedom zone which surrounds any behaviour that is oriented by plans, and also unobserved by the theory, that on the average I have to stick to the amount of dollars allocated for this purpose. The global character of future needs also has little to do with the time element. Similarly, it is rather insignificant that, with the expiration of time the zones of the various degrees of specification of behaviour move farther away (either regularly or erratically). The assumption of such an automatic extension does not lead to a gain in insights into the relationships of the elements that form an exchange period. The questions of foresight and the possibility to foresee are, of course, of great import-ance for the economy and for all social sciences and deserve exact explication.[7] However management in time cannot be explained by merely graduating foresight. It should be noted that the claim that there exists a uniform degree of diminution of the specification of all wants is at most a first approximation. Empirical observation of man teaches us rather that there are some wants which are determined in detail over very long time intervals while others become already foggy after a few hours. At this point one should be warned not to make the mistake of assuming that needs which can be specified on a long range basis are necessarily of a higher rank than other wants not itemized or not capable of specification. Rather, we will be able to show conclusively that these things, perhaps contrary to expectation, do not have to indicate any connection with each other. The part that future needs have the tendency to move out of focus is neither a necessary nor a sufficient mark of management in time. The proof that many transactions of tomorrow are not at all organized to the last detail and made clear and that on the other hand I know exactly that in 3 months I will go to a health resort for a week in order to lead a well defined life in an exactly specified sanatorium, etc., that is, that I will be able to determine this more accurately than where and what I will eat for dinner in a week, i.e. in a much shorter period, will lead one to discard the assumption that the crux of the matter had been hit by those writings which have hitherto been pre-occupied with the more global nature of future needs seeing in it a solution to the problem of time in value theory. In addition, from these correct but inconsequential statements no further evaluation processes can be deduced – as was to be expected, whereas everything just depends on such a possibility.

10. Compensation of expectations of wants and expectations of income
For a complete classification of the relationships of foresight and manage-ment as well as of the problem of the so-called inferiority of future goods it is necessary to examine the income aspect. It is rather strange that the moments of expectations concerning future incomes has played such a subordinate role in the theory in general and that in value theory in particular it has not played any role at all. The thesis of the constant increase of the growing global character which is concomitant with the length of the time space should have been accompanied by a correspond-ing statement concerning future incomes. For this first exposition it is not necessary to enlarge too much upon this observation that future incomes

as a rule become more uncertain and blurred as to kind and magnitude and that great differences occur in the various population types and occupational classes (e.g. artists vs. government officials) and so forth. But even if one is concerned with an income that remains uniform and regular, the expectations become gradually indefinitely low for large time spaces. From the apparently peculiar fact that, as a rule, except for the case of the typical miser, not even a substantial part of the presently available income is allocated for the future, it follows that the individual has certain fixed expectations with regard to future incomes.[8] A large part of the present income or even the whole income is used up in the present time period E_1, although it may be known by experience that the present or a similar or even a worsened want situation will usually re-occur, perhaps many times in succession. In the case where future known and accepted needs in period E_1, i.e. in a later income period are not provided for in period E_1, we have before us a compensation of : a) the urgency for providing for the future caused by the expected wants and b) the likelihood W_1, which the individual attaches to the receipt of a corresponding income E_1 or to the possibility of obtaining those parts of his income with which to satisfy these needs. Each behaviour with respect to future income periods which may consist in exchanges or in a conscious failure to trade, presupposes such a judgement by the individual concerning the compensation or non-compensation of both magnitudes which are in a figurative, but very decisive sense, complementary. One can say without exaggeration that we are dealing with the determination of a relationship of complementarity or dependence, until now unknown to economics. The likelihood of W_1 of the income E_1 implies that all preceding incomes are equipped with a likelihood of at least the same magnitude as W_1, if, as in the preliminary frame of this discussion some regularity of the income structure is assumed, e.g. in the sense of dependence of income on continued production. From the findings above results that Böhm-Bawerk's thesis of the inferiority of future needs as well as the opposite thesis of the nonexistence of this inferiority have to be rejected as incomplete splinter statements. Both lack a precise economic sense. This economic sense is only realized when the above indicated relationship of complementarity of both moments of expectation are taken into consideration.

At the same time, the many, partly quite strange paradoxes which have accompanied the literature concerning this problem disappear. Besides, with the claim of 'inferiority,' we are dealing with a case of an impermissible value judgment (in the sense of a 'deficient,' 'non rational' behaviour) while a later falling apart of the want structure and of the income magnitude, which does not result in compensation, contrary to expectations, merely causes the appearance of a moment of error. The statement of the

331

individual that at a later point in time a complete or partial compensation will occur can thus be true or false, just as any of his other statements; a special value element does not occur. It is shown, now, that it is no longer contradictory or even peculiar when the individual satisfies his most important needs today perhaps to a high degree and above that other less important wants, despite this knowledge of the periodic return of these needs. By no means does he underestimate the urgency of these same important desires at a later time, only he assumes at the same time that then he will be in command of at least the same income that he spent on these needs. That such an income estimation is undertaken can be proved by the fact that the householder uses up any part of his commodity stock, measured as a flow of income, at all, although perhaps he expects to live for a long time, yet. Should that phenomenon exist, that critics used as a counterargument against Böhm-Bawerk's thesis, it would cause a behaviour which is empirically not observed. Naturally it should be noted that in time the expectations of future needs as well as the expectations of future incomes begin to become hazier and that, further, the extent of foresight and expectation may become very unequal. But all this follows from the general principle, mentioned above, which manifests itself everywhere in human behaviour. One could hardly explain interest on the basis of error. It would be interesting to pose the question if the same conclusions of which Böhm-Bawerk's had a vague notion could not be drawn if one would assume, in his sense, a systematic superiority of future desires, instead of the inferiority. Without a basis of particular facts there is no reason why one claim should be preferred to another.

The observation mentioned at the end of 6 is now that of compensation. Thus, it does not suffice that successive income periods are congruent on the part of needs, but the further assumption on the part of the consumer must be added that compensation will occur so that any management will be excluded. Should one consider the congruence of the structure of wants of each period as given, but further count on a gradually uniformly or otherwise sinking income, compensation could not occur and a genuine allocation would take place to equalize welfare over time in spite of the congruence of the periods. In this discussion which gives only a preliminary, summary account, the variations of the basic assumptions will be disregarded for the sake of convenience, although these extensions would lead to most interesting results. Without going into further debate, it must have become clear to the alert reader how invalid, and even how absurd is the claim rejected earlier that by means of the want analysis one could do no more than come up with the empty phrase: 'the individual behaves the way he behaves.' The analysis of the behaviour over time is especially rich in counter arguments – if they should still be necessary.

In the case of an individual moving in an exchange economy, we have in addition to the elements which comprise the compensation effect several others of which we will mention merely expected price changes. Under certain assumptions shifts in behaviour will result which will break through the frame just set up. However, it can be seen upon closer examination than in essence everything depends on the question of compensation of the two magnitudes and that all other statements are ultimately such that they can be reduced to those of the kind made hitherto.

11. The process of evaluation in allocation

Now it is necessary to investigate a series of important details in connection with management, which up to now could only be drawn in rough outlines. Above all, we must construct the contact with the evaluation processes as they have been described hitherto by the theory. In this there are generally no difficulties worth mentioning with the exception of the current thesis that the consumer wants to maximize his total welfare. Apart from the fact that this aim has never been defined precisely and unobjectionably in spite of earnest efforts, it can be seen that using a more precise notion of time rather substantial complications appear to such an extent that perhaps we have a case here in which a change in the concept of value as such is called for. To decide this question would however lead too far, since before that the problem of the maximization over time by the entrepreneur, which in many respects is analogous to the present problem, would have to be examined. This also leads, in addition, to a number of new views in the region of pure theory and it contains a number of profound differences, vis-a-vis the theory of management over time which is applicable to the householder. It must therefore be treated separately somewhere else.

Whatever way one judges Gossen's so-called second law of marginal utility, the cautious formulation that the consumer moves toward a higher possible equalization of utility and that he would therefore always have the tendency to maintain a uniform level may be tenable. That this is not obtainable because of various circumstances determined by the criticisms does not distinguish this law from other laws or from those in other sciences. It is therefore permissible to apply the basic thoughts of the most feasible utility equalization also to the evaluation processes in time. The explanation has to proceed along the following lines:

a) the part of income allocated today to the future need x at the future t_i has a greater value in that use than if it were expended today in addition to other expenditures of today. But b) this does not mean that the need x_i in period E_i which has thus been covered is the most important one of this period, although perhaps it may receive the largest expenditure in E_i. In this lies an important observation which is intelligible only by reason of the theory of the judgment of the compensation developed in the previous section. The expenditure for x_i, therefore does not come from the income at t_i, and if it does, then only to a small extent, but it is formed by the sum of the preceding perhaps even numerous acts of allocation in various income periods. The needs x_i can rather be a luxury want of E_i (e.g. a trip). Then the other needs, which are in comparison much more important to the consumer, and whose significance at that later point in time must then actually be in agreement with the meaning attached to them and expected, are not pre-arranged, is, as should be clear now, not a fault or even a contradiction, since, on the contrary, exactly all the income expected in period E_i is allocated to these needs. Thus the most urgent needs are not necessarily pre-arranged as it might seem at a superficial glance! For the process itself, it is completely irrelevant just where on the scale of rank the need, which is considered for the purposes of allocation, is situated. The decision about this depends on two factors, one, on the ranking and second, on the rhythm. The latter acts on the decision with regard to the compensation. On this occasion we may point to the fact that only the simultaneously occurring estimations of both the compensation in the expectation of the future income and the future needs depends on the structure of ordering and periodicity and that it makes sense only if each time the total magnitude and not just some marginal value is compared.

If, then, the evaluation processes did not distinguish themselves from those hitherto constructed in the basic principles, some nevertheless interesting modifications do show up. Disregarding the problem of imputation where difficulties arise because of the question of quantitative units, we may mention the following example: If at the time t_i (i.e. the time before t_i when the need makes its appearance) the consumer has already at his disposal several pre-allocated units of a commodity, the above mentioned utility calculus remains valid, contrary to our expectations, since the individual merely needs to compare the quantity added to this stock with its next best use. The probable existence of goods extending over his income does not alter in any way his consumption plans of the contemplated period. This stock plays the same role as other property which is not assigned to consumption uses. If he still uses it up prematurely because he is unstable or because he is given to spontaneous moods, thus setting into motion another process of evaluation, no actual compulsion is expressed in this, but he simply rearranges his plans, causing a new set of facts to become relevant. The further actions can be explained, again, in a corresponding manner. However, the main question that should be dealt with is that of the value phenomenon in the case where the consumer adheres to his original plan.

For a series of questions it is also of importance that this theory of allocation brings up the first beginning of all the diverse problems of elasticity, at least for the simple economy. When pre-allocation takes the form where concrete commodities (i.e. non-monetary) are retained or earned successively, or are earned at unequal times, or that a natural income exist which shifts in time in its composition, then it is clear that narrower limits are set for the reaction possibilities to the various changes of data, because of the inherent technical nature of the different commodities. This 'rigidity' of the household is at the same time a form element. No special comment should be required to point out that the general problem of national economic liquidity which has been regarded hitherto exclusively as a bank problem although it manifests itself in all stages of an exchange economy, should be approached most conveniently from the consumer side as it is done with the problem of time.

In the above presentation the possible and actually observable variations were kept within a small limit. It seems therefore appropriate to indicate the directions of further variations. If we disregard the introduction of increasingly larger rhythms, either of natural or of institutional origin (e.g., explainable again by a production build-up whereby the contact with other time problems that appear is established immediately) which makes it necessary to consider increasingly numerous income periods for the construction of congruence groups, whereby the ability to oversee becomes less and less to such an extent, even, that maximization becomes a special problem, then our attention must be turned to the income side. It requires only a repeated reference that even with complete homogeneity of needs over time allocation is difficult for the consumer, if his income is subject to its own rhythms. This would also influence his judgments about compensation. Empirically, of course, both factors, need and income, are subject to constant changes and the problem to attain a uniform state of welfare over time is evidently different in degree of difficulty according to the various layers and cases of consumers. In addition, economic managements take place usually in an unstable environment of changing prices. The components of expectation thus become more and more complicated. This is certainly a field that opens up a myriad of possibilities before the theorist.

12. Sharpening of the principle of marginal utility, and of the conditions of complementarity by the inclusion of the time moment

Each formulation of the principle of marginal utility and of Gossen's law, however stated, contains at the same time some statement concerning some time space to be examined more closely. An examination of the question whether the formulation of the principle of marginal utility remains independent from the contemplated time space, or what other variations result with a lengthening of this time space, leads to a series of interesting inferences. We distinguish 1. the planning of acts of choice, 2. the execution of these acts, and 3. the chronological sequence of acts of consumption. Evidently several possibilities of combinations of these three elements are given. Each describes completely different processes. As a first type the coincidence of the three elements at one point of time may be mentioned. Such a condition, however, is not in agreement with the existence of an economic plan, i.e. complete aimlessness would rule and any arbitrary order of acts of consumption falling together with the acts of choice would be permissible. This results in a confusion which excludes the possibility of this combination.

The second variant consists in the chronological separation of the economic plan from the completion of the economic acts which again would be identical with acts of consumption. The implication of this quite possible case is that the consumption goods are without exception non-durable, and from this results the identity of the order of acts of choice with the significance attached to them and to the corresponding acts of consumption. This corresponds broadly to the current value theoretical assumptions. If one could observe an individual of such behaviour on the market in the short term, then it would be legitimate to make inference about the significance of acts of choice which are attached to them in the planning, from their order of choice, and one would obtain a complete picture of his order of wants by mere external observation of his behaviour. The existence of only immediately usable consumption goods would, however, presuppose an essentially different universe than those universes known to us hitherto, where doubtless the greatest part of all consumption goods is of durable nature. If the individual owns but one single durable consumption good the necessary identity of the order of acts of choice with their inferred significance is disrupted and there exist quite different, much more complicated relationships which have hitherto not been investigated in value theory. In its chronological arrangement the economic plan shows nothing but the existence of order in economic behaviour per se. This order is not conceivable if it is not fixed chronologically in advance of the various acts (of behaviour) in some general manner.

The third variant consists in the fact that the construction of the plan as well as the execution of the acts of choice (e.g. purchases on the market) and the acts of consumption take place separately in a chronological sense and that between the two latter new orders with different variations are included. Durable consumption goods are permitted where 'durable' means nothing else but that the commodity can be used for new consumption acts between which others fall to an arbitrarily greater or smaller extent. Thus in every income period acts of consumption are completed which are in no way sustained by an allocation of a current income from this period to the respective need. This is on the order of the day; a possible exclusion of these acts as 'non economic acts' would be quite nonsensical. The existence of the economic plan and the presence of durable consumption goods makes it possible now to obtain them for example in completely different sequence than corresponds to their significance and to the point of time at which the first consumption act took place and which is attached to these. From the mere observation of the individual, e.g. on the market, one could hardly make any significant inferences about his economic ordering. Should such inference be drawn in any case, all acts of choice in an exchange period – not just income period – would have to be put together in order to obtain a picture about the distribution of important things. Where the starting and end points of this exchange period lie could not be determined other than by questioning directly the observed householder, (thus also by introspection). The introduction of time into the law of marginal utility sheds light on all this.

It would lead much too far here to indicate in detail the far-reaching consequence which results from the observations just made. It suffices for the purpose of this paper to point to the fact that also in the case when no management is present the above mentioned description of importance and the chronological sequence enters in the most elementary value relationships. Nevertheless, it may be emphasized that the existence of durable consumption goods has a corresponding influence on the complementarity relationships in such a manner that the complementarity must not only be determined for those goods earned in the corresponding period, but that it also depends in various ways on the complementarity conditions created by the already existing goods (for which e.g. no more expenditures have to be made). In this appears a principle of 'form value' for the household in which, in this way, the former and the future states of welfare are closely connected in a manner which can be made more precise and should be investigated more closely. It is thus no longer sufficient to examine the single welfare stages (conditions) isolated from each other. Rather, an interdependence not only of all momentary relationships, but, for a long series also, a relationship with respect to time is given. The evaluation processes proceed along the principles of marginal utility but this can be interpreted correctly only if proper attention is given to the connections with earlier welfare conditions in the mentioned sense. The known theorems of complementarity still require completion and it is to be hoped that many of the contradictions made hitherto will be cleared up by following the lines drawn up above. At the same time it should be understood with what difficulties of principle the idea of maximization and the

337

thesis concerning total economic utility will meet under this point of view.

The chronological ordering of acts of choice is of course free only to a more or less limited extent. All acts of choice which are bound to those periodically recurring needs which can only be satisfied by non-durable goods, are only connected with their appropriate needs whereas the degrees of freedom of other acts of choice may rise substantially. In this way additional points of view and insight can help determine the exact circumstances and the final point in time at which the receipt takes place, when the question of the acquisition of the various goods arises.

Just as there are substantial indeterminances in this aspect because of this, there are also some such uncertainties in the case of acts of consumption whenever more or less intensive utilization of existing durable goods is at hand, partially with and partially without the inclusion of goods that originated from the process of allocation just taking place. Evidently, the consumer has free choice to utilize some goods to a greater or lesser degree. On this arbitrary factor which is not at all considered by the analyses of the household which have been used hitherto and which can also not be understood by them, depends, however, the success of the current economic acts carried out at present. Nobody could deny that the management of goods, originating from earlier periods is a question of householding in a rigorous sense, so that no complete determination of the economic process is given, if only those acts are investigated which apply to the current income period in an isolated manner or if no clear time period is specified. The analysis of these connections will thus have to proceed along somewhat different ways than would correspond to the paths followed by the value theory hitherto.

C. *Conclusion*

From the thoughts developed above with utmost brevity one may, as far as one can see now, deduce a number of assertions about the connection of time and value, in as much as it is a worthwhile task to unite the different investigations about the time moment which has been undertaken by different outstanding authors. A complete survey of the problems arising from the inclusion of time in value theory and the ways to their solution requires, however, a further, separate treatment of time management by the entrepreneur, because they show up a number of peculiarities. From the management of time by the consumer and by the entrepreneur, then, results a genuine inclusion of the time element in the theory of the exchange economy. Such an approach penetrates the problem much more than some introduction of time-parameters into some system of equations and the tagging of all economic processes with time indices.

The time element presents one of the most urgent problems with which economic theory is faced. About the immense difficulties there can be no doubt. For this reason the intensive collaboration of many investigators has become very necessary.

NOTES

* This essay reproduces part of a speech given to the Vienna Economic Society in June 1933. A number of thoughts which are touched here only very briefly as well as further thoughts which result from them especially for price theory and monetary theory were developed elaborately in my lectures 'Time and Economic Equilibrium' in the summer semester 1934 at the University of Vienna.

1. *Zeitschrift für Volkswirtschaft und Sozialpolitik,* vol. i and ii, 1921–2.
2. M. Schlick, *Fragen der Ethik* (Vienna, 1930), pp. 38–9. Compare also K. Menger, 'Das Unsicherheitsmoment in der Wertlehre', *Zeitschrift für Nationalökonomie*, vol. v, p. 485, where (in an application of value theoretical facts to the law of motivations) the question concerning the alleged tautology of the theory of wants is also settled.
3. Article 'Zurechnung,' *Handwörterbuch der Stastswissenschaften*, 4th edn.
4. Op. cit., vol. ii, pp. 14–15. Italics in the original.
5. This is perhaps an appropriate place to refer to the exposition by J. Tinbergen, 'Bestimmung and Deutung von Angebotskurven', *Zeitschrift für Nationalökonomie*, vol. i, pp. 677–8 (8) which though it moves in a somewhat different context, is nevertheless worth mentioning.
6. The treatment by Böhm-Bawerk of the present and the future are by no means satisfactory; considerable objections must be raised to his distinction between present and future goods.
7. Compare O. Morgenstern, *Wirtschaftsprognose* (Vienna, 1928), where a number of aspects of the time moment which are not treated here are presented and where, further, the moments of expectation and of foresight are examined in the broader context of questions concerning the theory of knowledge.

339

8. The expectations of income are in the centre of *The Theory of Interest* (1930), by Irving Fisher. This splendid work contains valuable inspirations, especially for the broader topics of the variation of incomes, e.g. through borrowing, etc. in connection with the questions treated here which are not treated in his book in our manner.